GOLF IN SCC
HIDDEN GEMS OF
SCOTLAND AND WALES

by Bob and Anne Jones

[Hidden Gems II: Scotland and Wales
Revised]

TABLE OF CONTENTS

Chapter One: Getting Started, p. 4

Chapter Two: Southwest Scotland, p.11

Chapter Three: Scottish Highlands and Islands, p. 36

Chapter Four: Northeast Scotland, p. 74

Chapter Five: Heartlands of Scotland, p. 105

Chapter Six: Southeast Scotland, p. 169

Chapter Seven: Central Scotland, p. 192

Chapter Eight: North Wales, p. 223

Chapter Nine: South Wales, p. 252

Map of Scotland and Wales, p. 280

Index, p. 282

Pyle and Kenfig GC

CHAPTER ONE: GETTING STARTED

The day was not going to be the weather we really wanted when playing a world class course like Royal Porthcawl in southern Wales--it was fiercely windy, spitting rain in squalls, and completely overcast. We also knew by the friendly greeting we got in the golf shop from pro Peter Evans that it was going to be a great day of golf despite the weather. We weren't disappointed.

Rain gear, including jacket, pants, gloves, hat, and bag cover on from the start, we headed to the first tee. I like it better when we can start fully prepared rather than having to interrupt play to don our gear; it's always easier to shed rain suits than to put them on during the round. The first hole, the one seen in the Wales tourism commercial with duffers and

Wee Welshman Ian Woosnam teeing off in glorious conditions, is a fair starting hole. A demanding drive, but not too demanding, followed by a tricky second onto an elevated green with interesting slopes. The wind, howling at a steady thirty miles an hour straight into us (measured with a portable anemometer), added character to the shotmaking. Bogeys were good on this championship start, but the score really isn't that important. Anne and I are retired after more than thirty years of teaching, we're in Wales, the land of at least my paternal ancestors (although there's English on that side as well), and we're playing golf on one of the world's great golf courses. Bogey, double-bogey, or even birdie doesn't much matter. The rest of the round was a little better than the start. The wind stiffened a little, but the rain lightened and stopped while we were still on the front. One curiosity was we kept coming into greens with the flags pulled out. The first couple downed flags we ran into we cursed the inconsiderates in front of us. Then as we continued to find flags down and realized it was the wind blowing them out, we apologized under our breaths.

As we came off the tough 410-yard 18th with dips and hills and lush rough, we talked to the visitor who had played in front of us. He was leaning against the building catching his breath. As we approached him, he smiled and said, "The course won." But he was smiling! We told Peter about the four flags we found down on the greens. He responded, "Oh, an average day at Royal Porthcawl. Only a four flag day; we often see six or eight flags out in a round." And he was smiling!

From the golf course it's only a few miles back to the Prince of Wales Pub in Kenfig near the interesting Pyle and Kenfig GC we'd played a couple of days before. We'd heard about the pub from the golf pro at P&K who said, "It should be in your book"--a phrase we'd heard several times before referring to this pub, that restaurant, or yon attraction. After a drink in the 16th century (rebuilt in 1808) Prince of Wales Inn we knew he'd been right. This pub needed to be in the book. We enjoyed a pint, Guinness for Anne and local ale for me, heard about the ghosts, talked to a few locals who said "Good day for golf, isn't it." And they smiled! With a little adjusting of our itinerary, we planned a return trip to the pub for a meal, and then headed out for the hour drive to tonight's B&B in Laugharne.

Laugharne has a ruined castle and a literary heritage. It's the literary connection that gives the Boat House Bed and Breakfast its name-- the Boathouse (around the corner from the castle along the water) was where poet Dylan Thomas did much of his writing. We arrived in time to take a quick peek at the castle before checking in at the B&B. We rang the bell and introduced ourselves to Angi, who looked at us a little strangely, but showed us to the Towy suite. When we asked about her husband George a look of recognition came over her face. Ann then introduced herself and her daughter Jenni who recently bought the B&B from Angi and George. They said Angi and George had left our reservation, but no details or contact information. After a good laugh we were told the dinner we had arranged would be in the dining room in about an hour.

Whenever we can we take advantage of B&Bs who do dinners--a nice change from always eating out. The dinner at Boat House was superb! A special smoked haddock appetizer started the meal for us and three other guests. The starter was followed by a main of chicken breast in special sauce served with potatoes and fresh veggies. Dinner ended with a scrumptious homemade pear pie. My Anne and I sat for an hour after dinner visiting with Jenni and Ann about the process of starting up a B&B.

Windy golf on a fantastic course. Pub ghosts and Guinness. New friends in a marvelous B&B. All in a day of touring in Wales.

Every day touring in Scotland or Wales isn't as good as the day we visited Royal Porthcawl and discovered the Boat House in Laugharne, but every day could be the day you find a great golf course, have a meal you'll write home about, or learn a little piece of history in the picturesque ruins of a castle. We hope this guide will help you find that special golf course, pub or restaurant, B&B, or tourist attraction.

HOW TO USE THIS GUIDE

Chapters 2 through 9 will guide you to golf, eateries (pubs, restaurants, and tearooms), lodgings, and attractions. Chapters 2 to 7 are about Scotland and use the same geographic distribution of courses as the *Golf Scotland* guide, produced yearly by the Tourist Board and available at any Tourist Information Centre. Chapters 8 and 9 are about Wales, the North and then the South. In each section we give details, some directions (most importantly the Post Code to put into your GPS). For golf courses we hope that the description of a few holes will give enough idea about whether that's a course you want to seek out.

Golf. The "golf" section of each chapter contains the following information for each course in alphabetical order:

GOLF COURSE: The name of the course.

ADDRESS: The address which includes the postal code. Use this code when trying to find a course using a GPS--the code will be the exact location you seek.

PHONE & WEB: The course's phone number (usually the golf shop or golf manager if there is no shop) and the course's website, if it has one. To phone from the US to Scotland or Wales dial 011-44-drop the 0 and dial the rest of the number.

STYLE, LENGTH, PAR, PRICE: Whether the course is links, parkland, heath or moorland, or a combination. The length from the members' tees, which are the tees most courses want visitors to play from. The par is from the members' tees. Price is given in £s (Great Britain Pounds) for the 2013 season.

AMENITIES: Notes on amenities include information about the golf shop (if there is one), clubhouse, and any special facilities (driving range) or lack of (no trolleys).

COURSE COMMENTS: Comments include notes about the history of the club or course, about the type of trouble you can expect to find, a description of several holes which typify playing the course, and any special information.

COMMENTS FROM THE FORWARD TEES: On the courses she played, Anne gives notes for ladies on playing the course, including length and special considerations.

Pubs, Restaurants and Tearooms. The section on eateries contains brief details for each establishment. The information here must be considered with our bias, although we try to think about what we would tell friends about the eateries.

NAME: The name of the establishment and what kind it is if the name isn't descriptive enough.

LOCATION: Enough description of the location of the eatery so that you can find it.

COMMENTS: Our comments will try to give you a brief word picture of the pub or restaurant to help you decide if it is a place you want to visit.

Lodgings. This is our description of the B&Bs, Guest Houses, or small hotels we've stayed in at least once, and often more than once. Again, this section is very subjective. We are not terribly picky, but do want value for our money. Lodgings details include the following:

NAME: Name of the B&B.

ADDRESS: Location of the lodging and most importantly, the postal code for GPS.

PHONE & WEB: Phone, website, if available, and price either per person per night (pp) or per room per night (per room).

COMMENTS: Our notes about the type of B&B, its amenities or special features.

Tourist Attractions. In this short section of the chapter we list some of the sites you may want to visit before golf, after golf, or on non-golfing days. Much more information will be available at local B&Bs, Tourist Information centers, or pure touring guidebooks like the Rick Steve series, *Lonely Planet*, or *Secret Places*.

SPECIAL TRAVEL NOTES

(1) As you seek some of the fine small out-of-the-way courses like Traigh and Durness as well as some of Scotland and Wales' interesting attractions, you'll encounter small **single-track roads**, wide enough for one vehicle. The trip to Durness, any way you go, will include fifty miles or more of these narrow roads with passing places (short pullouts to allow another vehicle to pass). On Isle Arran we encountered one tourist who was absolutely terrified of the oncoming traffic when there was little room to pass. In one instance when facing an oncoming lorry (truck) she just stopped and wouldn't move. The lorry driver finally pulled around her by going off the road, gesticulating all the while. I blinked lights at her for miles before she stopped so I could pass. When I drove around she had the most terrified look on her face.

Driving single-track lanes need not be so traumatic. A few simple rules make single-track driving, if not easy, at least manageable. First, If the passing place is on the right and you reach it first, stop on the left side of the road (remember, you're driving on the left in the UK) opposite the passing place. If the passing place is on the left and you reach it first, pull into it and wait for the approaching car to pass. Second, be careful when coming up to blind corners--you should drive as if you will meet a refuse lorry in the middle of the corner. Third, use the passing places to allow faster (mostly locals) vehicles to pass. Fourth, do not use the passing places as parking areas. Find another place to stop or skip the photo. Finally, when going downhill try to be considerate of the traffic going uphill. Driving single-track is a slightly stressful adventure, but it needn't be traumatic.

(2) If you book your golf ahead (and on all the major courses you should) be sure to take **documentation** with you (email confirmation, phone dates with contact names). We book 95% of our golf ahead and have been grateful of having copies of emails with us. For example, neither Moray Old nor Loch Ness had us on their books, but when we showed them our email confirmation we got right on. Even a grand course like Kingsbarns can have problems with reservations. We arrived, as we always do, well ahead of our scheduled tee time and checked in at the golf shop. The assistant pro had no record in the fully booked time sheet of our visit. When I showed him the email confirmation from the golf manager, he did some quick checking, shuffled a couple of groups, and had us on the first tee within five minutes of our scheduled time. We got an email apology later from the golf manager who had put us down for the next Sunday. Only once in 24 trips have we had a tee time arranged at a course (Borth in southern Wales) that wasn't honored even with the email documentation. If there are slight problems most courses handle them very professionally, but being prepared with documentation helps.

(3) **How much golf to plan** on a trip is a difficult question to answer. Our first self-guided trip was the result of our club's proposed 10-day Scotland and Ireland trip which would have included twelve rounds and no sightseeing. Now, we plan to play about four out of five days, but think that three out of five is more realistic for first trips or when you want to do more touristy things. Besides, you can always add more golf; the courses are everywhere.

(4) Plan to **play in the wind**. Twenty mile per hour breezes are to be expected almost every day, and 30-40 miles per hour winds are quite common. Be prepared by practicing low shots, run-up shots, and having proper clothing for cool winds. In Scotland they say, "If it's nae wind, it's nae golf."

(5) Play from the **proper tees**. Most clubs want visitors to play from the members' tees (the tees everyone plays almost every day) rather than the back or medal tees (those used only for competition). Honor the club's wishes; nothing gives American golfers a bad name quicker than doing something locals don't like. If you are a low single-digit player and want to experience the competition course, ask the pro or golf manager for permission to move back, and then respect his/her answer. Remember, golf should be fun--it's not a test of manhood.

(6) **Clubhouse lounges** are almost always good bets for food. Some, like Macrihanish, Aberfoyle, Ashburnham, St Andrews, Edzell, and St Fillans, are excellent. In our pubs section we mentioned a couple of the

clubhouse lounges, but we almost always feel the golf course is a good bet for a meal. After all, the club lounge has to keep the members happy.

(7) Finally, we suggest you **play a diversity of courses**. The problem with playing only the famous or Open Rota courses is that you never get to see what the Scots themselves play. A couple of years ago we played Gleneagles Queens course one day and Tillicoultry 9-hole the next-- and thoroughly enjoyed both experiences. One may be bigger, better groomed, and have more amenities than the other, but your golf ball doesn't know or care whether you paid £150 or £15. Both will have interesting shots and both will have their own set of tests. Both have a place in a good golfing itinerary.

NOW, START YOUR TOUR OF SCOTLAND AND WALES.

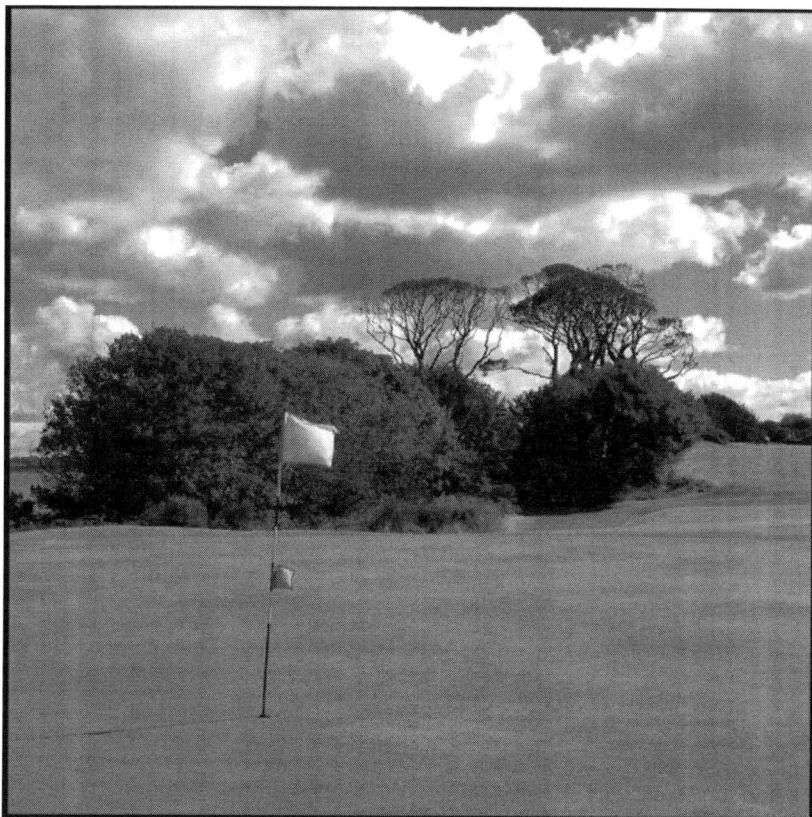

Stranraer GC

CHAPTER TWO: THE SOUTHWEST

<u>GOLF</u>

The southwest region of Scotland, in accord with the Tourist Board's golf guide, takes in the lands west of the M74 to the west coast and north along the coast to Oban. It's a diverse area with small villages like Moffatt and Portpatrick and more metropolitan areas like Ayr. The Kintyre peninsula and the Isle of Arran are different still with miles of single-track road and the mountainous regions of Arran. For the most part the golf is parkland with the exception being courses like those along the Solway Firth, near Macrihanish, and along the Ayrshire coast although there are more links courses either described in *Golf in Scotland: the Hidden Gems* or yet to be written about by us. Our picks for not to be missed courses in this region would be the two seaside gems in the southwest corner, Stranraer and Portpatrick. With a limited time they would be the ones to make time for. All the courses have their own charms and a round on any of them could be a grand day of golf.

DUMFRIES & COUNTY GOLF COURSE
Edinburgh Road, Dumfries DG1 1JX
01387-268918 www.thecounty.org.uk
Parkland, 5782 yards, par 69, £45

AMENITIES: Comfortable clubhouse serves regular hours summer and winter. Small fully stocked golf shop run by pro Stuart Syme.

COURSE COMMENTS: The course, only a mile north of town, was originally opened in 1883 and then redesigned in 1912 by Willie Fernie. In 1929 famed architect James Braid made alterations to the course. The design is a little unusual for an older Scottish course in that the routing comes back to the clubhouse at nine. During World War II much of the course's land was used for wheat and potato production; the course was reconstructed after the war. The course you play today offers some significant challenges, especially from the more than 40 greenside bunkers. Interestingly, there is only one true fairway bunker on the course and no real water hazards, except a burn beside the tee at the 7th and the River Nith (OB) beside the 5th and 7th. Greens are well conditioned and demanding to putt because of significant slopes, including a couple which are tiered.

All the holes at Dumfries & County are good, but we found several worthy of note. At the 5th, *Spion Kop* (a battle in the Boer Wars), 360-yard par 4, you drive from an elevated tee to a broad fairway with trees left. The elevated green is guarded by the River Nith (OB) and a pot bunker on the left. Next is *The Dell*, the 168-yard par 3 sixth. The elevated tee box provides nice views of the course as well as the six bunkers surrounding the large green (shared with the 1st). The short 6th is followed by the relatively long (510 yards) par 5 seventh called *Burns Walk.* You need to drive straight as the River Nith borders the right side all the way to the green. The green is two tiered but bunkerless. *Lea Rig*, the 425-yard par 4 eighth, is the fourth strong hole in a row. The bilevel fairway has trees on both sides demanding a precise drive. The green is guarded on both sides by traps and slopes back to front. On the back we liked the 12th, *Nunholm*. This 422-yard par 4 also requires a precise drive to avoid the railway (OB) right. The undulating fairway leads to a green with bunkers on both sides and some interesting slopes. An interesting very short hole is *The Wee Yin*, the 14th. It's so short at 90 yards that it should be an easy wedge, but five deep bunkers and small sloped green make a fun challenge. *Braid's Tree* is the tough dogleg right 365-yard par 4 fifteenth where your tee shot is key to the hole. A massive tree at the corner on the right, named for the architect, will affect your approach if your drive is short. Three traps guard the small raised green. Dumfries & County is certainly a course to make a special trip for.

FROM THE FORWARD TEES: The course is a lovely parkland golfing experience as the course is big and open. For ladies it's 5420 yards long with a par of 72. Each side has two par 5s and two 3s. The longest par 5 is the 7th at 496 yards with a stroke index of one. The longest par 3 is the 179-yard 16th. The 14th is very short at only 90 yards and requires a precise shot or deal with five deep bunkers. The hole had been called *The Wee Yin*, but in 2014 the name was changed to *Turner's Way* recognizing that local member David Turner has had 10 holes-in-one here. A delightful course.

GLENCRUITTEN GOLF COURSE
Glencruitten Road, Oban, Argyll PA34 4PU
01631-562868   www.obangolf.com
Moorland, 4452 yards, par 61, £25

AMENITIES: The small pro shop stocks all the essentials for your round, and the pleasant clubhouse lounge is fully licensed and serves meals all day

COURSE COMMENTS: One of the prime tourist destinations in Scotland is Oban, the ferry-terminal town, which is a jumping off point to the western islands, particularly Mull, Iona, Coll, and Tiree. As popular a tourist destination as Oban is, it's surprising that there isn't more golf in the area. What golf there is nearby is very worth the time to seek out. Glencruitten Golf Club at Oban is one of the most distinctive courses in Scotland. The James Braid 18-hole design is a complex mixture of par 3s and par 4s (long and short) which play up, around, over, and through knolls, knocks, ravines, canyons, and cliffs. The course guide, a worthwhile investment for this unique layout, describes an almost "lost world" feeling to the course. Don't take me wrong, Anne and I on our first visit discovered Glencruitten to be eminently playable and a great deal of fun, even if it is a little quirky.

With eleven par 3s, Glencruitten GC is certainly not going to overwhelm anyone with its length. Players may, though, be overwhelmed by the variety of shots they will have to invent to get around the course. Leave your driver at home (or for travelers, in your car) and stick in an additional wedge; this is a course which will reward short game accuracy and imagination over length. One of the only examples of where length will help is on the first hole, the longest of the par 4s at 445 yards. A drive of about 210 yards is needed to carry the two burns which cross the fairway. Here you want to be long while staying to the right side of the fairway--too far right, however, will end up in the rough and trees. The blind second shot is testing. It's a shot of 200 yards or more up a steep hill to a sunken green. Once you've successfully (and that's a relative term) negotiated the first hole, you should have an idea of what to expect for the rest of your round.

Glencruitten is hilly, rivaling Scotland's Switzerland at Pitlochry GC in Perthshire, with numerous blind shots which make the short holes even more difficult. One player thought the club ought to provide mountain goats as caddies. Though a hilly course, the Braid layout has a far more natural feel than Glencorse GC near Edinburgh, another steep up and down course. Burns come into play on ten holes and the course is dotted with a few bunkers, but both burns and bunkers are avoidable (and the bunkers aren't frightening if you do get into one). Because of the terrain, all holes on the course are unique, but some have special qualities. The 5th, a 163-yard par 3, which would be a simple shot from an elevated tee to a large flat green, except the right of the green is blocked by impressive rock outcropping about two-thirds of the way to the green. Even though the pin was on the left side of the green, both our shots were still drawn towards the rock. The 8th is a short par 4 (263 yards) which plays blindly uphill over a knock or knoll and down to a narrowing fairway which funnels balls down toward the green. For those who don't want to (or can't) hit over the knoll, a sliver of fairway to the left provides a longer alternate route. At the 10th, a 150-yard par 3, be aware that the green is directly behind the aiming post and a saving bunker is behind the green--a shot hit directly to the post should end up in good position. At the 12th the course crosses a road for four holes. Twelve is a brutal uphill par 4 (Cardiac Hill, it's called), but the other three are more captivating. Number 13 is downhill all the way from tee to green (185 yards) with rolling swales of fairway and rough in between. Pick two or three less clubs than your normal for the distance and pray for a favorable bounce. At 14, a 318-yard par 4, you drive to a fairway bisected diagonally by a troublesome burn. It takes an accurate shot of 220 yards or more to cross the burn and find the fairway.

The second shot is steeply uphill (blind) to a green protected by two bunkers. The 15th at Glencruitten is like the fourth at Anstruther, *Redan* at North Berwick West, and *Clivet* at Royal Tarlair--once you've played it, you'll never forget it. This 125-yard par 3 plays from a plateau tee box across a steep side slope with OB left (the uphill side) to a tiny plateau green (six yards wide and twenty deep). The green has the steep heavily grassed slope above to the left and a small menacing pot bunker on the downhill side. Hit the green or hit into trouble are your only options. A few years ago the hole was even harder with a tee shot of almost 180 yards. In that configuration, too many balls were landing in a private garden next to the course. The garden's owner got an injunction against the course, and the club decided that it was cheaper to move the tee closer than to move the green.

Glencruitten is busy with local members, but it is far enough out-of-the-way to be fairly easy to arrange a game. It is certainly not easy to play or to walk, but the unique James Braid design is worth the effort.

COMMENTS FROM THE FORWARD TEES: For ladies Glencruitten is short at only 3933 yards, but the challenges are many. Besides the hilly terrain there are burns, numerous blind shots, and slopes and angles on the greens. I found the back nine to be far more difficult than the front with more severe slopes and tricky shots. The 15th demands a 151-yard shot to the green because there is almost no other landing area other than a bunker. The land between the tee and green is all rough covered and severely slopes to the right. This is a course you could play over and over because it would be hard to play it perfectly. One side note for women: there are no toilets and not many good woods to hide in.

KIRKCUDBRIGHT GOLF COURSE
Stirling Crescent, Kirkcudbright DG6 4EZ
01557-330314 www.kirkcudbrightgolf.co.uk
Parkland, 5412 yards, par 69, £28

AMENITIES: New clubhouse built in 1987 has good views to the 17th and 18th. Serves pub food usual hours. No golf shop.

COURSE COMMENTS: Originally designed as a nine-hole course in 1893 and redesigned as an eighteen in 1978, Kirkcudbright (kirk-COO-bree) golf course is a pleasant parkland track with views of the Galloway Hills and River Dee estuary. Located at the southern end of the artist town of Kirkcudbright, the course is just off the A711. Several local hotels offer Stay-and-Play packages. As a relatively short track Kirkcudbright still offers plenty of challenges. A few more than ten bunkers (mix of greenside and fairway) will affect play, but it is really the water--ditches, burns, ponds--that will be noticed on four holes. The greens are small to moderate with interesting gentle slopes, but a couple of holes have tiered greens.

Most of the holes at Kirkcudbright are interesting and a few stood out to us. The 2nd, *Knowes*, is a 355-yard, par 4. On this longish two-shotter you tee off towards an aiming post 205 yards out. Also about 200 yards out on the left is a large tree with the end of a ditch (doesn't cross the fairway) just behind. The fairway has several mounds which will provide entertaining bounces. The shot into the green tucked behind a grass mound is blind, but there is an aiming post on the mound about 40 yards from the putting surface. *Jessie Robertson*, the 477-yard, par 5 eighth starts from an elevated tee to an inviting fairway, but beware of bunkers right at 220 yards out and left at 230 yards out. The small green is tiered and guarded by OB behind. Next comes the *Pond*. The 9th is picturesque 176-yard par 3 with ditch and pond left and and OB behind. When you find it the green has subtle slopes. On the back we especially liked the 11th called *Burn*, for obvious reasons. On this short (279-yard) par 4 you drive from the highest point on the course. The hole is short but testing with a small burn left near the green and a large pond front and right of a moderate sized green with significant back to front slope. A tough hole is the 12th, *Plantation*, a 439-yard par 5. The drive over a ditch and gully which shouldn't be a problem, but bunkers right at 220 yards and left at 240 yards might be. The narrow sloped fairway will be a challenge for second shots and the small kidney shaped green is protected by a trap on the right. A downhill one-shotter with OB left is the 16th, *Glebe*, at 174 yards. Stay away from OB and the tiered green with a bunker behind will still be a tough putt. In an area rich with fine golf, Kirkcudbright fits right in.

FROM THE FORWARD TEES: This is a beautiful parkland setting for a course--set in the hills with wonderful views of the Dee estuary and surrounding village. With all these distractions, it is important to keep your focus on the golf since there are many challenges. The course isn't long at 5321 for the red tees, but the hills and slopes, water, trees, and well-placed bunkers will test ladies' skills. There are three par 5s on the front and two on the back. Par 3s aren't too long on the front nine, but I thought the three par 3s on the back were more difficult, especially the 15th at 179 yards and the 16th at 175. Even with all the challenges, I thought Kirkcudbright was an enjoyable course.

LARGS GOLF COURSE
Irvine Road, Largs, Ayrshire KA30 8EU

01475-673594 www.largsgolfclub.co.uk
Seaside parkland, 6140 yards, par 70, £36

AMENITIES: Before or after your round treat yourself to a pint or dram in the plush clubhouse lounge which looks out over the first tee and the final green. The lounge serves good food most usual hours.

COURSE COMMENTS: Along the North Ayrshire coast in the seaside resort town of Largs is a striking parkland course with superb views of the shore, Cumbrae Isle, and Isle Arran. Though built on a raised ancient beach, Largs Golf Club is a parkland track with excellent drainage (only six to ten days a year does the course use winter greens). The course is an easy walk through a mixture of mature and young trees which define the holes. The greens are small to moderate in size and were in good condition when we played even though they had been recently "punched" (we'd say "plugged and sanded"). Besides the trees and the wind typical of an oceanside location, the main trouble for players will be caused by the 53 bunkers in play (several deep) and the five burns in play.

The Largs GC, which some have called "deceptively challenging," is an enjoyable test of shot-making skills. An interesting start is *Haylie*, the 150-yard par 3 first--yet another example of a short hole starting a full course. Your tee shot is uphill (the hole plays about 20 yards longer than the marked distance because of the hill) and over a burn. The bottom of the flag is not visible from the tee, but a slope behind the green acts as a backstop to aggressive shots. Not a difficult hole, but it does serve to get you up to the sandy soil of the ancient raised beach. The 3rd at Largs, *Killincraig*, a 476-yard par 5, is a great driving hole (as is the second). This hole begins with a tee shot which must negotiate an alley between tall trees to a generous fairway. Stay to the left off the tee because the slope of the fairway will push the ball to the right toward a bunker and row of trees. Be warned, though, you can't go too far left because a burn runs the length of the hole crossing the fairway just in front of the green. Not only do you need to be mindful of the burn on your second shot (or in my case, the third), but you also need to avoid two bunkers on the right of the green.

More so than on other courses with large landing areas, the tee shots are key at Largs. A couple more good examples of this are the tee shots at the 6th and 9th. *Castle*, the 365-yard par 4 sixth, begins with a blind tee shot to a fairway which turns left about 220 yards from the tee. A tee ball in good position in the fairway still leaves a difficult mid-iron to an elevated, well-bunkered green. An approach shot short of the green will tend to bounce right into a bunker on that side. A tricky par 4 is the 9th, *Waterside*, a 392-yard slight dogleg left. A long accurate tee shot (220 to

240 yards) to the middle of the fairway is needed to set up the second shot which must cross a burn and avoid stands of trees on both sides. A short drive brings the burn more into play on the second. Whether you go for the green or lay-up, the raised, two-tiered green is not an easy target.

Following the challenge of the 9th is the spectacular 10th. *Arran*, a par 4 of 401 yards, is my favorite hole at Largs. Another dogleg left, the hole plays through a beautiful avenue of mature trees with a burn crossing about 95 yards in front of the green. Your approach shot should stay to the left side of the plateau green, which slopes back to front. The tee box of the 11th is a good spot to pause and enjoy the beauty of the twin rows of trees planted in the 1880s by the Kelburn Estate in honor of the visit of Queen Victoria to the estate. *Bowencraig*, the 16th, is where Anne and I met Hugh, a local member. Whereas, in the States to speed play serious efforts are made to "pair up" groups or individuals into foursomes (fourball in the UK), in Scotland such combining of groups is unusual. Anne and I will usually be scheduled to play as a two-ball, though, whenever we can, we ask to be paired with locals. Take every opportunity you can to play with local players. Not only can they guide you around the course with their local knowledge, but they can be a fount of information about where else to play, where to stay or eat, what to see, or what to avoid. Often, too, they have stories to tell--about the course or themselves. In the three holes we played with Hugh, we got recommendations for good places to eat (better than the place we had reservations for), recommendations for where to stay next time we are in the area, a lead on a course we hadn't planned to play, and the history of Largs GC. From Hugh we found out that the club, organized in 1892, has had the Earl of Glasgow as Honorary President since its inception (the 10th Earl currently occupies the office). The course, like many others, began as a 9-hole course which was later expanded to 18 (1953). In 1981, the membership arranged to purchase the land the course plays over from the Kelburn Estate. Hugh also proudly pointed out that European Ryder Cup Captain (2001) Sam Torrance played much of his early golf as a junior member of the club, and still comes back to play when he can. Sad to say, he wasn't there the day we played. One of the reasons we avoid golf tours (not the only reason) is that on the lesser known or out-of-the-way tracks we are more likely to get to play with locals. If you are calling ahead for a booking, don't be afraid to ask to play with some locals. Very often courses can make that arrangement.

It's decision time on your drive at the 16th, a 340-yard par 4, with a burn crossing the middle of the fairway. Either hit it 230 to carry the burn or lay-up short--or miss hit a going-for-it shot, land short of the burn, and say you planned it that way (at least, that's the way I played it). The green is tucked a little to the right behind trees and protected by four bunkers. The 17th hole affords you a view of the Round Tower of Bowen Craig, known locally as "The Pencil," to the west of the course near the harbour. The 18th, *Kelburn Home*, at 356 yards is a demanding and fair finish to a round at Largs GC. This hole requires another long and straight drive; long enough to clear the burn 180 yards out and straight enough to avoid the OB left and the rough and burn on the right. The approach to the green is just as testing. Two bunkers left guard the significantly raised, tiered green. Don't be short or you may find your ball rolling back off the green and into the bunkers or the rough. It took us seven trips to Scotland to discover the beautiful Largs GC, and I guess that's the description of a hidden gem.

COMMENTS FROM THE FORWARD TEES: This parkland course is a good challenge for ladies. It has pleasant scenery, lots of trees, a burn or two to cross, a few hills, and decent length (5450 yards). The sunny day we played it made a nice walk in the park. Because the course is so close to the Firth of Clyde it could certainly be more difficult on a windy day. Even with all the golfing obstacles the course will be very playable for ladies, and with a 73 par I was able to play to my handicap. The five par 5s range from 422 yards on the 3rd to 368 yards on the 11th. The downhill 3rd is reachable, but trees and a dogleg make 11 play harder than its yardage. The par 3s are all short, but are not without hazards. The 1st is only 110 yards, but it's all carry uphill to a green which runs off on three sides into bunkers or rough and trees. Largs GC is a good choice for ladies.

LOCHGILPHEAD GOLF COURSE
Blarbuie Road, Lochgilphead PA31 8LE
01546-602340/510383 www.lochgilphead-golf.com
Parkland 9-hole, 2259 yards, par 32, £20 day

AMENITIES: A modern clubhouse, which offers refreshments during the week and a licensed bar on weekends, provides some golf supplies and a few articles of clothing for sale. An honesty box is available if the lounge (where you check in for golf) is not open. Changing rooms are open most usual hours.

COURSE COMMENTS: The Argyll region of the west coast of Scotland is rich in historical attractions and is dotted with worthwhile golfing experiences. Above the resort town of Lochgilphead located on the Loch Gilp finger of Loch Fyne, known for its wonderful Loch Fyne oysters, is the Lochgilphead Golf Club. Sitting just north of town above the hospital, the course designed by Dr. I. McCammond plays along the hill sides next to Kilmichael Forest.

The course itself, though short, offers plenty of challenge. With no bunkers, the difficulty at Lochgilphead comes from water in play on the last four holes, small greens (although they are relatively flat), and numerous uphill, downhill, and sidehill lies. One gent coming off the course summed up our feelings when he said the course was "well worth the day ticket price." Number three, *Mount Druim*, is a dramatic 131-yard par 3 which plays straight uphill. Take at least two extra clubs to reach the green. Another uphill par 3 is *Graveyard*, the 177-yard 5th. The tee shot, though not as extreme as at the 3rd, is much narrower with trees tight on the right. From here you go to the tee box of the most exciting hole on the course. *Rifle Range* is a 392-yard par 4 from a very elevated tee. Even though a downhill hole like this should play shorter than its measured distance, a good tee shot still left a long second shot to a green with a burn in front and OB (and sheep) behind. The prudent play for me was a lay up and a chip, but vacation golf isn't always meant to be prudent. I went for the green from about 180 and found the sheep field, instead. My next shot was the lay-up I should have hit the first time. The 8th, *Cuilarstitch Bends*, is a 264-yard par 4 demanding a precise opening shot. Your shot needs to clear a bog with water both left and right. Your second shot then is to a green fronted by more water. Though the hole isn't as difficult as it may sound, you need to be thinking here. Lochgilphead GC is an inviting 9-hole track set into a lovely area of Scottish countryside and well worth the time to play.

The town makes a convenient location from which to explore this region of Argyll, the Kilmartin Glen (with a myriad of ancient sites), and the Crinin Canal. The town has also eschewed modern shopping developments and retained the old Scotland shopping experience--it's like stepping back in time to visit shops like the Dalraida DIY Hardware Shop.

COMMENTS FROM THE FORWARD TEES: At 1963 yards the course is not long and has a par of 33, but I thought it was difficult to score on. Each time water comes into play it required an extra shot for a lay up. The lack of flat lies also gave me fits. The only par 5, the 6th, is only 354 yards, but as Bob described above, is not an easy hole. The water at 8 makes the hole tough. It is challenging golf, but it is a course I'd stop at anytime.

MOFFAT GOLF COURSE
Coatshill, Moffat DG10 9SB

01683-220020 www.moffatgolfclub.co.uk
Parkland, 5259 yards, par 69, £25

AMENITIES: Moffat GC boasts a classic clubhouse with a very comfortable lounge which serves snacks most usual hours. No golf shop, check in at the bar.

COURSE COMMENTS: The drive down the M74 from Central to Southern Scotland is lovely with the Southern Uplands to the west and the Border Hills to the east. Intriguing golf adventures are not far off the highway as well. Closest to the motorway is one of Scotland's true hidden gems. I know the term "hidden gems" is used far too often by golf journalists (I'll unashamedly admit my guilt), but in the case of the Moffat Golf Club the monicker is deserved.

An April 1905, article in *The Moffat News* describes the newly opened Moffat Golf Club:

"The site of the new course, from a spectacular point of view, could hardly be surpassed. Only half a mile from the town, it is standing at an elevation of 670 feet above sea level, and is a breezy and undulating tableland of fine old turf, noted for the salubrity of the air, while having a framework of mountain ranges, the scenery is most attractive." [*The Moffat Golf Club*, Drew Grieve, 2000]

That description remains accurate today. Built on Coates Hill, with grand views of the award winning Moffat village, this 18-hole Ben Sayer designed moorland course is aptly known as "the Jewel of the South." Were it located closer to metropolitan areas (as it is, it's only an hour from Glasgow or Edinburgh), it would surely be crowded all the time. Located in the rural south, the course is relatively free of congestion and very welcoming to visitors. The Moffat course is both picturesque and entertaining. Locals say that the Solway Firth is visible on an exceptional day. Though we enjoyed pleasant views of the town, the hills, and a castle to the west, the scuttling clouds on the windy, showery day we played blocked the distant views. The weather didn't interfere with our enjoyment of the course, which is well-protected with 32 bunkers (most in play), some quite large and many steep-sided. Combine Sayer's bunkering with small, quick, well-conditioned greens, a burn in play on a couple of holes, and numerous elevation changes, and Moffat will play tough enough to challenge any player's game.

The first hole, *Craigbeck*, is a 199-yard par 3 for both men and women. Even though the hole plays slightly downhill, it's a daunting task to begin with a long-iron shot. It is interesting to us that so many of Scotland's good village courses (Crieff, Peebles, Boat of Garten, Largs) begin with strong short holes. Number four is a short, but tricky, par 4. At only 292 yards *Roman Road* requires a tee shot to land about 60 yards short of the green at the bottom of a steep hillside of heavy rough. The second shot is then blind to a small green. An ancient Roman road crosses the middle of the fairway, hence the name. The 7th, *Annandale*, a 334-yard par 4, could be called the blind leading the blind. Again, it's a blind shot off the tee which this time leads to a blind second shot to a green flanked by three bunkers. The bowl shaped green is one of the most undulating on the course. Even with good shots, the hole is an adventure. Finish the hole and then reward yourself with a moment to take in the fine vista to the west. *Port Arthur*, the 125-yard par 3 ninth, starts with one more of the eight blind tee shots at Moffat GC. The hole rises steeply then drops sharply to the green. Trust the yardage rather then your eyes on this shot. Too little club leaves an almost impossible shot up the cliff face. Too much club leaves you lost in the heavy rough behind the green. This is a hole that really will get easier the more you play it (or so we've been told). Moffat also boasts one of the more interesting greens we've encountered. The 13th is a 141-yard par 3 which plays downhill to a "fortress green" (a square green with grass dykes in front and left, a stone wall on the right, and a grass hollow behind). The 18th is a classy finishing hole. At 271 yards this downhill par 4 won't scare you with its length, but it is definitely not as easy as it looks. For most of us, the tee shot needs to stay short of the burn fronting the green (about 240 yards). Big hitters can try to drive the green, but a burn, a greenside bunker, and rough behind await those who miss. A quality first shot will leave an easy chip or pitch, and maybe lead to a birdie to end your round. A fun hole!

COMMENTS FROM THE FORWARD TEES: When there isn't a panoramic view on this hilly course, the view of the hole itself will be engaging. The slopes are gradual enough that I didn't get worn out too fast. Yardage of 4794 yards isn't long for women and the par is 68. The par 5 fourteenth is very long at 476 yards, but the other par 5, the 8th, is only 390 yards. The 8th is still a challenge with a steep drop-off at 162 yards. Shot management is extremely important. The six par 3s at Moffat are all good holes. It's a course where experience will reward you with better scores.

PORTPATRICK GOLF CLUB, Dunskey Course
Golf Course Road, Portpatrick DG9 8TB

01776-810273   www.portpatrickgolfclub.com
Clifftop links, 5913 yards, par 70, £32

AMENITIES: Pleasant clubhouse with changing rooms and lounge on one level. The comfortable lounge looks out onto the first tee--and yes, everyone watches those teeing off. Wave to the audience. Small, but fully equipped golf shop.

COURSE COMMENTS: The course opened in 1903 and is playable all year because of the local microclimate. Set 150 feet above the sea, Portpatrick Dunskey GC offers great views of the Irish Sea and Sandeel Bay (from the 13th). On a clear day you can see the Belfast area and the Mountains of Mourne in Northern Ireland. The course is often viewed as a "holiday fun course," but the lush rough and gorse can be difficult and the wind (especially a south westerly) will seriously change the complexion of the course. Thirty-one bunkers, mostly greenside, are a welcome recent addition to Dunskey. Most of the bunkers are easily playable and four holes have no bunkers. The greens are small with some contours and tiers, but are easy to read. A burn on one hole is not a major problem, but on two holes it's a concern all the way. A deep ditch (playable) is a problem on 4 and 7, both par 3s. Dunskey is hilly and there are several blind shots. Even if you play badly, the views make it worth a visit.

Even though we enjoyed all the holes at Portpatrick, we chose six to highlight. The 3rd, *Muckle Skelp*, is a 544-yard par 5, which begins with an uphill drive toward an aiming post on a narrow fairway. The approach will also be blind over another hill with an aiming post. Approach with care because the green slopes away from you. Take plenty of club at the short, 160-yard 4th. This is one of the holes fronted by a deep ravine. Tee off well back in the gorse to a steeply sloped right-to-left fairway on *Flyover*, the 377-yard par 4 eighth. Stay as high as you can because your ball will run down to the left toward a burn. The green is tucked left, but has no bunkers. The premier hole on the Dunskey course is the 293-yard par 4 thirteenth. Enjoy the view before teeing off sharply downhill with Sandeel Bay (OB) on the left. Depending upon the wind, the green and trap front right and two to the left are all reachable. The green, which looks tiny from the highly elevated tee, has quite a bit of slope and is tricky to putt. Fourteen is the same yardage, 293-yards, but plays completely differently. Drive steeply uphill toward the aiming pole. Past the pole the slope goes down to the green. Stay to the right because the fairway slopes to the left. The green, which is guarded by one bunker left, is also a putting challenge. The last hole we note is the 16th, *Rickwood*, a 393-yard two-shotter. Into the wind the drive is fraught with trouble: gorse on both sides, a burn crossing the fairway, and a knob directly in your line. The narrow green has no need of bunkers. As one player noted, "Portpatrick Dunskey is a course where you can spend time looking at the views (the Isle of Man to the south and the Mull of Kintyre to the north) instead of looking for golf balls."

COMMENTS FROM THE FORWARD TEES: Portpatrick GC is a course which requires quite a bit of good course management from women; many subtle shots and plenty of wind. Several holes have visually interesting drives (some can be quite intimidating). The 13th is a stunning hole, but I was afraid my ball would hang up on the slope leaving me a terrible downhill lie. Luckily I had one of my better drives on this hole and reached the bottom. Although the course is up and down, it was an easy walk for the most part.

STRANRAER GOLF COURSE
Creachmore, Leswalt, Stranraer DG9 0LF
01776 870245   www.stranraergolfclub.net
Coastal parkland, 6308 yards, par 70, £30

AMENITIES: 1994 clubhouse has changing rooms downstairs and a lounge upstairs. The lounge has spectacular views of the 1st, 18th, and the sea loch, and serves good food the usual hours. The club has no golf shop, but some supplies are available in the starter/secretary office.

COURSE COMMENTS: The club has been in existence since 1905 and has played at several locations. The War Department requisitioned the course land in 1940 and it would be 12 years before a new course was built. The current course at Creachmore is the last design work of famed architect James Braid who was convinced to come out of retirement for the project in 1949 (he died in November, 1950). The course opened in June, 1952 and it's the course you play today. Stranraer is very welcoming to visitors and therefore can be busy; call ahead so you won't be disappointed. The course offers magnificent views of the sea loch, village, and surrounding farmland, ferries leaving to or returning from Ireland are an added distraction. Don't be distracted though by the more than 50 greenside and fairway bunkers strategically positioned on Stranraer. A few of the bunkers are deep and some are built into typical Braid Bumps (purpose-built mounds with facing bunkers). The moderate to small greens are mostly flat, but are in good condition and quick with subtle breaks. A burn comes into play on five holes, and the sea loch is a dramatic feature (OB) of the 5th. Lastly, as on most Scottish seaside courses, the wind is always a condition of play. One of the nice features of Stranraer is that it is playable all year without the use of alternate tees or greens.

The Stranraer Creachmore course is a joy to play with great variety in the holes to keep your interest the whole round. We like the course so much that it is difficult to narrow down the holes to describe; so many are that good. On 2, *Lea Rig*, a 338-yard par 4, you drive slightly downhill to a left sloping fairway. A burn, trees, and two greenside bunkers will complicate the approach to a moderate sized green. The burn again is in play on the 420-yard par 4 third. A dogleg left to right over the burn (off the tee) to a generous landing area begins the hole. The uphill approach has the burn along the right and a fairway which slopes toward the burn. The raised green has a large bunker on the left. A fantastic hole listed by *Bunkered Magazine* as one of the hardest in Scotland is *Corunna*, the 397-yard par 4 fifth. Drive from a very elevated tee (actually the top of a cliff) down to a crescent fairway which bends right, has heavy forest on the left, and Loch Ryan (the sea loch) as OB on the right. Two saving bunkers on the right are within easy reach on the drive. One more bunker guards the elevated green on this beautiful and challenging hole. I count my par here as one of my golfing highlights in Scotland. Next is *The Wig*, a 160-yard par 3 with an uphill tee shot to a relatively small green with five fronting bunkers. Be sure to take enough club. *Craw's Nest*, the 346-yard 10th, is the hole Braid liked best on the course. The hole doglegs right around a stand of trees from a slightly raised tee. A big hitter can try to cut the corner, but the safe play is to the center of the fairway. The lifted green is guarded by trees and two traps. In the spring beware of the crows nesting in the trees between the 10th and the 11th. *Bluidy Burn* (a name we've seen on other holes) is the 11th. This 377-yarder plays along the side of a hill on the right and then uphill to the green. Add an extra club on your approach because of the hill and watch out for two bunkers and OB right of the green. Despite the name, there's no burn in play on the hole. *Lang Whang* (another name you'll find on many courses) is a great right to left dogleg 513-yard par 5 around trees and a large mound. Traps and a sloped (to the left) fairway add challenge to the approach. The last, aptly named *Braid's Last*, is the final hole designed by Braid in his illustrious career. The 343-yard par 4 is a true gem which doglegs left around a large bunker with plenty of room to the right. The slightly raised green has three bunkers left and two right. Nothing fancy here, just good golf. Stranraer GC is well south, but certainly worth the effort to play.

COMMENTS FROM THE FORWARD TEES: The distances between the men's tees and the ladies' isn't that great, but women get four more strokes which helps equalize play. The numerous bunkers can cause some real trouble, especially the ones that are steep-faced and built into elevated greens. A number of approach shots are steeply uphill, especially at 10 and 11. The par threes are short, but they all have bunkers to trip you up. All the problems of the course are made up for by the beauty of the tree-lined holes and the vistas from the men's tee at the 5th.

Courses in this region listed in *Golf in Scotland: The Hidden Gems***:** Belleisle (Ayr), Brodick (Isle of Arran), Carradale (Kintyre), Colvend (Dumfries), Dalmally, Dundonald (Irvine), Girvan Municipal, Lamlash (Isle of Arran), Lochgilphead, Machrie Bay (Isle of Arran), Machrihanish (Kintyre), Machrihanish Dunes (Kintyre), Maybole, Powfoot (Annan), St Medan (Newton Stewart), Sanquhar, Seafield (Ayr), Shiskine (Isle of Arran), Silloth on Solway (England), Southerness (Dumfries), Turnberry Kintyre (Ayr), Whiting Bay (Isle of Arran), Wigtown & Bladnoch (Wigtown), Wigtownshire & County (Glenluce).

PUBS, TEAROOMS, & RESTAURANTS

Several of our suggestions in this chapter are either Isle Arran or the Kintyre Peninsula even though we don't list any golf courses in those areas. They are places we have played golf before and keep going back to play. As we go back we find new pubs or restaurants to recommend. In a way, this edition becomes a companion our first guide, *Golf in Scotland: The Hidden Gems*. The restaurant gems in this chapter are the Waterfront Fishouse Restaurant in Oban, Crown Hotel in Portpatrick, and the Brodick Brasserie on Isle Arran.

Abbey Cottage (tearoom) in New Abbey next door to Sweetheart Abbey (Historic Scotland). A tearoom and gift shop serving soups, sandwiches and sweets.

The Bistro Bar in the Selkirk Hotel just off the main street through Kirkcudbright. Recommended by our B&B, the hotel has several bistro rooms and a main restaurant (same menu throughout). Good food, good service in a busy place.

Bladnoch Inn (pub/restaurant) in Bladnoch by Wigtown and across from the distillery. Great place for lunch or dinner after a visit to Bladnoch distillery, Scotland's most southern facility. Good pub menu with specials.

Brig o' Doon House Hotel (restaurant) in Alloway on the River Doon. Located just in front of the bridge over the River Doon (Robert

Burns' Brig o' Doon from the poem "Tam O'Shanter"), the hotel restaurant provides great meals for just above pub prices. One of the best dining choices in the area.

Brodick Bar and Brasserie (bistro/restaurant) at the north end of the village of Brodick on Isle of Arran. Recently remodeled the Brasserie continues to serve excellent meals off a large entertaining (chalkboard) menu. One of the best bets on the island.

Carradale Hotel (pub/restaurant) in Carradale on the Kintyre Peninsula, just up from the golf course. Pub meals from an extensive, upscale pub menu and inexpensive set price two or three course dinners make the Carradale Hotel a good stop when in the area.

Catacol Hotel Pub at Catacol on the northwest coast of Isle of Arran. Sited directly on the Kilbrannan Sound looking across to the Kintyre Peninsula, the Catacol Hotel is a rustic hotel and pub. Food is basic, tasty pub fare and the locals are friendly.

Cavens Arms Pub on Buccleuch Street down from town square in Dumfries. A Victorian-style pub with a large menu and a large page of specials. Pub of the Year for the area at least seven years running. Excellent food and good prices--deserving of its awards.

The Chartroom II Bistro and Arduaine Restaurant at the Loch Melfort Hotel near Oban. Next to the Arduaine Gardens (National Trust for Scotland), the hotel has two fine eateries. For more casual (and cheaper) dining try the Charthouse II Bistro famous for its fresh langoustines and fish chowder. The more formal Arduaine Restaurant serves set price meals with some unique items.

Coasters (pub) on the seafront in Oban. This is a good place to catch the local flavor and have a drink. Not really an eatery.

Crown Hotel (pub) on the harbour front in Portpatrick. Pub in the front, a more formal restaurant in the back (with a slightly different menu than the pub), and a front patio for good weather. Scotland's Seafood Pub of the Year for 2011, the Crown Hotel pub has great local seafood specials. Food lived up to the awards.

The Drift Inn (pub) in Lamlash on Isle of Arran next to the bowling green. We enjoyed our first night's dinner here so much we came back the next night. The pub food is good and the place is usually very busy.

Eilean Mor (restaurant) on the main island road through Brodick, Isle of Arran. Bistro-style restaurant with wood tables, some with nice view of the bay. You can't miss the restaurant with its distinctive red facade. Large menu, good food, especially pizzas, and friendly staff are the drawing cards.

Glenisle Hotel Restaurant on the main street of Lamlash, Isle of Arran, facing the bay. Modern (recently refurbished) lodge-style dining with several small eating areas and a large dining room. The menu is limited but the food is delicious. There is a nice lounge for coffee or drinks after dinner.

Harbour House Hotel (pub) on Main Street in Portpatrick near the lighthouse. A comfortable pub with a slightly upscale menu.

Highland Laddie in Glasson, the **Hope and Anchor** in Port Carlisle, and the **Kings Arms** in Bowness-on-Solway are all wee village pubs on the England side of the Solway Firth near Silloth-on-Solway GC. Each is a good example of an English village pub and each serves decent pub food. Frequented by plenty of Hadrian's Wall walkers, the pubs are lively and friendly.

Huntingdon Hotel (pub) on St Mary's Street in Dumfries near city center. Newly refurbished in 2005, the small bar serves high quality food off a limited menu to residents and nonresidents.

L'Aperitif (restaurant) on the edge of the downtown section on London Road in Stranraer. The name may sound French, but the restaurant serves a full Italian menu. Excellent food and service in a building which was originally the postmaster's home.

Lagg Inn (pub/restaurant) in Kilmory on the southern end of Isle of Arran. Established in 1791, the inn is a little out of the way, but worth the effort to visit. The very interesting menu is served both in the pub and the more formal restaurant. Interesting food at fair prices. Take the short hike (500 meters) up to the ancient cairns by the inn.

The Lighthouse (cafe/restaurant) in the village of Pirnmill south of Lochranza on Isle of Arran. Cafe by day and restaurant on weekend evenings, The Lighthouse has a well deserved reputation for good food. Be sure to book for an evening meal, especially if a little out of season, since they won't open if there are no bookings.

Loch Fyne (pronounced Fine) Oyster Bar (restaurant) on the west side of Loch Fyne about nine miles from Inveraray. Excellent variety of quality seafood, and a seafood shop and garden store.

Machrihanish Golf Club Lounge (pub) at the golf club about six miles northwest of Campbeltown. There are only a few times that we'll recommend a golf club lounge for eating, although usually golf club food is good. Machrihanish's lounge is one of the special ones. Some of the best food in the area and the lounge is open to non-golfers as well.

Morris's Steakhouse (restaurant) on the bay front in Largs. Touted as the best steaks in the area, Morris's was a disappointment. The food wasn't bad; it just wasn't anything special and the service was mediocre. Try someplace else.

The Old Clubhouse Pub across from Machrihanish GC. The pub is literally in the old Machrihanish GC clubhouse, which for years has been a low-scale pub of another name. Newly refurbished by the owners of Machrihanish Dunes as part of their complex, the pub is a lovely golfer's hangout and serves upscale pub fare at upscale (though not outrageous) prices.

Pierhead Tavern on shore Road (the main road around the island) on Isle of Arran. Tasty pub grub in large portions, especially the haddock and chips. The new dining room is a strong addition.

Powfoot Golf Hotel (pub/restaurant) next to the Powfoot Golf Course in Annan. Three eating rooms means you'll find the type of food your looking for, from pub fare to full restaurant menu, at Powfoot Hotel. Good food, fair prices.

ReadingLasses Cafe on the main street in Wigtown. A bookstore with tearoom/cafe tables in each room. Eat among the books. Interesting menu items and a motto of "Read, Eat, Dream."

The Royal Hotel (pub) in the center of Kirkcudbright (kerk-COO-bree). Set in the middle of the artist town of Kirkcudbright, the hotel bar serves lunches and dinners from a typical pub menu.

Sea Bed Restaurant at the Anchor Hotel on the harbour at Tarbet. Both the restaurant and pub bistro serve the same extensive menu which is heavy on seafood. Everything we've had is excellent and the service always fine.

Steamboat Inn (pub) in Carsethorn near Dumfries on the firth. Historic inn, 1813, was the emigrant embarkation point for many heading for a new life. Now it is an inn with an extensive menu for today's travelers.

Stable's Restaurant on Bank Street in Fort William. Nothing fancy, but the window tables do have a good view and the food was tasty.

Suie Lodge (pub) in Glen Dochart near Crianlarich. We found Suie Lodge by accident--nothing else in the area was serving at 3:00 in the afternoon. It was our good fortune. The pub serves homemade food and specializes in local game. Good food and friendly people.

Waterfront Hotel and Bistro (restaurant) near the harbour in Portpatrick. Interesting menu and well-prepared food in a lovely setting. Good choice when in the area.

The Waterfront Seafood Restaurant on the docks of Oban harbour. Housed upstairs in the old Fisherman's Mission, the restaurant specializes in fresh seafood, of course, and offers great views of Oban Bay. To tell you how good the food is, we thought it still smelled good after we were stuffed and on our way out.

Wildings Hotel (restaurant) in Maidens by Turnberry GC on the Ayrshire coast. We had a great meal here several years ago. The restaurant now serves only set price lunches and dinners.

LODGINGS

The Anchor Hotel
Harbour Street, Tarbert, Loch Fyne, Argyll PA29 6UB
01880-820577 www.lochfyne-scotland.co.uk £90
Conveniently located in the heart of the village on the harbour, the Anchor Hotel has recently been refurbished and offers lovely rooms at reasonable prices--ask for the the sea view, a little higher but well worth it. Serves a great breakfast with good choices.

Barr Farmhouse B&B
The Barr, Dumfries DG1 3LJ
01387-711384 www.barrfarmhgouse.co.uk £76
This early 1800s farmhouse (modernized) offers two rooms, friendly hosts, and is 10 minutes drive from town.

The Broom Lodge
5 Broomfield Place, Largs, Ayrshire KA30 8DR
01475-674290 www.broom-lodge.co.uk £55
With good views of The Cumbraes, Arran, and Bute, The Broom Lodge has a great location and comfortable rooms, although we had a few small problems with our room the night we stayed. Breakfast is hearty and tasty.

The Burlington
Shore Road, Whiting Bay, Isle of Arran KA27 8PZ
01770-700255 www.burlingtonarran.co.uk £55
Built as a guest house in 1904 in the Arts & Crafts-style with Edwardian features, The Burlington has comfortable rooms and reputation for fine food (book ahead for an evening meal). The restaurant is part of

Scotland's "Slow Food" movement (organic and locally grown) with a three course dinner for about £25.

Craigard House Hotel

Low Askomil, Campbeltown, Argyll PA28 6EP
01586-554242 www.craigard-house.co.uk £90
Craigard House Hotel is a recently converted Victorian mansion with an interesting history. Accommodations are first class throughout and the food, both breakfast and evening meals, are top rate. The house began as a whisky distiller's home and then was run as a maternity home by the local Council from   1942 to 1973. In 1998, after extensive remodeling, Craigard House opened as a small hotel. An elegant and historic stay when playing Machrihanish and southern Kintyre courses.

Ferintosh B&B

30 Lovers Walk, Dumfries DG1 1LX
01387-252262 www.ferintosh.net £60
Emma and Robertson, your hosts, do an excellent job of making guests comfortable. The rooms are comfortable and the B&B is an easy walk from the centre of town and good restaurants. Breakfast is lovely and the craic (conversation) a joy. Definitely a top notch stay.

Glenaldor House B&B

5 Victorian Terrace, Dumfries DG1 1NL
01387-264248 www.glenaldorhouse.co.uk £56
Once you find Glenaldor House it's worth the effort. The lovely, centrally located home has spacious comfortable bedrooms and serves great breakfasts. On the same terrace, next to Glenaldor is a house where J.M. barrie (author of "Peter Pan")lived while attending Dumfries Academy. Several good restaurants are within easy walking distance of Glenaldor House.

The Glenisle Hotel and Bistro

Lamlash, Isle of Arran KA27 8LY
01770-600559 www.glenislehotel.com £116
In the heart of the charming village of Lamlash, the Glenisle opened in 1849. In 2008 the hotel and bistro underwent a major remodel. The rooms are nicely appointed and the breakfast is delicious. A good choice if our favorite B&B, Lilybank, next door isn't available.

Greenan Lodge
39 Denure Road, Doonfoot (by Ayr) KA7 4HR
01292-443939 www.greenanlodge.com £70
Greenan Lodge is a large modern B&B with huge rooms (our double was actually a suite) and a lovely guest lounge. Located on the main coastal road between Turnberry and Ayr, the lodge is convenient to most of the tourist sites in the area (five minutes drive from the new Burns Museum) and all the golf courses. Howard is a knowledgeable golfer and Helen a friendly host. Breakfast is delicious.

Harbour Lights Guest House
7 Agnew Crescent, Stranraer DG9 7JY
01776-706261 www.harbourlightsguesthouse.co.uk £50
Conveniently located on the harbour road and a short walk (10 minutes) from the downtown area, Harbour Lights is a good place to stay in the area. Rooms and breakfast is nice, and Rhone and Colin are wonderful hosts.

Hazeldean House Guest House
4 moffat Road, Dumfries DG1 1NJ
01387-266178 www.hazeldeanhouse.com £60
Only minutes walk from town, this 1898 Victorian villa has lovely gardens front and back. The house is near the rail station and has a lovely guest lounge.

Hillcrest House
Wigtown, Newton, Wigtownshire DG8 9EU
01988-402018 www.hillcrest-wigtown.co.uk £70
The house, at the corner of Midland Place and Station Road, is a short walk from the main shopping area. Built in 1875, hosts Deborah and Andrew Firth have retained much of the house's Victorian character. The ensuite bedrooms are comfortable as is the lounge and large dining room. Breakfast is top notch and evening meals can be arranged. Wigtown, with its numerous bookstores, is a great town to wander and the little village golf course is worth a round.

Kilmichael Country House Hotel
Glen Cloy by Brodick, Isle of Arran KA22 8BY
01770-302219 www.kilmichael.com £163
Believed to be the oldest house on the Isle of Arran, Kilmichael is as rich in historic associations as it is in elegant accommodations. The five star facility has been featured as a Best of Britain Hotel and is past winner of

the Taste of Scotland's "Country House Hotel of the Year." The tariff is not cheap, but then nothing is cheap about Kilmichael House. Rooms are nicely appointed and each has a distinct style. We stayed in a lovely room which was once the stable and were greeted with fresh flowers and a generous tipple of malt whisky. The restaurant, which has been called "Arran's finest," is highly recommended (though it is expensive). Breakfasts are excellent and the service deserves its five star status. Certainly, Kilmichael House is one of Scotland's premier lodgings.

Lilybank Guest House
Lamlash, Isle of Arran KA27 8SL
01770-650000 www.lilybank-arran.co.uk £65
Situated on the shores of Lamlash Bay overlooking the Holy Isle, Colin and June Richardson's Lilybank Guest House has an ideal location for the golfer wanting to play the several courses available on the Isle of Arran or just to explore the sites of the island or both. Most rooms are ensuite and have bay views. The dining room as well overlooks the bay and breakfast is delicious.

Linthorpe B&B
14 Arden Road, Twynholm by Kirkcudbright DG6 4PB
01557-860662 www.linthorpebandb.co.uk £75
Simon and Sue make Linthrope an accommodation with a difference. Linthrope has lovely rooms and a large guest lounge. The location, about four miles from the artist town Kirkcudbright is only slightly inconvenient, but the quiet situation in Twynholm and the fantastic breakfast makes up for it--be sure to have the fresh smoked trout if available (Sue teaches fly fishing).

Wallsend Guest House
The Old Rectory, Bowness on Solway, Wigtown, Cumbria, England CA7 5AF
01697-357055 www.wallsend.net £70
Yes, we know it's in England and this book is about Scotland golf, but Wallsend Guest House at the west end of Hadrian's Wall is excellently located for exploring the golf in the Dumfries-Gallway area, as well as visiting the very Scottish-like course Silloth-on-Solway. Accommodations are lovely and breakfasts are great. There are some pleasant village pubs in the area for meals as well.

The Warren
Machrihanish, Campbeltown PA28 6PT
01586-810310 www.thewaqrrenmachrihanish.co.uk
£64

Built originally as a golfing lodge in the 1890s, The Warren is a great location for playing the wonderful links at Macrihanish or the new Machrihanish Dunes. Rooms are lovely and spacious and the breakfast is delightful. Bryan and Judy McClements are great hosts, ready to see to all your needs.

TOURIST ATTRACTIONS

Brodick Castle, Brodick, Isle of Arran. Home of the Hamiltons since 1503, the castle overlooks Brodick Bay and the Firth of Clyde, while behind it stand   Goatfell Peak, the tallest point on the island at 2866 feet. Brodick Castle is a fine example of a Victorian Highland estate with a lovely garden and forest walks.

Caerlaverock Castle, near Dumfries. The substantial ruins of this 13th C Maxwell family castle has a complete moat around it. The grounds of the castle also host a locally   run   tearoom   known   for   its homemade baked goods.

Castle Kennedy Gardens, near Stranraer. The more than 200-acre estate offers gardens, lochans, sweeping lawns, and tree-lined avenues for visitors. Particularly lovely in the spring.

Crossraguel Abbey, near Maybole. The abbey, built in 1244 as a Clunic Monastery (one of only two in Scotland), has several parts still in good condition. The tower house is mostly complete with good views of the surrounding countryside from the upper floor windows. The abbey is a good place to search for mason marks, marks in the stones left by the masons who cut and placed the stones.

Culzean Castle and Country Park, near Ayr. The former Kennedy estate was redesigned at the end of the 1700s by neoclassical Scottish architect Robert Adams. The setting is awe-inspiring as the castle hangs on the cliffs overlooking the Firth of Clyde and the Isle of Arran. There is plenty to see in the interior and on the grounds of Culzean (pronounced "cullayne") Castle.

Dumfries has numerous attractions connected with Scottish poet Robert Burns, including The Globe Tavern and Burns Museum.

Isle of Arran Shops, Brodick, Isle of Arran. The island, known as Scotland in Miniature, possesses some interesting shops to explore. There's a fine chocolate shop in the heart of the village of Brodick, and just north are two more special shops. Arran Aromatics specializes in locally made soaps and l o t i o n s , w h i l e Island Cheese Company is famous for its hand-crafted cheeses.

Logan Botanic Garden, part of the Royal Botanic Garden of Edinburgh, is located south of Stranraer on the peninsula of the Mull of Galloway. Considered the most exotic of all the gardens in Scotland.

Mull of Galloway Lighthouse on the southern tip of the mull is a spectacular site with a nice tea room.

Robert Burns' Museum and Cottage, Alloway. The new Burns' Museum is very well done with interesting exhibits. The Scottish national poet's birth house is only a short walk away and shows the living conditions of a tenant farmer family in the mid-1800s. Just up the street across from the museum is Alloway Kirkyard and Brig O' Doon--all with strong Burns associations.

Stones of the Isle of Arran. The Isle of Arran hosts numerous standing stones, stone circles, and pictish stones, and most are easily accessible. The cairn at Torrylin (in the south near Kilmory), Moss Farm, and Machrie Moor stones (near Blackwaterfoot) are fascinating.

Sweetheart Abbey, New Abbey near Dumfries. The 13th C Cistercian abbey gets its name from founder Dervorgilla who had the abbey built in remembrance of her husband, John Balliol, hence the name Sweetheart. The ruins are spectacular with great striding arches, semicircular arches, and the stout tower.

Threave Castle, near Castle Douglas. Three-quarters of a mile walk from the parking area is well rewarded by the impressive ruins of the 14th C former home of the Black Douglasses. Ring the bell at the small dock and the Historic Scotland boat takes you to the castle on an island in the river. Worth going out of the way for.

Wigtown. Modeled after Hay-on-Wye, the Welsh border Booktown, Wigtown is a small village which hosts more than 20 bookstores and book related companies. For bibliophiles this is a dangerous place.

Durness GC

CHAPTER THREE: SCOTTISH HIGHLANDS AND THE ISLANDS

GOLF

This chapter covers a most diverse landscape; from the edge of the Cairngorm Mountains west and north. The golf is diverse as well with big courses like Spey Valley and Nairn contrasting with isolated intriguing nine-holers like Durness and Traigh.

ABERNETHY GOLF COURSE
Nethy Bridge, Inverness-shire PH25 3ED
01479-821305   www.abernethygolfclub.com
Heathland 9-hole, 2534 yards, par 33, £22 day

AMENITIES: One of the charms of Abernethy GC is, as one player put it, the "friendly natives." When we played, we spent time chatting with then club manager Shirley Herridge in the clubhouse tearoom (which has a great reputation for tasty soups, sandwiches, and sweets). Shirley was very helpful telling us how to get around the course as well as sharing the history of Abernethy. No golf shop, check in at the bar.

COURSE COMMENTS: The 115-year-old Abernethy Golf Club in the small village of Nethy Bridge is a heathland track set amongst farmland and forest (a grand stand of old Caledonian pines is to the left of the seventh hole), with pleasing views of the Grampian Mountains. Even though the course is in the village of Nethy Bridge, where the old military bridge crossed River Nethy, it retains the historical name of the parish, Abernethy. An interesting historical note about the course is that since the First World War until today, Abernethy counts an inordinately large number of left-handed golfers in its membership.

The course, while not difficult, does offer enough challenge to be enjoyable by all levels of golfers. The greens are small to moderate in size with several having two levels. Though the course has a few bunkers (none too severe), the rough can be demanding and a pond comes into play on one hole. The second hole, *Castle Roy*, a 115-yard par 3, starts with a tee shot which must clear a pond and a public road--more visually intimidating than physically challenging. The green has bunkers on both sides protecting the tiered putting surface. The most difficult hole on the course is *Balnagowan*, the 414-yard par 4 seventh. The first and second shots are both blind and some fairly dramatic moguls front the green and hide the pin. Walk up to take a look before hitting your second shot. The next hole, *Monument*, may be unique in Scottish golf. In the middle of the fairway is a large World War I obelisk. We've seen similar memorials on other courses (Maybole, Anstruther, and Strathlene Bucky come to mind), but they weren't in the middle of the fairway and used by players to aim their tee shots. Local rules say that if your tee shot hits the memorial, it may be replayed with no penalty. Be warned, though, other than on the tee shot the obelisk is an integral part of the course and in play. We had intended to play the course only once, but so enjoyed our round that we changed plans and went around again.

COMMENTS FROM THE FORWARD TEES: This 9-hole course is much more than it seemed when we drove up. Each hole is unique, and the course isn't too long at 2420 yards (par 36). The water adds difficulty and it's hard to convince yourself to "not see the water." I especially like the 8th and 9th. The 8th is fairly straight forward. You do have the monument in play, but it's not as much of a concern for women.

The uphill 9th has a difficult approach over bunkers while holding the green. A fun short course not to be missed.

BALLINDALLOCH CASTLE GOLF COURSE
Lagmore, Ballindalloch, Banffshire AB37 9AA
01807-500305   www.ballindallochcastle.co.uk
Moorland 9-hole, 6495 yards (played from distinct sets   of   tees),
par 72, £20/18

AMENITIES: The Old Lagmore Farmhouse has been remodeled into a modern clubhouse with changing facilities, a reception area, and a licensed clubroom which offers snacks, lunches, and light refreshments. The club has no golf shop, but some essentials are available in the clubhouse, and the club offers a complete driving range.

COURSE COMMENTS: As you drive up to the golf course, don't be put off by what looks like a simple, uninteresting course. There is much more to Ballindalloch Castle GC than you might at first think. Set along the glacial banks of River Avon amongst 150-year-old oak trees, the Donald Steel and Tom Mackenzie design with two distinct sets of tees allows you to play eighteen different holes from the tees while playing familiar greens the second nine. Opened in April 2003, Ballindalloch is yet undiscovered, but it is a top quality facility and won't remain undiscovered for long. While playable by all golfers, the course is certainly no tame Jane. On an 18-hole round 56 bunkers are in play, plenty of rough is around to grab wayward shots, large quick greens will challenge your putting stroke, and water must be avoided on eight holes.

You won't find a weak hole on the course, but several will highlight your round. Number 4/13, *High Drive*, plays as a par 5 of 502 yards and 528 yards. From either tee, the hole will get your attention. The first shot is a long lay up (200 to 230 yards) to the edge of a cliff which drops down to a lower fairway. The heavy, steep rough is marked OB to keep people off the slope for safety reasons. Once on the lower fairway, the green is guarded by a series of four bunkers on the right. *Tall Pines*, the 188-yard par 3 seventh, is a tough downhill shot over a burn to a green protected by one bunker and a tall pine on the left. From the 16th tee, the hole is a relatively mild 105-yard downhill shot where the tree is no longer in the way. The next hole is *Avonside*, a 395-yard par 4, where the tee shot is key. The shot demands either a strong fade or a bold stroke straight over a bunker to a narrow fairway with a chapel ruin left (OB) and thick bushes right (also OB). Bunkers left and right add to the difficulty of this winding hole. The configuration for the 17th makes the hole a 476-yard par 5 with a much straighter (and easier) drive. Our feelings for the course were eloquently expressed by Michael Parkinson in the *Daily Telegraph*: "Ballindalloch was the perfect place to find escape from an imperfect world. The 9-hole course designed by Donald Steel who, by imaginative use of alternative tees, has achieved the illusion of making 9 holes into 18. Purists who scoff at the idea would be missing a treat if they pass it by."

COMMENTS FROM THE FORWARD TEES: This course is more than you see from the highway or as you drive in. The 1st is a wide open uphill par 5, but after the first the course gets interesting. Several challenges await at Ballindollach Castle including the length (5593 yards for 18). Tee placements are very different front and back, but the yardage is almost the same. Holes 5/14 and 6/15 require accuracy because the rough is exceptionally deep. The 7th/16th is fun. Your tee shot must cross a burn and land on the green or you find yourself in the woods. The course is interesting straight ahead golf with some challenge as well.

CARRBRIDGE GOLF COURSE
Inverness Road, Carrbridge, Inverness-shire PH23 3AU
08444-141415   www.carrbridgegolf.com
Parkland/heathland 9-hole, 2682 yards, par 35, £21 day

AMENITIES: The club doesn't have a golf shop, but golfers will find a few essentials in the pleasant tea shop which serves snacks all day.

COURSE COMMENTS: About four miles north of Boat of Garten, that wonderful James Braid designed heathland track, is the village of Carrbridge (at the junction of A938 and B9153). Carrbridge, the home of Landmark Forest Heritage Park (30 acres of ancient Caledonian pinewoods with water slides, nature trails, and a working steam sawmill), was built where the main road from Perth to Inverness crossed River Dulnain. The main reason for building a bridge at this ford was to insure that funerals did not have to be delayed when the river was in spate and unfordable. The other attractions of the village include the annual Porridge Festival early in September to select the best porridge-maker for the year and, more to our point, the fine Carrbridge Golf Club. The oldest records extant show the club has existed at the same location just north of town since at least 1905. By the late 60s or early 70s, the course was nothing but grass fields. In 1979, local citizens discovered that the Carrbridge Hotel (which had been managing the land on which the course lay) didn't own it. The city reclaimed the land and, after being cleared by a local farmer, found the original holes. Carrbridge GC was opened under city management in 1980. The combination parkland and heathland course is no pushover. Challenges abound at Carrbridge with water in play on every hole, small quick greens, and plenty of bunkers to snare off-line shots (fairway, fore, and greenside). Fairways are generous, but the heather rough can be difficult to get out of. Carrbridge is definitely a thinker's course with some shot on every hole which must be planned with trouble in mind.

The par fours at Carrbridge play particularly tough. The 2nd, *The Nest*, a 334-yard par 4, begins with a blind tee shot over a hill to a large landing area. The second shot is where the challenge begins. A burn about 70 yards from the green and a narrowing fairway spell trouble for all but the best shots. With most placements the hole is hidden from the second shot. The 4th is a 331-yard two-shotter which starts out relatively easy with a downhill tee shot to a wide fairway (a shot of 150 yards is all that's needed to find safety). The second shot must cross a burn and climb steeply to the green which can't be seen from the fairway. From the members or visitors tee, the shot (227 yards) looks like you can reach the green or at least the slope in front. The prudent play, though, is to lay up short of the burn (about 160 yards) and pitch up. A less difficult par 4 is *Badengorm*, the 258-yard 5th. The tee shot is over a valley with the inevitable burn at the bottom. Your first shot is key to the hole. A shot of about 230 yards is needed to reach the top of the far side of the valley. This hole can be a solid birdie opportunity. The finishing hole at Carrbridge is a 231-yard par 3 called *The Birches* (a stand of birch trees sits on the right of the hole). An elevated tee plays down to a fairway with yet another burn running the length of the hole at the right and directly in line with the green. Unless you can fly the green, aim to the fairway left and chip on. Carrbridge GC can be a demanding track, but the views of nearby hills and more distant Cairngorm Mountains along with blooming heathers and silvery birches, will make every round enjoyable.

COMMENTS FROM THE FORWARD TEES: This course was a big surprise. It looks simple, but there are challenges at every hole. The course is short at only 2401 yards, but will still require good course management to score. I especially liked the 4th even though I played it badly. You tee off over bushes and then the fairway drops down and over the burn to the green. On the drive hit over the bushes and carry the burn. This leaves a mid- or short-iron to the green. The course is worth the time to play.

DURNESS GOLF COURSE
Balnekeil, Durness, Sutherland IV27 4PN

01971-511364   www.durnessgolfclub.org
Links 9-hole, 2762 yards, par 35, £20 day

AMENITIES: The comfortable no-frills clubhouse lounge offers grand views of the beautiful bay and the sea. Snacks and soup (homemade and delicious) are available most usual hours, as are a few golfing essentials. No golf shop, but golf manager Lucy Mackay (a playing member) is a wonderful host and a fount of information. Honesty box for when no one is about.

COURSE COMMENTS: Without going to the islands, Durness GC is about as far off the beaten track as you can get in Scotland. It's worth the trip! The 9-hole course is built on ancient dunes which rise above the beach only a few miles from the northwestern most corner of the Scottish mainland, Cape Wrath. When we played the 1988 course, we thought it reminded us of some of the great links courses in Ireland. As we sat in the clubhouse lounge after our round talking to golf manager Lucy Mackay, her husband, and two other members, we knew we'd played one of the great 9-hole links courses in the world. We've played several stunningly good 9-hole courses: St. Medans, St Fillans, and Corrie (from *Golf in Scotland: The Hidden Gems*); Rush, Connemara Isles, and Cruit Island (from *Ireland's Small Greens*); and Newport (Pembs), Traigh, and Durness (in this book). Most would acknowledge Cruit Island as perhaps the best in the world, but I would say that Durness could rival or surpass Cruit Island, if you saw them both in good weather. We played Cruit on a gorgeous day, and trekked around Durness in 30 mile per hour winds and driving rain (though Lucy e-mailed to me that after we played, the course had almost a full month of shirt sleeve weather). Both are excellent courses, with Durness presenting more straight ahead demanding golf, while Cruit Island has a couple of quite unique holes. Each has a hole where you dramatically hit over the ocean, but at Durness it's the last. The views from the course are fantastic, and not just the ocean views. On our first visit we could barely see the fairways, but the next year when we played and the weather was reasonably clear the views of surrounding hills were stunning.

It's not just the location that makes the golfing good at Durness; there's plenty to test the best of your game. The course has 19 heavy sand fairway and greenside bunkers. None of the bunkers is too severe except for one behind the green on the 6th. A loch is in play all along the right side of six and two small ponds are in play on the fairway. The sea is crossed off the tee of 9/18 (more about this in a minute). The greens are small to moderate with interesting slopes and borrows. All are easy to read and putt very true. Most holes have either blind drives or approach shots, and 8 is double blind. Significant elevation changes will affect play on most holes. Most importantly the wind and weather will be a matter of concern.

All holes at Durness, the most northerly course on the British mainland, are great fun to play and have challenges for all golfers. The following should give a good feel for the course, of course from our biased view. The 5th is a 344-yard par 4 where you drive (or try to) over a large hillock or go around to the right. If you try to go over and don't make it, you will be left with a 130 yard shot from a steep up slope. The green is elevated and is a small target. No bunkers are needed here. A classic golf hole is the 443-yard par 5 sixth. Start from an elevated tee on this sweeping dogleg right. The landing area is wide, but a small pond sits toward the right about 220 yards out and the loch is farther on the right the length of the hole. Big hitters with a good drive can take an iron across the loch to a two-tiered green tucked around the loch to the right. A menacing bunker awaits shots left of the green (behind the green if you're coming across the loch). Eagles are possible, but so are doubles or others for those who are short or who find the bunker. The 8th is a downhill blind 377-yard hole. The tee shot is down to a fairly level landing area from which you may or may not see the flag further downhill over a drop-off. The putting surface is defended by three traps and backed by the sea. The 9th at 108 yards or the 18th at 155 yards finishes your round. If you only go around once, play this one from the 18th tee. Shoot across a sea chasm to a small green guarded by two bunkers. It's a lovely, visually intimidating hole. A picture postcard finish! Lucy told us a story about a golfer who the week before had left £2.50 in the Honesty Box when nobody was around, and wrote on the envelope, "What a fantastic position for golf. Took 3 shots on the 18th--made the Atlantic on all three." Two Canadian golfers came in soaking wet while we were getting soaked on our first visit. They told Lucy to tell the American writers they loved the course despite the weather, and to be sure to put it in the book. Those are the kind of reactions Durness GC inspires. The second time we played was very windy and on the tee box of the 8th we let a single play through. As he teed off he looked over and said, "It's madness to be out in this." If it was, it was a fine madness. Be sure to play it!

COMMENTS FROM THE FORWARD TEES: What a fantastic 9-hole course. Yes, it's worth the effort to get to this far northwest corner of Scotland. If the weather is bad there's always the Cocoa Factory for the most decadent hot chocolate ever. We played the course in two different fall trips. The first time it was raining and quite windy and there were only limited ocean views. The second trip we played with heavy wind, but dry and partly sunny weather. In good weather there are gorgeous views in all directions: mountains and moorlands to the southeast and ocean views to the southwest and northwest. Every hole on this 9-hole links course is unique. The yardage is short at 2473 yards, but there are challenges on every hole. Some shots are very steeply uphill to elevated greens. The 9th is a fair but daunting shot over the ocean. Durness GC is an exciting course to play.

FORT WILLIAM GOLF COURSE
Torlundy, Fort William, Inverness-shire PH33 6SN
01397-704464 www.golfhighland.com
Heathland, 6217 yards, par 72 (5464 gents and visitors, par 68), £25

AMENITIES: Pleasant, friendly lounge in the small clubhouse offers drinks and snacks, and (when we played) a group of friendly members eager to find out how we liked their course. No golf shop, but a few essentially are available at the bar where you check in for golf.

COURSE COMMENTS: The Fort William GC is a reasonably interesting course. Played from the medal tees at 6217 yards into the prevailing wind the course can be a stern test for the lowest handicappers. Played from gents' or members' tees, 753 yards less than the medal, it's still a challenge for all players. Sited at the foot of Ben Nevis, Great Britain's tallest mountain, the Hamilton Stutt 1974 design heathland course is an easier walk than the one on the Ben Nevis hiking/climbing path that runs through the course. Besides the wind which will usually be blowing, seven holes have bunkers, almost all greenside, to confront your shot-making. When we played in the late summer of 2007, several of the bunkers had heather growing down into them, which added difficulty to bunkers which would normally be easy to play from (good sand). A small burn comes into play on many of the holes, and sometimes you can't see it until you're in it. Greens at Fort William are small, well conditioned, speedy (even when wet), and have tricky borrows or slopes. Expect to play in the wet; this area receives a large share of damp weather. To its credit, the course plays well in the wet, as we found out. The course throws a couple more tricks at players. First, you will face several blind shots, including approaches; and second, holes 4 and 7 share the same fairway. What's unusual about the shared fairway is that they share it in the same direction. Unfortunately they both play into the wind and significantly longer from the medal tees. On the day we played with 20 to 30 miles per hour gusts into us, I'm not sure I could reach the fourth's members' tee (393 yards) from the back tee (566 yards). Between the two tees was nothing but marram and heather. True, it's a par 5 from the back and a par 4 from the front, but I'm not sure that's much consolation. Fort William is a tough course in competition.

From whichever tees (or mixture of tees) you play, the course keeps your attention. The second is a 385-yard par 4 which begins with a blind shot over a large mound, don't be short (less than 210 yards) or the hill stops your ball. The second shot is down and over a burn to a fairly large (for this course) green with bunkers on each side. The green is quite sloped back to front. The 3rd at 110 yards is not extremely difficult, but is very picturesque. The tee shot is through a gap in the trees to a small target with a burn and large bunker in front. Take your camera! Another picture postcard hole is the 125-yard par 3 sixth. The tee shot is over a meandering burn to a moderate sized putting surface with traps left and right. Pick the correct club for the wind and par or birdie can be yours. The finish on the front nine (which comes back to easy access to the clubhouse) is a 401-yard par 4 (from the gents' tee) or a 527-yard par 5 (from the medal tee). Nine is a tough hole from either tee into the prevailing wind. From an elevated tee box (gents') hit to a snaking sloped fairway. Your second shot must contend with a fairway bunker left and burn winding on the right about 60 yards from the green. Several mounds before the green can affect your approach. On the back we liked the 387-yard par 4 eleventh with a blind tee shot over a knoll (aim at the post) which will throw your ball to the right on this gentle dogleg left. Forest and heather trouble is all the way down the left. The green is protected by one large trap on the right and is surrounded by trees. Thirteen is a 284-yard par 4 for men (from either tee) and a 147-yard par 3 for ladies. The hole looks like it belongs more on a links course than inland. Hit into a series of hillocks toward an elevated green. Tee from an elevated box on the 156-yard 16th to a raised green fronted by two large bunkers. There's a hill left of the green, but plenty of area to the right. You'll find a friendly greeting in the Fort William GC clubhouse before your round and again when you finish.

COMMENTS FROM THE FORWARD TEES: The front and back at Fort William are very different in look and feel. The front is only 330 yards longer, but has a par of 37 while the back is a 34. The front has several holes with blind shots that hide the burn that runs through most of this side. The par 3s are quite varied, ranging from an extremely short 91 yards to a 191-yarder that's uphill. I tend to see long par 3s often because there is usually only one tee box for ladies, which must be used for daily play and medals or competitions. Par 5s here are not too long, but in the wet conditions which are common you don't get much roll even from the moorland fairways. Fort William is the kind of course that makes me want to go back and do it again now that I know what to expect and where the trouble is.

GAIRLOCH GOLF COURSE
Gairloch, Ross-shire IV21 2BE
01445-712865 www.gairlochgolfclub.com
9-hole seaside heathland, 2072 yards, par 31, £20/ 9, £25 / day

AMENITIES: Clubhouse contains a pleasant tearoom and bar which serves food all day. It's a popular eatery with the locals, non-golfers included. No golf shop, but an honesty box for when no one is around.

COURSE COMMENTS: The 9-hole seaside track was built in 1890 and hasn't changed a lot since. The course has inviting holes, and a beautiful setting with lovely views of the surrounding hills, the loch, and the isles of Skye and Harris on a good day. Gairloch is a very small, tight course. In fact, the new Spey Valley GC in Aviemore which we played a couple of days after Gairloch has areas of rough on one hole almost as big as the entire Gairloch course. The course has some trouble on it including thirteen bunkers, all greenside and none too penal. A small pond is sort of in play on the 1st and 2nd, and the sea (beach) is OB on the 8th. Most of the greens at Gairloch are small with subtle slopes, but a couple have serious swales. On this small course be aware that several holes cross over. One feature of the course, not really a hazard, is a deep depression next to the 1st tee called the Preacher's Hole because a local preacher used to hold services there in the time when golf wasn't allowed on Sunday.

We enjoyed all the holes at Gairloch, but several really got our notice. *Blind Piper*, the 209-yard par 3 fourth, begins with a blind tee shot with trees and a hill on the right which is the direct line to the hole. Locals play the 3rd as a dogleg par 3. The ladies hit down left to a patch of fairway and then up to the green. This hole is tough enough without bunkers. The 6th, *Westward Ho!*, is a 193-yard par 3 where you tee off from very good mats on an elevated tee box through a tunnel of trees. Two bunkers right and one left complicate the hole. On the 7th you again tee off the top quality driving mats. The shot is only 91 yards, but it is absolutely blind over a rough-covered mound. The green is directly beyond the mound and is guarded by a bunker right and another long left. It's some kind of wedge and hope. *Traigh Mor*, the 488-yard 8th, is the only par 5 on the course. Though not long, the hole is tricky, especially the first time you play. It's a tough dogleg left along the slope above the beach. Left is OB and lost, but there's plenty of room to the right. For your second a rough-covered gully encroaches from the left in front of the mounded fairway. Your third shot (I understand very few go for the green in two) will be a long drop to a green with one trap on the right. It's all about placement on this hole. Gairloch GC is quite a ways off the beaten track, but interesting golf holes, wonderful views, friendly members, and a comfortable tearoom make the trip worth the effort.

COMMENTS FROM THE FORWARD TEES: Gairloch is a short, challenging course with nine unique holes. It's hard to know where to aim unless you have a local guide. Distances on the par 3s are reachable for most ladies, but hills, trees, dunes, heavy grass, and heather will all present problems. The green on the 4th is over trees on a hill to the right, so the best plan is to aim for the fairway of the third and then play up to the green. The only par 5 on the course is the 8th which can be parred with good shots, but can also give a very big score especially on a windy day.

INVERNESS GOLF COURSE
The Clubhouse, Culcabock Road, Inverness IV2 3XQ
01463-233422   www.invernessgolfclub.co.uk
Parkland, 6256 yards, par 69, £42

AMENITIES: The classy clubhouse has changing rooms down and lounge and dining room upstairs. Locals say the food is excellent, but it is only available to members and players. The complete golf shop has a full range of clubs and clothes.

COURSE COMMENTS: The Inverness Golf Club was formed in 1883, but it took until 1908 before the club settled at today's Culcabock site. During World War II five holes were lost to garden or farm cultivation, but were restored fairly quickly in 1946. Golf at Inverness is classic golf, played through tree lined fairways and over small burns. The challenges, too, at Inverness are classic. Seventy-six bunkers, most deep and penal with inconsistent sand, will test your accuracy and sand play. Five holes have a small burn to cause you trouble. The moderate to large greens are quick with subtle borrows (on a couple the borrows aren't so subtle). The course's residential setting never intrudes on the golf, perhaps because the course is heavily forested with a wide variety of trees. All these conditions add up to testing, but a fair and beautiful course with several memorable holes.

The 6th is a 313-yard par 4 with a blind tee shot starting this dogleg left. A mid or long iron is all that's needed to reach the prime landing area.

The approach will be a short iron over a small burn to one of the smallest greens on the course. The only hole without a bunker is a real birdie opportunity with a safe play. On *Kelly's Copse*, the 208-yard par 3 ninth it's a challenge to find the correct club from an elevated tee to an elevated green guarded by three bunkers. The burn which crosses the hole half way to the green shouldn't be a concern. The 12th starts with a dramatic downhill tee shot. Bite off as much as you can on the angled drive on this 394-yarder, but be sure to clear the trees on the right. The green is tucked in the trees and protected by hummocks and one bunker. It's my favorite hole on the course. The toughest hole at Inverness is *Midmills*, the 475-yard par 4 fourteenth. The tee shot is the key to your score on this dogleg right. A large tree on the inside of the dogleg creates the target to go over or around. If you stay left of the tree, the fairway runs out at about 200 to 220 yards. Second shots are to a narrowing fairway with a trap about 30 yards short of the green. The 15th, *Curling Pond*, is a demanding 188-yard par 3. The narrow two-tiered green is a tight target from any of the tees. Bunkers on the left and a drop-off right and back add difficulty. Inverness GC is a beautiful, venerable challenge which should definitely be on a Scotland golfing tour.

COMMENTS FROM THE FORWARD TEES: The yard-age for the ladies at Inverness GC is almost exactly the same as for the men. The course is classic in style, and though long, the ball gets good roll. Some of the par 3s are almost impossible to reach without a lay up or shooting into trouble. As challenging as the course is, it is also a joy.

ISLE OF SKYE GOLF COURSE
Sconser, Isle of Skye IV48 8TD
01478-650414   www.isleofskyegolfclub.co.uk
Seaside parkland 9-hole, 2406 yards, par 33, £25 for 18, £35 day

AMENITIES: Small clubhouse has coffee and tea available in the club room, and pop and candy available in the office along with a few golf essentials, including some hats and shirts.

COURSE COMMENTS: Isle of Skye GC affords some outstanding ocean and mountain views, and the golf on the 1964 design course is good as well. Playing between the sea and the cuillins (Gaelic for mountains), the course is relatively flat and exposed to the wind and weather. Don't expect much roll on the usually damp course, but then it's not long anyway. If you've made it this far out-of-the-way and you have time, play 18 because there are distinctly separate tees for three holes, the 10th, 14th, and 16th. In fact, the tee for the 14th is 90 degrees or more off the tee for 5. Only three bunkers add sand trouble--behind 1/10, to the side of 6/15, and a vicious pot bunker in front of the 9/18 green which was created when the old greenskeeper removed a large boulder. There are burn crossings on 8/17, twice on 6/13, and on 10. The greens come in two sizes, small and tiny; as small as 15 yards deep. Thankfully, most have little slope. As at Traigh, distractingly grand vistas at every shot.

All the holes at Isle of Skye are fun, but we'll highlight three. The 3rd is an uphill 153-yard par 3 at the far corner of the course near the quarry. The green is a tiny target (15 yards by 17 yards) and slopes back to front, with sticky rough all around. With the mountain in the background, it's a picture postcard view. A small burn crosses the fairway of the 349-yard 6th twice. Land between the burns and approach the green protected on the left by one bunker. OB and the sea are all tee to green on the right. Our last hole, the 268-yard par 4 ninth, is uphill all the way. Aim over the right side of a large mound on the left or out to the flats on the right. The green is raised and guarded by a mound and dangerous pot bunker. It was on this hole that we heard an unusual phrase. Our playing partner, local Alister Grant, directed me to "hit to the shades" (meaning trees) near the right flat area. The Isle of Skye has many wondrous attractions, including the cuillins, Talisker Distillery, and the sea. Count Isle of Skye GC among those attractions.

COMMENTS FROM THE FORWARD TEES: A scenic walk along the sea with grand views of Skye and Ramsay is the Isle of Skye GC. The course is fun without being complicated. Fairways are wide, but the small greens keep the golf challenging. First nine par 3s are longer than the second nine, but still the longest is only 162 yards. The par 4s aren't long either, but since it's usually wet here, you don't get much roll. The views are worth more than the price of golf.

LOCH NESS GOLF CLUB, New Course
Castle Heather, Inverness, Inverness-shire IV2 6AA
01463-713335 www.golflochness.com
Parkland, 5907 yards, par 70, £32

AMENITIES: The Castle Heather facility which houses the Loch Ness Golf Club is full of amenities. Besides a fine practice range, the clubhouse has probably the best golf shop in the area. After your round plan to browse in the nicely stocked golf shop, then stop in at the Fairways Pub and Restaurant (sandwiches, snacks, and full meals). Staff and members at Loch Ness GC are helpful, friendly, and very proud of their facility. While I was in the golf shop talking to the pro about the course,

Anne was in Fairways where local members were telling her about the course and area.

COURSE COMMENTS: One of the more interesting layouts in Inverness is the Loch Ness New and Old Golf Courses and Castle Heather Golf Club. Only three miles from the heart of the Capital of the Highlands, as Inverness is known, is the Castle Heather facility with its two eighteens, a 9-hole course, practice range, quality golf shop, indoor bowling green, pub and restaurant. It was the two main courses, the New and the Old, which fascinated us. Discounting the 9-hole course, which is good for a quick round or some practice, there aren't 36 holes at Loch Ness GC, but there are two 18-hole courses. Confused? So was I at first. After we'd played the New Course on a stormy September morning, I finally caught on.

The Old Course at Loch Ness is a configuration used only for competitions. It's composed of thirteen New Course holes and five holes that are only played when the Old Course layout is used. It's really a brilliant idea. Club members, for the most part, play a different course in competition (for example, the third on the New Course ends up being the sixth on the Old Course), and not just the back tees of the same everyday course (for instance, the 332-yard par 4 sixteenth on the New becomes the 503-yard par 5 seventeenth on the Old).

Since Anne and I weren't playing in a competition (though, we do have a side bet on our game occasionally), we can only comment on the New Course at Loch Ness. In general, though, both configurations have burns and ponds which definitely affect play, a mixture of large flat and small penal bunkers mostly around greens, and moderate sized quick greens. Fairways on this parkland layout are generous with a wide, manageable first cut of rough. Anything beyond the first cut is in serious trouble. Number two (on both the New and Old) is a 557-yard par 5, which has the fairway split by a burn with heavy rough and trees right. The fairway slopes left, but the right side is where you want to be for your approach to an elevated green with a burn in front. The 16th on the New (17th on the Old) is an intriguing par 4. The 332-yard hole begins with a blind drive to a wide fairway. A good drive leaves a short-iron second shot to a green tucked left behind a hill and protected by a deep bunker on the right. The long holes at Loch Ness are good, but some of the par 3s grabbed the spotlight. The 7th on New (not played on the Old configuration) is a 111-yard one-shotter which plays uphill. The pin is hidden from the tee and trees encroach on the right side. At almost twice as long, the 208-yard 9th (11th on the Old) has a steeply downhill tee shot over a deep chasm. The green slopes right and is protected by a bunker on the left. With the normal wind, choosing the correct club can be a guessing game. The 195-yard 17th (not played on the Old) again has a steeply downhill tee shot. This time, though, there is a pond on the right of the green. The prevailing wind will blow your ball directly toward the pond. When we played the hole, the wind was 20 miles per hour with higher gusts. I thought starting my ball twenty yards to the left of the green would be enough, but I ended up well right of the green (luckily missing the pond). Two grounds crew members ensconced in the cab of a pickup truck, watched my play and just shook their heads. The course (or courses) can be quite windy, but if the weather cooperates, the views are superb--Inverness, the Moray Firth, and the Black Isle. In the spring and early summer the course is a riot of yellow with gorse and broom in full bloom.

COMMENTS FROM THE FORWARD TEES: On my first look at the course I thought it was going to be easy, but it's harder than it looks. The course is on the side of a large hill, with numerous sidehill shots. Some of the course, though, plays in an open meadow. The front side (2941 yards, par 37) is harder than the back (2446 yards, par 34). We played the course on a rainy day, and I'd like to play it when I could get some roll. From the top of the course we got a couple of glimpses of the fine views you'd get on a good day.

THE NAIRN GOLF COURSE
Seabank Road, Nairn, Nairnshire IV12 4HB
01667-453208   www.nairngolfclub.co.uk
Links, 6436 yards, par 71, £90

AMENITIES: Plush bar and dining room upstairs with good food served usual hours. Modern changing rooms downstairs along with a very complete golf shop.

COURSE COMMENTS: The Nairn GC has hosted many major events over the years, with winners such as Colin Montgomery and Willie Achterlonie. It is considered one of the two premier courses in the north of Scotland, with Royal Dornoch being the other. Nairn's reputation is justly deserved and its pedigree is superior. First designed by Old Tom Morris of St. Andrews in 1887, the course was updated by both James Braid and Ben Sayers. During the season you must book ahead, but in the off season you can find spots during the week.

The course, host of the 1999 Walker Cup matches, is a stern test with over 100 steep-sided bunkers in play. The bunkers, in range for big hitters, moderate hitters, and women, are easy to get into and difficult to get out of. Most of the greens are moderate to large and very quick. The greens, except the very swaled 14th, are flat with subtle breaks. On five holes a burn will be a concern, and the wind will be a concern on all the holes. A problem at Nairn, that we've seen on a few other courses, is that tee boxes may be in the line-of-fire of those players behind. All these difficulties can be forgotten in the beauty of Nairn, built along the beaches of the Moray Firth. The views over to the Black Isle and Caithness coast are stunning.

Stunning, too, is the golf at Nairn. For example, *Nest*, the 373-yard 3rd, is a moderate length dogleg left two-shotter where your tee shot needs to avoid the "nest" of bunkers on the inside corner to be safe. The approach to the raised green is over a major swale while avoiding four more traps. The 5th, *Nets*, has only one fairway bunker on this 377-yard hole, but the fairway slopes toward the bunker. The two-tiered raised green is protected well by six bunkers. The 13th is the number one stroke index hole at Nairn. This 423-yard par 4 is an uphill narrow fairway with alternating right, left, right bunkers. The fairway gets narrower and the bunkers more numerous as you approach the tiered green. A fine par 3 is *Kopjes*, the 211-yard 14th. This long one-shotter is all uphill to a raised green guarded by plenty of sand. The green has more slopes than any green on the course making three-putts common. A benign fairway doesn't prepare you for the trouble around the green on the 417-yard par 4 sixteenth. Three large bunkers surround the green which is fronted by a burn and three nasty pot bunkers. For years Anne and I had played all around Nairn GC, but hadn't had the opportunity to try out the course. We now wish we'd played years ago. It's a course we will definitely want to play over and over.

COMMENTS FROM THE FORWARD TEES: Nairn is a difficult course for most ladies. It's easy to have shots roll into trouble-- heather and gorse. The many bunkers seemed particularly hard to get around or over. The big greens were tricky to read with subtle slopes. With all that against it, it is a beautiful course in a spectacular setting. It's the kind of course I want to play again so I can do better.

NEWTONMORE GOLF COURSE
Golf Course Road, Newtonmore, Speyside PH20 1AT
01540-673878 www.newtonmoregolf.com
Heathland/moorland, 6031 yards, par 70, £30

AMENITIES: The two-section clubhouse lounge is fully licensed and was very busy the Sunday we played. If the lounge is too crowded, Newtonmore has numerous choices for meals and lodging. There's no golf shop, but limited supplies are available in the clubhouse.

COURSE COMMENTS: Located on the A86 four miles south of Kingussie is the Highland town of Newtonmore. The town fits neatly between the Badenoch region to the south and the Monadhliath Mountains north. At the northeast terminus of the A86 to Fort William, Newtonmore is the gateway to "Monarch of the Glen" country. Settings in Newtonmore, as well as others along the A86 (such as Laggan and Loch Laggan), have been used in the popular BBC television program.

Newtonmore is also home to Newtonmore Golf Club, a heathland/ moorland track surrounded by Highland scenery dramatic enough to be a pleasant distraction to a visitor's game. The club celebrated its centenary in 1993, and, with periodic upgrades, has kept pace with the modern game and equipment. Like a couple of other courses in the area, Newtonmore proudly boasts a higher than normal number of left-handed members. [Could it be something in the Highland water?] The course also boasts of fifty-six bunkers (a good mix of fairway and greenside) in play. Several holes are defined by their bunkers, such as the 5th and 9th which have large, deep face bunkers fronting the greens. Burns are in play on four holes, but will be serious hazards only on the 6th and 16th. Newtonmore's greens are small to medium in size, and early in September when we played, were in great condition, quick and true. The railroad line separates holes 1, 2, 17, and 18 from the rest of the course, but is not really a condition of play.

As you walk from the second green to the third tee, be sure to take a moment to look at the sign posted about "Newtonmore Golf Course--A Special Habitat." It shows the variety of birds and flora you can find at Newtonmore. One of the more interesting holes on the front is *Strone Dell*, the 332-yard par 4 sixth. A drive of only 210 yards is needed to reach the prime landing area on the dogleg left. The second shot is over a burn to the green backed by a stand of trees. A pond to the right of the green should not be in play. A simple shot fraught with dangers is an apt description of Newtonmore's par 3 eighth. *Spey* is only 163 yards, but a huge steep-faced bunker fronts the green and a narrow crescent sand bunker wraps around the right side. The left side of the green isn't defenseless, having a grass bunker complementing the crescent sand bunker on the other side. Take an extra club because long is greatly preferable to short on this fun hole. Three holes stand out on the homeward nine--numbers 13, 15, and 18. Between the 12th green and the 13th tee, at the furthest distance from the clubhouse, sits a small caravan. Obviously used as a snack shop during the busy season and on weekends, the caravan sported an interesting sign: "No food. No money. Don't bother breaking in." The 13th, *Black Rock*, is a 392-yard par 4. Long and tough, this straight fairway has three strategically placed bunkers to cause trouble on the first and second shots. Two more small bunkers guard the approach to a fairly small green. It is bunkers and more bunkers which define play on the 159-yard 15th, aptly called *Sand Folly*. The green, big for this course, is long and narrow (as much as three clubs different depending upon the pin placement), but it is the six bunkers ringing the green that will give you shivers. *Craigdhu*, the 331-yard par 4 eighteenth, is an interesting finishing hole. A drive 225 yards is needed to reach the top of the fairway ridge. It's probably best to stay short of the top of this ridge because a deep grass depression past the ridge will make your second shot more difficult. If you are in the correct spot with your drive, it's only a short-iron shot to the green immediately over the road coming into the club across the fairway. A ball landing in front has a chance of bouncing over the road and onto the green like Anne's did, but that wouldn't be the preferred plan. Four saving bunkers are sited around the right and back of the green. It makes the hole even more interesting when you realize that everyone in the pleasant, modern clubhouse lounge can watch how you come in on 18.

The course is well worth a visit, and the village also hosts a couple of interesting non-golf attractions--"Waltzing Waters," a water-light-and-music spectacular, and the more sedate Highland Folk Museum.

COMMENTS FROM THE FORWARD TEES: Newtonmore is set in beautiful meadowlands in the Highlands along the banks of the River Spey. The course is well adapted for women with an overall yardage of 5210 yards and a 73 par. Interesting challenges are what give the course its higher par rating. Although the course is flat, there are many mounds and slopes as well as water and trees to contend with. On the 1st, for example, ladies must carry a tee shot 106 yards just to get over the mound and reach the fairway and at 126 yards is a big grass bunker. It takes planning and good execution. I was able to score well on this course and found the four par 5s all playable. Newtonmore is a fine meadowland course which is fun to play.

(Macdonald) SPEY VALLEY GOLF & COUNTRY CLUB
Dalfaber Village, Aviemore, PH22 1ST
01479-815100 www.speyvalleygolf.com
Moorland/heathland, 7017 yards, par 72, £70

AMENITIES: Construction on a new clubhouse for Spey Valley GCC began in April 2008. The new clubhouse contains complete changing rooms, a bar/lounge, restaurant (The Scottish Steak Club), and fully stocked golf shop. The amenities already include extensive practice facilities.

COURSE COMMENTS: One of Scotland's newest premier golf venues, Spey Valley course was designed by Dave Thomas, architect of The Belfry, and opened for play in July 2006. We played the course shortly after it opened and it was already behaving like a mature course. Spey Valley is sited on land similar to Boat of Garten and Granton-on-Spey, but is much larger. Built as a championship course, Spey Valley has challenges which might frighten some, but is really playable by all levels (especially if they remember to play from the correct tees). Huge deep bunkers on almost every hole, both greenside and fairway, will create problems for those who can't avoid the sand. Huge also are the quick greens with plenty of interesting slopes. A loch is in play on both the 15th and 16th, and several holes play along the Spey River which is OB on number two. Much of the course plays on a hillside which means there are good views of the Cairngorm Mountains and surrounding hills, but also means that the wind can be a factor of play. One feature of the course that can be positive or negative is that it is designed as a "buggy course." This will appeal to those seeking a resort golf experience (including circulating beverage buggy). The downside is that the course loses some of its Scottish Highland feel by playing in a buggy. Whether you like this aspect of the course or not, riding in a buggy does not diminish the quality of the course itself.

As fitting a top quality venue (making some lists of the top 100 in the world), all holes at Spey Valley are alluring and demanding, and several caught our notice. Number 5, *Creag Eabraich*, is designed to be the longest hole in the Highlands. It is indeed that at 621 yards. Not only is it long, but the hole begins with a blind shot. Trees right and bunkers left can be seen, but the landing area is hidden. Several traps cause more trouble than the distance. If you stay out of trouble, a par is possible even for modest hitters. *Carn Dearg*, the 409-yard par 4 seventh is another hole that begins blind. From the tee it looks like you should aim to the right of the visible fairway bunker, but what isn't seen is a second bunker more in the middle of the fairway. Either lay up short of the bunkers or get lucky and find a small ribbon of fairway left of the bunkers like I did. More bunkers front the swaled green. It's from about this hole that you can see a notch in the Cairngorm Mountains in the distance. The golf manager said that if we walked as the crow flew it would be only 22 miles to Braemar. It's amazing how close things in Scotland really are. Next is *Carn Daerg Mor*, the 396-yard par 4 eighth. Drive to the corner of a sharp dogleg left around two large trees (even big hitters can't cut the corner). A trap on the right side of the dogleg shouldn't be in play, but greenside bunkers will be. The 9th, *Carn Beinn Glanilben*, is a short (330 yards) downhill par 4 which doglegs around trees and bunkers. A long iron is all that is needed to set up a short approach over bunkers. The last of a really great set of four central holes is the 196-yard 10th. This longish one-shotter is a drive across a large heather patch and two large bunkers. Mature trees at the sides add difficulty. Twelve, *Dalwhinnie* (which means "meeting place"), is a 464-yard par 4. This very typical heathland hole plays between copse of birches and firs and is beautifully lined with heather. The green is protected by a fronting bunker on the right. A dramatic downhill dogleg left is *Ord Ban*, the 422-yard par 4 fifteenth. This tricky hole is difficult to describe because the first time I got caught up in the rough on the left that was brutal to get out of. Both Anne and I agree, though, that the combination of bunkers, a loch, and elevation drop makes a great test. One which I failed! *Loch Meghan*, the 202-yard 16th is a Redan-like one-shotter. A loch is on the right, but not much of a concern. Of more concern are the two bunkers fronting the right side of the angled green. It's a fine par 3.

The course was already growing up the second time we played, and given a few years to mature and a new clubhouse, MacDonald's Spey Valley Golf & Country Club resort will become a much sought after golfing destination.

COMMENTS FROM THE FORWARD TEES: Spey Valley is a long course for women where off the tee the holes are fairly wide, but second or approach shots often seem like American target golf. The heathland turf was easy to hit from, but as on links courses it was hard sometimes to predict where your ball might go. Par 5s are long with the 5th being the longest at 513 yards. For me the 13th, 462 yards, set up as the most difficult hole both times I played. It's a dogleg right which rises a little, plateaus, and goes over a ridge about 80 yards from the green which is slightly elevated. The rough around this hole is quite penal. I still want "do-overs" on this hole. The views from the course are spectacular. Spey Valley GC is a course I want to play again.

STRATHPEFFER SPA GOLF COURSE
Golf course Road, Strathpeffer, Ross-shire IV14 9AS
01997-421219 www.strathpeffergolf.co.uk
Parkland, 5001 yards, par 67, £30

AMENITIES: The club hosts a very comfortable lounge with views of the 18th green. Serves good food all day. There is a small, but well-stocked golf shop.

COURSE COMMENTS: The course was designed in 1888 by Willie Park Jnr and then was extended to 18 holes in 1896 by Old Tom Morris. The course has been periodically updated, but the original Park/ Morris routing has remained the same for over 100 years. Trees, gorse, deep rough, and dramatic elevation changes add difficulty to one of the Highlands most scenic courses. The course, especially the first seven holes, is a hard walk, but the views down to Dingwall and out towards Inverness are worth the effort. Five holes have burns in play and three have ponds. The greens are tiny to small with the largest only 26 yards deep. Most of the greens have slope and three are multilevel. Eighteen has the most dramatic tilt. For a short course, all the holes are quite unique and the drama starts at the first.

Castle Leod, a 330-yard par 4, is considered the longest drop from tee to green in Scotland. Tee it high and let it fly, but don't be right (OB and trees). The green is relatively flat, but a mound in the middle of the fairway can cause trouble. The 3rd, *Pavilion*, is a 197-yard one-shotter uphill over a large pond. The only bunkers on the course flank this green. The tee shot plays longer than its distance, so take an extra club to reach the back-to-front sloped green. The 7th is a tricky, short, uphill 288-yard par 4 hole called *Rockies*. The hole demands a well-positioned drive. Two-hundred twenty-five yards will reach the base of the steep rough-covered 70-yard uphill slope leading to the flat green. Your approach will be blind. Don't let anybody tell you short holes are easy. The 159-yard 10th certainly isn't. You must thread your tee shot between trouble left and right and over a pond to a small green with gorse behind. You need a great iron shot and a little luck to par here. An interesting par 5 is *Ord*, the 475-yard 15th. Here you drive steeply uphill and then decide what to hit on the blind second shot. Beyond the crest of the hill is 60 yards of steep rough-covered downhill slope. If you're not confident about flying all the way to the bottom of the hill, lay back to the top of the ridge and have a look. From the top of the ridge it's about 130 to the small green with OB behind. *Home*, the 323-yard par 4 eighteenth begins with a dramatic downhill tee shot to an angled fairway. To find safety requires a shot of about 220 yards, short of that ends up in heavy rough. Now the fun starts. The green is tucked behind a ridge (left over from a stone fence) and is wildly sloped back to front--never give a downhill putt on this green. We played Strathpeffer Spa GC in a Couples Open competition and ended up 15th out of 17 couples. The locals really took us to task on their home course, but they did it in a friendly manner. At the awards over a beer we won the award for traveling the farthest--there were only two other non-club couples and they were both from neighboring clubs. In a competition or not, we'd certainly play Strathpeffer Spa GC again.

COMMENTS FROM THE FORWARD TEES: Everyone will get plenty of exercise on this course in a charming setting in the hills. The challenges are hills, steep hills, blind shots, gorse, trees and some water. I especially liked having to plan the placement of each shot, but some holes are quite open. The 6th is a short (113 yards) blind par 3 over a hill. It's a fun hole and typical of several for women. The holes are very doable, but trouble is near if you are off line.

STRUIE COURSE, The Royal Dornoch Golf Club
Golf Road, Dornoch, Sutherland IV25 3LW
01862-810792 www.royaldornoch.com
Links, 6276 yards, par 72, £50

AMENITIES: Dornoch Struie shares the great clubhouse of Royal Dornoch Championship Course (reviewed in *Golf in Scotland: The Hidden Gems*) with the beautiful upstairs lounge which serve fine food all day. The golf shop is below the lounge and is one of the best in the north. Check in at the golf shop; the Struie first tee is across the road past the first tee of Royal.

COURSE COMMENTS: In 1877 the course was known as the Ladies' Course and was an easier track for the lady members. Much of that course was lost during the war years. When the course was rebuilt it was as a relief course for Royal. Struie was significantly strengthened in the 1980s when it was extended to 18 by Donald Steel. In 2003, five holes were rebuilt by Robin Hiseman. Now the Struie course should be considered a true championship track, longer and in some ways more difficult than venerable Royal Dornoch.

Since everyone wants to play Royal, Struie is often there for the taking. Don't make the mistake of taking Struie lightly; it has teeth. Forty-six fairway and greenside bunkers, most of which are steep-sided, will exact a toll. The greens, medium to large, are quick and quite undulating. Water in play on four holes (a burn on the 3rd, 16th, and 17th, and a pond on the right side of the 6th) adds a challenge not found on Royal. Add in the length and the wind and Struie is a formidable test. With great vistas of the firth across to Tain and Portmarnoch, the hillsides, and the views of the village of Dornoch with its prominent cathedral, placed anywhere but beside Royal Dornoch, the Struie course would be golfing destination. As it is it's a wonderful course and a great value for your money.

None of the Struie holes are easy, but *Gizzen Briggs*, the 399-yard par 4 fifth is a standout. On the tee shot stay left of the two bunkers on the right to have a fair approach to the green. The bilevel green has a bunker and trees in the way when coming in from the right. The green also has a couple of unusual humps in the back. Follow that hole with *Plantation*, a testing two-shotter of 367 yards. Trees left and a long pond on the right means that driving accuracy is highly important. The swaled green is guarded by three bunkers. The 9th, *Dornoch Firth*, is a long, 545-yard par 5, with seven bunkers to add difficulty to the length. The last set of bunkers almost completely cross the fairway about 100 yards out from the green. Lay back to a good distance and have a go at the narrow green which has no bunkers around it. At *Tarbet Ness*, the 527-yard par 5 thirteenth, again it's all about the bunkers. Six fairway traps and two more by the green create plenty of challenge, and the green with three distinct levels adds even more. The final hole is interesting. *Witches Pool* is only 125 yards long, but is very demanding. A pond is in play from the medal tee, but not from the member's tee or the ladies'. The shot is all uphill to a green which slopes back to front and has three fronting traps which need to be carried. After playing the long course it's a relief to finish with a finesse hole. Royal Dornoch may be King of the North in Scottish golf, perhaps the best course in Britain not on the Open Rota, but Dornoch Struie is turning into a real Prince.

COMMENTS FROM THE FORWARD TEES: Dornoch Struie is a long course for ladies (especially the new holes 9, 10, 11, and 13), but it has wide fairways. All the par 3s are long, except the 18th which is short and straight up. The 3rd has the most trouble with a burn and the road in the way for most women. The challenges are different at Struie than at Royal Dornoch. My first choice would always be Royal, but I'd never pass up a chance to play Struie.

TORVEAN GOLF COURSE
Glenurquhart Road, Inverness Inverness-shire IV3 8JN
01463-711434   www.torveangolfclub.co.uk
Parkland, 5799 yards, par 69, £28

AMENITIES: Very pleasant clubhouse with panoramic views of six holes. Snacks and sandwiches are available most of the time, and the club has a chef who prepares evening meals on weekends. The course comes back to the clubhouse after the 8th, so a quick stop is possible. Torvean has no pro, but a small golf shop is housed in the original small clubhouse.

COURSE COMMENTS: The Longman Municipal GC was located near the site of today's Torvean GC, but it shut down in 1939 because the land was taken over by the RAF for a base. Torvean was designed and built by Jack Blackburn as a 9-hole track in 1962, and then expanded in 1988. The current parkland course, named for the 6th century missionary St. Bhean (*Torr Bheathain* means "Hill of the Bean"), plays below Torvean Hill which contains ancient grave sites. The club's emblem is a distinctive decorated Celtic cross. The course, welcoming to visitors, has some simple holes, but plenty of interesting and challenging holes as well. The 48 fairway and greenside bunkers are generally unfriendly, but playable. Five holes have water trouble. The burns and ponds will be of most concern on the 15th and 16th. The smallish greens are hard and fast with some being narrow. Some of the putting surfaces are quite sloped and all have subtle borrows or breaks. The tight course has some open tee shots. On some of the holes you need to watch out for other golfers coming at you. We played in a wet year and the course was in excellent condition. Besides the views of surrounding hills and great spring and autumn colors, you may see the unusual sight of the tops of boats going by on the Caledonian lock next to the course.

The first three holes at Torvean are fairly straight ahead, but starting at the 4th the course gets far more interesting. *Birches*, the 270-yard par 4 fourth is a short potential birdie hole that can bite. The wide fairway is tree-lined which can catch any off-line balls. The green is shallow and protected by two bunkers. Be below the hole because putts from above can easily roll off the front. Next is the par 5 fifth of 565 yards, one of the longest holes in northern Scotland, which is both long and tricky. The right side has tree trouble while the left has trees, heavy rough, and left to right slope. The approach is uphill and the green is guarded by four traps. Look for the old dynamite shed in back of the green (and hope you aren't around when it blows). The 6th, *Magazine*, is one of those holes you'll only find in Scotland. It plays as a 277-yard par 4 from the medal tees and the members play it as a 249-yard par 3! The hole plays downhill with heavy forest left. The best approach is to try to clear the bunker 33 yards out from the right side of the green and your ball will roll left to the two-tiered green with a bunker left. Four is a good score from whichever tee you use. On the 157-yard 7th hit from a very elevated tee down (one or two less clubs) to a small green which slopes seriously left to right and is guarded by bunkers front and left. With *Loch Na Sanais* (loch of whispering) on the left and trees on the right, the 8th is a very narrow fairway. Bill and George, our playing partners, pointed out that the smart shot is an iron down the middle. On your approach avoid the large tree on the right and the traps left and right. The long, narrow green slopes back to front. On the back side at Torvean (the last ten holes) we found three holes to mention. The 13th, *Collie Bheag*, is a tough 410-yard par 4 with fairway bunkers right and left to collect wayward shots. A burn crosses the fairway about 90 yards from the green which is hidden over a hill. Be careful of the bunkers surrounding the back to front sloping green. One more problem is that OB runs all the way tee to green on the right. The seven-yards-wide putting surface is a hard target to find on the 174-yard 15th. Bunkers on both sides and a pond to the right edge just before the green make a hard shot even more testing. After the 15th make one of the three road crossings as you play Torvean. It was about here that we saw a beautiful grouse who let us get as close as about ten paces. The 16th, *Tigh Dhubh*, is a tough 471-yard par 4 which begins with a blind drive over an aiming post. The fairway bends slightly left and drops to a green protected on three sides by traps. The pond about 90 yards from the green is definitely in play. Along with Inverness Golf Club, be sure to include the friendly and challenging Torvean GC on you itinerary.

COMMENTS FROM THE FORWARD TEES: Torvean GC has an interesting front and a long, harder back with pars of 34 and 37. The back is 642 yards longer. The first 8 holes, before you cross the road, are set in old forest beside a loch and planted with a wide variety of trees. The feeling is comfortable and inviting. The 260-yard 4th is especially fun and can be an easy par except for the slope of the green and tricky pin placement. The back is newer, open, and wider, but not easy. Besides being longer, the bunkers are particularly well placed to be troublesome for ladies. Torvean is an interesting course with the Caledonian Canal running beside several holes. We noticed a couple of boats passing by while we played. Our playing partner, Bill, told me that before they laid the concrete for the canal they lined it with sheep fleece. It's a good parkland course for ladies.

TRAIGH GOLF COURSE
Arisaig, near Mallaig, Inverness-shire PH39 4NT
01687-450337 www.traighgolf.co.uk
Seaside 9-hole, 2456 yards, par 34, £20 day

AMENITIES: Cokes, candy bars, and changing rooms as well as a few golf essentials are available in the small clubhouse. If nobody is around use the honesty box. I noticed that the course had quality sets of clubs for hire, unlike many other small courses.

COURSE COMMENTS: Traigh is one mile north of Arisaig off A830, the Fort William-Mallaig road. Golf has been played at Traigh for the last 100 years, but this course is the work of John Salveson and James MacDonald (Head Greenskeeper at Royal Lytham & St Annes) in 1994. Traigh (pronounced "Try") means "beach" in Gaelic. The name fits the course which plays beside sandy beaches and rock outcrops, with spectacular views to the islands of Eigg and Rhum, and the Cuillins (mountains) of Skye. It's drop dead gorgeous enough that one recent newspaper article called the course, "Probably the most beautifully sited nine-hole golf course in the world." After playing nine on a delightful September morn, we'd be silly to disagree. When I first booked a tee time on Traigh (not always necessary, but a good idea to avoid societies or competitions), I was told that it was just a small track, out-of-the-way, but very pretty. What I wasn't told was that the golf would be highly entertaining as well. Only two holes have bunkers, the 4th and 6th, with only one fairway bunker. Water is in play on three holes: 9 has a small ditch in front of the green, and a wide burn (wider at high tide) is crossed in front of the green at 5 and off the tee at 6. Elevation changes and weather, especially the wind, will add difficulty to the course which can play both wide and tight depending upon the hole and the shot. The other difficulty at Traigh is the distracting views; the beauty makes it hard to concentrate on your golf.

For a small course, the variety in the holes helped keep our attention. The course calls itself a "seaside course," but it would be easy to describe it also as linksy or moorland. Number two, *Spion Kop*, is a 452-yard par 5. Big hitters can aim over the marker pole and significantly shorten the hole, but short will mean you're on a hillside of very nasty rough. Those less adventuresome play along the dogleg right around the hill and up. The approach to the links-like green will be blind. *Jimmy's Choice* is the 257-yard par 4 fourth which begins with a dramatic uphill tee shot with a stand of gorse on the left at the top of the hill. You need an uphill shot of 230 yards to clear the gorse. The more normal route is to lay back of the top to the right and have a short shot in. The green is one of Traigh's largest. Next comes *The Bridge*, a 135-yard par 3. Take one or two more clubs into the wind on this downhill one-shotter. The tee shot is over a wide burn (almost a pond) to a relatively small target. The second par 5 is *The Lang Whang*, the 479-yard 7th. This is a classic straight hole. A hillside with heavy rough is on the right and rough and OB is left. The green is tucked tight to the right. Eagles and birdies are possible, par is likely, but stray right or left and big numbers come into play. What we found at Traigh GC were wonderful views, interesting and testing golf, and friendly members. I can't think of much more to look for in a golfing experience.

COMMENTS FROM THE FORWARD TEES: Traigh is an absolutely beautiful course with panoramic views until the 6th which turns inland and presents the vista of the Mhor Mountains. As you come up over the hill to the green at the 8th you are again in sight of the beach and sea. The course is short for ladies, only 2103 yards, but is filled with unique challenges. Several of the drives and second shots are up and over hills or ridges. To reach the 4th green you must hit through a narrow gap with gorse on one side and the hillside on the other. Par 3s are reasonable distance, but on the 5th you must fly the ball about 100 yards over the burn/pond. The two par 5s are relatively short, 390 and 382 yards, but they are tricky. All in all, Traigh GC is a great small golf course with fantastic views. A course any woman would like.

ULLAPOOL GOLF COURSE
The Clubhouse, North Road, Morefiled, Ross-shire IV26 2TH
01854-613323   www.ullapool-golf.co.uk
Seaside moorland 9-hole, 2731 yards, par 35, £25 for 18

AMENITIES: The club has a pleasant clubhouse with lounge, but services are limited and only if someone is there. Don't count on being able to get anything. No golf shop, but there is an Honesty Box for when no one is around.

COURSE COMMENTS: Ullapool had a course as early as 1903, but that was lost during World War I and never rebuilt. The current course, sited along the Ullapool River (really a sea inlet), was opened in April 1998. When we played in the autumn of 2007, a light mist was falling for part of our round, but there was no wind (unusual for the course). When I sent a picture of the course to the club secretary, he said he's never seen the flag on the third green hanging so limp. The downside of the windless round was that we met the scourge of Scotland, the Midges.

Midges or midgies are small biting flies that appear in mid to late summer, especially in the Highlands and around water. In the northwest we would call them "No See 'Ems" or gnats, but ours don't bite. This was our tenth trip to Scotland, mostly in April/May and September/October, and it was the first time we'd been introduced to the midges. We thought we were prepared with *Off!* insect repellant, but I was in for a surprise. By the time we reached the tee of the second, we knew we needed protection. We sprayed our necks and heads and played on. The repellant worked fairly well, except that I didn't think about the fact that I was wearing short sleeves while Anne had on long. Even though I hadn't felt a single bite, by the end of the round there were a few welts on my arms and they were beginning to itch. By that evening I was putting on the only anti-itch medicine we had. By the next morning I could count more than forty bites per arm! A midge bite is not like a mosquito bite which welts up, itches for a couple of days, and is then forgotten. Midge bites itch for a month! Literally! Businesses have refused to move to the Highlands because of the midges. Scotland loses millions of pounds in lost work-time a year at Highland outdoor employment because of the "wee beasties." This painful reminder is not meant to be a knock against Ullapool GC. The wind usually keeps the little monsters at bay (they can't fly in a seven mile per hour breeze). We just happen to hit a windless day which also happened to be the first midge day of the season, and they were voracious. Be prepared, especially in the northern Highlands, with good repellant and protective clothes.

Apart from our experience with the midges, we enjoyed our round at Ullapool GC. The course has nine bunkers, three on the 9th, and all are playable. A burn is in play beside the 1st and 9th, and it crosses the 5th. The river (sea inlet) is in play on the 3rd and 4th. The greens are small to moderate, and mostly flat, except for the 9th which is two-tiered. Elevation changes at four holes add a little difficulty and keep the round interesting. During your round, you'll have beautiful views along the river and down to the village. The 3rd, *Loch Broom*, a 338-yard par 4, is a tight hole. With the loch or river on the left and rough-covered steep hill on the right, the fairway is a narrow target. The green is long and narrow as well. *Gully*, the 251-yard par 4 fifth plays from an elevated tee. Drive over the gully (filled with brush and burn) to a steeply uphill fairway--in the wet, the ball will stop dead where it lands. The second shot is up to the raised green backed by gorse. Avoid the large bunker in front of the green. The 2nd, *An Teallach*, and the 4th, *Summer Isles*, are both short par 3s (about 165 yards) which play off bluffs down to the greens. Fun holes. Don't miss left on 4 or you're on the beach. You end the round at *Rowan Over*, the 298-yard 9th. Shoot to a narrowing fairway with a small tree in the middle. If you're off-line right and short, a burn comes into play. The green is two-tiered and three bunkers on the right lead up to the green. Mounds on the left add difficulty.

COMMENTS FROM THE FORWARD TEES: The course is harder to score on than it seems. It initially appears to be a simple course by the sea, but there are many obstacles to good scores. The first has a burn to cross. Two is a long carry downhill over gorse. The 3rd requires precision to avoid water left or the hillside right. Four has gorse bushes to carry. The 5th is steeply uphill with a huge bunker in front of the green. Number six has a sharp dogleg near the green, and 7, 8, and 9 are all long, especially in wet conditions. Ullapool is a good course, but not as easy as it first appears. And oh yes, the midgies didn't get me!

WICK GOLF COURSE
Reiss, by Wick, Caithness KW1 4RW
01955-602726   www.wickgolfclub.com
Links, 6123 yards, par 69, £25

AMENITIES: A warm welcome awaits visitors to this course in the far north of Scotland; that is if someone's around. If nobody is about, drop your money in the honesty box and have a go. If the attractive clubhouse lounge is open, check in for play there. Good pub food and snacks are served in the clubhouse lounge most of the time it's open. No golf shop.

COURSE COMMENTS: Wick GC established in 1870 is older than Royal Dornoch, and that much further out-of-the-way. Recently an early club medal turned up for auction on eBay. A club member bought it and returned it to the club. The medal was dated 1871. Like Raey GC, even farther north, wind accosts you almost every day at Wick. The fall day we played the skies were sunny, but the wind was whipping through the course at 30 to 40 miles per hour. It brought to mind the old Scottish saying: "If there's nae wind, it's nae golf." What's nice at Wick is that the prevailing wind is against you going out and with you coming in. Besides the wind, trouble exists as quite a few small deep bunkers, several fronting and some fairway. The traps are particularly troublesome on the par 3s, like the 14th with four. The greens are medium to small with a good bit of undulation. Thirteen is dramatically two-tiered. The small Burn of Lyth comes into play on several holes, but the trouble is always visible. The first cut of rough is very penal and balls are often hard to find. Off the first cut consider it lost in most cases, it's that deep.

The front side plays long into the wind and through flat linksland. Tee shots are fairly open with wide landing areas. On a calm day (of which they have very few) it would be the easy side. Three holes on the back, which plays more in the dunes caught our attention. The 9th, *Tern*, is 141-yard par 3, with a drive which is all carry over a small burn and heavy rough to a green guarded by two vicious fronting bunkers. A little bailout room can be found long, but don't end up too long or you'll find a dune and the Westerloch River. Number 10, *Bay View*, a par 4 of 381 yards, offers great views of Sinclair's Bay from the elevated tee. A dogleg left, with the prevailing wind blowing right to left, takes a drive of 200 to 210 yards to reach the corner. The second shot is to a relatively defenseless green. The test will be can you stop your ball downwind on the small green. The 13th, at 414 yards, is a great links hole with a rising hummocky fairway; great for blasting drives downwind, but be careful of the links bounces. The approach is through more swales to a wonderful two-tiered green. You really want to be on the correct level! From the middle of the fairway it looks as if the burn crosses in front of the green, but it is only in play to the left and right, not in the center. In the first week of September we played at 1:00 p.m. after a men's game and had the course to ourselves. Views of nearby farmlands, the river, the sea, a lighthouse, and a castle added to wonderful uncluttered links golf and make Wick GC a fun find.

COMMENTS FROM THE FORWARD TEES: When we played at Wick, we played some tees together even though the card had more separation. Especially into the wind the course played very long. The rough was particularly tough and wiry; it took all my strength just to get the ball out. The clue is just stay out of the rough. There definitely wasn't much yardage break for ladies on the par 3s. Some were almost impossible to reach in one. On the longer holes, though, the links grass gave good long roll. The views of the dunes and the sea are magnificent. The course is certainly worth your time to visit.

Courses in this region listed in *Golf in Scotland: The Hidden Gems*: Boat of Garten, Brora, Buckpool (Buckie), The Dragon's Tooth (Ballachulish near Glencoe), Fortrose & Rose-markie, Garmouth & Kingston, Golspie, Grantown-on-Spey, Helmsdale, Hopeman, Kingussie, Nairn Dunbar (Nairn), Orkney (Kirkwall), Reay, Royal Dornoch, Spey Bay (Fochabers), Strathlene Buckie (Buckie), Tain, Tarbat (Tain).

PUBS, TEAROOMS & RESTAURANTS

There are numerous quality eateries in this large section of the country. Some of the best dining is in small villages like Boat of Garten, Durness, Gairloch, and Ullapool. It is the restaurants we ate in on the Isle of Skye, the Sconsie Lodge Hotel next to Isle of Skye GC and Sea Breezes in Portree, that make the top of our list. The one though that we would say you have to find a way to get to is the Storehouse Restaurant and Farm Store in Foulis on the way to Dornoch on the A9--stop for the shopping and the great food.

Anderson's Restaurant on Desher Road in Boat of Garten, just a few blocks away from the golf course. The best bistro-style fine dining in the area. Emphasis is on local products and seasonal items. Very nice selection of malts and delicious meals. Try the homemade ice cream for dessert. Be sure to book ahead.

The Arch Inn (pub/restaurant) along the seafront in Ullapool. Modern, bright, lively pub section and more formal restaurant. Small but interesting menu. Good value.

Birsay Bay Tearoom at the end of the road in Birsay Village, Orkney (follow the signs). Cottage tea room serves local produce (from greenhouses next door) and homemade sweets.

Ben Mhor Hotel (pub) on the main street through Granton-on-Spey. Comfortable old pub with upscale pub food and reasonable prices.

Cafelolz@21 (tea room) on Albert Street, Kirkwall, Orkney, in the heart of the shopping district. Limited menu, but good food.

Cairngorm Hotel (pub/restaurant) on the main road through Aviemore. Large menu from sandwiches to full meals. The staff is friendly and efficient, and the food is always good.

The Ceilidh Place (pub/restaurant) two blocks up from the seafront in Ullapool. Lunch menu, dinner menu, and sweets menu served in the pub or dining section. Music hall on occasion.

Cocoa Mountain Cafe & Chocolaterie north of Durness on the way to the golf course. Located in the Balnakeil Craft village, the sinful chocolate shop has the most decadent hot chocolate in the world. Our other favorite shop in the village is a great local bookshore.

Cromdale Bar and Restaurant (pub) in the Hough Hotel on the main road through Cromdale. Excellent pub food in the bar which mostly caters to locals. Recommended to us by local golf manager.

Dornoch Patisserie and Cafe on High Street in Dornch, behind the cathedral. Tearoom where all the sweets are homemade. Good spot for a snack or light lunch before or after golf.

The Eagle Hotel (pub) on the main street of Dornoch ten minutes walk from Royal Dornoch GC. A noisy golfer's pub which serves good pub grub at good prices. Occasionally has music.

The Garden (tearoom) near the ferry terminal in Mallaig overlooking the water. Complete lunch menu and both indoor and outdoor seating.

Garth Hotel and Restaurant on the main street through Grantown-on-Spey. Fine dining, excellent food, and prices to match. Reservations recommended.

The Glenmore Cafe on the main road up to the Cairngorm Funicular Train and across from the Glenmore Visitor's Centre. Alpine-style cafe with simple booths and tables serves good soups, sandwiches, and sweets--especially known for its homemade apple strudel. Outside the cafe windows are feeding areas for birds, red squirrels, and the occasional pine marten.

Julia's Cafe across from the ferry terminal in Stromness, Orkney. Seaside tea room serving breakfast and   lunches. The fish pie is a specialty and the apple pie is very good.

Kirkwall Hotel (pub/restaurant) on the harbour in Kirkwall, Orkney. Highly recommended as the best in town. We had tasty lamb and chicken dishes. Try the crispy fried cheese as a starter.

Lucano (restaurant) on Victoria Street in Kirkwall, Orkney. Very tasty Italian dishes, but a little light on the protein. Good service.

The Keeper's Kitchen on the main road through Newtonmore. The gift shop and tea room in the middle of the village has a garden in the back with a pond and small eating area. Nice selection of sweets.

Myrtle Bank Hotel (restaurant) on the shores of Gairloch. Known locally as The Myrtle, the hotel has 3 bars and a fine dining room known for its excellent sunset views. Great menu specializing in local caught seafood and highland venison. Try the seafood platter as a wonderful meal for two or more.

Mountain Coffee Company & Hillbillies Bookstore on the square in Gairloch. Funky coffee shop with good hot chocolate and great cheese scones. Eclectic book shop is fun to wander.

North Kessock Hotel (pub) off A9 just north of Inverness. With a nice location near the Moray Firth and the   Dolphin Centre, the pub serves good food at decent prices. So good we ate there two nights in a row.

Old Bakery (tearoom) in Carrbridge across from the photogenic Packhorse Bridge. Good sweets and coffees and teas. Good place to pick up local events. Be sure to have a good look at the locally made quilt on the wall.

Old Bridge Inn (pub) behind the train station in Aviemore. Good pub food in a pleasant setting.

Roos Leap (restaurant) in the heart of the village of Aviemore across from the Cairngorm Hotel. Modern cafe/restaurant in a part of the old rail station serves unremarkable burgers, sandwiches, steaks, and a few Aussie items.

The Rowan Tree Country Hotel and Restaurant between Aviemore and Kingussie. One of the best places to eat in Scotland, The Rowan Tree Restaurant in the 18th C coaching inn serves elegant large meals in a beautiful rustic setting. Must book ahead.

Sango Sands Oasis (pub/restaurant) east of Durness by the sea. Nautical themed family restaurant with some sea view. Complete menu with all the usual pub items.

Sconsie Lodge Hotel (pub/restaurant) just past the Isle of Skye Golf Course. Small menu, but not the usual pub fare. Lodge-style dining in the hotel bar and dining room. Popular with locals and recommended for tourists.

Speyside Heather Centre & Clootie Dumpling (tearoom) on the road between Aviemore and Grantown-on-Spey. The Heather Centre is worth a look and the Clootie Dumpling (a specialty cake with custard sauce) Tearoom serves soups, sandwiches, and sweets including 21 kinds of dumplings. Always a pleasant stop.

Storehouse Restaurant and Farm Shop (tearoom/cafeteria) at Foulis Ferry on A9 between Inverness and Dornoch. Great food and interesting shopping in the middle of nowhere. Recognized as one of the Top Ten Breakfasts in Scotland.

Sutherland House (restaurant) five minutes walk from Royal Dornoch GC. As far as we're concerned it's the best food in Dornoch. Always top quality and fair prices.

Trenabies Bistro (cafe) Albert Street, Kirkwall, Orkney, toward the harbour from the cathedral. Typical town cafe with good food.

The Winking Owl (pub) on the main road through Aviemore. Typical pub and pub food. Can get noisy in the evenings.

LODGINGS

1 Janet Street B&B
1 Janet Street, Thurso, Caithness KW14 7AR
01847-895906 www.1janetstreet.co.uk £60
Lovely listed building houses some large nicely appointed rooms. Easy walk to the downtown area. Catrione and Andrew Tait are excellent hosts.

Ardlogie Guest House
Dalfaber Road, Aviemore PH22 1PU
01479-810747 www.ardlogie.co.uk £62
Off the main highway yet close to the shopping area, Ardlogie only a short ways from the Old Bridge Inn. Very comfortable 1909 home turned into a B&B in the 1970s and has been pleasing guests ever since. B&B actually faces the River Spey.

The Auld Alliance B&B

An Taigh Donn, Lonemore, Gairloch IV21 2DB
01445-712122 www.auldalliancebandb.co.uk £60
On the hill out of town this lovely modern B&B has grand views over the bay from each of the two rooms for let. The Duncans are wonderful and helpful hosts. The B&B makes a fantastic stay in the area.

Ben Tianavaig B&B

5 Bosville terrace, Portree, Skye IV51 9DG
01478-612152 www.ben-tianavaig.co.uk £80
Lovely terra cotta building only a minutes walk from the heart of Portree's shops and restaurants. Charlotte and Bill Johnson run a very comfortable B&B. Good choice in the area.

Brooklyn Licensed Guest House

Grant Road, Grantown-on-Spey PH26 3LA
01479-873113 www.woodier.com £84
Awarded Taste of Scotland accreditation and a Four Star accommodation rating, Brooklyn is one block of the main street of Grantown. Everything in the B&B, from rooms to food, is first class. Dinners can be arranged.

Carnoch B&B

14 West Argyle Street, Ullapool IV26 2TY
01854-612749 www.carnoch.com £ reasonable
A lovely, well-appointed B&B next door to the Ceilidh Place and very central to the town. Mrs Robbie Mackenzie is a great host and was very helpful when contacting the golf local course.

Catlina B&B

Aultivullin, Strathy Point, by Thurso, Caithness
01641-541395 www.a1tourism.com/uk/catalina £52/room
As out-of-the-way as Catalina B&B is, on Strathy Point surrounded on three sides by ocean (as the crow is blown, half way between John O' Groats on the east and Cape Wrath on the west) a mile or so toward the ocean from the main road, A836, it's worth every effort to stay there. Listed in the *Good Bed and Breakfast Guide* as one of their "Top 20" in Britain, Catalina is definitely unique. Only one room is available and it's a suite of bedroom, lounge, dining room and bathroom. The fact that Jane and Pete Salisbury take only one or two people (no children, no pets) means that you are guaranteed peace, quiet, and personal service. Oh, and

No Smokers (not even a hint of smoking) are allowed--Catalina has received the prized Gold Clean Air Award and works to keep it. Breakfast is great and you can book for a dinner as well (we did and it was superb). If that weren't enough, Jane and Pete are fascinating hosts. Go to the Catalina website and read the comments from guests if you're not sure about staying here.

Craigiewood B&B

Black Isle, near Inverness IV1 3XG
01463-731628   www.craigiewood.co.uk £80
Lovely country home about four miles from Inverness, but fairly isolated in the   country setting. Hosts Gavin (who organizes garden tours in the area) and Araminta (who cooks with famous chef Claire Macdonald) work hard to make your stay enjoyable.

Docharn Lodge Guest House

Boat of Garten, Aviemore PH24 3BT
01479-831779   www.docharn.com £90/night 2 night min.
The restored steading is an excellent B&B with views of Strathspey and the Cairngorms. Owners Neil and Catriona work hard to insure guests have a comfortable stay.

Eagle Hotel

3 Castle Street, Dornoch IV25 3SR
01853-855558   www.eagledornoch.co.uk £ moderate
A golfer's hotel with a good pub for drinks, food, and craic. Not high-style accommodations, but decent for the price. With touring golfers the hotel can be noisy, but the staff works hard to not let things get out of hand.

Gairloch View Guest House

Achtercairn, Gairloch IV21 2BN
01445-712666 www.gairlochview.com £75
Alan and Sheena Weston will give you a warm and friendly welcome. The modern purpose-built home provides nice accommodations and the lounge and dining room, as well as some bedrooms, have a grand view over the water to Isle of Skye.

Garadh-Nan-Ros B&B

24 Sutherland Ave., Fort William
01397-703861 www.visit-fortwilliam.co.uk £25pp

Panoramic views of Loch Linnhe and a warm welcome from Mrs. Marjorie Kennedy greet you at Garadh-Nan-Ros B&B. The modern house has pleasant rooms and Mrs. Kennedy serves a hearty breakfast. Phone contact only.

Glengolly B&B
Durine, Durness, Sutherland IV27 4PN
01971-511255 www.glengolly.com £26pp
Labeled by guests as the "best stop in the Highlands," Glengolly's proprietor, Martin Mackay, will look after you well.   Rooms are comfortable, the breakfast is great, and Martin is a wonderful host. The 120 year old house has been nicely modernized yet retains the charm of the original house.   When here you must try the whisky porridge--it will get your day off to a brilliant start.

Glentower Lower Observatory
Fort William PH33 6RQ
01397-704007 www.glentower.com £58pp
Luxury accommodation five minutes from Fort William High Street overlooking Loch Linnhe and the Ardgour Hills in a historic building which received telegraph meteorlogical transmissions from the high observatory on the summit of Ben Nevis four miles distant. Serves a good breakfast, but the price is high for the room.

Greystones B&B
13 Dalreich Road, Oban PA34 5EQ
01631-358653 www.greystonesoban.co.uk £110
Described as a luxury boutique B&B, Greystones is a baronial home five minutes walk from the heart of town.   Modernized by owners/architects Mark and Suzanne McPhillips, besides lovely rooms the house has stunning views of Oban Bay. Not cheap, but worth the price.

Hildeval B&B
Easthill, Kirkwall, Orkney KW15 1LY
01856-878840 www.bedandbreakfast-orkney.com £68
Hildeval is a 4 Star B&B with lovely views especially from the large breakfast room lounge and convenient to the town.   Very nice breakfast options, including huge Orkney kippers.

Luib House B&B
Luib nr Broadford, Isle of Skye IV49 9AN

01471-820334 www.luibhouse.co.uk £24pp
Nestled in the shadow of the Red Cuillins on the shore of Loch Ainort on
the main road (A87) between Broadford (six miles) and Portree (19 miles),
Luib House is nothing pretentious. It's just a fine B&B hosted by friendly
and helpful Marilyn and Phillip Wright. Comments from guests include
"great hospitality," "perfect," and "honest advice." Besides a good
breakfast, Luib House has a fully equipped kitchen where you can prepare
an evening meal for yourself (a nice feature). A great place to stay on Skye.
When we asked Marilyn for recommendations for a dinner out, she
suggested a couple of places and then added, "You won't go far wrong
anyplace on the island--it's too small an island for a bad restaurant to
survive long."

Macrae Guest House
24 Ness Bank, Inverness IV2 4SF £60
01463-243658 www.scotland-inverness.co.uk/macrae
Small pleasant Victorian house on the banks of the River Ness only five
minutes walk from city shops and restaurants.

Roskhill House Guest House
Roskhill, Dunvegan, Isle of Skye IV55 8ZO
01470-521317 www.roskhillhouse.co.uk £80
This 1890 croft house only three miles from Dunvegan is absolutely
beautiful inside and out. Close enough to large villages on Skye yet
isolated enough to have great dark skies, the Rawlings will make sure your
stay is enjoyable.

Ruthven House
Kingussie PH21 1 NR
01540-661226 www.ruthvenhouse.com £70
Up a quiet lane north out of town, Ruthven House overlooks the historic
Ruthven Barracks. Within walking distance to town and near the local golf
course, the house makes is a good place to stay in the area. Hosts are very
helpful.

TOURIST ATTRACTIONS

Cawdor Castle & Gardens, Cawdor by Inverness. Just a couple of miles
off the A9 south of Inverness, Cawdor owes much of its fame to
Shakespeare's play *MacBeth*. The real history of the castle is
much different than the Bard's, and the castle is good for touring.

Clava Cairns, near Cawdor. A field of cairns (burial mounds) and standing stones from the late-Neolithic or early-Bronze Age period. The cairns are extremely evocative and date from before the Great Pyramids.

Culloden Battlefield, near Cawdor. One of the most important historical sites in Scotland, the Drummossie Moor, where the Battle of Culloden took place in 1746, is the site of the last battle on British soil. The battle ended the dreams of Scottish independence and Bonnie Prince Charlie) to the throne. A new Visitor's Centre does a very good job of making the history understandable.

Distilleries, up the A9. Eduador by Pitlochry, Dalwhinnie, Tomatin, and Glenmorangie by Tain are all good distilleries to visit, with nice tours and a tasty dram after. They are all easily accessible from the A9.

Dunrobin Castle, between Dornoch and Brora. The ancestral home of the Earls and Dukes of Sutherland, Dunrobin is the most northerly of Scotland's great houses. Many rooms are open to visitors as well as a formal garden.

Moray Old GC

CHAPTER FOUR: NORTHEAST
SCOTLAND

GOLF

The northeast corner of Scotland, bounded on two sides as it is by the North Sea, is home to some wonderful old-style links courses, but the moorland heathland tracks like Ballater and the parkland village courses at Keith and Huntly are not to be slighted. The gems of the area are the fine, challenging links courses at Cruden Bay and Fraserburgh. A wonderful week long visit can be made by staying at one of a number of good B&Bs or small hotels and playing the coastal courses from Murcar near Aberdeen to Fraserburgh on the Buchan Ness, with a longer day trip to play a fine inland course like Ballater or Braemar.

ALFORD GOLF COURSE
Montgomery Road, Alford AB33 8AE
01975-562178   www.alford-golf-club.co.uk
Parkland, 5128 yards, par 69, £22

AMENITIES: New clubhouse built in 1994 replaced the original clubhouse which was a school moved from Aboyne to the course. Clubhouse serves good meals usual hours. No pro shop, but the starter's office has the usual essentials.

COURSE COMMENTS: Alford had a course before World War II, but the land was given over to the MOD during the war. It wasn't until 1982 that a 9-hole course (designed by David Hurd) was built on the current land and then ten years later it was expanded to 18. The current tree-lined parkland Alford course has more than 30 greenside and fairway bunkers to cause trouble. They are well placed, but none are too penal. Greens are small and while some have slopes only a couple are tiered. There is water in play on the course in a ditch which is at the side of several holes and pond and lochan in play on the 14th. The course has lovely views of the hills and is lined by a nice variety of trees. The Alford Valley Railway, a small tourist train, runs by and through the course on summer weekends. For relief there is a toilet near the 10th tee. Alford has many good holes and we'll highlight three on each side. The 4th, a 325-yard par 4 called *Village Grun*, has one of the narrower fairways. Try to stay out of the trees on both sides. Bunkers on each side guard the small green. *Wee Dunt*, the 130-yard 6th is a pretty one-shotter. The green is protected by one bunker left and two right. The 9th, *Lang Stracht*, begins with an interesting shot which almost makes a dogleg left of a straight hole. On this 388-yard par 4 hit out to the right to leave a good approach into the green with one bunker on the left. On the back the 11th, *The Oaks*, a short (275 yards) par 4, is a true dogleg right around a copse of trees-- your drive is key to the hole. Three bunkers on the left side of the dogleg are good aiming points as long as you stay out of them. One trap right makes an approach over the copse more difficult. Short and challenging. Another dogleg right is the 14th, *Boglowster*, a 323-yard par 4. Dogleg around a mound of trees--I found out that there is room right between the trees and a lochan. The second shot must contend with a burn and a pond. A tricky short hole is *Ca Canny*, the 145-yard 16th. It's even trickier at only 76 yards for ladies. A burn runs down the right and crosses directly in front of the hole. A bunker left makes the shot even harder. Alford GC can hold it own as a challenging, fun course against other Dee-side tracks.

FROM THE FORWARD TEES: Alford is a flat course in the heart of farming countryside. The holes are interesting with bunkers and trees to test your skills. The course is not long at 4982 yards with a par of 70. There is only one par 5 and two par 3s on each side. The 14th was one of my favorite holes. You must stay to the left in order to avoid the mound and trees on the right. A hundred yards from the green is a small pond on the left and a burn crossing the fairway. Good hole where some strategy pays off. Food in the clubhouse is quite good.

BALLATER GOLF COURSE
Victoria Road, Ballater AB35 5QX
01339-755567 www.ballatergolfclub.co.uk
Heathland/parkland, 6059 yards, par 70, £30

AMENITIES: Very comfortable lounge with views of the 1st and 18th green. Meals served the usual hours. One of the better golf shops we've seen at a village course.

COURSE COMMENTS: As many village courses, Ballater started as a 9-holer (1892), but soon expanded to 18 (1905). Like Braemar GC further west on A93, Ballater is closed much of the winter at just under 1200-feet elevation. Surrounded by mountains, Ballater is brilliant in the autumn, and lovely any time of year playing along the Dee River. Each hole is visually attractive and challenging. Fifty-three bunkers will keep players honest. All are playable, but there are a few quite penal. A burn is in play on three holes, but is only a concern on the 1st. The Dee River is a nice attraction but should not come into play except on very wild shots. Greens are small to moderately large, but mostly on the small side. The excellently conditioned greens have subtle slopes and a couple are tiered. They putt very consistent. Wind can be a concern on this high course, but most will be more affected by the scotch broom lining many holes. We hear, too, that midges can be a problem on the holes beside the river. The best views are from the 10th tee.

Ballater GC is a lovely course to play with interesting holes. The 3rd, *The Dooker*, is a 223-yard par 3. The tough one-shotter has trees left and right and two bunkers guard the green which slopes back to front. Next is *Invermuik*, a 410-yard par 4. The #1 stroke index hole is more difficult than it first looks. A slight dogleg left with trees and broom on the left has more open trees on the right. The approach is complicated by a large moguled dip covering the last 80 yards in front of the relatively flat green which runs off left. It's easy to pitch up to the green only to have your ball roll back into the front hollow. Another challenging par 3 is the 186-yard 5th named *Glengairn*. The green is a small target to hit through large trees. The narrow green has two bunkers right and a severe drop-off left. The ladies' tee (112 yards) comes in from a different angle. A good par 4 is the 8th, *The Knocks*, at 328 yards. Avoid the series of bunkers on the left of the fairway. The green has bunkers on each side and drop-offs at the back. A birdie chance with good shots. The 12th, *Red Brae*, a par 4 of 402 yards, is a dogleg left with large trees on the inside of the turn. Stay to the right for the best approach, but avoid the bunker at 270 yards from the tee. The green has one bunker left and a drop-off into trees behind. A drive can run out of fairway on the 319-yard dogleg right par 4 fourteenth. Trees give problems on the inside and outside. A 200-210 yard drive to the left side of the fairway sets up the best birdie opportunity on the course. The green is flat and has one bunker on the right and OB not far behind. Last comes *Hame*, the 328-yard par 4 eighteenth, and it's a fun finish. The drive is over broom to a fairway dotted with bunkers. The green, fairly large and flat, is offset to the right and protected by large mounds. The green sits just outside the large clubhouse picture windows and everyone inside watches the action outside. It's like finishing your round in a fishbowl. This beautiful elevated moorland track, it is not a bad fishbowl to be in.

COMMENTS FROM THE FORWARD TEES: This is a lovely heathland course set along the Dee River and surrounded by beautiful mountains, but the course is actually in a large meadow. It's a nice layout with holes weaving between each other, which means you have to be aware of oncoming golfers on a few holes. Both the par 3s and the par 5s are reasonable distances. Ballater more than some other courses requires accuracy. Some of the trouble is hidden and right where ladies tend to hit. The course is a visual delight with a good variety of trees and interesting mountain views.

BRAEMAR GOLF COURSE
Cluniebank Road, Braemar, Aberdeenshire AB35 5XX
01339-741618 www.braemargolfclub.co.uk
Moorland, 4935 yards, par 64, £25

AMENITIES: The new clubhouse opened in 2000 and has a delightful view down the 1st hole. Serves food all day. The small starter's room in the clubhouse has most golf essentials.

COURSE COMMENTS: Set in the Deeside (River Dee) Highlands, Braemar GC is not far from Balmoral Castle, the Queen's private Highland retreat. When in the area one year when the Queen was in residence (her flag flies at the castle) we asked a local if there would be a chance to see the Queen. He said that if we would stop on the highway toward Ballater we might see her as she went from her car into the church on Sunday morning. We chose instead to play Braemar GC. The professional at Cruden Bay, Mr. Weir, was responsible for designing the first Braemar GC in 1902. Joe Anderson of Perth redesigned the course in the 1930s. It is the Anderson course you play today. Braemar GC is the acknowledged highest 18-hole course in the UK at 1200 feet, which explains why the course is closed from the end of October until the beginning of April. The early October day we played was lovely with sun, dramatic clouds scuttling through the surrounding mountains, and the occasional spit of rain. The course can be busy anytime it's open, but is really busy in prime tourist season around the first of September when the Queen's Highland Games come to Braemar. It is wise anytime you want to play to call ahead. Beside the gorgeous setting of the course in the Grampian Mountains of Cairngorm National Park, Braemar is worth a visit for the golf. The short course, with eight par 3s and no par 5s, will still be an engrossing challenge to all players. At one point the course had bunkers, but they were difficult to maintain. Now there are grass bunkers and berms where bunkers once were. If there had been bunkers on the course I would have found several of them. The present berms do affect chipping around the greens. You might think that without bunkers play would be easy, but that wouldn't take into account the water on every hole, although sometimes not significantly in play. The Clunie River and burns are serious considerations on eight holes. The greens are small and well-conditioned, and several have distinct levels. Mild elevation changes add difficulty on four holes, and some holes cross over.

We played the course with Dr. Eve Soulsby, a professor of Geography at St Andrews University and author of the Braemar GC centenary history, who provided details of the names of holes on the course. *Clunieside* (plays with the River Clunie on the right), the 369-yard 2nd, is a tough par 4 with the river beside and a burn in play at about 260 yards out. The approach is up a two level incline 50 feet higher than the fairway--take at least one extra club, but don't be too long since there are large mounds at the back. Rated as the hardest hole on the course. Five, 6, and 7 make a stimulating set of 3s (5 and 7 play as par 4s for ladies). The 5th, *Cavan's Park* (named for the 9th Earl of Cavan who used to rent the area) is 231 yards with a tee shot over a burn to a narrow green. *Queen's Drive* (the hole looks toward the road of that name), is a blind 92 yards up to a small green with trees and rough on three sides. Seven is a 191-yard hole called *Tom a' Chait* (meaning hillock of the cat). The hole is fairly long, but downhill. Watch out for golfers playing across on the 4th and teeing off on the 8th. The tricky green slopes back to front. The 10th, *Callater View* (looks towards Glen Callater) is a little like the 1st at Machrihanish. You tee off on the 409-yarder at an angle over rough--decide how much of the angle you want to take on (or cut off). Two mounds on each side of the fairway make the approach tricky. The 15th is named *Kirk Spire* (indicates the best line for the drive from the men's medal tee), crosses a burn on the drive (not a problem) and again in front of the green (more of a problem). A good drive still leaves a tough second shot between trees and over the burn to a two-tiered green. The final hole is the 122-yard *Port Arthur* (may be a reference to a battle of 1905 in the Russo-Japanese War in the news about the time the course was built). The short, but tricky hole is severely uphill with a large tree on the right. The two-tiered green can be very quick. As you drive into Braemar from the south the lovely meadow course on the left looks easy and uninteresting. Don't be fooled. Braemar GC will keep your attention from start to finish.

COMMENTS FROM THE FORWARD TEES: Braemar is a delightful Highland setting. The course for ladies isn't long at only 4497 yards and a par of 72, but is full of difficulties with river and burn crossings, strategically placed grass bunkers, and tough rough. The longest of the four par 5s is only 369 yards but you have to cross the river. The 18th is the toughest par 3 because you have to carry over rough to a very elevated green. We played on a calm day, but I could tell that wind could add significant challenge. It's a fun course to play and it's one where you can score well.

CRUDEN BAY GOLF COURSE
Aulton Road, Cruden Bay, Peterhead AB42 0NN
01779-812414   www.crudenbaygolfclub.co.uk
Links, 6291 yards, par 70, £95 for 18 or 27

AMENITIES: Modern clubhouse with changing rooms and golf shop downstairs. The upstairs lounge has great views over the course and serves full meals and snacks all day. Food was very good. Cruden Bay GC provides excellent practice facilities including a covered-bay driving range, putting and chipping greens. St Olaf is a 9-hole course built inside the big course. It's tougher than your normal practice track with some demanding bunkers, a burn in play, and lots of humps and hollows on the fairways (2463 yards, par 32, £25/day).

COURSE COMMENTS: Tom Simpson and Herbert Fowler redeveloped the original Old Tom Morris layout in 1926. Cruden Bay GC is sited along the North Sea about half way between Fraserburgh in the north and Aberdeen in the south and was built in the great railways expansion era by the Great North of Scotland Railway. The course is consistently ranked in the top 40 in Britain and the top 100 in the world. As far out-of-the-way as Cruden Bay is, it's still a very busy course; plan ahead.

Plan, too, for an entertaining challenge. Even though the fairways are generous, all your game will be tested at Cruden Bay. Fifty-two greenside and fairway bunkers will catch your attention, especially because most are deep and steep. Some of the fairway bunkers will give you a chance to advance the ball to the greens which are small to moderate in size with a good bit of borrow. Several of the greens are tiered and have false fronts. Currently, the course is working to return the greens to bent and fescue grass which will make them harder and faster. You can see the North Sea on most holes, but several will have other water in play. The river will come into play on 4; burns cross on 6, 10, and 11; a burn is the major problem in the middle of 13; and a burn runs down the right side of 18. As on most seaside links courses, the wind can make or break your round. The second time we played the wind was howling and it always seemed to be in our faces until we reached the last few holes, then it died down. Besides the views of the sea and river, the course affords a good look at the village and out to ruined Slains Castle in the distance. Slains Castle is supposed to have been Bram Stoker's inspiration for the castle of Count Dracula.

On the drizzly morning we first played, my first drive was significantly less than spectacular. The starter, who had come to the tee with us, suggested I take a "breakfast ball." When I asked he said it was an early morning mulligan which could only be granted by the starter. I was grateful and did find the fairway with my breakfast shot. Cruden Bay GC is so full of wonderful holes it's hard to narrow down our list of favorites. Our picks start at one of the most beautiful holes in golf, *Port Erroll*, the 195-yard par 3 fourth. Set along Cruden Burn (a small river), the hole starts from an elevated tee out over a valley to an elevated green. Take plenty of club because anything short of the green risks rolling back into the one trap on the hole. Par is a very good score here. Six, *Bluidy Burn* (guess where the name comes from), is the only par 5 on the front. The hole is a 525-yard dogleg left with the green tucked behind a rough-covered hill and a troublesome burn. After a drive over a small hill to a narrow fairway your second shot should be a lay up to the left of two bunkers about 115 yards out from the elevated green. Anything short runs back into the "bluidy burn," so take an extra club on your approach. *Whaupshank*, the 380-yard 7th, is a sharp dogleg left. Unless you can turn the ball left, you need to be aware that the fairway runs into tough rough about 250 yards out. Stay out of trouble with your drive to have a reasonable uphill approach to the narrow green which slants back to front. Don't miss right because the slope will kick your ball further right. After climbing a bit on the 8th and 9th, you tee off from the top of the headland on *Scaurs*, the 380-yard par 4 tenth. The hole is a dramatic downhill tee shot to a wide landing area. The bunkers on the left are around the 11th green. A burn crosses the fairway about 65 yards from the putting surface, but it is reachable because the shot is so downhill from the tee. From the member's tee it is about 300 yards to the burn, but my normal 230 yard drive left me only 15 yards from the burn. The green is raised, two-tiered, and has three bunkers around it. A fun hole! The hardest hole on the back is also my favorite. *Whins*, the 389-yard par 4 fourteenth, is a dogleg right (near the green) with the left side of the hole a whin or gorse-covered hill. Your second shot will be blind off a narrow, uneven fairway. The green is almost directly below an aiming post and a vicious bunker sits on the right above the green. It's a hole you'll want to play over and over. The next hole reminds me of the 7th at Shiskine on Isle Arran, except longer. *Blind Dunt*, a 236-yarder, begins with a blind drive over a rough-covered hill-- aim over the marker post and hit more than you think you should. The raised green has some intriguing slopes, but no traps are needed to make the hole plenty tough. Cruden Bay GC may be a chore to get to, but the Tom Morris/Tom Simpson design is not to be missed.

COMMENTS FROM THE FORWARD TEES: Wow! What a wonderful links course set along the North Sea. We have played twice and will play whenever we are in the area. The course has great variety throughout with elevation changes, dunes, gorse, water, and plenty of distracting vistas. The overall yardage for Cruden Bay is 5606 yards with a par of 73. The front side is more difficult for me with holes 5, 6, and 7 giving the most trouble. Five and 6 are long par 5s which play with the wind and/or rain in your face, bunkers, dunes, gorse, and water to cross on the 6th. The 7th is a 336-yard par 4, but severe slopes, a double dogleg, and an elevated green are the challenges here. Then you go up the big hill to play the 9th and the views of Slane Castle and the village of Cruden Bay are wonderful. The holes on the back are unique, starting with the 10th with a long drop to the fairway and a burn to cross, the hole plays longer than it looks. The burn comes into play on several holes on the back. The 15th has a blind drive and requires a well placed shot to have a good approach. The par 3 sixteenth (180 yards) also requires a high long carry over a gorse and heather hill. Short of the green will run towards the green, but a shot landing on the green could run off the back. Cruden Bay GC is thought to be a very difficult course for women, but I love it. There are definitely holes that push the limit of my game, but it's a beautiful challenge that I would take on any day except in a howling gale.

FRASERBURGH GOLF CLUB, Corbie Course
Philorth Links, Fraserburgh, Aberdeenshire AB43 8TL
01346-516616   www.fraserburghgolfclub.org
Links, 6308 yards, par 70, £40

AMENITIES: The new 2005 clubhouse (the old one burned down in 2003) provides views from the lounge out to the Rosehill 9-hole course, the 1st and 18th of the Corbie, and the dunes. Meals and snacks are served most usual hours.

COURSE COMMENTS: Fraserburgh is one of the oldest centers of golf in Scotland's north with Parish Kirk Session records of 1613 containing details that one John Burnett was ordered to "the Minster's stool for correction" for "playing at the gouff" on Sunday instead of going to church. After playing on an earlier course on the links of Philorth (1891), James Braid was commissioned to design a new course which would play over Corbiehill and along "The Golden Strand." The new course opened in 1922 and is essentially the course you currently play. The Fraserburgh GC is eager to share its courses (the 18-hole Corbie and the 9-hole Rosehill) with visitors. During WW II, the club had a training camp and a rifle range on the course, but play continued. Both courses were dotted with large poles meant to deter the landing of German gliders. One pole still remains on the 1st hole of the Rosehill as a reminder of those times. The views of the North Sea, surrounding farmland, and the town of Fraserburgh are only part of the charms of the Corbie Course. About 30 bunkers, mostly greenside with some being tough pot bunkers, are spread over 16 holes (2 and 5 are unbunkered). The small, well conditioned greens play quick and significant undulations make putting tricky. A burn runs down the first, but shouldn't be a concern. The wind (more playable in the wind than nearby Cruden Bay), significant fairway mounding, and elevations changes over Corbiehill create the character of Fraserburgh GC. The best compliment we've heard about Fraserburgh was made by a Cruden Bay GC Board member who called the Corbie Course "the purest links course in the north of Scotland." The whole course is a joy to play, but we picked out six holes as our favorites. Three, *Whyte's Shelter*, a 331-yard par 4, tees off from the highest spot on the course (the top of Corbiehill) down to a wide fairway. The hole then goes up to an elevated green with two fronting traps. A great blind par 3 is *The Hump*, the 183-yard 5th. Your tee shot must clear a large hill to find the green, only a tiny corner of which is visible from the tee. Ample room exists to the right for the faint of heart or the smart. Another fun one-shotter is the downhill 165-yard 7th, *The Well*. Hit to a long green with three bunkers at the front. An absolutely diabolical pin placement is at the front in the middle of the triangle of bunkers. The 10th, called *Solitude*, is a 322-yard par 4. Starting with a semi-blind tee shot where some of the landing area is hidden makes choosing the correct club on this short hole difficult. The approach is slightly to the right with only part of the green visible between dunes. Be wary of the hidden pot bunker left and front of the green. The 13th, *Hillocks*, elicits the comment, "Wow, what fun!" On this 322-yard two-shotter, two large bunkers backed by hillocks look to be directly in front of the green. Actually, they are easily in reach of a good drive and are out about 120 yards from the green. The hillocks you see from the tee are backed by even more hillocks. A great Braid hole! When on the tee box at 14, go up to the top of the dunes (about 50 yards) to get a view of "Golden Sands Beach." *Bents* is the 508-yard par 5 fifteenth. A fairly wide beginning narrows as you get closer to the green. On the left is Corbihill and on the right are the sea dunes. Watch out for the pot bunker at the back left of the green. You don't want to be there!

In 2006 when we played Fraserburgh we were told about their oldest member. Jack Presley, 90 years old, has been a member for 85 years! After playing the Corbie Course we can see why you'd want to play it for that long. It's that good.

COMMENTS FROM THE FORWARD TEES: The course is fantastic with grand views of the town of Fraserburgh, Inverallochy, and the North Sea. Good adjustments are made for ladies while still maintaining the character and difficulty of the hole. Several tee shots require a strategic placement of the ball. Second shots are often affected by the lay of the land. The par 3s are not too long, but bunkers and mounding can make them tough. There are six par 5s on the course, and the hardest for me was the 2nd. Not extremely long at 361 yards, it goes up and up. It also requires a high approach over grassy dunes to reach the elevated green. The course is an interesting combination of tough and easy holes. Along with Peterhead, Cruden Bay, and Inverallochy, Fraserburgh is great golf along the northeast of Scotland.

HUNTLY GOLF COURSE
Cooper Park, Huntly, Aberdeenshire AB54 4SH
01466-792643   www.huntlygc.com
Parkland, 5359 yards, par 67, £18

AMENITIES: The Huntly GC clubhouse was built in the 1920s, but has been well modernized. Lounge serves snacks and light meals during the day on weekdays in season and has longer hours on the weekends (limited hours off season). A separate modestly equipped golf shop has friendly, helpful staff.

COURSE COMMENTS: The original 9-hole course was an Old Tom Morris 1892 design, but that course was lost to the war efforts in 1914, and not reopened until 1923. The course extended to 18 in 1938, and then promptly lost the new nine during World War II. Huntly did not become an 18-hole track again until 1966. The undulating parkland course is an exhilarating walk, but not nearly as strenuous as a course like Pitlochry. Beside elevation changes, trees can cause trouble on every hole. The 55 tough, but playable bunkers will keep you thinking (only the 14th has no sand). A burn comes into play at 1, 11, and 15, and the river is a distinct hazard all the way down the left of 14. Because of the hills, a number of holes will play with side-slope fairways. Huntly GC affords pleasant views of the surrounding hills and farmland, as well as some glimpses of the River Deveron and River Bogie.

From the start of your round you'll find interesting holes at Huntly. The 1st is *Brig*, a moderate length, 352-yard dogleg left slightly uphill. On your approach you must miss trees, three bunkers, a burn, and find the correct side of a double green (shared with 8). A challenging beginning. The 153-yard 3rd is a one-shotter which plays down and then up to a green guarded by two fronting bunkers and backed by more sand. Next is *Devil's Elbow*, a 393-yard par 4. A blind tee shot over a fairway mound starts this dogleg left with OB all along the left. The putting surface is sunken left with two traps on the high side and a drop-off left. The hole requires precision and luck. You return to the clubhouse after nine, always a convenient feature. On the back, we liked the 11th, a 387-yard two-shotter listed as the #1 stroke index hole. Drive over the burn (only a concern on missed shots) to a left to right sloped fairway. Your approach is significantly uphill to the plateau double green (shared with 7) protected by the slope and traps on each side. The bunker on the right, which is significantly below the green's surface, is particularly difficult. At the 15th, called *Burn*, the water is especially troublesome for men because we should be able to clear it (230 yards from the medal tee, 162 from the members' tee), but it has a way of grabbing balls. For ladies it's 155 yards to reach, encouraging a lay up. The green is long and narrow and flanked by two bunkers and backed by a thick copse. *Pirriesmill*, the 381-yard 16th, is a tight dogleg right with trees on both sides (the river is also left, but you'd have to be really wild to find it). Bunkers right and left at the narrowest part of the fairway complicate the drive. The green has a large bunker left and two smaller ones right. The last hole is a short uphill par 4 with trap trouble. The most interesting thing about the hole is a comment from one of the members we talked to. He said his favorite hole was 18 "because I know there's a pint waiting for me at the end."

COMMENTS FROM THE FORWARD TEES: Huntly GC is a lush parkland course with a wide variety of deciduous trees, as well as hills and plenty of sloped lies. The course is relatively short at 4316 yards, but you must hit all the way because you won't get much roll. The par 3s aren't long, but you must fly the ball to the green or deal with hazards such as bunkers, slopes, and thick rough. The only par 5 is the 8th at 395 yards where the only difficulty is the length. A fun, challenging course similar to nearby Keith GC.

INVERALLOCHY GOLF COURSE
Whitelink, Inverallochy, Fraserburgh AB43 8XY
01346-582000 no web
Links, 5340 yards, par 67, £20

AMENITIES: The welcoming lounge in the clubhouse is fully licensed and enjoys views of the course and the North Sea. Take a moment while in the lounge to read the framed news clippings on the walls which tell the story of Inverallochy's fishermen golfers. No golf shop.

COURSE COMMENTS: An idea foreign to most American golfers is playing from one town or village to the next. We'd done it in Scotland at Strathlene Bucky, then we found it again at Inverallochy GC about four miles south of Fraserburgh. This old links club [I couldn't find an exact date, but probably late 19th Century.] plays from the village of Inverallochy to the next village, St Combs, a mile and a half south. When we checked in at the clubhouse lounge, the barkeep/course manager directed us to the first tee by saying, "The first tee is just in front of where those clothes are hanging on the line." I don't want to leave the impression that this is backwater golf. It isn't. Inverallochy is just simple, rural Scottish golf with great views and interesting holes.

The course was rebuilt in 1953 and over fifty bunkers were added a couple of years ago. The course might have been a little tame before the bunkering project, but now can be quite a challenge. Some of the bunkers, both fairway and greenside, are deep and tough to advance out of. For the most part, though, players will be able to maneuver around them. Greens are moderately sized with plenty of undulations. This greatly adds to the difficulty of the course because the well-conditioned linksland greens can be speedy. Quick greens, North Sea winds, and tough links rough can make playing Inverallochy an adventure. The highly exhilarating 5340-yard 18-hole course is built on two kinds of linksland. Several holes play on the flat land separated from the sea by typical dunes. These holes have gently rolling fairways with small hummocks and swales. The other holes play in and around low dunes and usually have elevated tees.

The 6th at Inverallochy, *Bents*, is a 470-yard par 5 (played as a 442-yard par 4 from the member tees), which is rated the toughest on the course, mainly because of the OB on the right all the way to the green. The downhill tee shot needs to avoid the OB and large bunkers on the left. The green is a difficult target to find, tucked into the hollow of a large dune and protected by bunkers on two sides. Once you reach the putting surface, it's easy to three-jack the dramatically undulating green. The 6th may be the hardest hole, but the next hole is no easy play. At *Whitekirk*, a 198-yard par 3, the locals may know what club can hold the green fronted by two bunkers, but for the rest of us it's a guessing game. The safest play is to hit slightly short and left of the bunkers. Plan well and it's an easy chip--par is still available. One of the most interesting drives on the course is at *Trenches*, the 278-yard par 4 ninth. Three bunkers line the left side of this short hole and two more guard the green. The fairway is severely swaled and the humps and bumps can send your ball far off line. Another longish par 3 is the 11th at 199 yards. At this hole's elevated tee you look down toward the flag and the houses of the next village, St Combs. It's a daunting drive with OB right, but fun as well. The 17th, *Allochy*, is a par 4 (419 yards) which shares a fairway with the final hole. A burn crosses the fairway about 250 yards from the tee. On this hole (and the 18th) is an interesting set of fairway bunkers on the left. The bunkers can serve as an aiming point for your drive, but you must be careful. Because of the way they're built, 18's bunker can't be seen from the 17th tee, and its bunker can't be seen from the 18th tee. The second shot at 17 must climb to a raised green--take plenty of club, the pin looks closer than it is.

Not only is Inverallochy GC fun to play, but it is beautiful as well, with views of the North Sea from every hole. On the holes which play next to Whitelinks Bay, the view south stretches all the way to Peterhead Lighthouse. When in this corner of Scotland, don't make the mistake of overlooking this fine course.

COMMENTS FROM THE FORWARD TEES: This is a short course where you actually walk from one village to the next and back. The course looks straight and easy, but it is links and the gentle mounds and slopes will surprise you. I think the back is more difficult, perhaps because it plays closer to the sea and in more hilly dunes. There are nine par 3s which range from 118 to 179 yards, but the hazards and the layout add more difficulty than the length. Wind will definitely add to the challenge here as you walk along the sea, but it's a fun course and on a sunny day has great views of the North Sea and Fraserburgh area.

KEITH GOLF COURSE
Fife Park, Keith, Morayshire AB55 5GF
01542-882469 www.keithgolfclub.org.uk
Parkland, 5802 yards, par 69, £15

AMENITIES: The small clubhouse lounge opens from 5:00 PM to 11:30 PM daily and during the day on weekends, and only provides bar service with catering by special request. No golf shop, but visitors are encouraged and an honesty box is in the men's changing room for when nobody is around. No trolleys are available.

COURSE COMMENTS: Keith GC is typical of numerous village golf clubs--unpretentious, friendly, and offering interesting golf. An earlier 9-hole course on the Burn of Drumbuilt was built by local members, and was returned to agriculture during the war. A new course was built by members, literally. Tees and greens were made by allocating the task to two or three people per hole, who then rotovated the site and hired small boys with baskets to remove stones (which often formed the base for a tee box). "The ground was then harrowed, rolled and finally seed sown and carefully nurtured by the team, who personally greeted every emerging blade of grass" ["A History of the Present Club at Keith," by William Ettles]. The hand-built Keith GC, a Roy Phimister design, provides challenges aplenty. Most holes have bunkers, mixed fairway and greenside. None are too penal, except for a couple of greenside pot bunkers. A burn or ditch will cause problems on a couple of holes, and the various sized greens are quick with some serious undulations. Trees lining most holes are the biggest hazard at Keith. An early member named Dodd planted many of the trees on the course, and now when members get in trouble with a tree, they say it's another of "Dodd's Damned Trees." The rough will affect shot-making, but it's not lose-your-ball thick.

For a small village track, Keith has more than its share of fine holes. The 3rd, *Kynoch's Corner*, is a 215-yard long par 3 with a green hidden by tall fir trees (more of Dodd's work?). Go around the copse which makes the hole a dogleg, or go over and hope. At the tree-line is a small burn which is only a concern if you rattle your ball into the trees. For the ladies, the hole plays as a 210-yard par 4 with the burn and the dogleg as the problems. The green needs no other protection. Another interesting one-shotter is the 237-yard 7th. This very long par 3 goes down and then back up with OB left and one bunker at the green. Length here is the challenge.

Midtowers, the 282-yard par 4 eighth is short but still a test. This uphill hole has a large berm or dyke across the fairway about 10 yards in front of the green. At the edges of the dyke are two bunkers. The second shot is semi-blind to a large green. Next is *The Beeches*, a 465-yard par 4. A very classic hole, the 9th curves around two mature beech trees and up to a green with traps on each side. *Firs*, the 10th is a fine risk-reward 284-yard par 4. The hole bends right (with OB left) around a copse of trees. You might shorten the hole by taking a tee shot over the trees, but two bunkers await and shots that are short can bounce around anywhere in the trees. The green only has one bunker left for protection. The 13th, *Treetops*, is a long 441-yard par 4 which gently doglegs to the left up and then down to the putting surface. A burn about 30 yards from the green adds difficulty to the long second shot. Anne and I played with two local members, Dorothy and Sandy, who were eager to show off their course. A beautiful fall day playing with two locals on an interesting course can't be beat.

COMMENTS FROM THE FORWARD TEES: The par threes at Keith are shorter than on many courses, but a hole that is very difficult from the women's tee is the 14th, *Wee Widdie* (meaning the "small woods" beside the course). Only 130 yards, the difficulty comes from a burn in front of the green and a bunker on the left side. For men it's a simple short iron, but for me it was hard to find a club to be safe. The course is set up well for women with good distance breaks on some holes without losing the character of the hole. Keith is a "feel good" course which still has plenty of challenges.

MORAY OLD GOLF COURSE
Stotfield Road, Lossiemouth, Morayshire IV31 6QS
01343-815102 www.moraygc.co.uk
Links, 6687 yards, par 71, £45

AMENITIES: The Moray courses (the second course is the New Course and plays inside the Old) have everything necessary to provide a great golfing experience. A small, but complete, pro shop, run by PGA head professional John Murray, sits next to the first tee of Moray Old. Both courses play over tremendous linksland with dramatic dunes and share inspiring views of the Moray Firth and coast. Both also offer challenging golf adventures. When your round is done, enjoy the ambiance of the hundred-year-old clubhouse which overlooks Old Moray's 18th, one of the best finishing holes in all of golf.

COURSE COMMENTS: Founded in 1889, the Moray Golf Club Old Course is one of the highlights of golf on Scotland's Morayshire coast.

Situated just west of the town of Lossiemouth, which was once the fishing port for the cathedral town of Elgin and is now a popular yachting marina, the area is reputed to have a very favorable climate where golf can be played almost 365 days a year. The course is far enough north to be able to schedule "midnight golf" on midsummer days. With the addition of the New Course in 1976, Moray GC would be considered one of the prime destinations for links golf in Scotland if it weren't so far out-of-the-way. Instead, it should be on every links golf aficionado's list of places to visit. The Old Course at Moray comes with a magnificent pedigree having been designed by Old Tom Morris in 1889. Bunkering, gorse, glassy greens, and the ever-present coastal winds are the great challenges at Moray Old. Bunkers, too numerous to count, line fairways (nine on the par 5 second, six on the shorter par 4 eleventh, for example), and surround greens (the short par 3 sixth has five bunkers around the small green). Gorse, beautiful when in bloom in the spring and early summer and impossible to play out of anytime, lines most holes. The greens are small to moderate in size and play quick with challenging borrows common to most. Though this corner of Scotland often has better weather than much of the rest of the country, the sea breezes can be expected to play havoc with your game. We enjoyed playing the Old Course on a gorgeously sunny, windless day. When I told the pro at Cruden Bay about the day we'd had at Old Moray, he said, "My God, how could you not be under par on a day like that?" I shrugged and chose not to remind him of the bunkers, the gorse, and the tough greens.

In describing the Old Course at Moray, an overriding premise is there are no bad holes on the course--all holes are interesting and demanding, such as the seven par 4s longer than 400 yards. We did watch a player sneak onto the course at the 3rd tee, play a few holes, then leave before the 9th (Shame! Shame!). Number four, *Coulart*, a 197-yard par 3, looks benign, but plays far tougher. Three bunkers guard the small raised green. The left side sees action because the two bunkers and gorse there act as ball magnets. On the 7th tee, we had to hold up our tee shots because two RAF/NATO Tornado jets were using a flight path that brought them in to land directly over our heads. I swear I could have hit the plane with a high pitching wedge shot. Many players complain about the jets as a nuisance disturbing their games. I think the locals get used to the noise and, at least, tolerate the distraction. Anne and I have encountered jets making low-level runs through the hills (St Fillans, Killin, Moffat, Boat of Garten, Alyth), practice bombing runs (Royal Dornoch, Tain, Tarbat), and takeoff/landings (University of New Mexico South Course, Hopeman, Strathlene Bucky, Moray Old and New). In each of these instances we've been fascinated and awed by the screaming jets. Certainly, they disturb a shot or two (I had a ball knocked down by jet wash at the 16th at Moray Old), but we view these instances, as one player commented, as "an unusual nuance to be savored and enjoyed." The 9th at Moray Old, a 310-yard par 4, is called *Ditch* because the fairway is divided by two rows of mounds (creating a ditch about 200 yards out from the tee). Even a short pitch shot will have a tough time finding the green safely as it's protected by five bunkers. Another well-bunkered hole is the 11th. *Lighthouse*, at 423 yards, is a difficult two-shotter with six fairway bunkers in play before you get to a burn which crosses the fairway. Avoid these problems and the green is only protected by one bunker on the right. *Road* (most of the good courses seem to have a Road hole) is the 358-yard par 4 sixteenth. Mounding and a long carry over rough add difficulty to the angled tee shot. Gorse on the right side of the hole awaits any drives that run through the fairway. A road is in play on the second shot into a green with five small bunkers surrounding it. The premier hole at Moray Old is the 18th. This hole has been variously described as, "one of the toughest holes I have ever played," "superb," "the best single hole I have ever seen," "one of the finest holes you'll ever see," and "simply an awesome hole." [You can guess how young a player made that last comment.] Does the hole live up to all its accolades? You're damn right it does! *Home*, a 406-yard par 4, has a narrow fairway with heavy rough and OB all the way down the right, five fairway bunkers along the left, and mounding down the center. The green is elevated and protected by two bunkers, one of which has earned the moniker "Hell Bunker." This hole is a serious challenge at the end of a round. I count my par here as one of the highlights of my golfing career.

Moray Old is as fine a course as you will find in this area of Scotland, and with competition like Nairn, Dornoch, and Fortrose, that's saying a lot.

COMMENTS FROM THE FORWARD TEES: I love links courses and Old Moray is a grand example. It's right on the Moray Firth and we were lucky enough to play on a warm calm day. I'm sure it could be much more demanding on a windy day. We were enchanted with the jets taking off and landing just over our heads. The course is long at 6114 yards, but the par 3s are very reasonable lengths. The 6th (136 yards) has five traps, two grass valleys, and a mound that surrounds the small green. A good target shot is required. All the par 5s are over 400 yards with longest being the 454-yard 2nd with a long gorse-lined fairway protected by nine bunkers, slopes, mounds, and a slightly elevated green. As tough as the course is, I think it is both playable and enjoyable.

MURCAR GOLF COURSE
Murcar, Bridge of Don, Aberdeen AB23 8BD
01224-704354   www.murcarlinks.com
Links, 6504 yards, par 71, £78

AMENITIES: The newly remodeled clubhouse lounge overlooks the first hole and the North Sea. The golf shop with the clubhouse is complete with all your golfing needs. Get the code for the changing rooms in the golf shop. A popular 9-hole course is also part of the facility

COURSE COMMENTS: This 1909 club is sited next to Royal Aberdeen GC which is visible from the 12th. Both courses play over the same kind of linksland, but Murcar, though busy, is much easier to get on. Archibald Simpson designed the original course which was later revised by James Braid. During WW II much of the course was turned over to agricultural uses and then rebuilt after the war. Currently the course is undergoing renovation to take the course back to the original Simpson/Braid layout, including removing much of the gorse that has spread over the years (the same kind of program as is going on at St Andrews).

The course shares something else with its more famous neighbor--difficulty. Murcar is a serious challenge to the average or better golfer, and beginners would be better served by the 9-hole course. More than 70 bunkers, many very deep and steep-sided, are spread throughout the course. All the bunkers should be considered penal and would best be avoided. The greens are top quality; moderate in size, fast, with many having interesting slopes. Burns are in play on 16 holes, but are only a real concerns at 7 and 15. Blind shots and the ever-present wind will also affect play at Murcar. Perhaps the defining feature of the course, though, is the linksland. Murcar plays through small steep dunes which means plenty of uphill, downhill, and sidehill lies especially at the edges of the fairways. Don't get me wrong, Murcar is eminently playable by low and mid-handicap players.

On the dreich day (cold, wet) we played, I stayed within three of my handicap and greatly enjoyed the challenges like those at the third. On *Ice House*, a 401-yard par 4, stay as close to the line of the aiming pole as possible because what little fairway there is tilts left. The hole doesn't have much fairway, just a series of ridges and flat areas. The green is protected by two bunkers right. *Serpentine*, the 423-yard par 4 seventh begins with a drive that needs to clear a burn ("Serpentine") 180 yards out and find the fairway to have a chance at the green. The fairway has a slight dogleg left around gorse and a bunker. The narrow green has three bunkers fronting it. The bit of fairway you drive to on the 383-yard 8th runs out between 250 and 280 yards. From there to the green you enter a series of hummocks and hollows with nary a flat lie. The raised green is guarded by two traps left and one right. A completely blind tee shots begins *Tarbothill*, the 402-yard par 4 tenth. A good tee shot over the aiming pole will run down to a flat fairway and leave a short iron shot which also may be partially blind. The green is a challenge to putt; large with two distinct levels. On the 13th (386 yards), take the club that will get you to the top of the hill (about 215 from the medal and 190 from the members' tee). From there you can see over the large rough-covered valley to the green. My favorite pick at Murcar is *Field*, the 383-yard par 4 fifteenth. You begin from an elevated tee and drive out to a fairly open fairway--its an over 200-yard carry and bunkers left and right add challenge. On the second shot you need to take plenty of club to carry to the steeply raised putting surface. Anything even slightly short will roll back toward the second burn crossing. The green is surrounded by five bunkers. *Field* is a stern test. The final hole of note at Murcar is the 16th, a 160-yard one-shotter. *Nipper* is almost all carry across the 15th fairway to a green with a false front and four bunkers around it. Murcar GC will definitely hold your attention from the first to the last.

COMMENTS FROM THE FORWARD TEES: This is a very difficult course for women. The club's pro said that only the top women players in the area (single digit handicaps) play the big course, while most play the 9-hole course at the facility. The difficulty is that many of the holes have drives which need to carry at least 160 yards to find fairway, and others with shorter carries are visually intimidating. The higher handicap women who do play Murcar need to know where in the rough to place their shots. While Bob enjoyed the challenges of Murcar GC, my advice to ladies would be to play the 9-hole course or go shopping.

NEWBURGH-ON-YTHAN GOLF COURSE
Beach Road, Newburgh, Aberdeenshire AB41 6BY
01358-789058 www.newburgh-on-ythan.co.uk
Seaside links, 6423 yards, par 72, £35

AMENITIES: The beautiful nine-year-old clubhouse has tall windows in the lounge from which you can see 15 greens (all except 3, 5, and 15). Food is served all day. Uniquely, the club members raised all the money for the clubhouse before starting construction and then even dug ditches for the power lines. The club has a fully stocked golf shop for all your golfing needs.

COURSE COMMENTS: The original 1888 9-hole Newburgh-on-Ythan (pronounced NEW-bro-on-EYE-than) course wasn't extended to 18 until 1996. The original course was laid out over links while the second nine was built by club members on the headland beside the links (plays very links-like). As with most seaside links courses the wind will completely change the nature of play. Significant wind from any direction will bring the numerous areas of gorse or whins (known locally as funze or furze) even more into play. Along with the gorse and rough 34 bunkers spread over the course (seven holes have no bunkers) will add difficulty. Most are at the front of holes and many are penal. A couple of small ponds aren't much concern, but the Ythan River flows beside the 16th and is OB. The greens are small to moderate with plenty of subtle borrows. Several greens are multilevel and all are well conditioned. The 15th hole has an alternate green for wet conditions. This green was used for a time in the spring of 2008 because a skylark nested by the regular green and club members chose not to disturb the mother and chicks. The course is home to plenty of seabirds (the club's emblem is the Arctic Tern), as well as deer, stoats, and weasels. The views of the Ythan River estuary and sand dunes of the Forvie National Nature Reserve (an Area of Specific Scientific Interest) are a fine feature of the course. One unusual distraction at the course is a plethora of large helicopters flying over. It seems that the flight path from the mainland out to the North Sea oil rigs is almost directly over the course.

Newburgh-on-Ythan GC offers some interesting golf as well as wildlife and views. The 3rd, *Pitscaff*, is a short (467 yards) par 5. A blind uphill tee shot begins this dogleg right. The best line is to aim directly for the marker post (without hitting it). Over the hill the fairway goes down and then back up to the reachable green protected by two fronting bunkers. If you're not sure, a layup in front of the bunkers is wise because the green is the smallest on the course. Next is *Drovers*, a 285-yard par 4. OB all along the left of this downhill dogleg left adds challenge, as does the old drovers' stone corral reachable at only 204 yards in the middle of the line from tee to green. Four bunkers behind the stonework protect the three-tiered green. It's a fun short hole, and so is the 7th, *Funs Gap*. A strategic layup of about 150 yards is all you need at this 288-yard two-shotter. Big hitters can try to drive the gap between the gorse hills or mounds, but off-line shots are dead. From a decent layup the green is an easy target. Another good short par 5 is the 9th, *Corf House* at 482 yards. The hole is a dogleg left with a fairway that runs out at about 260. From that point the fairway drops into an area of rough. With your first shot if you are on the right and in the fairway there's a chance to go for the green in two, but any drive on the left will be blocked by a hill. The prudent second shot is to lay up about 80 yards short of the green, chip on, and have a putt for birdie, which is what Anne did while I ended up in the gorse to the right. The 13th, *Majuba*, is one of two holes named by members for battles in the Boar War (the other is *Springbok*). It's important not to hit past the aiming post (about 220 yards) on this 316-yarder because beyond the post is a deep depression which is difficult to hit out of. At the 15th, *Boathouse*, you can't see the fairway from the tee, only mounds and bumps. The best approach on this 305-yard par 4 is from the left and the green slopes back to front. *Short* is the name of the 148-yard 16th. Because of mounds of gorse, the tee shot is blind--only the top of the flag and the face of one of the three protecting bunkers is visible. Hit and hope, but the green is receptive. Newburgh-on-Ythan GC is fairly quiet during the week, and is much more player friendly than the nearby Murcar GC.

COMMENTS FROM THE FORWARD TEES: Newburgh is a wonderful track with hills and dunes on the front and flat links along the Ythan River on the back. The par 3s are easily reachable, but bunkering and small dunes make them intimidating. Using a course guide is a good idea here because the course has many hidden surprises. For instance, the green on the 6th is at the top of a hill and tucked left behind a dune. The overall distance of 5416 yards isn't long, but it will keep you challenged at every turn.

PETERHEAD GOLF CLUB, Craigewan Links
Craigiewan Links, Peterhead, Aberdeenshire AB42 1LT
01779-472149   www.peterheadgolfclub.co.uk
Links, 6173 yards, par 70, £40

AMENITIES: Half the original clubhouse was washed away in big storms in 1937. The new clubhouse was then replaced by the present modern facility in 1997 and includes a full bar with all-day catering and excellent changing rooms. The lounge and dining area provide views over the course, the beach, and the North Sea. A complete golf shop is also housed in the clubhouse. A 9-hole practice course sits beside the Craigewan Links course.

COURSE COMMENTS: Park in the car park and walk across the bridge over the River Ugie to reach one of the most natural links courses in Scotland, Peterhead's Craigewan Links. A 9-hole course was designed by famed Willie Park Jnr in 1892, and expanded to 18 in 1908. A second 18-hole course was designed by Laurie Auchterlonie of St. Andrews in 1923, but was neglected in WW II and reopened later as the present 9-hole track.

In 1929 James Braid redesigned the Links, mostly with additional bunkering. The course is very welcoming to visitors, but is much in demand by societies and golfing groups. Be sure to plan ahead.

Craigewan Links remains true to the work of Parks and Braid and is a perfect fit for the land. Almost 90 bunkers dot the course, with the 9th the only hole with no traps. True to Braid's design, many of the bunkers are steep and penal, including fairway bunkers. The moderate to small greens have plenty of interesting slopes, but all are readable. A burn is in play on a couple of holes, and the North Sea is deemed "in play," but only on really wild shots. Wind here will always affect play and the fescue grass can be heavy and wet. The views, though, of the beach, the North Sea, and the town are a pleasant distraction.

In the clubhouse after a wet round, as we enjoyed a dram of Scotland's finest thoughtfully provided by a gentleman playing ahead of us who scored an ace, we were told an interesting story. One day when they knew some Americans were playing, a member took out four drams of whisky to the 18th green and waited for the Americans to come in. He said that it was a Peterhead custom to meet their American friends on the last hole with a dram. It isn't, by the way, but he said that when they left the clubhouse later they were all blotto! Not only that, the Americans had bought most of the drinks!

It's wise to be clear headed when playing the challenging links course at Peterhead. *Mount Zion*, the 392-yard par 4 fifth, is the first hole we choose to highlight. It's the first hole where you really feel you're getting into the dunesland. Drive out toward the dyke that crosses the fairway 50 yards from the green. The putting surface is quite sloped with four bunkers on the right. Stay left and mounding will help the ball onto the green. The 7th, *Valley*, has a dramatic downhill start to this 343-yard two-shotter. Stay off the right hand rough-covered bank and play toward the two center traps (reachable by some at 280 yards). The relatively small green has five bunkers protecting it. The 8th is a 488-yard par 5 from the tips, but a 470-yard par 4 from the members' tee. Golf isn't always fair! It's a tight driving hole with three bunkers waiting to grab your drive. The second shot is complicated by fairway mounding and bunkers on each side of the green. *Cottage*, the 10th, is one of two fine short holes at Peterhead. Hit across a large gully containing a burn to a small platform green with five bunkers around it. Plenty of challenge for only 133 yards. The 14th has a burn in play directly off the tee and another about 100 yards from the green. The 421-yard par 4 is named *Burn* (Duh!). Four bunkers dot the fairway and the burn runs the length of the left hand side of the hole. Four more traps surround the green. The hole is rated the most difficult on the back side. *Target,* the 16th, is an apt name for a hole where only the flag and back of the green are visible from the tee. This 174-yarder, the other fine par 3 we mentioned, plays over a ridge to a green with five bunkers around it (most are hidden from view on the tee shot). Take enough club because all the trouble is short. The last hole of note is *Craigewan*, the short par 4 seventeenth. A blind tee shot uphill begins the 316-yard challenge. An iron is all that is needed to find the fairway; play to the right of the hill on the left. Plenty of mounding fronts the small green. Peterhead GC is a true hidden gem, natural and unknown except to the locals. Include it in your itinerary and you won't be disappointed.

COMMENTS FROM THE FORWARD TEES: Peterhead offers great North Sea and wild beach views and though the course doesn't play long, the wind and bunkers make an average score a victory. The par 3s are short by Scottish standards (typical by American standards), but all are challenging with elevation changes, bunkers, and burns (at the base of the 10th). At Peterhead's 3s, success for me was landing near the greens without finding a bunker. Ladies need to be aware that the 9th tee is directly behind the green on 8, so watch for approaching golf balls. The 18th is an extremely long par 5, but if you can stay out of trouble the green is reachable in four shots. A very enjoyable course when playing the northeast coast.

ROSEHEARTY GOLF COURSE
℅ Masons Arms Hotel, Castle Street, Rosehearty AB43 7JJ
01346-571250 No web
Links 9-hole, 2231 yards, par 31, £15 day

AMENITIES: A clubhouse with changing rooms sits next to the first tee, but to book a round you need to pop over to the bar at the Masons Arms Hotel across from the club parking lot. The course doesn't have any golf shop or supplies available, though at the bar they did lend a member's trolley to Anne. (Normally, no trolleys are for hire.)

COURSE COMMENTS: Near the northeast corner of Aberdeenshire, the notoriously windy area called the Buchan, are the attractive communities of Crovie, Pennan, and Rosehearty. Crovie and Pennan have specific attractions discussed in other sections of this book, but Rosehearty (probably named from the Gaelic *"Rossachdair"* meaning "the anchorage ground near the promontory") is the only one with a golf course. We had heard the Rosehearty Golf Club described as "cow pasture golf" by one American visitor. That description, though, didn't put us off, having enjoyed golf at Leadhills, Spean Bridge, Sanquhar, as well as other golf-with-no-frills-attached local courses. After the round we were glad we'd played Rosehearty GC, even on a squally fall day.

The course at the east end of the village on the coast road through town is very rustic. Rosehearty provides natural links golf much like it must have been early in the games' history. The greens are small to tiny with a few steeply sloped (you need to stay below the hole on those greens). Only a few bunkers will bother play and those aren't too penal. A burn crosses into play on three and five. The main difficulties on the course are the small greens and, of course, the coastal winds.

The green on number one, a 186-yard par 3, is as natural a green as you could find anywhere. It's flanked on three sides by dunes and was created by mowing the valley formed by the convergence of the dunes and some of the sides of the dunes. They say that you are never more than a hundred yards from the sea at Rosehearty, Most of the time the second hole will be the featured hole on the course, but we played to a temporary green on a shortened version of the par 4 because earlier in the year a freak wave had washed up and over the green, inundating the ponds in front with sea water. When repaired, the second shot will again play over three small linked ponds to an elevated green. Number three, *Bents*, a 428-yard par 4, starts with an elevated tee shot (above the ponds on two) to a fairway which narrows about 220 yards out. The hole then doglegs right around the edge of a dune. The next hole, *Craggie Neuk*, is a shorter two-shotter (299 yards) which plays between dunes to a green again tucked left behind the dunes. *Airman's Leap* (I wish I knew the story behind that name) is the par 3 sixth of 106 yards. It's a wedge downhill to a green backed by a dune and fronted by a small bunker. The wind and the tiny green are the only tricks here.

The North Sea can be seen from everywhere on the course, and many holes give vistas down to the busy Rosehearty harbour. Two ruined castles, Pitsligo and an unnamed castle, are visible from the course, as well. After your round, be sure to drop over to the Masons Arms Hotel bar; it's where all the local golfers hang out.

COMMENTS FROM THE FORWARD TEES: We played this course on a wet day, but the sun came out as we teed off on the 8th hole. It's a short course of only 2077 yards, with no par 5s and three par 3s. The longest hole is the 3rd (376 yards) which doglegs right around a dune and crosses a burn. A bogey on this hole is good. The course has water on three holes, some blind shots, dunes to go over or around, and some sidehill shots if you stray from the fairway. Even with these challenges and bad weather, I'd play here again.

TARLAND GOLF COURSE
Aberdeen Raod, Tarland AB34 4TB
01339-881000   www.tarlandgolfclub.co.uk
Parkland 9-hole, 5528 for 18, par 66, £18 for 18 holes

AMENITIES: Small clubhouse open usual hours serves bar food and golfers snacks. No pro shop.

COURSE COMMENTS: We kept hearing about Tarland GC as a real gem, but it took us until 2013 to try it. The promoters are correct, this 1908 Old Tom Morris designed nine-hole course is definitely worth the time to play. Tarland is a classic track, fun yet challenging. About 25 bunkers, mostly greenside or fore bunkers (a classic design motif of Old Tom Morris), will be of concern, but none are too penal. The greens are small to moderate in size and mostly flat. A few have entertaining slopes. Holes 1, 4, and 9 have a small ditch or burn in play. For a small course the fairways are quite wide and when we played late in the season the course was in great condition. Views of the nearby farmland and local parish church (which dominates the 1st and 9th holes) are quite lovely. So too is the play at Tarland--the course has no bad holes.

The 1st, *Springbank*, a 293-yard par 4, is an entertaining start as the middle third of the fairway is 80 yards of hummocks which create interesting bounces and lies. The green has three bunkers around it. *Curling Pond*, is the 170-yard par 3 third, but there's no pond to be seen. The slightly downhill tee shot leads to a green protected right, left, and behind by bunkers. Next is probably the best hole on the course, *Yule's Brig*, a 373-yard par 4. This two-shotter goes up and over a rise and down to a burn about twenty yards in front of the green. To the left, and not really in play, is a pond which is probably the original curling pond. Traps left and right add to the difficulty of the approach. Before you leave the hole look through the trees on the right to see if you can spot the Tomnavarie stone circle on the hilltop across the fields. The 6th, *Lang Whack*, is the number one stroke index hole on the course. This 410-yard par 4 bends right around the hillside--tee shots high right can come to the left. Be careful of a bunker on the right side about 200 yards out which isn't visible from the tee. Your second shot will be slightly down to one of the larger greens with bunkers on both sides. Classic golf hole. Last is *Lochnagar*, a 368-yard par 4. A bunker on the right about 200 yards off the tee is to be avoided as are the two bunkers in front of the burn which fronts the green. It's a lovely finishing hole to a wonderful short course.

FROM THE FORWARD TEES: Tarland is a very interesting, challenging 9-hole course. The course is 2590 yards long with a par of 35.

There are some hills and side-hill shots, but the course is very playable. My favorite hole was the 4th, a 304-yard par 4. Tee off to a wide, almost flat fairway which drops about 150 yards out. A burn in front of the tiered green adds difficulty. I will return to this course whenever I'm in the area.

Courses in this region listed in *Golf in Scotland: The Hidden Gems*: Aboyne, Banchory, Cullen, Duff House Royal (Banff), Elgin, Kintore, Moray New (Lossiemouth), Peterculter, Portlethen, Royal Aberdeen, Royal Tarlair (MacDuff), Stonehaven, Torphins.

PUBS, TEAROOMS & RESTAURANTS

We found some nice tearoom/coffee shops in this region, but two pub/restaurants are worth planning a trip around. On the Deeside at Aboyne is the Boat Inn with some of the best pub fare in a rustic pub setting. Not quite as isolated, Poacher's Rest near Ellon is both friendly and fine dining. When in the area be sure to stop at the Cock and Bull north of Aberdeen just to see the place (and the food is good as well).

Birdhouse Cafe on High Street in Banchory. This tiny tea room serving specialty sandwiches and cakes gets rave reviews for good reasons. Excellent food and friendly service.

The Boat Inn (pub) on Charleston Road in Aboyne. Traditional pub setting and menu which specializes in local produce. Lots of pub favorites and specials. Always busy and always good.

The Bothy (tearoom) on the main street (A93) in Ballater. Typical tearoom popular with the locals and usually busy. Best choice in town.

The Bothy (tearoom) on Grant Street, Burghead. Newly opened tea room with back patio for nice weather. Breakfast items all day and delicious sweets.

The Broken Fiddle (tearoom) on Straith Path Street off the main shopping street in Banff. Situated in a late 1700s building, this little cafe serving typical tearoom fare is popular with locals. Be sure to notice the "Broken Fiddle" mural on the back wall.

Covesea Cafe on the coastal tourist route a couple miles east of Moray Golf Club, Lossiemouth, practically beneath the Lossiemouth Lighthouse. A driving range, golf shop, par 3 course, gift shop, and cafe, Covesea Cafe has an unusual menu. The half-lobster salad was outrageous for only £9. A better stop than it looks.

Cock and Bull Bar and Restaurant on Ellon Road, Balmedie, near Cruden Bay. Over-the-top kitsch decor--you could spend an hour browsing the lounge-- but good food. Worth a visit.

The Creel Inn (restaurant) in the historic fishing village of Catterline just south of Stonehaven. One of Scotland's premier seafood restaurants. Pricey, difficult to get to, but well worth the effort. Specializes in fresh lobster and crab caught in Catterline Bay. A Must Stop.

Crossroads Teahouse on High Street in Buckie. Very popular with locals. Tasty food, and inexpensive as well.

The Falls of Feugh Tearoom and Restaurant just past the falls bridge in Banchory. Very full menu of breakfast and lunch items. Lovely inside and out with pleasant views of the river. Food is homemade and outstanding.

Gordon Arms Hotel (pub) on the square in Huntly. Good pub fare, and an especially nice Sticky Toffee Pudding.

Gordon's Tearoom and Restaurant at the edge of the village of Braemar. Good food when we visited, but we've heard negative comments recently. Check with locals before stopping here.

Kilmarnoch Arms Hotel and Falcon Restaurant (pub/ restaurant) on the main road through Cruden Bay just down from the Cruden Bay GC. Classy place with good food and fair prices.

Kimberley Inn (pub) on the bay in Findhorn. We have loved the fresh seafood here, but our last visit was definitely below par and locals say it's only average. Check before making the drive.

La Mangiatoia Restaurant and Pizzeria on Bridge Square in Ballater near the River Dee Bridge. A slightly limited Italian menu, but the quality is excellent. Nice wine list.

Lunan Farm Shop and Cafe by the dunes at Lunan Bay between Arbroath and Stonehaven. A beach cafe with porch for good weather serves some unusual items (ie., smokey chowder, port schnitzel, crab cakes sandwich). Great location with excellent food.

The Mains of Drum Garden Centre (tearoom) in Drumoak near Banchory. Cafeteria coffee shop with snacks and full meals.

Noah's Ark Wholefood Cafe on the main street of Dufftown, a half block from the tourist Centre. Funky decor and an interesting menu are the attractions here. One of the best fish soups I've ever had.

Pennan Inn (pub) in the small village of Pennan along the Morayshire coast. Recognizable from the movie *Local Hero*, the village of Pennan is nothing more than a row of buildings along the steep-sided shore. Most notable is the Pennen Inn, a small pub (reopened in 2009) serving interesting pub food in a spectacular setting. Visit for the experience as well as the food.

Poacher's Rest (pub/restaurant) at a crossroads in Denhead near Cruden Bay. A friendly pub and restaurant with good food and good prices. It's not the easiest place to find, but worth the effort.

Prince of Wales Restaurant and Lounge Bar just off the main square in Ballater. The pub menu includes some very interesting sandwiches. Great for lunch.

The Seafield Arms Hotel (pub/restaurant) on the main street of Cullen. Pub has a large selection of single malts and the restaurant is fine dining with decent prices.

The Ship Inn (pub/restaurant) on the harbour in Stonehaven. Always busy, the pub with small tables and nautical decor is crowded and boisterous. The separate restaurant is bight and inviting. Plenty of choices of excellent seafood--the crab claw and mussel platter was delicious.

Skerry Brae Pub in Lossiemouth overlooking the 18th hole at Moray Old. Pub/restaurant with several eating areas, including a great outside patio. Typical pub food, but good quality.

St Olaf Hotel (pub) on the main road through Cruden Bay. Along with the Kilmarnock, St Olaf's is a good bet for dining in Cruden Bay. Good menu selections.

The Three Kings (pub) just up from the beach and golf course in Cullen. Small pub menu in an old pub. Stop for the friendly atmosphere and interesting ceiling.

LODGINGS

Academy House
Schoolhouse Road, Fordyce, Moray AB45 2SJ
01261-842743 www.fordyceaccommodation.com £70
Dating from the early Victorian period, Academy House began life as a school and schoolhouse. The house was refurbished in 1977 by present owners Sandra and Richard Leith. Rooms are well-appointed and spacious, and the breakfast plentiful and tasty. Dinners can be arranged.

Braeside B&B
Braeside, Strachan, Banchory AB31 6NL
01330-820688 www.braesidebandb.co.uk £60

A modern small family-run B&B a short drive from Banchory and across the road from the River Feugh. Friendly and comfortable.

Cedars Guest House
339 Great Western Road, Aberdeen AB10 6NW
01224-583225 www.cedarsaberdeen.co.uk £70
Small private hotel on a busy residential street has access to the heart of town, about a mile away, via local bus service. Rooms are comfortable and breakfast is good. Since Cedars mostly serves business people, weekend rates can be lower.

Gleniffer B&B
Stonehaven AB39 2EH
01569-765272 www.gleniffer-stonehaven.co.uk £70
Four Star accommodation within easy walk to main town area and harbour. Very nice rooms and breakfast.

Greenmount Guest House
Huntly, Aberdeenshire AB54 8EQ
01466-792482 www.devonfishing.com £50
The welcoming Greenmount Guest House is a Georgian building providing lodging to anglers and other travelers (including golfers) since 1978. A good stop in whisky and castle country.

Inchgeal Lodge B&B
Tullich Road, Ballater AB35 5SH
01339-753849 www.inchgealbandb.co.uk £65
Spacious historic house across the road from River Dee is close to town. A great value.

Kilmarnock Arms
Bridge Street, Cruden Bay AB42 0HD
01779-812213 www.kilmarnockarms.com £85
Serving guests (including Bram Stoker, author of Dracula) for more than 120 years, the Kilmarnock Arms is a good choice for this golf rich area. Close to clubs such as Cruden Bay, Trump International, and many others, the hotel provides pleasant accommodations, good meals, and boosts more than 80 malts in the bar.

Links Lodge Guest House
Stotfield Road, Lossiemouth, Moray IV31 6QS
01343-813815 www.linkslodge.co.uk £70
Awarded "Scotland's Friendliest B&B" by one group, Links Lodge is a 150 year old home which is now a grand B&B. Rooms and breakfast are excellent, but it is the location overlooking the fabulous 18th hole on Moray Old GC that makes this a special stay for the golfer.

Milton of Grange Farmhouse B&B
Forres, Morayshire IV36 2TR
01309-676360   www.forres-accommodation.co.uk £70
The farmhouse B&B is on a working farm. Rooms are very comfortable and we had a nice view out to the fertile fields as a storm swept through. Hilda Massie fixes a grand breakfast and the B&B is near the coastal village of Findhorn and the Kimberley Inn, usually a good spot for fresh seafood.

Twentyfour Shorehead B&B
24 Shorehead, Stonehaven AB39 2JY
01569-767750 www.twentyfourshorehead.co.uk £ reasonable
Great location on the harbour at Stonehaven and lovely rooms with grand views are the prime attractions of 24 Shorehead. The breakfast room is unique with breakfast fixed right beside you. A top choice when in the area.

TOURIST ATTRACTIONS

Castle Trail. The Grampian and Deeside regions are home to numerous castles and great houses. Huntly Castle, Fyvie Castle, Kildrummy Castle, Drum Castle, Crathes Castle, Craigievar, and Braemar are all within easy reach. Each is distinct and worth a visit.

Dunnottar Castle, Stonehaven. The ruins sit impressively on a promontory looking out to the North Sea. Present structures date back to the 1300s and were captured by both William Wallace ("Braveheart") and Cromwell. There's much history here, but it's quite a walk to reach (not recommended for small children). You might recognize the dramatic ruin as the setting for Zeffirelli's *Hamlet*.

Elgin Cathedral, Elgin. A lovely 13C cathedral, which at one time rivaled St Andrews Cathedral in importance and power, is in the heart of the town. Rich in carvings Elgin is a must stop in the area. Only a few blocks away is Gordon MacPhail's Whisky Shop, another must stop.

Malt Whisky Trail. The area is the heart of Scotland's distillery business. Glen Grant, Glenlivet, Glenfiddich, Glenfarclas, Cardhu, Straathisla, and Benromach are a few of the distilleries in the area. All offer nice tours. Dallas Dhu by Forres is a silent distillery now run by Historic Scotland. As a closed facility the tour is self-guided and unique--there's still a dram of spirit at the end of the tour.

Museum of Scottish Lighthouses, Fraserburgh. Home to an interesting collection of lenses and prisms, the museum has interesting exhibits relating to Robert Louis Stevenson's father and grandfather, builders of many UK lighthouses. While you're there tour the Kinnaird Head Lighthouse.

Kingsbarns GC

CHAPTER FIVE: HEARTLANDS OF SCOTLAND

GOLF

Comprised of Perthshire, Angus, and Fife, the Scottish Heartlands is not only geographically the heart of the country, but it is the heart and soul of the golfing world with the Old Course at St Andrews. Much fine golf will be found throughout the area, from historic 9-hole courses like Bridge of Allen to the heathland jewels around Blairgowrie and the glorious Gleneagles Resort with three fantastic tracks. The variety of courses in this region is phenomenal--links tracks like Panmure, parkland beauties like Forfar--and then there's Fife. We can easily see why Scottish golfers tend to not stray far from home, especially if they live near Fife. So many great courses are within an hour drive that the choices become mind boggling. Whether you play the Old Course or not, don't pass up a round on the New or the Jubilee. And don't dare by-pass Kingsbarns. You really can't go wrong with any of the courses in this region.

PERTHSHIRE AND ANGUS

ALYTH GOLF COURSE
Pitcrocknie, Alyth, Perthshire PH11 8HF
01828-632268   www.alythgolfclub.co.uk
Parkland/heathland, 6205 yards, 70 par, £25

AMENITIES: Alyth offers a large practice area, a modern well-stocked golf shop, as well as a beautiful clubhouse (built in the 1960s and refurbished in 2003). The clubhouse upstairs lounge is fully licensed and serves food all day.

COURSE COMMENTS: Twenty-one miles northeast of Perth is the charming, challenging Alyth Golf Club (one mile southeast of the village on B954). The course is rarely crowded weekdays and thus is a good choice for a drop-in round.   Alyth GC, though, should be on everyone's list of must play courses. Established in 1894, the original 9-hole course, built on the heathery muir, was designed by Old Tom Morris for the munificent sum of less than £1.50 (less than $3.00). A tee shot slicing out of bounds at today's 8th would land on Old Tom's course. A new 9-hole layout was built in 1896 on land used for the present course. Two more major developments took place to give us the present 6259-yard par 70 heathland track. New land was acquired and the course was extended to 13-holes in 1928. The final change came in 1934 when famed architect James Braid designed six additional holes (and took out one short one) to leave us with today's course.

Alyth GC uses some great design techniques to challenge players. The excellently put together course has 62 bunkers (many steep-sided and all strategically placed), large greens with subtle contours, tree-lined fairways, and a burn which crosses three holes to create a fair test for any golfer. Number three, *The Teuchat's Tryst*, is a visually intimidating 169-yard par 3. The pin can be placed so that it is directly behind a large pot bunker--there is more room behind the bunker than it appears from the tee. Two large bunkers protect the left side on this hole. The signature hole at Alyth is *The Brig*, 454-yard par 4, which is also the most difficult hole. A dogleg right, with OB on the right from tee to green, the 5th hole is diagonally bisected by a troublesome burn. A strong tee shot of about 240 yards will carry the burn, but trees encroach on both sides. The second shot is to a long, narrow raised green, which more than one golfer has called "amazing." No bunkers are needed on this hole. In the clubhouse lounge after your round, don't be surprised if you are asked how you played the fifth. It's always a lounge topic of conversation, like at Boat of Garten people will ask how you played *Gully*, the fifteenth. Great holes, like the fifth at Alyth or the fifteenth at Boat, help define the character of a course. Another fine hole at Alyth is *Heathery Muir*, the 255-yard par 8th, where you can slice out to the original Tom Morris land. OB on the right can affect play on this short hole, but the biggest challenge is the nest of three bunkers around the green, especially the large bunker covering the entire front of the green. It was on the tee box of this hole, with great vistas into the surrounding hills, that Anne noted that the view seemed to invite us into the Highlands. Don't think about the name when playing Alyth's 326-yard par 4 thirteenth. *Tyke's Shank* (I hate that word!) is a dogleg left with three bunkers lining the right side (at 180, 230, and 250 yards). A thicket of trees protects the left side--you only have to be into the trees a couple of feet to not have a shot forward. Only the top half of the flag is visible on your second shot to a green with bunkers on both sides. Alyth's 17th is another visually daunting one-shotter. At 202 yards, *The Cairn* is another example of strategic bunkering. Golf course architect Robert Trent Jones, Jr., in his book *Golf by Design* (Little, Brown & Co., 1993) describes the use of fore-bunkering to create an illusion of a more difficult shot. Like the 8th, a bunker placed in front of the green at the 17th makes it look like the green is directly behind the bunker; but it's almost twenty yards from the back of the bunker to the front of the green.

"A little piece of golfing heaven," is how one golfer described Alyth GC. Anne and I can't disagree with those sentiments.

COMMENTS FROM THE FORWARD TEES: Alyth is a beautiful birch and evergreen lined course set in the Highlands with views of the Cairngorms. The trees impact your golf because the fairways are fairly narrow. The course is very fair for ladies and it's possible to score well here. Par 3s are reasonable length and the only two par 5s are on the back. I especially like the par 3 third with two bunkers near the tee and three around the green. It's a good challenge with very little safe landing area other than the green. The 5th fairway is divided into three segments by two burn crossings. Good course management is required to score well, and it feels good when you succeed. There is a convenient toilet after the 12th. This course is high on my list to return to.

BLAIRGOWRIE GOLF CLUB, Lansdowne Course
Rosemount, Blairgowrie, Perthshire PH10 6LG [For all courses.]

01250-872594 www.theblairgowriegolfclub.co.uk [For all]
Heathland, 6834 yards, par 73, £65

AMENITIES: [For all courses.] The older clubhouse was remodeled in 2003 without losing any of its venerable character. The lounge serves good food all day and offers lovely views out to the courses. The well stock golf shop is shared by all three courses that make up Blairgowrie GC--the Lansdowne, the Rosemount, and the Wee (9-hole) Course.

COURSE COMMENTS: There is much discussion about which of the two Blairgowrie big courses is the best. The Rosemount tends to get the most publicity, but a lot of local players say that Lansdowne is the better. Everyone agrees, though, that both courses are superb and that visitors should skip neither. By the way, the Wee Course is no slouch, playing over much the same ground on the 450 acre Blairgowrie Club property.

This description, though, is of the Lansdowne Course, the newer 1977 Peter Alliss and Dave Thomas design. Tighter and longer than its sister, Rosemount, the Lansdowne Course plays over similar heathland turf through lovely woods. Plenty of challenges make Lansdowne a championship track which is fair for all level of golfer. The 59 bunkers on the course are not too penal or deep but are strategically placed to catch wayward shots. Though there is no water trouble on Lansdowne and the rough is fairly forgiving, the trees which line most fairways and surround many greens will be cause for concern. Into the trees is a lost shot or two. The greens range from small to large, but are relatively flat and, even with subtle undulations, putt very true. At Blairgowrie the wind is not the problem it is on links courses, but it can still be a problem on a windy day, especially as it can be blocked by trees at one spot while another spot is wide open to the wind.

All the holes on Lansdowne are top quality, but we did pick out six to help give a feel for the course. The start at Lansdowne's 490-yard par 5 (played as a 461-yard par 4 from members' tees) is challenging. Drive up and over a rising fairway which doglegs left around two bunkers which can be carried with a good shot. The fairway drops gently to a small green protected by a fronting bunker and flanked by two others. Number five, *The Pines*, is a fine 164-yard par 3 with most of the trouble at the front. Tall pines line the tee shot to a teardrop shaped green with a narrow opening guarded by a pot bunker right and large bunker left. Try not to be too long because mounds and a drop-off are behind the green. *Moorfield*, the 8th, is another good three-shotter. This long (537-yard), narrow hole has OB (a fence) all along the left. Trouble comes from the heavy rough off the narrow fairway. Two bunkers come into play about 80 yards from the green which has one bunker left. Stay straight and birdies are very possible, but never be disappointed with a par on this one. A convenient toilet is accessible from the tees of both 10 and 16 (check for the code on the scorecard). On the back we liked *White Loch*, the 404-yard 12th. There's no water, so I don't know where the name came from. The tee shot is tight with trees on both sides, but the fairway opens up about 230 yards out--just about where a bunker lurks on the left. The green has no sand trouble, but trees front the right side of the approach. Next is a fine moderate length par 4 of 369 yards. A slightly downhill drive begins this dogleg left with a large bunker on the inside corner. Approach the green with care because it is well guarded by three large traps, as well as being long (as much as three clubs from front to back) and narrow. Last is *Lincroft*, the 357-yard par 4 eighteenth. The strong finishing hole is a downhill gentle dogleg left with OB along the right and forest left. The raised two-tiered green has four fronting bunkers to make a testing end to your round. Lansdowne is a straight hitters paradise where the ball will roll nicely even when the course is wet. Regardless of how you play, Blairgowrie's Lansdowne Course is a beautiful walk in the woods. The wildlife is interesting as well. When we came to the 16th we had seen several lovely pheasants wandering the course. Off the tee I noticed a large bird which I thought might be some type of grouse in the fairway. I took several long range photos of it. When we got closer and the bird practically crawled into my golf bag, we recognized it was a colorful rooster I'd wasted film on. After the round I learned from the ranger, Ron, that the bird had shown up about six weeks earlier and was now very good at dodging golf balls.

COMMENTS FROM THE FORWARD TEES: Lansdowne is a long beautiful forest course where trees are definitely an issue. Straight shots will help you score on this 5986 yard course. The rough isn't easy to play out of, but you can find your ball. The par 3s are between 131 and 145 yards and good scores are very possible with accurate shots. The front has three par 5s while the back has only one and two long par 4s at 365 and 367 yards. My favorite hole on Lansdowne is the 14th, a 136 yard par 3. The hole is lined tee to green with trees and is visually very narrow (there's plenty of room even though it doesn't seem so). The green is raised with two large fronting bunkers. Your shot must be very precise. A good challenge.

BLAIRGOWRIE GOLF CLUB, Rosemount Course
Heathland, 6600 yards, par 72, £65

COURSE COMMENTS: The Rosemount Course is the older and busier of the two Blairgowrie big courses (be sure to book ahead). A 9-hole course was built by the club in 1889 and then extended to 18 by Alister Mackenzie (of Augusta National and Cyprus Point fame) in 1927. In 1935 the design was revamped by Scotsman James Braid (a master of inland golf); therefore, the ancestry of the course is superior. The challenges of Rosemount show its heritage starting with a mix of 84 fairway and greenside bunkers. Some of the bunkers are deep and penal, and all are troublesome. The course is littered with typical Braid fairway bunkers which are difficult to hit full shots from. Black Loch is sort of in play on 15 and definitely on 16 from the back tee. A burn crossing the 17th shouldn't be a problem, but it's there. The greens are moderate to large with only the 14th being small. The putting surfaces here have enough subtle slopes to be interesting, and a few are multi-tiered. Like the Lansdowne Course, Rosemount is a beautiful forest walk, as long as you keep your ball out of the forest. One of the features we liked about Rosemount is the sense of isolation you get while playing; each hole is completely separate from the others and not shared (on our round we saw only one golfer who had hit through the trees onto our fairway). It should also be mentioned that the quality Wee Course (9-hole) has some of the original 1889 holes, especially *Fairy Dell*. Though we haven't played it yet, we hear it's quite a charmer.

The Rosemount Course is made up of quality golf holes, and we picked out a few to highlight. The 2nd, *Woodfold Dell*, a 339-yard par 4, begins with a drive up over a ridge, but you need to stay left to avoid a menacing fairway bunker. The next shot is down and then up to a two-tiered green four-posted by bunkers. One more long bunker fronts the green on the right. *Meikleour* (you probably drove past the Meikleour Beech Hedge on your way to the course), is the 553-yard par 5 fifth. The hole is long and straight, but a nest of traps can cause trouble on the drive. The fairway has one more trap on the right about 140 yards from the green which is tiered and has three fronting traps. A chance for long hitters to reach the green in one is offered at the 293-yard 12th called *Straight Away*. The preferred play, though, is a safe shot and a pitch to the green with three bunkers around it. The finishing four are the premier holes of Blairgowrie's Rosemount Course. Fifteen is *Wee Dent*, a 129-yard one-shotter. The tri-level putting surface is surrounded by five bunkers, with the large fronting bunker about 20 yards from the front of the green. Left are trees and heavy rough and right is the loch. Take dead aim; anything missing the green is severely punished. Next is *Black Loch*, a 475-yard par 4 which demands a draw over the loch on this dogleg left with OB left all the way to the green. Stay to the right as you approach the green because the fairway runs off left as does the green. Five is never a bad score on this hole. The 17th, *Plateau*, is a spectacular par 3 of 165 yards, one of the top rated short holes in Scotland. The large green angles sideways to the tee which brings a large right-hand bunker well into play. The green is tiered and three-jacks are very possible. A strong finish is the dogleg right 18th, *Mount Blair*, which comes up and then down to the green 390 yards away. Left is the best approach because there are three traps on the right and only one on the left of the two-tiered green.

Whether you play the more venerable Rosemount or the younger Lansdowne, the courses at Blairgowrie GC will both challenge and delight. Keep in mind the club's motto, *Longe et Certe* (Latin for "Far and Sure") as you play these wonderful woodland tracks.

COMMENTS FROM THE FORWARD TEES: I very much enjoy the evergreen and birch forest setting of this beautiful championship course. The course is long at 5959 yards (2885 and 3074), but it is possible to score well. The six par 5s vary in length from 431 to 471 yards. My favorite is the 16th hole with the pretty loch on the left not really in play. The tee shot is uphill and to the right with trees defining the fairway. The hole then doglegs slightly to the left as it narrows towards the green. It's important to set yourself up to fly the ball to the green. Of the four par 3s on Rosemount the 3rd is very challenging. At 192 yards the hole is too far for me to reach with a drive and the natural layup area is made more difficult by three bunkers. I learned early on this course that the ladies' tees are set so that I could succeed, but that I had to think and plan the placement of my shots. It's definitely a play again course.

DOWNFIELD GOLF COURSE
Turnberry Avenue, Dundee DD2 3QP
01382-885226   www.downfieldgolf.co.uk
Parkland, 6817 yards, par 73, £59

AMENITIES: The golf shop is one of the best supplied we've visited, and the comfortable clubhouse lounge is a great place for a dram, a pint, and a bite as you watch other players tee off on one or come in on eighteen.

COURSE COMMENTS: Five time Open Champion Peter Thompson calls Downfield Golf Club, "One of the finest inland courses I have played anywhere in the world." Not too many who play the James Braid designed combination parkland/heathland course would disagree.

Located just two miles off the A90, the main road through the outskirts of Dundee, this golf adventure was used a Final Open Qualifying venue for the Open Championship at Carnoustie in 1999 and again in 2007.

This fine test of shot-making began in the early 1900s as a 9-hole course when Downfield was a village separate from Dundee. The course, like many others in the UK, was lost during the First World War when the land was converted to agricultural use. Rebuilt in 1932 with James Braid as the course architect, Downfield was modernized in 1964 with extra attention to letting as much of Braid's work stand as possible, especially his signature bunkering. More than sixty bunkers are in play, and though some are quite large, none are overly penal. The greens here can be more problematic than the bunkers, with eight multilevel greens which can be quite tricky. Small burns and ponds, including the new pond on the 4th, will affect play on nine of the holes. Many of Downfield's fine holes are doglegs. If you can stay out of the more than one hundred varieties of trees which line the fairways, your game can be a pleasant forest walk. The fall colors at Downfield can be distractingly gorgeous, especially early to mid-October. Don't wait too much later to play because November to March the course uses winter (temporary) greens on most holes.

As you would expect on an Open Qualifying course, there are no weak holes at Downfield GC, and it's a chore to pick favorites. We suggest several considerations, though, to keep in mind when playing here. First, this is a thinking-person's course which will ask you to use all the clubs in your bag. Second, short of the greens can be good--it is better most of the time to run a chip shot up to the pin than to play from behind the greens. Third, when we played in early fall, mats were used for teeing ground on the par 3s. Anne and I didn't find that to be a problem, but some golfers might. We did find six holes to be particularly interesting. We think these will give you a good sense of the quality of the course. On the front, the 3rd is a prime example of the tough par 3s at Downfield. *Lucky Slap*, at 228 yards, needs more than a lucky slap to score well. This long downhill one-shotter has a bunker which collects any shots left of the narrow green. A bank on the right can help kick stray shots towards the putting surface. A three at the 3rd is definitely a good score. *Templeton Trail* is the 497-yard par 5 seventh (plays as a 435-yard par 4 from the visitor's tees) which is a favorite with straight hitters. Trees and bunkers on both sides of the fairway await wayward balls. About 130 yards from the green a burn crosses the fairway which can cause concern for those chipping out of trouble. The green has bunkers on both sides and is sloped enough to create problems if you're above the hole. After coming back to the clubhouse at the 9th green, a feature not often seen in Scotland's older courses, the back nine contains its share of quality holes. The 12th, *Davy Jones' Locker*, is a 182-yard par 3, with a green tucked into a stand of trees and protected by three bunkers. A wide pond-like burn further complicates the first shot. A burn also comes into play on *Witches' Brew*, the 515-yard par 5 fourteenth. The burn flowing down the right side of the fairway demands your drive stay left on this dogleg left. The fairway is narrow and the tiered green is well bunkered. Number sixteen, *Round the Bend*, does just that. Don't be tempted to get greedy with your drive on this sharpest dogleg right which is only 354 yards long. On the second shot short hitters will have two options: first, try a full high shot over the corner trees, or second, lay-up past the corner trees and have a straight chip into the green for your third. If you are long enough, try to stay to the left on the cut grass (a burn comes close to the fairway on the left) and leave yourself an easy chip to the green only protected by one bunker. The finishing hole isn't very long (a par 4 of 384 yards), but can cause even the best players trouble. *Journey's End* is a sharp dogleg right with two bunkers on the inside corner (215 yards to clear both) and a burn which collects short miss hits. The two-tiered green has tricky breaks and is surrounded by three bunkers. Whether you visit in late spring, summer, or early autumn, Downfield GC is a course worth a visit.

COMMENTS FROM THE FORWARD TEES: Downfield is a nice long course for women (5839 yards with a par of 74). There are six par 5s which range from 400 to 444 yards. The longest is the 14th, a tree-lined dogleg left with a burn flowing down the right side. The hardest par 5 for me was the 486-yard 4th which plays over a hill with a pond/burn in front of the green. The par 3s are testing and fair. Downfield is a pleasant walk in the woods where ladies can score well if you plan your shots.

DUNKELD & BiRNAM GOLF COURSE
Fungarth, Dunkeld, Perthshire PH8 0HU
01350-727524   www.dunkeldandbirnamgolfclub.co.uk
Parkland/heathland, 5511 yards, par 69, £25

AMENITIES: The clubhouse, built in 2001, has changing rooms and a comfortable lounge which serves special homemade sweets, as well as food most usual hours. The food is so good that the club has quite a clientele just for meals. No golf shop, but there are a few essentials in the reception office.

COURSE COMMENTS: The first club was formed in 1892 and played on a course built along the River Tay until commandeered by the military in 1914 for practice trench digging. The new hilly course at

Fungarth was opened in 1922 and consisted of the current 1 to 8 and 18. In 2000 the course was extended to 18 with the addition of holes along Loch of Lowes. The present Birnam and Dunkeld plays as two very distinct nines; the hilly front and flat second. Elevation isn't the only difference between the nines. Twenty-three bunkers (none too penal), all on holes 1 to 8, add challenge to the elevation changes. No bunkers were placed on the new holes because of the many environmentally sensitive areas (all OB) in play around the loch. The new holes also have burns seriously in play on four holes, while there is no water trouble on the front. The greens are fairly consistent front and back and have subtle breaks on most holes with a couple of tiered greens on the back. The views at Birnam and Dunkeld of the Highland hills, the beautiful Dunkeld Cathedral in the village, and Loch of Lawes, where Ospreys breed every spring, are marvelous

The play on the course is worthy as well. The 2nd, *Marshes*, is a 281-yard par 4, with a drive from the elevated tee down to the bottom of a hill which rises steeply to the green. The approach is blind to a green with one bunker left and two behind. A great challenge, even at 402 yards from the members' tee (par 4), is the fourth, *Lawes* (the loch), which plays as a 442-yard par 5 from the medal tees. The hole plays uphill with a bunker on the right about 225 yards from the tee. Your second shot must clear a ridge of rocks about 50 yards from the raised green. The 6th, *Gully*, is a wild hole. At 303 yards big hitters may try to go for the green (243 yards from the members' tees), but could easily get stuck in the tall bank in front of the green. A mid-iron is all that is needed to reach the bottom of the hill from the tee. The shot to the green is blind and three traps guard the putting surface. The best views of the cathedral are from the 6th green and the 7th tee. On the back, *Osprey*, the 508-yard par 5 tenth, is a dogleg left to right over a knob to a wide fairway. Your next shot will be challenged by a burn crossing about 85 yards out from the green. A second burn crosses just in front of the tiny green. Another short challenging two-shotter is the 12th. It's a par 4 of only 274 yards which begins with a drive over a burn and lochan (small pond or loch) to a mounded fairway. Another burn crosses in front of the green makes trying to drive the green fraught with risk. The final hole, *Whinney Brae*, is the shortest par 3 on the course at 123 yards. Most of the whins or gorse is now gone from the original 9th hole, but trouble still remains. Tee off down across the road and up to a small green surrounded by three bunkers. The members of Birnam and Dunkeld GC are friendly to visitors and eager to share their treasure. The ladies' club and men's club hold an annual competition against Dunkeld GC in Dunkeld, Victoria, Australia. The trophy is mailed back and forth.

EDZELL GOLF COURSE
High Street, Edzell, Angus DD9 7TF
01356-648462   www.edzellgolfclub.net
Parkland, 6367 yards, par 71, £40

AMENITIES: Nice clubhouse with changing rooms inside. The lounge, recognized for serving the best food in town, has good views of the first tee and the 18th green. A very complete golf shop is at one end of the clubhouse. The facilities include the 9-hole West Water Course opened in 2001.

COURSE COMMENTS: The first Edzell course was near the town's spa and Victorian ladies were afraid of getting hit by stray golf balls as they walked around the spa. The spa stayed in the same place and the club moved. Bob Simpson designed the new course (1895) and then the design was revised in 1933 by James Braid. The course is a wonderful village track at the foot of the Grampian Mountains, but can be busy on the weekends. One of Edzell's unique features is its history of girl caddies. The club had a cadre of young female caddies until they were replaced by caddy cars (trolleys). As would be expected at a Braid course bunkering is a prime feature. More than 100 fairway and greenside bunkers frame your shots at Edzell. Thankfully, most are playable and only a few are steep-sided. While the West Water (a river) flows beside two holes, no water is in play at Edzell. The greens are small to moderate with a fair amount of borrow or break and they putted very true to what we could see. The other condition of play is the heavy forest off the fairways. Edzell is a beautiful tree-lined course, almost like playing in a pine forest on some holes. The course also affords pleasant views of the village and historic Edzell Castle can be seen from two and seventeen. Edzell is a very player friendly course, with at least three water fountains, a toilet after nine, and numerous shelters for inclement weather.

The play at Edzell is equal to its amenities. *The Ridge*, the 310-yard par 4 third, begins with a blind tee shot--aim at the trees that look only to be about 150 yards away, but are really behind the green. Bunkers right and left can't be seen, but if you aim at the top of the path you can avoid them. Two cross bunkers 50 yards short of the green could catch a big drive. The green with four bunkers around it slopes back to front. Another good par four is *The River*, the 354-yard 8th. Bunkers left and right off the tee are reachable on this dogleg right. The best line is out toward the shelter. Trying to cut the corner brings more trees into play and is not worth it (believe me, I know). The approach to the two-tiered green guarded by one trap right is downhill. You end the front side at *The Deep End*. With two good shots it's possible to reach the green on this 478-yard par 5, but you must stay in the fairway. Crossing bunkers are visually intimidating, but should not be a concern. The green has some slopes, but only one bunker left. Good potential for birdie here. Next is the 369-yard par 4 named *Hamewith*. The easy, open tee shot leads to a visually challenging second shot over two huge, deep bunkers crossing most of the fairway about 20 yards short of the green. Three more bunkers around the green add to the difficulty of the approach. The 155-yard par 3 fourteenth got our attention with an uphill tee shot. Take at least one extra club because you must clear two fronting bunkers enough not to roll back on a green which slopes back to front. Three more bunkers guard the sides. If that isn't enough to challenge you, OB is all along the right if you miss hit. *The Deil's Neuk* (the Devil's corner), the 15th, begins with a blind shot where the green is visible 338 yards away, but the landing area isn't. OB left and right and plenty of bunkers help the hole earn its name. The 16th, *Spion Kop* (lookout), is a 316-yard par 4 with a very elevated green protected by two large bunkers and a rough-covered approach. You only need to avoid the fairway bunkers left and right on your drive to leave a fun approach shot with only the top of the flag visible.

Scotland's big courses, the St Andrews and Gleneagles, are marvelous, but the small village tracks like Edzell and Keith (in the northeast) are worthy of play as well. Edzell is a course to which we will definitely return.

COMMENTS FROM THE FORWARD TEES: Edzell is a wonderful visually challenging course. Many of the approach shots are particularly difficult for women, especially on the back side. Many require lay ups and seem as difficult as water hazards. The par 3s are reasonable distances, but bunkers add problems on all. The course is a pleasant walk and the members we met were particularly friendly and accommodating.

FORFAR GOLF COURSE
Cunninghill, Arbroath Road, Forfar DD8 2RL
01307-465683 www.forfargolfclub.com
Seaside/wooded heath, 6066 yards, par 69, £34

AMENITIES: The pleasant clubhouse has a comfortable lounge which looks out over the course. Meals are served usual hours. The separate golf shop is well stocked and staff is helpful. Forfar's Managing

Secretary is Stuart Wilson who brings a strong amateur career to the club being a 2003 Walker Cupper, 2004 British Amateur Champion, and 2004 Low Amateur in the Open.

COURSE COMMENTS: Only 15 miles from Carnoustie Golf Links, Forfar GC can be quite busy, but is very welcoming to visitors. The Old Tom Morris design of 1871 was redesigned by James Braid in 1926. The course continues to modernize to meet the demands of the modern game. The 70 bunkers at Forfar are playable, but can be penal especially around the greens. The only water on the course is a burn in play at the left of 10. The smallish greens are interesting with subtle undulations and swales. A few, like the 13th, are definitely tiered and a couple have steep fronts. One green has a brutal pin position for competitions right at the edge of the front slope. Even though it's fifteen miles to the sea, the ocean influence is felt in the almost constant west or southwest wind. Several of the holes have unique regular undulations, called "rig and farrow," from flax farming in World War One. The fairways, though, are great to play off and have a links turf feel. Trees will also be a condition of play because every hole is tree lined to some extent. With tree-lined fairways, pleasant views of the surrounding farmlands and hills, Forfar is a lovely forest course.

The first hole, *Restenneth* (named for a nearby ruined priory), a 341-yard par 4, is a gentle start to give a feel for what's to come. Drive down slightly between copse of trees to a rolling fairway. Your second shot can be partially blind to a green with bunkers on each side. With only one par five on the course (the 478-yard 14th), it's the strong par 4s that make Forfar a fine track. For example, *Dunnichen*, the 381-yard 3rd, is a dogleg left with bunker and trees at the inside. The "rig and farrows" which give the rolling effects on 1 and 2 are now parallel with the ball's line of flight. Approach the green with fore and side bunkers with care. Next is *Cat Law*. Heavy forests on the sides and a large trap left make for a daunting drive on this 393-yard par 4, especially into the wind. Around the corner of the left dogleg the swaled green has no extra bunkers. If the 4th is into the wind, the 6th will be a downwind shot to a wide fairway with two bunkers on each side. Three more bunkers protect the green where the best approach on this 376-yard hole is from the left. *Gate*, the 359-yard 10th, has the thickest rough on the course left of the narrow fairway. A burn, also on the left, runs about half way down the hole. A false front and large swales make putting a challenge. *Braid's Best*, the 412-yard 15th is a gentle dogleg right with room on the outside and heavy forest on the right. The crux of the hole is the raised green with three fronting bunkers. If you don't make it well onto the green, you are in danger of rolling back into the bunkers. The penultimate hole is *Pitreuchie*, another demanding par 4 (344 yards). The fairway starts wide and narrows down between 150 and 180 yards out with traps on each side. Four more traps and plenty of trees complicate the approach to the narrow green.

We had driven by Forfar GC on our first trip to Scotland in 2000. It wasn't until our ninth trip that we finally played the course. It certainly won't take us that long to play this interesting track again.

COMMENTS FROM THE FORWARD TEES: I'm not usually excited by parkland courses, but was pleasantly surprise with this course. It has a great setting and is visually attractive. Some holes have ridges that send your ball further along and the moorland type grass helps as well. At 5435 yards with a par of 72 this is a long course for ladies. Par 3s range from 128 to 164 yards--very reasonable distances. Par 5s are also reasonable length. A definitely do again course for me.

GLENEAGLES RESORT, Queen's Course

Gleneagles, Auchterarder, Perthshire PH3 1NF [for all courses]
01764-662231 www.gleneagles.com/golf [for all courses]
Heathland/moorland, 5965 yards, par 68, £160

AMENITIES: [for all courses] All the amenities of a world class golf resort with hotel, restaurants, and the Dormy Clubhouse with lounge and restaurant, changing rooms, and well stocked golf shop with all the logoed supplies you'd ever need. The golf shop also hosts a specialty women's shop. The Gleneagles Golf Academy offers excellent practice facilities.

COURSE COMMENTS: As befitting the world's number one (from more than one source) destination golf resort in the world, everything at the Gleneagles Resort is first class and friendly. The three big courses, The Queen's Course, The King's Course, and the Jack Nicklaus designed Centenary (where the Jorhnnie Walker Classic Tournament is held each August and which hosts the 2014 Ryder Cup), are world renowned, and deservedly so. All the courses are championship quality, yet all three are different. The resort has a challenging 9-hole track as well. The Queen's Course, designed by Scottish architect James Braid in 1919 with the King's Course, is the shortest and most player friendly at Gleneagles. The course, though, has plenty of bite. A mix of 93 strategically placed bunkers challenge your sand game and your score. Most of the bunkers are large and deep; to get in one can easily cost a shot. A pond could be in play with missed shots at 13 and 14, and you cross a small loch, Deuk Dubs, off the tee at 18. The greens are mostly large with subtle borrows, but several are quite sloped or tiered. The Queen's is easy to walk and what elevation changes there are enhance the play. The bunkers and heavy rough, including broom and heather, are the real difficulties on the Queen's Course.

Regardless of what you score, the beauty of the course, surrounding countryside and resort grounds (including the other courses) will make your round enjoyable and memorable. All the holes on the course are top quality (no weak holes), but several stood out starting at the first, *Trystin' Tree* (Lover's Meeting Place). When we played we were guided around by head teaching pro John Murray (now head pro at Moray Old) who had the starter clear the first tee for us. While all the waiting golfers watch, Anne and I had to follow the tee shot of John. Thankfully we both hit the fairway. As we headed down the fairway, we could hear muttering about "so who were those two?" The tough 409-yard par 4 opener starts off over a large drop and back up to a fairway with a bunker on the left. Stay to the right on this dogleg left with a small green tucked around trees and guarded by a fronting bunker on the right. It's the flattest green on the course, and one of only two with no protecting bunkers. The 4th, *Warlock Knowe* (The Hill of the Male Witch), is a 355-yard dogleg left with a bunker on the outside of the bend. The approach is over a humped fairway with the green guarded by two bunkers left and one right. Be sure to take enough club into the green. *Drum Sichty* (Sight of the Hills, offers good views west) begins with a long carry over light rough to a fairway that opens up past the two traps on the right (225 yards). On this 437-yard par 4, three more bunkers are set to catch wayward approach shots. The plateau green is quite large with very entertaining subtle slopes. Next is *Westlin' Wyne* (the hole farthest from the start) is a 491-yard par 5. The sloped fairway doglegs left about 200 yards from the green. Four bunkers call for you to place your second shot well. The putting surface is protected by three bunkers, drop-off behind, and is sloped toward the back and left. It's a challenging hole where double or worse is just as likely as birdie. On the back nine we found some of the most interesting holes on the Queen's. The 10th, *Pint Stoup* (Scottish for a jug holding one pint, the hole before the halfway house), is a 421-yard par 4 which has a dramatic bend left just before the green. On the drive three bunkers across the fairway are intimidating, but won't cause concern to a good drive. You need to be on the right to hope for a look at the putting surface tucked well left behind trees. The green is long and narrow, but on the flat side. Between the 10th and the 11th is the Halfway House, which has snacks, burgers, drinks, and toilets. At the Halfway House you can make a short stop or choose to get out of the rotation for a longer stop. A phone on the 10th tee allows you to order food to be ready at the snack shop.

After a relief stop you head to *Muir Tap* (top of the muir or woods), the short 318-yard 11th. Aim over the right of the two bunkers on the left dogleg. Big hitters who stay too far right can run out of fairway and leave an approach out of the rough. The swaled green is protected by four traps towards the front and a hidden one behind. The last two holes on the Queen's Course provide a spectacular finish. The 17th, *Hinny Mune* (probably a reference to the crescent moon shape of the green), is a wonderfully demanding 204-yard one-shotter. A visually terrifying hole with a deep drop-off right, three dangerously deep bunkers left, this long narrow green is a tough target. A pin placed in the back can add another 20 yards to the shot. Then comes the 18th, *Queen's Hame*, a 412-yard par 4, which starts with a grand vista out to the clubhouse left and the King's Course right. The tee shot is from an elevated box down and across the loch and heavy rough to a generous diagonal fairway. The approach is to a large, relatively flat green fronted by bunkers right and left. The clubhouse balcony is left of the green and everyone there can watch you take two to get out of the deep bunker (at least that's what they saw when I played). The Queen's Course is fun, but it is definitely not a lightweight track. To find a similar design that will provide even more challenge, check out the King's Course.

COMMENTS FROM THE FORWARD TEES: This wonderful course is well set up for ladies. It's 5495 yards long with a par of 74, but it isn't easy. On the front, the par 3s are short and not too difficult, but the back side 3s present many challenges, such as water, bunkers, and severe rough. They are still fun, and it's extremely rewarding to score well. The par 5s on both sides are long and difficult. The toughest par 5 for me was the 4th at 469 yards. The most difficult part was the approach to the green which appears to hang at the back edge of a hill. It would be easy to turn the approach shot into two or three by not trusting the distance. The second nine on the Queen's is shorter, but trickier and requires more accuracy. The course starts out challenging and doesn't let up, but it's fun all the way around.

GLENEAGLES RESORT, King's Course
Moorland, 6471 yards, par 70, £160

COURSE COMMENTS: Built at the same time as the Queen's and also designed by James Braid, the King's Course at Gleneagles plays over similar, but more dramatic ground. The 110 bunkers on the King's will be a major concern to all level of players. Both larger and smaller than the bunkers on the Queen's, the sand here is a serious hazard. We watched one quite decent player in the group in front of us take four shots on the par three 11th to get from one greenside bunker into another. Thankfully, he got out of the second bunker in one. Unlike the Queen's, there is no water trouble on the King's. The greens range from moderate to large and most have tricky slopes, though only two are two-tiered. The trouble on the King's is the sand, of course, elevation changes, and the heavy moorland rough, gorse, and broom off the fairways. This is definitely a case where it pays to be long since most of the trouble is short of the green. Set between the Ochill Hills and the Grampian Mountains in central Scotland, the King's is a stunning tribute to the design skills of Braid, and each of the 18 holes will be stern test.

The first, *Dun Whinny* (meaning the gorse covered hill) is a departure from Braid's usual gentle beginning. Braid's designs often start soft and toughen as you get into the round. Gentle is not a descriptor when you consider the rising 362-yard hole has five fairway bunkers and the elevated green is protected by four more. An even sterner test is the 374-yard par 4 third, *Silver Tassie* (referring to the cup-shaped hollow in which the green is found and the nearby silver birch trees). Tee off down to a narrow fairway with a rough-covered hill on the left and rough on the right. The approach is over a steep rough-covered hill (steep enough that a stable stance is almost impossible) about 50 yards from the quite difficult to putt two-tiered green with one bunker on the left. A shot just over the top will run down toward the front pin placement, while two or three more clubs are needed if the pin is in the back (check the pin placement layout which comes with your scorecard). A drive in the fairway and selecting the correct club to the green are the keys to the hole. *Het Girdle* (hot griddle), the 5th, is a challenging one-shotter of 161 yards. Alignment is important as some of the tees don't line you up well. Be precise with club selection to this plateau green fronted by four traps. Long will be better than short. The 7th, *Kittle Kink* (tricky bend), is a long dogleg par 4 which earns its name. Tee off to an angled (left) fairway which runs down a narrow valley. You must clear a ridge to see the green on your second shot, but crossing the ridge further left means a longer initial carry. Two bunkers short of the valley fairway can cause trouble on missed shots, but the biggest trouble is the five more bunkers faced on the approach. Take plenty of club because all the trouble is short of the deceptively long green. The Halfway House after the 10th, the same one servicing the Queen's, offers a welcome respite. When the course is busy, rangers will be there to help keep the groups moving smoothly. *Deil's Creel* (the devil's fishing basket) is the

230-yard par 3 eleventh. Of the six bunkers around the green, the front two tend to gather shots that look like they would run onto the green. Take enough club to be well up to the green. Twelve, *Tappit Hen* (an old Scots' pewter ale or wine measure), should be an easy hole, but a poor first shot can create a disaster. Drive blind over a tall ridge laced with bunkers. A high shot of only 190 yards is needed to clear the ridge, but anything short hangs up on the slope. A good drive should stay left of center for the best line into a well guarded green. Again all the trouble is short of the green with tough slopes. When we played in 2002 with our B&B hosts John and Jacky Clifford, we stood on the tee of the 15th and introduced John to GORP (Good Old Raisins and Peanuts; actually raisins, peanuts, and chocolate M&Ms). Since that first time, we've had to bring GORP to John for our golfing outings. The 17th, *Warslin' Lea* (Troublesome Valley) is a 377-yard narrow challenge. Think about taking an iron off the tee on the narrowest fairway on the King's Course and try to stay left. Your approach needs to negotiate four traps to the green which is very sloped at the front. *King's Hame* is good finish to your round. On this par 5 of 525 yards, if you can carry the ridge (about 275 yards) you'll get roll and have a chance to reach the green in two. For those of us moderate hitters, it's a true three-shotter. The course guide says, "No prize for being short" on your approach because all the trouble is there. Take enough club into the largest green cut in half by a formidable ridge. The front of the green has severe slopes, while the back is more subtle. The hole ends below the window of the Dormy Clubhouse pub. The King's Course is definitely more demanding than the Queen's [Should there be some sexist comment about that?], but with good course management it's playable by almost everyone.

COMMENTS FROM THE FORWARD TEES: This is a beautiful, difficult golf course where course management is vital. The red tees are only 5220 yards with a par of 71, but the course is a tough track. The challenges begin on the first hole where the second shot has to be planned so that you can reach the green on your third shot over the deep bunkers that surround the elevated green. Most holes have strategically placed bunkers which need to be avoided. I especially enjoyed the 6th. The setting is lovely with a great view of the Strathearn Valley from the tee. I was glad to find the halfway house for refreshments and a toilet after the 10th--a convenience not often found in Scotland. The second time I played was easier than the first, but anytime I can play the Kings it will be great.

MONIFIETH GOLF LINKS, Medal Course
Medal Starter's Box, Princess Street, Monifieth, Angus   DD5 4AW

01382-532767 www.monifiethgolf.co.uk
Links, 6655 yard, par 71, £55

AMENITIES: Three clubs have clubhouses at the links; the Monifieth Club, the Grange Club, and the Broughty Club. The golf manager suggests that the Broughty Club lounge is the best. The private golf shop, located between the Medal Starter and the Aushludie Course along the row of clubhouses, has all your needs. The Ashludie Course, a second full course at the facility, is easier to get on than the Medal Course.

COURSE COMMENTS: A 9-hole course on the Monifieth Links, designed by St Andrews' professionals Allan Robertson and Alexander Pirie, was built in 1845 and was the course for the Panmure Club, the Monifieth Club, and others. In 1898 the Panmure club moved to its Barry location because of crowding at Monifieth. The Monifieth Club became the custodian of the links, which had been extended to 18-holes in 1880. A second course was initially laid out as a 9-hole track in 1912 and extended to 18 in 1930. Several alterations have been made to the Medal Course, the last in 1968. *Golf World*, in a 1991 article, described the Medal Course as "the most scenic links on the east coast of Scotland." Although I may not completely agree with *Golf World's* comment, the Medal Course is a championship track, an Open Qualifying course, and fun to play.

As a championship course, Monifieth Medal has plenty of challenge. Seventy-five bunkers, a good mix of greenside and fairway, most penal, and some very deep, will give players concern. The 5th with six and the 17th with nine have the most bunker troubles. A pond is in play on the 10th and a burn on two holes, but is only a major threat on the 7th. It's the same burn that's in play at Panmure GC next door. The greens are mostly large with several being long and narrow. Some greens are flat and few have significant slopes, but all are speedy and a challenge to putt. Twice we saw tanks on the military road to the west of the course. Though, we never saw them point their guns at us for bad shots.

We picked out several holes which demonstrate the kind of play you'll find at Monifieth Medal. The 4th, *Featherbed*, is a long, demanding 456-yard par 4 with fairway mounding, trees on each side, and OB (the army base) right. As you approach the green, high mounds are on the left from about 75 yards out and then practically surround the large amoeba-shaped green. On *Lucky Daddy*, the 382-yard par 4 sixth, you tee off over the burn (which continues over to Panmure GC) which is in play on the left for as far as 215 yards from the tee. The rolling fairway is a little downhill to a moderate green with one bunker left. OB is all along the right. The par 5 ninth, *Long Hole* (547 yards) begins with a drive to a narrow fairway which runs into rough-covered mounds about 300 yards out. The second shot is over mounds to a rumpled fairway with a little slope toward the green protected by two traps. On the back we liked the par 3 eleventh, a narrow 183-yard one-shotter where gorse, mounds, and one of four bunkers cuts off the view of the putting surface. The 13th is named *Pyramids* and is a 432-yard par 4. You tee from one of two boxes separated by trees and gorse to a narrow fairway which is quite mounded. More mounds and several bunkers will encroach on your approach to the sloped green. The last Monifieth Medal hole we note is the 376-yard 15th. It's an uphill tee shot to a wide fairway with mounds on both sides. Your second shot will go slightly down to a green with three fronting bunkers. Monifieth Medal, along with Panmure GC, means that there is more great golf in this area than just Carnoustie.

COMMENTS FROM THE FORWARD TEES: This is a links course with enough trees that you'd think you're on a parkland course until your ball takes that typical links bounce. The course is long for women at 5883 yards with a par of 73. Problems include trees and gorse. The par 5s are good, but I believe the 14th is one of the toughest par 3s I've ever played. You must carry all the way to green 139 yards away over gorse and mounds. If you're not one hundred percent accurate you will roll off into one of three bunkers. It's a good hole to walk up and look at before you hit. Monifeith is definitely a course where you'd benefit from playing more than once.

MONTROSE LINKS TRUST, Medal Course
Trail Drive, Montrose, Angus DD10 8SW
01674-672932   www.montroselinks.co.uk
Links, 6544 yards, par 71, £40

AMENITIES: Numerous clubs have come and gone at Montrose, but three remain vital today: the Royal Montrose Golf Club, the Mercantile Golf Club, and the Caledonian Golf Club. The clubhouses for all three are near the very complete golf shop and are welcoming to visitors. A very well-stocked golf shop serves both the Medal and Broomfield courses.

COURSE COMMENTS: Twenty-three miles south of Stonehaven and north of Dundee on the coast road (A92) is the harbour town of Montrose, with two 18-hole golf courses and three venerable golf clubs. The Montrose Links Trust Medal Course is the premier facility, while the Broomfield course is also worthy of a round. Golf has been played on the Montrose linksland for at least four hundred years, and can reliably be traced back to 1562, when local James Melville recorded in his diary being taught "how to use the *glubb* for *goff*." By 1810, an official club existed, The Royal Albert Club, which ranks in the top ten oldest clubs in the world. The course itself can lay claim to having at one time the greatest number of holes. In 1866, Montrose had 25 holes. The course played today as the Medal Course has holes which have been played for the past 350 years. It may not be as ancient as the Old Course at St Andrews, but it comes close. Much of the present Medal Course was designed by Willie Park Jnr in 1903 with advice from Old Tom Morris-- history and credentials! As a recognized great course, the Montrose Medal Course is predictably busy. It's not impossible, though, to get a game as a drop-in, even on a gorgeous, sunny Sunday afternoon in early September as Anne and I did. We only had to wait forty minutes, which we spent in the golf shop.

The Medal Course is a majestic links layout with twelve holes playing along the North Sea and where the sea is in view on most holes (holes 10 to 15 play away from the beach). Strong links bunkering typifies the course, with many deep and penal bunkers. Though no water hazards are on the course, the winds can be brutal and the large greens can be lightning quick with difficult borrows. The rough (grasses and gorse or whins) can be unforgiving.

"Absolutely terrific," was one golfers comment about the Medal Course after playing it and Carnoustie (a few miles south). Holes number one (*Scurdy*, 391-yard par 4) and number two (*Bents*, another 391-yard par 4) make a demanding start to a round at Montrose. The 1st doesn't always play as long as it says on the card because the prevailing wind will be behind. The wind can also bring a fairway bunker and whins into play. The semi-blind (you can only see the top of the flag) second shot is to a green with a bunker left and a gully right. "Nothing but bumps and hollows" is how some have described the moguled second fairway, which leads to typical links bounces. The only sand on the hole is the beach on the right which is in play. The green has some tricky breaks and the big gully behind the green makes an up-and-down from back there unlikely. A fantastic hole is *Jubilee*, the 444-yard par 4 ninth. The shot from the elevated tee must clear a large patch of rough and stay out of the gorse left and away from the OB right. To make it more of a challenge, you usually are driving into the wind. From the fairway, the long second shot is to a green both shallow and wide. The saving grace is that the green is flat. Twice Masters Champion, golf architect and historian, Ben Crenshaw says that the 16th, *Gully*, is one of the best one-shotters anywhere. Not many golfers will use an iron at the 235-yard hole with its green protected by gorse and an evil pot bunker. The large undulating green is a three-putt waiting to happen. Par is quite an accomplishment here. The penultimate challenge on Montrose Medal is a 418-yard par 4 called *Rashies*. It's important to find the narrow, undulating fairway with gorse on the left and OB right. It's a testing drive. Deep bunkers and gorse guard the large, angled green. Beware of the road and OB behind the green.

COMMENTS FROM THE FORWARD TEES: This is a long difficult course which is fun to play. Yardage for ladies is 5622 with a par of 73. Two of the par 3s, the 3rd and the 12th are reasonable length and have their own challenges, but the 16th is much longer at 192 yards and has plenty of trouble including a gully, gorse, and a pot bunker. Par is a very good score. The four par 5s are all over 400 yards and 15 is the number one handicap hole for ladies at 492 yards. Other challenges on this hole besides the length include a large ridge and bunker on your third shot and the slopes beyond the ridge that pushes balls into greenside bunkers. Three of the par 5s are on the back and make an interesting finish to the round.

PANMURE GOLF COURSE
Barry, by Carnoustie, Angus DD7 7RT
01241-855120   www.panmuregolfclub.uk.co
Links, 6340 yards, par 70, £75

AMENITIES: Beautiful venerable clubhouse, which opened in 1899, has modernized changing rooms. The lounge, which looks out toward the 1st and the 18th is where you can feel the history of the course. Very complete golf shop with friendly staff.

COURSE COMMENTS: The Panmure course opened in 1899, and the course members play today is the 1937 design work of James Braid. During WWI much of the course was lost because of a lack of work force. Competitions were suspended, but they couldn't graze sheep on the course because there was not enough grass on the tight linksland for a flock. They tried the sheep again in WW2 with the same negative results. The army was more successful billeting 100 soldiers in the clubhouse in 1940.

The course which plays through low dunes is a strong qualifying course for the Open Championship when its played at Carnoustie (as in 2007). Panmure GC has all the earmarks of a great links venue--fast mounded (drumlins) fairways, undulating greens, gorse, wind, the 90 bunkers in play. All the bunkers are real hazards with most quite penal. The greens, moderate for the most part, will seem large when you barely get on. Even the flat greens have subtle breaks, but all roll very true. Burns are in play on three holes, but are definitely a concern at 12 and 13. Out of

Bounds is a feature on twelve holes, and slicers beware because the OB is on the right at eleven of the holes! For all the challenge of the course it's a beautiful track with views of neighboring farmland, Monifieth course next door, and at least one view of the North Sea. It's very picturesque with several copse of trees planted as wind breaks. One other feature of the course is that between it and the sea is an active military base. We could hear rifle fire as we played, but really knew the base was nearby when a tank went rumbling down the road next to the commuter train tracks on the seaward side of the course. It really speeds up play when a tank runs by and turns its gun turret toward golfers!

Panmure is a true championship track, but is playable by all level of golfer if you choose the correct tee. Though I'll describe the course from the medal tees, I had a successful round (almost hit my handicap) when I played from the members' tees. The 3rd, a 405-yard par 4, is a straight hole with sets of ridges across the fairway. The drive will be challenged by three bunkers, two right and one left. The large green with runoff front and back is protected by three more traps. Between holes 3 and 4 is a pleasant "wee walk in the woods." A slight dogleg left with a drive over an expanse of rough to a very mounded fairway is the 387-yard 6th. The bunker 251 yards off the tee is a good aiming point if you stay a little left of it. The fairway narrows towards the swaled green with a large false front. Be careful of the tiny pot bunker on the right front of the green. There's plenty of reason this hole is listed as the hardest on the course. The 8th, a 360-yard par 4, is a dogleg left from the tee to a generous, but sloped fairway. Your second shot needs to be between (or over) some large mounds (drumlins) which hide the smallish green that tilts away to the right. Panmure's par 3s are all interesting, but the 171-yard 11th really attracted our attention. From the tee the hole looks like it's all bunkers. Five of them protect the green with the biggest covering the width of the putting surface about 15 yards in front. Next is the 363-yard par 4 twelfth. This wildest hole on the course begins with a drive (over a small burn, not really a concern) to a generous fairway with ridges and a meandering burn about 280 yards out from the tee. The second shot must contend with the burn, a raised green, a pot bunker, and a putting surface with interesting contours. Quite a challenge! On the next hole, a 398-yarder, you cross the burn off the tee and then again about 100 yards from the green. The rumpling of the fairway gets more dramatic as you approach the green. It's the only hole with no bunkers at Panmure. A fine par 5 is the 535-yard 14th. This long hole doglegs left just before the green. Four bunkers right and left down the fairway and heavy trees on the left add to the difficulty. The green, set beautifully in a copse of trees, has one more trap guarding the left. The Monifieth course next door is also an interesting track, but if you only have time for one, it needs to be Panmure GC.

COMMENTS FROM THE FORWARD TEES: This is a wonderful course for ladies, beautiful and fun to play. The course is visually appealing with greens tucked into stands of trees and even a view of the North Sea (or the firth) on 11. Women's tees have some advantages, but the character of the hole isn't lost--you must still hit a good shot or you will find the trouble. The par 3s are not long except for 15 which is 216 yards. There are plenty of bunkers and mounds to make even the shorter par 3s challenging. Panmure is one of the most enjoyable links courses I've played.

PIPERDAM RESORT, Osprey Course
Fowlis, Dundee DD2 5LP
01382-581374 www.piperdam.com
Hillside parkland, 6013 yards, par 72, £40

AMENITIES: Room with a View Restaurant and Howie's Bar in the Leisure Centre both serve from the same ala cart menu. Small, but well outfitted pro shop is run by professional Owen Leslie. The 9-hole Wee Piper par 3 course is quite popular.

COURSE COMMENTS: The Osprey 18-hole track was designed by owners and members in 1998 around the spectacular views the land affords. Several of the holes, while beautiful with grand views, are not great golf holes. When talking to pro, Owen Leslie, after our round he said that the management recognize the problems on the course and are implementing a plan to completely rebuild three holes and significantly alter five more starting over the 2013 winter. The plans we saw should make a great difference in the playability of the course. Our description will be of the course we played in the fall of 2013. The course currently has 42 fairway and greenside bunkers in play, and while none are very penal they are strategically placed. The bunkers may not be penal, but the water on the course definitely is. Ponds or the large loch (a 40 acre fishing loch) are in play on nine holes, burn crossings are on three others. Many of the greens you play are sloped and often front to back. We thought the greens on the front were more open to approach shots. The course climbs steeply at times and taking a buggy wouldn't be a bad choice. While playable by all levels of golfers, the course is really a big hitter's course. Regardless of how you play, the Osprey Course (we did see one osprey on our round) is a lovely, well-kept track. The views of the surrounding village and farmland are always nice, and from the tee at the 5th you can see Dundee and the bridge to Fife.

The golf challenges begin with the 1st, a par 3 of 133 yards. It's a difficult starting hole with your first shot of the round all carry over the loch. Be long--short on the back-to-front sloping green can still spin back off the green into the loch. Next is a par 5 of 471 yards. You drive uphill to a sharp dogleg right. Get the drive correct and the second shot to a green with one bunker left is much easier. The 11th is another all carry over water with some bailout to the right. Bunkers fronting the green on this 174-yard hole make the shot even more daunting. A good short par 4 on the back is the 13th, a 315-yarder which doglegs left around two bunkers. The second shot is down to a burn which crosses the fairway and back up to a raised green protected by bunkers left and right. It's a fun hole. With the planned improvements to the course and the great views, Piperdam's Osprey Course can become a gem in this golf-rich area.

FROM THE FORWARD TEES: There are some great views from the course, but because of some long walks between holes it's a good course for taking a buggy. The ladies' tees are well placed to be challenging yet playable. Water is the main concern with it in play on nine holes. The backside seemed easier with fewer side slopes and the toilet after the tee on the 12th can be a welcome relief.

STRATHMORE GOLF CENTRE, Rannaleroch Course
Leroch, Alyth, Perthshire PH11 8NZ
01828-633322 www.stathmoregolf.com
Parkland/moorland, 6454 yards, par 72, £32

AMENITIES: Clubhouse has changing rooms, a pleasant lounge (serves excellent food usual hours), and a small golf shop with all the essentials. A 9-hole course, Leitfie Links (1666 yards, par 29), is also at the facility.

COURSE COMMENTS: In the golf rich area near Blairgowrie, with two Blairgowrie courses, Alyth, and Glenisla, all within a few miles of Strathmore Golf Centre, the 1995 Rannaleroch Course with its smaller cousin is a positive addition. The big course is pleasant; not too difficult, but fun. The well groomed moorland turf on the fairways is easy to play from, and elevation changes keep the holes interesting without being difficult to walk. Fairways are generous, but trouble is there if you stray too far off line. A mix of 32 greenside and fairway bunkers are strategically placed forcing you to think your way around. The greens are large, quick, and have interesting contours. Water is in play on several holes, but will only be a concern on holes 5 and 6. The medal tees, used for competitions, are significantly more challenging than the normal member tees.

A good dogleg left 514-yard par 5 named *Tullyfergus* starts your round. Try not to be long to the green which drops off behind. Next of interest is *Lochans* the 468-yard par 5 fifth, which plays as a 400-yard par 4 from the member's tees. First shot on this narrow hole is over a small pond (only a visual hazard). The hole is a dogleg right with trees right and bunkers left. The large green has one trap front right. The 6th, *Dunsinane*, a short par 3, has an interesting green. It's like two separate greens with a valley between, and when we played the flag was in the valley. Twelve is a long, 547-yard, par 5 called *Tipperary* (you know, "it's a long way to Tipperary") which doglegs right with OB on both sides almost the length of the hole. Two bunkers on the inside of the dogleg can catch drives. Mounding and slopes add difficulty to your approach and putting. In my view the best hole on the course is *Pictillum*, the 469-yard par 4 fourteenth. This classic golf hole is a dogleg left with ditch and OB tee to green on the left. Your tee shot is blind, aim to the right of the marker pole, and the green is tucked tight on the left and protected by two fore bunkers right about 70 yards out and two more bunkers (left and behind) at the green. It's a pure challenge. A fun drive begins the 337-yard par 4 fifteenth called *Bunkerhill*. Aim at the wishing well in the distance and let fly on this sharp dogleg left. The raised green has only some mounding for protection. Definitely a birdie opportunity. The longest par 3 is *Kinpurnie*, the 224-yard 17th. It's a dramatic downhill shot to a large green with a trap on the right and OB left. The trees behind frame the hole beautifully. Strathmore's Rannaleroch Course shouldn't be taken lightly, but neither is it the challenge of the Blairgowrie courses or of Alyth.

COMMENTS FROM THE FORWARD TEES: Strathmore GC is a fun course. Though the women's distance is about the same as the men's, the two strokes more I got on par was helpful. Three of the four par 3s are short enough for success, but the 17th is very long even though it's downhill. The par fives tend to be long, but are open enough to allow you to cut some corners. This is a course to go back to for a stress free round in the area.

Courses in this region listed in *Golf in Scotland: The Hidden Gems*: Auchterarder, Blair Atholl, Brechin, Carnoustie Burnside, Comrie, Crieff Ferntower and Dornock, Dalmunzie (Spittal of Glenshee), Glenisla (Alyth), Killin, King James VI (Perth), Kirriemuir, Mains of Taymouth (Kenmore), Muckhart, Murrayshall Championship and Lynedoch (Scone),

Muthill, Pitlochry, St Fillans, Strathmore Leitfie (Alyth), Strathtay (Pitlochry).

KINROSS AND FIFE

ABERDOUR GOLF COURSE
Seaside Place, Aberdour, Fife KY3 0TX
01383-860256   www.aberdourgolf.co.uk
Seaside parkland, 5460 yards, par 67, £32

AMENITIES: Wonderful views from the upstairs lounge. From one end you watch the whole first hole, and the other end affords vistas out to the firth. Lounge serves good food usual hours, but only to players and members (not open to the public). A nicely stocked golf shop is below the clubhouse lounge.

COURSE COMMENTS: Especially on a good day, Aberdour GC offers some of the most fascinating views of any course we've played. As you play you can see the firth, Edinburgh across the firth, and Inchcolm Abbey on an island in the Firth of Forth. This wasn't the first location for the course which began as a 9-hole track. The club moved to the current beautiful spot in 1905 and expanded the course to 18 holes in 1914. A local member told us that in the first Open competition for the full course a shot struck a sheep and stuck in its wool. The sheep ran closer to the green and the ball dropped out a few feet from the hole. It was ruled that since the ball was still in motion, the ball was deemed to be in play where it came to rest. No penalty. [We've heard similar stories several times from other clubs. Either balls stuck in sheep's wool fairly often in golf's early days, or this is an example of a Scottish golfer's urban myth.] The course may be short, but don't confuse that with easy; Aberdour is a quite challenging track. The 35, mostly greenside bunkers, are not too penal, but a few can cost shots. Two burn crossings present slight problems, but the firth crossing on the 2nd is a major concern. The wildly sloped greens range from small to large and are fast to putt. Playing along the firth as the course does, the wind will usually affect play. Throw in a some elevation changes (nothing too difficult to walk), a few tilted fairways, a couple of crossover holes, and some blind shots, and you know why the course doesn't need length to test your game.

The tests begin with the two beginning par 3s. It may be an unusual start to have back-to-back one-shotters, but as lovely as they are, you'll be glad to be past them. The first is called *Bellhouse*, a 159-yarder. From directly in front of the clubhouse, drive down to a moderate sized green guarded by two bunkers and backed by interesting rock formations and the firth. It's tough to pick the correct club straight out of the car. Next comes Aberdour's signature hole, the 159-yard 2nd called *Firs*. A dramatic hole is followed by an even more dramatic hole! Shoot across the firth to an elevated green fronted by a road and backed by a hillside of trees. Your drive must carry to the green or you'll be left with an almost impossible up and down (that is if your ball doesn't go swimming). The rest of the holes may not be as spectacular, but they are fun. The 6th, *St Colme*, a 365-yard par 4, is a classic golf hole. It's a slight dogleg left with trees on the inside and a rough covered hillside on the right. The green is tucked right and is severely sloped back to front. Stay below the hole on this green. The hardest hole on the course (stroke index #1) is the 458-yard par 4 eighth. With a stone fence and OB all along the left, stay to the right while avoiding the two fairway bunkers. A burn crosses the fairway, but should not be too much problem on your second shot. The green has no bunkers, but it's hard enough to get there that they're not needed. Thirteen and 14 are two drivable par 4s. At 251 yards the 13th is uphill and the 318-yard 14th is down. Both greens are guarded by several traps. These two are followed by a fun one-shotter. The 15th, *Woodside*, is 171 yards downhill with bunkers all around, but the green is one of the easiest to putt. A blind uphill tee shot begins the 354-yard 17th. The second shot is downhill to a putting surface tucked left. Your best approach is from the center of the fairway or slightly to the right. The very picturesque green is guarded by three traps and backed by a stone fence and forest. Some pleasant forest or seaside walks between holes, gorgeous views, and quality golf challenges make Aberdour GC a course to put on your "must play" list.

COMMENTS FROM THE FORWARD TEES: This parkland course has a lovely setting by the sea (the Firth of Forth). It's hilly, especially on the front, with long walks between 4 and 5 and 9 and 10. The course is not long at 4892 yards with a par of 68, but it's set up fairly for women. Of the six par 3s, only the 18th is over 160 yards long. There are only two par 5s, but the 17th plays like a par 5 most days because it's uphill and into the prevailing wind. Aberdour GC is delightful with spectacular views, especially if you get a sunny day.

CANMORE GOLF COURSE
Venturefair Avenue, Dunfermline, Fife KY12 0PE
01383-724969   www.canmoregolf.co.uk
Parkland, 5376, par 67, £22

AMENITIES: The original farmhouse still serves as part of the clubhouse with extensions to the lounge in the 1970s and again in the 1980s. Grand views down the 18th. Good food served all day. Club also has a small, but complete golf shop.

COURSE COMMENTS: Canmore GC is a gentle course with several interesting holes. The course may not be a championship track, but then I'm not a championship player. One of the joys of golf in Scotland is that even the village courses are worth playing, and Canmore is no exception. The original 9-hole course was built in 1897. In 1914 the course was expanded to 18 holes by famed designer Ben Sayers. Canmore was redesigned in 1946 after much of the course had gone for agricultural use during the war years. Ten years ago the club undertook a project of planting over 1000 trees of more than 100 different varieties. At Canmore there is plenty of tree trouble if you stray off the fairways. Besides the forests, 45 bunkers will test your sand play; thankfully most of the bunkers are flat. Number ten is the only hole on the course with no sand trouble, but as I'll point out in more detail later, none are needed. A burn crossing on nine is the only water trouble, but on most days the wind will affect play. The small to moderate sized greens look flat, but have plenty of tricky slopes when you putt. Several of the greens are platforms with significant run-offs on the sides and back. Besides the lovely trees, Canmore provides views of the village and the Pentland Hills past Edinburgh.

Though Canmore is relatively short, the holes kept our interest. A good par 3 is *The Road*, the 155-yard 4th, where you drive over the road to a green with a trap in front and another to the left. The green is elevated and runs off on the right. The 6th is a drive slightly up a fairway lined with beautiful mature trees. The approach on this 351-yard par 4 is up to a green protected by two bunkers and tucked right. We think *The Loch*, the 375-yard 9th, is a very interesting hole. Drive over a hill and down towards a burn crossing about 235 yards from the tee. A steep levee on the left holds back a loch used by the Scottish National Water Ski Team. The green is a small target tucked at the back of the hole and guarded by one bunker right. We go from one interesting hole to another as we move to the 10th, a 375-yard par 4 called *The Burn*. It's difficult to know how to play this hole, especially the first time around. A slight dogleg left with OB (and the burn) all along the left and a high hill on the right. The narrow valley of fairway is easy to find as long as you don't go left because most shots right will bounce back down to the fairway. The green is tucked neatly into the end of the hill and fairway. The third of the intriguing turn holes is *Quarry*, a 374-yard par 4. The last two were interesting; this one is unique. You drive toward the marker post on the ledge at the edge of the fairway. A drive of 225 to 250 yards in the middle would be perfect. Walk up to the post and take a look at the rest of the hole which drops sharply down to a narrow bit of putting surfaces with sand right and left. It's a hole you'll want to play again no matter what you scored. The last hole is *Up the Hill*, a 323-yarder. Drive steeply uphill (hence the name) past or over the traps on each side of the fairway. Your approach continues up to a small green with two fronting bunkers. Smile when you're on the green because everyone in the lounge will be watching you finish.

Canmore GC is a busy course with a full membership, but is very accommodating to visitors. Not high powered, but definitely interesting and entertaining, it's a course to include in your plans.

COMMENTS FROM THE FORWARD TEES: Canmore is a parkland course full of surprises. It's a short course at 4836 yards, but has plenty of trouble with trees, water, hills, and bunkers. More than anything else I like that there are several unique holes, like the 10th which is very narrow and the 11th which has a green completely hidden by a high drop-off. The 13th is difficult because the green sits up at the edge of a hill which requires a precise shot to land the ball on the green 183 yards away. Canmore is a woman friendly course with enough challenge to hold your interest.

CRAIL GOLFING SOCIETY, CRAIGHEAD LINKS
Crail, Fife KY10 3XN
01333-450960 www.crailgolfingsociety.co.uk
Links-like cliff top, 6185 yards, par 72, £60

AMENITIES: Venerable clubhouse almost completely rebuilt and refurnished in 2009 has two bars and three eating areas with grand views of sea and the last four holes on Balcomie and at least one on Craighead. Clubhouse serves excellent fare. Pro shop, run by professional Graeme Lennie and a very knowledgable staff, is one of the best in the area.

COURSE COMMENTS: The design work of American Gil Hanse (TPC Boston), the course was built in 1998 as a relief course for the Balcomie Links. The course has been continually upgraded and today is a challenging tournament-worthy course. With panoramic views on almost every hole, Craighead features "Danes Dyke," a 1200 year old Viking built defensive wall in play on four holes. Besides the dyke, the main feature of the course is the more than 80 strategically placed bunkers (fairway and greenside) in play--many quite penal. Although there are no water hazards on the course, the sea is OB on a couple of holes. Greens are moderate to large and relatively flat with mild undulations, though a few have some real slope. Further difficulties comes from the wind and the heavy, sticky rough off the generous fairways. Though the course will test the game of the best golfers, it's an easy walk and playable by all levels. The views of Isle of May, Bass Rock, North Berwick Law, and the Lothian coast will keep all engaged.

The fine holes at Craighead will be engaging as well as demanding. After our latest round we picked several holes to highlight. The 2nd, *Windmill Corner,* is a par 4 of 364 yards which dramatically doglegs right around two large bunkers and gorse. Stay left of the corner bunkers unless you can carry more than 270 yards. The large green is protected by four more bunkers. The 6th, called *Barracuda Way*, is a straight, long par 5 (515 yards) with bunkers right about 260 from the tee and a stone fence encroaching from the left at the same point. The slightly raised green is narrow and has a nest of three bunkers left. The OB all along the right shouldn't be a major concern, but needs to be noticed. A twisting fairway snaking around two bunkers and gorse on the left characterizes the 9th, *Craighead*, a 347-yard par 4. The green is a small target well-bunkered. On the 10th, *Fife Ness*, a 300-yard par 4, it's all about the bunkers--nine on this short hole. From the tee it's a difficult decision whether to lay up or go for it. Whatever you chose, the green is small, well protected by four bunkers, and has some serious undulations. A fun short hole. Next is *The Muir*, another nice short hole (314 yards). With a stone dyke only 200 yards from the tee, this par 4 is a layup and then a blind approach to a deep green with two bunkers right. Not very classic, but it can be fun. The 13th, *Cat Ha Brae,* is one of the course's fine one-shotters. This lovely 139-yard hole plays with the shore edge (OB) left the whole way. A deep pot bunker fronts the relatively small green. A beauty! *Dane's Dyke* is the 512-yard par 5 fifteenth. The hole is a dogleg right with bunkers on both sides about 200 yards out. The next challenge is clearing the stone dyke 100 yards from the slightly elevated green. The modern Craighead course is very different from the 1895 Old Tom Morris designed Balcomie Links, but both share the lovely clubhouse, friendly members and staff, and most importantly both provide exciting golf challenges.

FROM THE FORWARD TEES: What a beautiful setting for a golf course--you can see the North Sea on almost every hole. The views on a clear day include the East Lothian shoreline, St Andrews, and the coastline east of Dundee including the Carnoustie area. The course, though, demands your full attention. It's big with wide fairways on the front and shorter, tricky holes on the back. The course is 5340 yards for ladies with a par of 74. There are four par 5s on the front and two on the back. I liked best the 10th, 11th, and 13th holes which are shorter, but require accuracy and strategy. The 13th plays along the sea with a steep drop on the left (OB). It looks like you'll be hitting the green or into the sea--an exciting hole.

DRUMOIG GOLF COURSE
Drumoig Hotel, Drumoig, St Andrews, Fife KY16 0BE
01382-541898 www.drumoigleisure.com
Parkland/moorland, 6835 yards, par 72, £25

AMENITIES: The hotel serves as a clubhouse and provides quality changing facilities and access to the hotel restaurant with great views over the loch holes on the course. The lounge serves a full pub menu with some interesting Scottish items. There's no golf shop, but a few essentials are available at the starters office next to the first tee. The course boast one of the finest practice facilities in the area, including a 24 bay driving range and a short game area. It also has a full complement of inexpensive buggies (pawer carts), but it is an easy, though long, walk.

COURSE COMMENTS: The Drumoig Golf Course and Hotel opened in July 1996. The course is maturing rapidly with 2500 trees planted in addition to those already in place and the greens were constructed to USGA specifications and plays well in wet weather. As should be expected of a championship quality course, challenges abound at Drumoig. The well-conditioned greens are of a wide variety of sizes, from only 20 yards deep to over 40 yards wide. Most of the greens are flat with subtle breaks, and the speed was moderate the day we played. A total of 41 bunkers, a mixture of fairway and greenside, are ready to catch errant shots. A few are steep-sided and penal, but most are easy to play from. Lochs are in play on four holes which is unusual for the area. The Drumoig fairways are generous, which is good because the rough beyond is tough.

This long course has a variety in its holes. The 5th, *East Quarry*, a 565-yard par 5, has two encroaching bunkers on the right side of the drive. The main feature of the hole, though, is the two-tiered green wedged left into an old rock quarry--a very striking setting. Thirteen also has a green set into the quarry, but is a far easier hole. *Downwind*, the 430-yard 6th, plays downhill (as well as usually downwind) to a narrow fairway with rough left and trees and rough right. A bunker 225 yards from the tee acts as a ball magnet. The green, which is sloped right, is guarded by two bunkers. A third good hole in a row is the 7th. *Marches*, a 379-yard par 4, is a narrow downhill hole with a bunker and marshland right to worry your drive. Three more traps near the green can cause more problems. The narrow, deep green can have some tricky putts. The 9th is the first of the loch holes. Named *Loch*, this 434-yard par 4 is a great driving challenge. Water is in play on the left at about 200 yards and on the right at about 260 yards. If you can stay in the middle with a good drive, your second will be a fairway wood or long iron over the loch to the green only nine yards beyond. The green slopes back to front and towards the loch. The second loch hole, *Comerton*, is next. The short par 4 tenth at 288 yards has a drive over the corner of the loch on the left with a smaller loch on the right if you stray too far that way. The green is almost surrounded by water. The longest hole on the course is the uphill 575-yard 12th. Three bunkers around the green demand an accurate approach, but it is length that is the test. Ladies start 150 yards out at the top of the first big hill, but its still a tough 420 yards to the green. The finish is a long one-shotter. *Tussocks*, a 220-yarder, has OB left, a loch behind, and a bunker right. The hole requires length and precision at the end of your round. Set in the lush Fife farmland, Drumoig GC is a busy course and well worth the effort to play.

COMMENTS FROM THE FORWARD TEES: Drumoig is a long course, but the turf allows for some roll so it's not too difficult for short hitters. Ladies' tees were well designed and appropriate length on most holes while still maintaining shot values. The par 3s seemed quite long, but water was in play on only one tee shot. I enjoyed the views, as well.

DUNNIKER PARK GOLF COURSE
Dunniker Way, Kirkcaldy, Fife KY1 3LP
01592-261599 www.dunnikerparkgolfclub.com
Parkland, 6091 yards, par 71, £20

AMENITIES: Small clubhouse serves meals from morning on and has a complete pub/cafe menu. Alasdair McDonald runs a small, well-stocked pro shop.

COURSE COMMENTS: The modern (1963) tree-lined parkland Dunniker Park Golf Course is a nice find in an area with plenty of competing courses. The course is quite busy and can be busy even in the off season. Significant work has been done in the past couple of years to help the course drain, so it is a popular choice in wet weather. Forty-three fairway and greenside bunkers are in play and some of them, especially the fairway bunkers, are large and penal. Greens are mostly moderate, but a couple are large. The 4th is dramatically tiered and several have distinct swales especially around the bunkers. The only water on the course is the new drainage ditch in play on about half the holes. Besides the great variety of trees lining broad fairways, several blind drives (well marked) add interest. Even though there is no 9-hole rate, the course does come back to the clubhouse after the 9th and toilets are next to the starter office.

We found several memorable holes at Dunniker Park starting with the opening pair. The 1st, *Alpha*, is a 393-yard par 4, and the 2nd, *Carberry*, is a 349-yard par 4. Both have blind tee shots (with aiming poles) and generous fairways. Over the hills both holes drop to their respective greens. The 1st green is protected by one bunker and the 2nd by two bunkers. Other holes may be more challenging, but these two are confidence builders without being too easy. Nine, *Lang Whang* (there always seems to be a hole named something like this one) is a par 5 of 502 yards. On the downhill tee shot you must contend with a fairway bunker right and the ditch about 225 yards out. The second shot is blind as will be the third if you don't carry the crest of the hill. The approach is downhill to a green protected by three large bunkers. A fine short hole is *Beech Tree*, the 158-yard par 3 eleventh. From the gent's tee it seems you have no choice but to clear the deep fronting bunker and miss the two side bunkers. It's a daunting shot to a fairly small green. The 15th, *Lina*, is the number one stroke index hole. This 358-yard par 4 goes down slightly with a steep-faced bunker on the right (very penal, I know). On the approach be aware of the ditch in front of the green with one bunker left. A birdie opportunity is *Birks*, the short (317-yard) par 4 sixteenth. It's down a bit from the tee to the ditch and then up to the green guarded by bunkers left and right. Dunniker Park is a track that we'd play anytime.

FROM THE FORWARD TEES: Dunniker Park is a parkland course with many hills, trees, and interesting holes. Water is at the edge of eight holes, but straight shots can avoid the small ditch. Red tees give ladies a fair advantage on the 5237-yard par 71 course, but tee placement doesn't take away the challenges of the holes. I enjoyed the testing par 3 eleventh which requires a very straight shot from the left of the tee box or fly the bunkers to land on a small green. A nice parkland course to play any day.

GOLF HOUSE CLUB (Elie)
Golf Course Lane, Elie, Fife KY9 1AS
01333-330301   www.golfhouseclub.org
Links, 6273 yards, par 70, £77

AMENITIES: The beautiful clubhouse houses modern changing rooms for members and visitors. Visitors are welcome in the mixed lounge with food service accessed by ringing a bell for kitchen service. Offers the normal pub menu, but the quality is excellent. The golf shop is across the road from the clubhouse at the first tee for the 9-hole sports club course.

COURSE COMMENTS: The land for the club, along the north shore of the Firth of Forth, was in dispute early. It was decided that the disputed area should be as wide as the best player could hit the ball. A poor shot resulted in the club acquiring a narrow neck of land for the course. The course is the work of famed Scottish architect James Braid who lived in Elie. The name, Golf House Club, comes from the group who put up enough money for the first clubhouse in 1912. The course is always busy, so plan to book ahead.

The Braid design is a fun links challenge. A mix of about 80 greenside and fairway bunkers are typical of Briad's work, and many are quite penal with a couple hidden. A quirk of the course is that most of the sand is on the right--a real problem for slicers. With wonderful views of the firth, no water comes into play. The greens are a joy; most are moderate in size, moderately undulated, and fairly easy to read. The course is open enough to be easily playable in the stiff winds on the firth. One of the challenges of Elie is its numerous blind shots, most of which are drives, but short off the tee may leave a second blind shot. All the holes with blind shots have well placed aiming posts. The views from the course are spectacular on a good day. You can see the Lammermoor hills, Bass Rock, the Isle of May, the Berwick Law, Firth of Forth, and East Lothian across the firth. The picturesque village is beside the course as it plays out to the beach and sea cliffs.

Golf House Club Elie is a strong links course with all holes interesting and fun. Even the easier holes present some challenge. The blind shot off the first tee is not the most unique aspect of the hole; that would be the vintage 1938 submarine periscope in the starter's shack used to see if the way is clear. If it's clear, the starter then sends you on your way. Be sure to ask for a peek through the periscope. Another blind tee shot (sans periscope) begins *Quarries*, the 315-yard par 4 fifth. The fairway is littered with five bunkers and the green is drivable because the second half is downhill. *Martin's Bay*, the 9th, is a 440-yard par 4 with again a blind drive, but this time you can see the four bunkers on the right of the fairway. The second shot is also blind for most, but comes down to a green with two traps on the right. A toilet is sited to the right of the 9th fairway near the green, but you need to get the code from the starter before you start your round. The short 288-yard par 4 tenth is wild. Steeply uphill for the first 210 yards, the hole then goes steeply down to a large green with one bunker left. Wait for the bell before you hit as the green is reachable. Architect James Braid called *Croupie*, the 380 yard par 4 thirteenth, "the finest hole in the country." This great hole begins with a slightly downhill tee shot and a well struck shot will run hard. A bunker in the center of the fairway is within reach of big hitters. The elevated green is guarded by bunkers and a large swale in front and runoff behind. The putting surface is a difficult target because the green is wide and not very deep. One good hole follows another at Elie. The 14th is a 414-yard par 4 which slightly doglegs left on both tee and approach shots. The green has bunkers on both sides. A good finish is the 359-yard two-shotter 18th. A slight dogleg right, the hole has five traps and heavy rough right. The mildly elevated green is approached from over (or out of) a bunker no matter where you land your first shot.

With a plethora of great courses within half an hour's drive (such as St Andrews, Kingsbarns, Crail, Leven, and Lunden), Elie tends to get overlooked in discussions of the great Fife courses. It shouldn't! Golf House Club, Elie is a wonderful track and worthy to be on any Scotland golf itinerary.

COMMENTS FROM THE FORWARD TEES: The views at Elie are fantastic and make it hard to concentrate. You need to concentrate because the day we played the women's course was only 200 yards shorter than the men's tees, which means the course played very long. Three of the four par 3s were reasonable in length, but the 7th at 217 yards was very difficult. A couple of other holes are tough for ladies. The 10th is a hard shot up hill and the 11th has a long carry to the fairway. Overall though, Elie is a course I would go back to any chance I could.

FORRESTER PARK RESORT
Pitdinnie Road, Carneyhill, Dunfermline, Fife KY12 8RF
01383-880505   www.forresterparkresort.com
Parkland, 6296 yards, par 72, £37

AMENITIES: The stone manor house styled clubhouse has a fine dining restaurant, but no real golfer's lounge. Snacks and drinks were available at a small bar in the golf shop which has only the essentials. The men's changing room, toilet facilities weren't up to standards with a leaky urinal (no pun intended) and loose toilet. The women's toilet was much nicer. It could be that more construction was planned, but nobody explained that. The course does have a covered bay driving range.

COURSE COMMENTS: The 2001 Forrester Park Golf Course was once part of the Keavil Estate. It plays over the natural contours of the local farmland; the farm next door could easily fit into the course. The course has quite a bit of elevation change, but much of the uphill is between greens and the next tee. There's an especially long walk between the 4th and 5th holes. The 42 bunkers at Forrester Park are not too penal, and the heavy sand is easy to get out of. You'll find no bunkers on the 6th, but ten on the 10th. Burns and/or ponds are in play on nine holes; seriously on seven of them. The greens at Forrester Park are the pride of the course being built to USGA specifications (the course is playable all year). Most greens are moderate in size, but a couple are small. Even greens which look flat have subtle slopes, and most have multiple borrows or levels. They were fun to putt. As young as the course is, the trees are not yet much of a problem, but I can see they will be as they grow up. Course routing brings you back to the clubhouse after the 9th.

Besides the pleasant views of neighboring farmland and the Pentland and Lothian Hills, Forrester Park offers up some challenging golf as well. After a wide open beginning hole, the 128-yard 2nd is a tight shot between stands of gorse to an elevated green with one bunker on the right. If the pin is on the right behind the bunker, play for the middle of the fairly flat green. The short 282-yard par 4 fourth is a tight drive over a burn and between trees to a fairway which bends right as you get close to the green. A long fade will position you for a wee chip into the green protected by one trap right. We thought that the back had the more demanding holes at Forrester Park. The 10th, at 358 yards, has ten bunkers guarding the fairway and green. Drive over the burn and up to a nest of five good sized traps in the fairway. A drive of 230 yards to the right will clear the traps, while the same drive to the left may find the next traps. After a safe drive, the two-tiered green seems defenseless, even though it has a bunker on each side. Next is the 11th, a great risk-reward 417-yard par 4. The hole is a dogleg left with trees left and OB right. Cut the corner downhill over the trees with a 270-yard shot to reach a flat area in front of a pond. One-hundred-thirty yards is all that is left to find the small two-tiered green with one fronting bunker. A straight hole at the top of the course, the 503-yard par 5 fifteenth plays over a roller coaster fairway of three hills. Second and most third shots will be blind. The green is sloped back to front and is completely fronted by a menacing bunker. On the 17th, a par 4 of 379 yards, the drive of 220 yards to get over the burn is difficult into the wind. Trees left and OB right complicate the drive. Three bunkers on the left near the green encourage you to approach from the right. Forrester Park offers up a tough finishing hole. The 342-yard par 4 begins with a downhill drive over a burn and wetlands area 225 yards from the tee. The approach is steeply uphill to a green with an extremely sloped front; your ball can easily roll back and well off the green. One bunker on the front left needs to be considered as well. The golf course is definitely worth a visit, but the ancillary facilities are not yet up to the level of the course. Hopefully they will get there to make Forrester Park GC a good addition to the older courses in the area.

COMMENTS FROM THE FORWARD TEES: This very young course is set on the hills with natural up and downs, but much of the climbing was between holes rather than during play. It was a clever, enjoyable walk. The panoramic view of the Forth Valley from the top of the course was wonderful. For ladies Forrester Park is a long course of 5601, but it does have a par of 74. The course has wide fairways with water, bunkers, and hills to catch the attention of your golf ball. The par 3s are all similar in that they have elevated greens which required a high shot to hold. The par 5s are fairly long, but I did really like the 17th at only 331 yards. You have to plan your drive to land on the top of a knoll to avoid running down into a burn. Staying to the right on your second shot will cut off some yardage and gives a chance for a birdie. The course is better than its first impression.

GLENROTHES GOLF COURSE
Golf Course Road, Glenrothes, Fife KY6 2LA
01592-750063 www.glenrothesgolf.org.uk
Parkland/heathland, 6223 yards, par 71, £18

AMENITIES: The clubhouse lounge is open to members and golfers only and serves during the day, except Monday--bar open 11 to 11. Small pro shop has all the essentials and is combined with the starter's office.

COURSE COMMENTS: Opened in 1967 Glenrothes GC is two courses--the first ten holes are flat, tight parkland and the last eight are more hilly and wider heathland, but only a couple of the hills are steep climbs. Some of the 30 greenside and fairway bunkers are penal enough to cost a stroke. A burn runs down the right side of the first, and on the back four holes have burn crossings--three of which affect tee shots. Greens are moderate to large with subtle borrows on the front and the greens on the back are more swaled. The lovely trees on the front draw the most interest, but on the back it is the small aircraft taking off and landing at the Glenrothes airport next to the course. Some might find the air traffic disturbing, but our home course is next to a small airport in Oregon and so we're used to it.

Both sides of the course have interesting holes, but we liked the front better. The 1st, *Benarty View*, a 365-yard par 4, begins with a dogleg left which bends uphill. Trees and a burn on the right make for a difficult tee shot since the right is where you want to be for your second shot. The hill and a bunker right of the green complicate second shots. It's a fair but demanding start. The 5th is *Whins*, a long (210-yard) one-shotter, but it's mostly downhill. Trees right and left and a bank right force a straight shot to a green protected by larger traps on both sides. A long par 5, *Lomand Loan*, the 564-yard 7th, is made tougher by a couple of fairway bunkers left then right. Trees and OB left add challenge. The green is guarded by bunkers on both sides. A par or birdie opportunity if you stay straight, but bogey is never bad on this hole. The first of the heathland holes is *Satan's Gateway* (343-yard par 4 eleventh) followed by *Stutt's Curse* (437-yard par 4). These two are mirror-image holes--downhill tee shots which need to clear a burn at the bottom and then uphill to greens protected by bunkers. The difference between the holes is that the 12th is longer and the uphill is steeper. Twelve deserves its Stroke Index #1 status. The back ends with *Hell's End*, a 359-yard par 4. Sort of like the 11th and 12th, the last hole is slightly down to a burn and then up to the green. Coming at the end of the round as it does, the green doesn't need any bunkers. While we like the forested front ten holes better than the hilly back, we don't think the back is "hell"--entered at the "*Gate-way*" and finished at the "*End*."

FROM THE FORWARD TEES: The course feels like two distinct courses--the first is tight parkland and the second course is wide open, hilly, with a meandering burn. The course at 5448 yards is long with a par of 73 (35 front and 38 back). I'd have rather played the more difficult back first and then relaxed more on the forested front, but then I stay out of the trees that Bob finds so often.

KINGSBARNS GOLF COURSE
Kingsbarns, St Andrews, Fife KY16 8QD
01334-460860   www.kingsbarns.com
Links, 6652 yards, par 72, £195

AMENITIES: Visitors to Kingsbarns GC are met by a lovely modern clubhouse with classic styling. The beautiful lounge/restaurant/bar serves high quality fare most normal hours, but is only open to players and guests. In the clubhouse is a golf shop very well stocked with golf essentials, clothes, and souvenirs. The golf shop staff is professional, efficient, and friendly.

COURSE COMMENTS: Golf has been played on the free-draining linksland now occupied by Kingsbarns GC since 1793. The original course on the land was gone by the mid-1800s, and a new course was built in 1922 and then taken over by the military in 1939. The rebirth of Kingsbarns golf came in the late 1990s when developers Mark Parsinen and Art Dunkley employed architect Kyle Phillips to design a course that would celebrate the best of Scottish links golf. Built along a mile and a half stretch of North Sea coast between famed St Andrews and venerable Crail Balcomie Links, the new Kingsbarns has admirably succeeded in its mission. With the Old Course at St Andrews and Carnoustie, Kingsbarns is a Dunhill Links Championship venue, and was recently rated 5th Best Golfing Experience in the World by *Golf World UK Magazine*. Beside the remains of several ancient sites (habitat and burial) on the land of Kingsbarns, an 18th century burn and stone bridge were found about ten feet below the placement for the 18th green. Both the burn and bridge were incorporated into the design of the hole.

Kingsbarns is a true championship venue over fine fescue-bent turf, but is eminently playable by mid-handicappers, though it can be a brutal test for even the best in the wind. With more than half the holes having the sea directly in the golfer's active frame of play, the 82 bunkers on the course range from tiny to huge, but all are very penal (often hitting out backwards is the only option). It's for sure that getting into bunkers will add strokes to your score. One burn crosses in front of the green at 18, and the sea is in view on every hole and in play on at least five. The greens are championship in quality and size. It's possible to have putts as long as 180 feet over small mountains and through deep valleys, or so it seems. Every green has significant contouring. The wide fairways are a bonus, but the rough can be unforgiving. As on most links courses, it is the wind which will present the greatest challenge. Hit the course on a beautiful day with light breezes, like we had in the autumn of 2007, and even I could get close to my handicap. By the way, Kingsbarns is one of the few Scottish courses with a USGA slope and rating (from the regular tees a rate of 70.7 and a slope of 132, for ladies a rate of 70.7 and a slope of 126).

With such a fine caliber course, we found no weak holes, but after much reflection selected four on each side to highlight on what is definitely a thinking person's course. The shortest par 5 is the 502-yard (played from the medal rather than the championship tees) 3rd which plays narrow along the sea. The first two shots for modest hitters shouldn't be a problem if you stay in the middle--off the fairway is heavy rough and gorse. Second or 3rd shots will be more challenging with a huge, deep bunker front and right of a green large enough to make it easy to three putt. One additional pot bunker on the right waits for shots which come too strong from the left. The 5th is a 370-yard dogleg right around a nasty pot bunker. The hole is best played from the left side, even though it means a longer approach. One of the flatter putting surfaces is protected by mounding left and right, but the opening is quite wide. The green, which has plenty of shape (it only looks flat), has one bunker back left. Next is the 318-yard 6th with its amoeba-like fairway. This short hole has plenty of trouble. Two large traps are set into the slope of the fairway in perfect position to catch short drives (200 and 235 yards). Beyond the traps is fairway, but not much of it. The smart play is to lay back safely and leave a wedge or short iron into the two-tiered, sloped green, though the shot will be blind from the left. Finish the front on the 536-yard three-shotter 9th. This long slightly double-dogleg (right then left) hole is gentle at the start and toughens nearer the green. Two bunkers in the middle of the fairway, 80 and 60 yards from the green, mean you must be precise with your approach. The raised green is protected by bunkers on each side and some wild undulations in the putting surface. If you are on the wrong level even relatively short putts are in danger of missing by a bunch. A welcome complete snack shop greets you near the 10th tee, and a toilet is behind the 11th green (also easily accessible from the 8th green). On the 11th, a 425-yard par 4, you must thread your drive between traps visible from the tee to have a wedge shot into a decently flat green. The interesting feature of the hole is a deep hollow on the front right of the green which acts as a magnet, especially when the pin is placed just beyond it. You can bet it will be there when you play. Next is my favorite hole on the course, the 566-yard 12th. It's a beautiful long dogleg left set along the sea. From the tee you can see south to one of my other favorite courses, Crail Balcomie Links. Three bunkers, two left and one right, come into play on most player's second shots, about 70 yards from the green. The green is long and narrow with three distinct levels. Bunkers on each side add challenge, but it is the size of the green that is most challenging. It's almost 80 yards long! It's easy to leave yourself a putt of over 100 feet that will have to negotiate interesting slopes. One of the signature holes on a course full of signature holes is the 185-yard 15th. The sea on the right shouldn't be a factor, but it will be on this short par 3, and so will the trees on the left. With a green that can be easily three or four clubs different just by pin placement, there's plenty of challenge. The trees may block wind from the tee, but not from the green. A smooth swing and a little luck is what's needed to score here. It's a hole you'll want to play over and over. The finish doesn't have the character of the rest of the course, with a blind drive up a featureless slope which hides three bunkers on the left, but the last 125 yards can take your breath away (as well as your score). The green is a plateau separated from the fairway by the cavernous burn found when the course was built. Both tiers of the green slope back to front toward the drop-off into the burn. It is fitting that the last few shots on this magnificent course are so demanding.

The beauty and quality of Kingsbarns GC, a pay for play course, is difficult to describe. At what point does admiration turn to gushing praise? The course and the facilities are top notch world class at Kingsbarns and I've probably never played a better course, although my personal favorites would still be Shiskine on Isle Arran, Royal Dornoch in the Highlands, and Carne in Ireland. But number five in the world and number four on my list isn't bad.

COMMENTS FROM THE FORWARD TEES: Kingsbarns is a beautiful course in a beautiful setting with fantastic views. There are no weak holes on the course and the ladies' tees are situated significantly forward of the men's, but none of the challenge of the holes is lost. There are always bunkers to watch out for, dips and rolls in the fairways, links bounces, and difficult rough if you miss the fairway. The course isn't long for ladies at 5171 yards, and good course management is rewarded. Laying up in front of the trouble is often the prudent play. The par 3s are all short, but are surrounded by trouble. Three of the par 5s are over 400 yards, but I found it was easy to score on them with accurate shots. I liked every hole, but think that 12 is especially fun. The views from the men's tee are wonderful and its good to view the hole from this higher tee. With the beach and sea to the left, the best play is out to the right. The green is large and we could see pin placements that would be really tricky. From a woman's point of view, Kingsbarns is at the top of the golf world. Kingsbarns has everything you'd want--beauty, challenge, playability--and it's just plain fun.

THE KINROSS GOLF COURSES, Montgomery Course (formerly The Blue)
2 The Muirs, Kinross KY13 8AS [for both courses]
01577-863407 www.golfkinross.com [for both courses]
Parkland, 6452 yards, par 72, £35

AMENITIES: [for both courses] Beautiful, recently upgraded lounge with views onto the courses. Bar meals available usual hours. New, fully equipped golf shop opened in May 2007. Friendly, helpful staff. Two hotels are part of the facilities, as well. Golfers staying at the reasonably priced Four Star Green Hotel or The Windlestrae get a special price on greens fees.

COURSE COMMENTS: The Kinross golf courses started as a 9-hole course, then was expanded to 18 holes. In the early 1990s, as we learned from owner Jamie Montgomery, the 18-hole course was split and two new 9s were added to make two 18-hole courses, called the Blue and the Red courses. After major upgrades in 2005, the two courses have been renamed, The Montgomery and The Bruce, after the two families who have owned the estate around Loch Leven for most of the last three centuries. The Montgomery Course gained several new tees, a pond in play on the 11th, and more sand trouble in the form of almost twenty new traps. The Bruce Course was made friendlier to the high handicapper, and several new forward tees were added.

Although quite similar in playability, challenging for low handicappers and fair to high handicappers, each course offers its distinct challenges. The Montgomery Course has a mix of 77 greenside and fairway bunkers to keep you on your toes. On many holes the fairway bunkers can be used as aiming points on drives. None of the bunkers are too penal. Mixed also are the green sizes, from small to quite large. Most have mild undulations, but some have distinct levels and platforms. Unique, at least to my knowledge, is the 2nd green which is also the 9th green on the Bruce Course. This is the only instance I know of one green shared by two courses. A burn is in play on eight holes, but only a real danger on six of them. A couple of ponds are also in play, and some of the water is hidden. The beautifully tree-lined course is wide, but into the trees is bad. On our round we saw a couple of black pheasants, which Jamie said were unusual. Jamie also said that about 30 roe deer wander the course.

The first hole is a relatively benign 161-yard par 3, which gets you out to the rest of the course. Don't take it likely, though; playing from bunker to bunker netted me a six. The 5th, a 300-yard par 4, is a straight ahead hole with a left sloping fairway and bunkers in reach on the right. The biggest problem is the second shot which must clear a burn in front of a small green with numerous interesting contours. Next is a 395-yard par 4 which is a slight dogleg right with two traps on the outside corner--the first is in reach for most players. The approach will be a long one to a three-tiered putting surface. Four bunkers around the green complicate the approach. Seven, a 340-yard two-shotter, has three bunkers left on the fairway which act as magnets for drives (at 185, 205, and 220 yards). On the next shot you must contend with a burn which crosses in front of a raised, but relatively flat green. The front side ends with a 408-yard par 4. Nine is a sharp dogleg right with trees on the inside and bunkers on the outside. Big hitters can try to cut the corner which is called the Tiger Line. The 150-yard marker on the left side of the fairway is a good aiming point for the less adventurous (or smarter) players, but the fairway is one of the narrowest on the course. Another narrow fairway is found at 11, a 498-yard par 5. A small pond on the left at about 200 yards and a large bunker on the right at about 225 make for a demanding tee shot. Trees, especially the large one in the middle of the fairway 160 yards from the green, are only part of the trouble on the approach. A burn and pond cross the fairway 90 yards out from the multi-sloped green guarded by two bunkers. Fifteen plays straight from the medal tees, but as a dogleg right from the members' and ladies' tees. Keep to the middle of the fairway because bunkers on both sides will worry your shots all the way down to the two-tiered green protected by two more bunkers. A long, classic two-shot hole is the 16th at 443 yards. The hole is straight over a slight hill to a large two-tiered green with bunkers right and left. No tricks, just beautiful golf. That's an accurate way to summarize The Montgomery Course; no tricks, just good, beautiful (especially in the spring with blooming trees or in the autumn colors) golf.

COMMENTS FROM THE FORWARD TEES: This course is the harder of the two for ladies as well as men. The ladies' tee boxes had recently been changed (2007) at the request of the Ladies' Club so that tee shots on the par 3s, for instance, had a chance to land on the green. I found that most tee shots were fair and that none were unnecessarily penal for misses. The water on several holes provided plenty of challenge, but shots were always fair and the variety was appreciated. Visually the course is very interesting with a wide range of views. This is certainly one of my favorite parkland courses in Scotland.

THE KINROSS GOLF COURSES, Bruce Course (formerly the Red)
Parkland, 6231 yards, par 73, £35

COURSE COMMENTS: Trees are the biggest hazard on the Bruce course, with some stands being very thick. Though not as many bunkers dot the Bruce (only 55), several completely cross fairways. Water is in play on seven holes, but only a concern on four of them. The greens aren't as large as on The Montgomery and are flatter, but all the greens on both courses are well conditioned. We heard a great description of The Bruce when one golfer in the lounge called it "a great walk in the forest."

That "forest walk" will challenge your best play. The second, a 308-yard par 4, begins with a blind drive--aim for the post in the middle of the fairway. A 210-yard straight drive can catch the down slope for extra run. A large bunker about 15 yards from the green protects the whole front with a smaller bunker on the right. Holes 4, 5, 8, and 9 are par 5s for a par of 39 on the front (the back has one par 5 and 3 par 3s for a par of 34). At 495 yards, the 4th is a double dogleg left then right with plenty of big trees. The middle of the left tree line is OB. The green is guarded by two small traps and has a hollow on the right which funnels shots towards the trap on that side. A tremendous short hole is the 272-yard par 4 sixth where the reward is probably not worth the risk of having a go at it. The fairway runs out at 220 yards with a pond crossing the fairway. A peninsula sticks out into the pond from the left and blocks the view of the rest of the pond beyond. The wide, shallow green runs off in front toward the pond and in back to rough. The 513-yard par 5 twelfth has a tri-part fairway divided first by a burn (290 out) and a rough covered ditch 100 yards beyond the burn. Three fairway bunkers scattered down the hole will complicate club selection for all levels of players. A long sweeping dogleg right where you can try to cut the corner is the 375-yard par 4 fifteenth. You run out of fairway at about 230 yards unless you stay to the inside, which brings the trees more into play. The narrow green is protected on each side by bunkers. Look for great golfing deals when staying at either The Greens Hotel or The Windlestrae.

COMMENTS FROM THE FORWARD TEES: The easier of the two courses is still fun, but not the challenge of the Montgomery. The Bruce provides the same quality course condition and interesting views, too.

LEVEN LINKS GOLF COURSE
The Promenade, Leven, Fife KY8 4HS
01333-428859 www.leven-links.com
Links, 6506 yards, par 71, £55

AMENITIES: The Leven Links clubhouse has changing rooms (ask the starter for a FOB or magnetic key) and an upstairs lounge which serves good meal usual hours. No golf shop, but essentials are available in the starters shack.

COURSE COMMENTS: Golf has been played on this ground since 1846 when a nine-hole course was built. The course expanded to 18 in 1868 and the inaugural competition was won by Young Tom Morris of St Andrews. In 1909, Leven and Lundin golf clubs split the land, and

Leven Links added a new nine as did Lundin Links to create two 18s back to back along the coast. Today, when you reach the fifth, sixth, and 13th tees, you are at Mile Dyke, and on the other side of the dyke is Lundin GC. Both course are now used as qualifying courses when the Open is held at St Andrews.

As should be expected of a true championship links, Leven is not easy, but it is playable by all levels of golfers. Besides the constant wind, the more than 120 bunkers in play, many very penal (as in play-out-backwards), are the major challenge. Several greens have more than five bunkers surrounding them. At the 18th, the Scoonie Burn which crosses in front of the green and is often called "demonic," is the only water hazard on the course. Most greens are moderate to large, but a couple are quite small. All are well conditioned and have significant undulations. The views are equal to the course challenges with vistas of the North Sea, the beach, and the village. A large "law" or hill dominates the view north.

It was hard to pick favorite holes at Leven, but we did take special note of several. The 2nd, *Knowe*, a 379-yard par 4, presents two distinct driving options. First, drive straight down the fairway which runs into rough at about 300 yards. Your approach to the green is then from the right and over rough and a bunker. Second, drive left over the two bunkers 205 yards out (the shot is blind). The longer approach from this angle is straight up the cut grass to the large green. The green is in a slight bowl protected by four bunkers in front. Seven is the second par 3 on the front and is a 182-yard semi-blind shot over mounds and whins to a moderate sized green with seven bunkers around it. Oh yes, behind the green is OB. *Bing*, the 350-yard par 4 eighth usually plays into the wind making a tough hole even tougher. With OB all along the right and mounds and gorse left, driving accuracy is most important here. Two bunkers cross the fairway as it narrows about 70 yards from the green and four more bunkers await greenside. The 10th, *Cattle Creep* (I never did find out about that name), a 383-yard two-shotter, starts with a blind drive. The aiming post will help, but fairway mounding will play havoc with your ball. You might not see the green on your second shot, but it is a big target with only three bunkers to protect it. The 11th normally plays downwind. This 368-yarder is a fun driving hole. The fairway is plenty wide, but three traps (two right and one left) are reachable. More sand awaits in front of the green, meaning your approach from anywhere will be over hazards. Two more traps are at the sides of the green, but if you've avoided trouble so far, why worry about them. Oh, and if you haven't avoided trouble, what's a little more. Eighteen, *Scoonie*, might not be the most difficult hole, but it will definitely demand your attention. The 456-yard par 4 shares the fairway with the first, with only a patch of rough and two bunkers running down the middle. Besides the length of the hole, the biggest problem is Scoonie Burn which runs in front of the very large green (almost 50 yards wide and deep). Don't let it bother you that locals in the clubhouse are betting whether you get over the burn or whether you two putt your hundred-footer.

Leven Links and its neighbor Lundin GC (see *Golf in Scotland: The Hidden Gems*) make a fantastic pair to play.

COMMENTS FROM THE FORWARD TEES: We played on an extremely windy day which made a tough course even more difficult. The par 5s are very long with the 6th at 542 yards (it's 555 for men). The par 3s are more reasonable distance, but all are surrounded by bunkers, especially the 7th with seven. Links turf with 124 bunkers and often windy makes Leven a real challenge. Do play the course and don't worry about score, just enjoy the experience and the fantastic views.

ST ANDREWS, Duke's Golf Course
Craigtoun, St Andrews, Fife KY16 8NS
01334-470214   www.destinationandrews.com
Heathland/hilltop, 7002 yards, par 71, £120

AMENITIES: The pay-for-play course (no membership) has a Five Star clubhouse as would be expected at a Kohler Co. resort (such as Whistling Straits and Blackwolf Run). The new clubhouse has changing rooms downstairs and lounge/restaurant upstairs. The views of the city of St Andrews and the firth are spectacular. The clubhouse also houses a beautiful fashion (no clubs) golf shop. The Kohler Co. of Kohler, Wisconsin, also owns the Old Course Hotel in the heart of the golfing mecca, but the hotel and The Dukes is not part of the St Andrews Links Trust.

COURSE COMMENTS: The rumor we must dispel about The Duke's is that it is a difficult walk and one should take a buggy (power cart) to play, a comment we heard from several who had played. Rubbish! Aside from mild climbs back to the clubhouse after 9 and 18, the course is a joy to walk with only mild elevation changes. The next rumor which needs to be laid to rest is that The Duke's course is brutally tough. Again rubbish! The course is indeed a championship track which will test all the clubs in your bag, but brutal it is not. It is eminently playable by mid to low-handicappers, and even high handicaps can enjoy the course if they play from the correct tee. The original Peter Thompson designed course was built in 1993, and redesigned by Tim Liddy a few years ago when Kohler took it over.

The Duke's will challenge all players with well over 100 bunkers. Many are massive and naturally shaped. The rough around the bunkers is often more difficult to play out of than the bunker itself, though some are steep-sided. A pond is in play (sort of) on 3, 12, and 17. A burn crosses on 10, 11, and 14 and is backed by a stone wall on both 11 and 14. The greens are moderate to large, and while many are flat with gentle borrows, others are significantly swaled or severely sloped. Being only a few miles from the sea and playing on a hilltop, The Duke's can be quite windy. The day we played, a beautiful May afternoon, avoiding the bunkers and the gorse which lines many holes was our major concern. Visually, the course is stunning with firs and pines, gorse and flowers, and the naturally sculpted bunkers. Great vistas of St Andrews and the North Sea don't hurt either. To us the course seemed like a cross between Gleneagles and Boat of Garten combined with the views of courses such as Kinghorn and Stonehaven.

We found many interesting holes on The Duke's, starting with the easiest. *Denhead*, the 159-yard par 3 third, listed as the easiest on the course, at first seems to be all sand, but really is quite open. The green is plenty big, but can be tough to putt. A classic long par 4 is the 470-yard 7th called *Denbrae*. The hole plays down to a wide landing area with one very large bunker on the right. The fairway bends gently around the bunker towards one of the smaller green. Three bunkers protect the multi-swaled green. Before you tee off, take in the great views from the tee box. The 9th, *Craigtoun*, has a generous fairway which slopes to the left. A shot down the center on this 396-yarder will run down leaving a flat lie for your approach to a two-tiered green almost surrounded by sand. After climbing back to the clubhouse you'll find the 10th tee on the left side of the 1st. *Burn Brig*, the 426-yard 10th, is a big bend to the left with a large trap (aren't they all) on the outside of the dogleg and a copse of trees on the inside. The trap at 250 yards is reachable off the tee by most. Your second shot must cross a small burn to reach the elevated green with sand front and left. Next is the 613-yard par 5 eleventh. This long hole is the hardest at The Duke's because of the length, the bunkers, and the burn. Watch out for the bunkers left on the drive and right on your second shot. The approach to the green is made more difficult by a burn and stone wall cutting across the fairway, and bunkers left of the swaled green. Accuracy more than distance is needed on the 405-yard 13th to set up the best approach to the large green with many levels and a small bunker behind. Last is *Ice House*. This 386-yard finisher is a slight dogleg left around a series of traps (only 175 yards to clear) to the base of a rising fairway. Whereas on the 9th you finished the hole and then climbed to the clubhouse, on the 18th you will find the green about half way up to the clubhouse with still a little climb left once you leave the green. Traps right and left and a tree on the left complicate getting to the very sloped putting surface. With five tee boxes on every hole, almost everyone can be challenged and yet enjoy a round at The Duke's. Whichever tee box you play from, we know you'll enjoy a pint in The Duke's clubhouse.

COMMENTS FROM THE FORWARD TEES: This course is set up well for ladies, except for a couple of holes where the red tees are set so that the interest or challenge is taken out of the drive. It's a short course from the red at only 5216 yards. I enjoyed the course but it was difficult to score well. Bunkers are strategically placed for both drives and second shots. The course is beautiful (I especially enjoyed the views of St Andrews and the North Sea) and there is good variety among the holes. The Dukes fits well with all of the great courses in the area.

ST ANDREWS LINKS TRUST, The Castle Course
Pilmour House, St Andrews, Fife KY16 9SF [for all]
01334-466666   www.standrews.org.uk [for all courses]
Links-style, 6759 yards, par 71, £125

AMENITIES: The modern bar and lounge serves until 7:00 p.m. daily (the bar is open later). The lounge has great views of the 9th/18th double green and the sea along St Andrews Bay. There is also a halfway house in the bottom of the clubhouse where you come off the 9th and head to the 10th. Complete merchandise shop with all your logoed needs.

COURSE COMMENTS: The Castle Course just south of town toward Crail on A917, was designed and built by David McLay Kidd. It's the seventh course at the Home of Golf and opened in June 2008. The symbol of the course is a Scottish peer's helmet which was the centerpiece in the crest of the Moneypennys, the family that owed Kinkell Castle which once stood on the site. The course, built on seaside agricultural land, is designed like and plays as a links course. If you didn't know that tons of earth had been moved to "create" the dunesland the course plays over, you would swear the course had been there forever. The views of St Andrews, the bay, the North Sea, and across to Carnoustie and Panmure from the clifftop course are gorgeous. The views below the cliffs on the western edge of the course are interesting as well, with Maiden Rock and the sea stack called the Rock and Spindle. It's not only the views that will bring you back to The Castle Course, the golf is equally exciting (too exciting for some, but more about that later). There are too many bunkers to count, and most can be quite penal (even the fairway bunkers). All are beautifully rough-sculptured. With as much as a mile of shoreline, the sea is in play on several holes, especially the 17th. A burn will cause concern on 4, 14, and 15, but it's never a surprise. Greens are very large (some will say huge), and heavily swaled (some will say mountainous). We heard from several locals who thought the greens were too extreme. Anne and I both took a couple of holes to get used to the size and undulations at The Castle Course, but on the 14th, which is considered the most extreme green, we each two putted from about 35 feet. We certainly didn't feel the greens were over the top, although I probably wouldn't want to play a competition without extensive practice on the the greens. Like on all links courses (or in this case, links-like) the wind will be a condition of play--the course will play extremely long into the wind. The fairways will provide plenty of roll, but will also give you interesting bounces off the humps and hollows. Especially the first few times you play, make use of the course guide to help you find the correct line from the tee.

The Castle Course is world class with no weak holes, although we did pick out several after our round which will highlight play on the course. Number 3, *Cathedral*, is a wonderful 202-yard one-shotter with a fabulous view of the town. There is plenty of bunker trouble short right and left of the putting surface. A huge problem is being long right. The deep depression there is difficult to putt out of (hard to persuade yourself to hit it hard enough) and almost impossible to chip out of. The green isn't as wild as some, but it's still significantly swaled. Take your camera. The 6th, *Pier*, a 421-yard par 4, begins with a true blind shot (some others seem blind because it's difficult to pick a target) on this downhill march to the sea. A shot over the aiming post or just left of it can run a long way towards the green. The approach is down to a green backed by the sea (there is room behind). An exciting birdie opportunity. Don't mess with the left on the seaside dogleg left 7th called *Maiden Rock*, a 456 yard par 4. Two bunkers on the left side are the only hazards within reach of mortals. The bunker on the right 314 yards out is a good aiming point. The green is tucked left and is backed by the sea--miss to the right. At *Boar's Chase*, the 454 yard par 4 twelfth, it's only 210 yards to clear the nest of bunkers straight ahead on the left of the generous right to left bending fairway. If you're not confident of reaching the green with your approach, the smart play is to lay back of the pot bunker fronting the green by 40 yards. The green will be hard to putt if you're not close because of some really tricky pin placements. The green at the 400 yard par 4 fourteenth, *Covenanters*, is the most controversial. One local we met said it was a joke, but he was there playing it. The landing area for your drive is large, but favor the left for the best approach to the huge, wildly swaled green. The hole has no bunkers to distract you from the real challenge--the green. Testing, yes. Unfair, no. Destined to be one of the most photographed holes in golf, the 17th at 184 yards is a marvelously demanding one-shotter. From the white tee it's a 175 yards of carry to reach safety towards the center of the green (165 from the yellow tee). Bail out left and the carry is 10 yards less. The green is large with plenty of slopes and interesting pin positions. A camera is required equipment on *Braes*. The 18th, *Rock and Spindle*, a 555 yard par 5, is a dramatic dogleg right finishing hole. A big hitter might want to cut the corner, but to miss right means disaster. It's better to hit to the center of the corner and let the slope add some yards. The fairway running down to the large double green by the sea (shared with 9) is studded with vicious bunkers, particularly on the right. Play the hole the safe way, and you too can walk away with par. Regardless of what you score on The Castle Course it's a beautiful, demanding track that will keep you engaged from the 1st to the 18th.

COMMENTS FROM THE FORWARD TEES: The course plays almost 900 yards shorter from the forward tees, but is still interesting and challenging. On this course it's extremely important to position the ball carefully off the tee because the landing area is links-like--expect to get unusual roll and bounces. The greens are hard to hold (links and new), so practice pitching up. Most of the short holes are visually intimidating, but fair. The course is difficult but fun to play. I finished knowing that I wanted to go around again to do a better job.

ST ANDREWS LINKS TRUST, Jubilee Course
Links, 6742, par 72, £75

AMENITIES: The clubhouse near the Old Course is shared by the Jubilee and New courses. The very pleasant lounge serves quality meals and snacks most of the day. Lounge is open to the public. Be sure to go up to the roof garden on top of the clubhouse for marvelous views. The golf shop in the basement of the clubhouse is great for clothing and essentials. Numerous shops in town sell clubs, shoes, and other hardware.

COURSE COMMENTS: The third of the St Andrews Links Trust courses, the Jubilee is thought of by many as the best and most challenging. The 12-hole course which opened in 1897, Queen Victoria's Diamond Jubilee year, was fairly basic. It didn't take long to start the upgrades. In 1902 David Honeyman, Old Tom Morris' right-hand man, suggested expanding the course to 18. The expansion was finished in

1905. The next major improvements came in 1938 under the direction of Willie Auchterlonie, who at the time was head professional to the R & A. Auchterlonie noted then that the course "would become a championship course." That prediction came true with the 1988 redesign by Donald Steel. Jubilee is the course which plays closest to the sea of all the St Andrews Links Trust courses, except The Castle Course (2008).

The course sits with the New Course (1895) and the Old Course (1400s) on one side and the North Sea on the other. Sixty-two bunkers, most steep-sided and penal, make the course a test of shot-making. Four holes, though, have no bunkers and are still plenty testing. The greens are large (as big as 55 yards from tip to tip) with the longer holes having the smallest greens. They all play quick with a good bit of undulation. The fact that there is no water on the Jubilee is made up for by elevated tee boxes which leave players more at the mercy of the wind than even on the Old Course. The other demanding feature is the gorse. Even though a program to cut back the gorse has been instituted, the stickery bushes will grab your attention, and your ball, and your shirt, and anything else available. The Jubilee has some great hole names, including #1, *Willie Auchterlonie* (St Andrews pro who won the first Open); #10, *Spires* (the first view back to the town spires); #11, *Treble-One* (squadron number 111 is stationed at Leuchars RAF across the estuary); and #13, *Hale Bopp* (named in 1997 for the comet which lit up the links sky in the course's centenary year).

As well as some interesting names, the holes are interesting to play. All the par 3s are strategically bunkered, but relatively simple until the wind blows--then they are diabolical. The second, *Whinny Knowe* (referring to the gorse covered hillock to the left of the green), is a 360-yard par 4 where accuracy off the tee is more important than distance because of OB right and heavy rough left. The best approach to the long, narrow green is from the left, but be aware of the bunkers on each side of the green. *Playfair*, the 498-yard par 5 sixth is named for Sir Hugh Lyon Playfair, a former Captain of the R & A. Stay to the right if you can on your drive to avoid having to approach over a particularly bothersome pot bunker in front of the green (one of five around the green). Staying right will also avoid the two fairway bunkers left. *Eden's Edge* is a challenging hole which follows the line of the Eden Estuary, hence the name. The 369-yard par 4 is one of the four without bunkers, but the gentle right to left dogleg with the green tucked in the dunes to the left is still demanding. Another interesting par 5 is *The Butts*, named for the WW I rifle practice range which at one time occupied the land. The long (538 yards), narrow fairway has more bumps and humps the closer you get to the green. The narrow two-tiered green is protected by bunkers right and left. *Steel's Gem*, the favorite of designer Donald Steel, is a 356-yard par 4. Stay as left as you can while avoiding the reachable fairway bunker (about 210). The green is hidden right behind a gorse-covered hill and has a deep swale in front. The 16th is named *Freddie Tait*, after a well respected St Andrews golfer, and plays as a 428-yard two-shotter. The tee shot is demanding even though the fairway is generous. The best line on this dogleg left is halfway up a gorse-covered hill. The green is huge and has two distinct levels; it's like playing a double green with only one flag. It also has a bunker left front and one in the middle behind.

The day Anne and I played, the wind was howling. Even though the course "ate my lunch," it's a wonderful track which I can't wait to play again.

COMMENTS FROM THE FORWARD TEES: The Jubilee is a long, long course for women (only 468 yards shorter than the men). It's plenty tough with lots of difficult bunkers, gorse all around, and the wind a constant factor. The course demands almost perfect shots. But then what would you expect from one of the world's premier courses? As demanding as it is, Jubilee is a course where, if I stay in control, I can hit my handicap. The Jubilee plays over the same land as the Old Course at half the price. Ladies, just because it's challenging doesn't mean you shouldn't play.

ST ANDREWS LINKS TRUST, New Course
Links, 6625 yards, par 71, £75

AMENITIES: Same as Jubilee
COURSE COMMENTS: Designed by B. Hall Blyth and laid out by Old Tom Morris in 1895, the New Course was the second course to be constructed at St Andrews. The course is a natural out-and-back layout and features shared fairways and at least one double green (3rd and 15th). The course is sited between the Old Course and the Jubilee, and between the town and the Eden Estuary. Fifty-eight bunkers will cause problems on the New, especially because most are steep-faced, penal, with soft sand. The good side is that the bunkers are easier to avoid than the ones on the Jubilee and are much more visible than the ones on the Old Course. Greens are quite large, though smaller than those on Jubilee or the Old Course. The greens have plenty of interesting borrows but putt true. Gorse, heather, swaled fairways, and the wind add to the difficulty of this venerable venue.

While the Old Course receives the most attention, locals and visitors alike argue about which is the best course--the Old, the New, or the Jubilee. Prevailing sentiment is that the Jubilee is the toughest course and that the New is the favorite to play. In the heavy wind the days we played, the New was definitely easier than Jubilee, but certainly no pushover. The first par 5, the 511-yard third, is long, narrow, and has a slight dogleg into the green. Bunkers right and left must be in your mind on the tee shot. Sand can also encroach on your second shot, but the large elevated double green (shared with 15) is bunkerless. The 5th, a 180-yard par 3, begins a fine series of holes in the heart of the course. It's an intimidating shot because of fronting bunkers left and right and a wide, shallow green. The putting surface is hard to hold because it slopes away from the tee; a run up shot is the best approach. Next is a 445-yard par 4 which has been selected by greenskeepers as the hole which best represents the character of the New Course. Six has no bunkers, but is still a testing hole. The drive through a gorse chute should stay left to give the best approach to the green. The fairway was best described by local golfer John Stewart as "rumpled" (lots of humps, bumps, and hollows). The green is one of the more undulating on the course with a multitude of nasty pin placements. Long hitters must be wary of the three fairway bunkers about 270 yards out on the 481-yard par 5 eighth. The approach to the sloped green is complicated by mounds and five more traps. The path to the green is between two dunes with fronting bunkers. It's a design much copied. Nine, a 225-yard par 3 with rough and OB left, rough and mounds right, and mounds in front of the green, is a daunting one-shotter. The wind can let the hole play as a mid- to long-iron shot, or make you use a driver. Thankfully the green is unbunkered and is set into a bowl which tends to gather in well struck shots. The only blind drive on the course starts the long, tough, 464-yard par 4 tenth. There are no bunkers to worry about, but then there are probably no level lies on the hole either. The rumpled fairway narrows as you approach within 100 yards of the green, but there are several humps and bumps before you get there. Finally, you come to the 408-yard par 4 eighteenth, a fun finishing hole with enough challenge to be interesting, yet easy enough to allow you to look good for the spectators watching at the clubhouse just beyond the green. Bunkers left and right can catch wayward tee shots, and two more bunkers can affect your approach to the large green with some interesting undulations. After your round leave some time to explore the university town of St Andrews, and see if you can find the graves of Old and Young Tom Morris and Allan Robertson in the church yard of St Andrews Cathedral.

COMMENTS FROM THE FORWARD TEES: The New Course (next door to the Old Course) is tough, but fair for ladies. Tee shots are particularly challenging at 2, 6, 10, and 11 which is the hardest driving hole for ladies. Par 3s aren't too long, but most have bunkers that come into play. The 17th at 192 yards is very difficult. I found, though, that down the middle (where Bob never plays) works very well, except on the holes with bunkers in the middle. Considering that the New is a world class course, it is very playable for women. On a good day with a little luck, when the wind is down, it is possible to beat your handicap.

Special Note: The St Andrews Links Trust wants women to play all the courses. I believe women would enjoy the courses and the challenges they present. Women need to be aware that the courses will be filled with men and to be faster because you will usually need more shots. To enjoy your round more, be smart--lay up rather than risk trouble.

TULLIALLAN GOLF COURSE
Alloa Road, Kincardine-on-Forth FK10 4BB
01259-730396   www.tulliallangolf.co.uk
Parkland, 5974 yards, par 69, £24

AMENITIES: Pleasant clubhouse with lounge and full restaurant open to the public in the evenings. Bar menu available all day in the lounge which has panoramic views to the 18th green. In fact, the club has had a few balls bounce up, but none have broken a window--yet. The very complete golf shop was refurbished in 2001.

COURSE COMMENTS: Tulliallan GC, near the Firth of Forth, is an established track which gets busy on the weekends, but can be virtually empty on weekdays. As many of the courses in this area, Tulliallan's history is linked to the world wars. Originally built as a 9-hole course in 1902, Tulliallan was closed down as part of the war effort in 1914. In 1918 a new 9-holer was developed, which was expanded in 1937 to the eighteen currently played. Though the course is mostly flat, what slight elevation changes that exist add variety to the holes. Fifty bunkers, some steep-sided, will be a concern to play, as will a burn which is in play on six holes (most seriously on the third). The small, flat greens have subtle borrows and can be tough for a first-timer to putt. There are pleasing views of surrounding farmland and hills, and seven counties can be seen from the highest point on the course. When we played there were numerous pheasants on the course and we even saw our first wild hedgehog between one green and the next tee. We also found out that as cute as they are, they are often heavily infested with fleas and other critters--look, but don't touch.

While Tulliallan has no bad holes, a few stand out in our after-round notes. The shortest par 3 at Tulliallan, the 145-yard 6th called *Damn End*, begins a enjoyable run of three holes. The small green is surrounded by five strong bunkers. Our playing partners, locals Dave and Eli, told us that a popular front pin placement is particularly tough. The next hole, *The Firs*, a par 4 of 323 yards, has a series of three fairway traps on the left which makes accuracy on the drive particularly important. The narrow green is further protected by bunkers on each side. The third in this series of holes is the 8th, *Broom Knowe*. The burn crosses the fairway at about 275 yards (big hitters beware!) on this 401-yard par 4 after running down the right side. The hole then goes down to a green with a fore bunker right and a pot bunker left which makes the green a small target. A burn is also in play on the short challenging 11th. With a large tree right and a copse of trees left, driving in the middle is vital on this 273-yard lay up hole. The burn crosses in front of the largest green on the course which has a trap on the left. The 16th, *Road Yett* (a "yett" is a gate), is the longest par 4 at Tulliallan. At 447 yards, the hole is the hardest on the back, but it does play downhill. The burn is in play for a duff off the tee. The narrow green is a tough target guarded by 3 bunkers. Tulliallan GC is frills free, no tricks golf which is a joy to play.

COMMENTS FROM THE FORWARD TEES: Tulliallan is a comfortable course even for average hitters. Only the burn on the 14th forces a lay up drive. That burn does cross seven fairways and lateral water is in play on 8, 9, and 11. Three of the par 3s are short and reachable, but the 4th is 200 yards and uphill making it the most difficult par 3. Visually lovely, the course is a comfortable walk in the park where I could score below my handicap.

Courses in this region listed in *Golf in Scotland: The Hidden Gems*: Alloa, Anstruther, Balbirnie Park (Markinch), Burntisland, Charleton (Colinsburgh), Crail Balcomie, Dunfermline Pitfirrine, Kinghorn, St Andrews Links Eden and Strathtyrum, Scotscraig (Tayport), Thornton.

PUBS, TEAROOMS, & RESTAURANTS

For the size of the Heartlands we don't have a large list of eateries to recommend for a couple of reasons. First, we have a Scottish family in Crieff who have adopted us--John and Jackie Clifford at Merlindale B&B. We spend so much time eating with the family that we tend not to go out as much. Second is the fact that we keep going back to the Moulin Inn in Moulin (near Pitlochry) and the Dreel Tavern in Anstruther rather than finding new places. [Both Moulin and Dreel were written up in *Golf in Scotland: The Hidden Gems*.] We do suggest a visit to the Anstruther Fish

Bar in Anstruther, regarded as the best chippy in Scotland, and Deil's
Cauldron in Comrie as great for their style. Perhaps the best bet is Yann's
in Crieff--always serving great meals.

PERTHSHIRE AND ANGUS

Breizh (restaurant) on High Street in the heart of Perth's shopping
district. French/Italian bistro which is very popular with locals.
Book ahead or stop in and book and then continue shopping. Great
food, decent prices.

Bridge of Balgie Post Office and Tea Room on the road through Glen
Lyon. Fourteen single-track miles from Fortingall this small
grocery/post office/tea room has a few tables inside and picnic tables
outside. Homemade soups and sandwiches can be welcome if
you're touring this out-of-the-way location.

Balgove Larder & Farm Store on the way into St Andrews on the A91.
Shop and cafe which is crowded and noisy because it's very popular.
Limited menu, but the food is delicious.

Carlton Hotel (pub) in the center of Montrose. Don't be put off by having
to enter through a side alley, the hotel has class. Friendly place
with a good menu and decent food.

Ciao Roma (restaurant) in the main shopping area of Perth. Traditional
Italian with full menu.

Cocoa Mountain on High Street in Auchterarder in the middle of town.
Delicious truffles, hot chocolate to die for, coffee specialties, and
sinful sweets. Forget your diet, you're on vacation.

The Comrie Cafe on the main street through the village. Typical tearoom
fare, good quality.

Courtyard Bar and Brasserie in The Mains of Taymouth shops in
Kenmore. Modern chalet-style lunchroom and formal dining
restaurant with a very complete menu and full bar. Great pizza and
soups.

Crieff Hotel, Haggis and Sporran (pub) on Perth Road in Crieff at the
east end of the shopping area of town. Typical hotel pub where
the food gets mixed reviews.

Crystal Tea Room & Coffee Shop at the Stuart Crystal Factory
Showroom on the south edge of Crieff. Airy and bright with
outside seating for good weather the cafe is a decent spot for teas,
coffees, sweets, and light lunch.

Deil's Cauldron (pub/restaurant) just off the main road through Comrie heading north. A top spot to eat in the Strathearn Valley. Food is exceptional and the service matches. Pricey, but a Must Stop.

Delivino's (lunch/tearoom) down from the main square in Crieff. A deli and wine bar (hence the name) with good lunches, fantastic sweets, and early dinners.

Drummond Hotel (pub/restaurant) on the main road through St Fillans just past the golf course. The food was good, but the service was abysmal--go to the golf course tearoom instead.

The Joinery (Meigle Cafe & Coffee Shop) on the Square in Meigle. Interesting cafe (good food) and gift shop with friendly, helpful owners.

Killin Hotel and Riverview Bistro (restaurant/pub) on the main road through the village. Classic hotel pub, nicely decorated which serves good food.

Lounge in Crieff (restaurant) on High Street in the heart of the shopping district. Combination coffee shop and bistro-style tapas bar owned by Yann and Shari (owners of Yann's). Excellent food and full bar.

Meadow Inn (pub) in Crieff on A823 (road to Perth) at the west end of town. A locals pub with typical, but good, pub food.

Old Tudor Coffee Shop & Bistro on Main Street, Auchterarder, in the middle of town. Great sweets and lunch items in a Tudor-style interior.

Paco's Restaurant and Sandwich Bar (restaurant) near the Opera House in Perth's downtown shopping area. Good quality food (huge menu featuring Italian, American Southwestern, and steaks) at good prices. Can be hectic.

Red Squirrel Cafe (tearoom and art gallery) on High Street, Crieff in the upper part of the shopping district. Some high quality art (including my photos) and sandwiches and sweets. Friendly atmosphere.

Royal Hotel (restaurant) in the middle of Comrie. Elegant dining at affordable prices. Order in the lounge and be taken to your table when the food is ready. The hotel also has a separate lively bar.

Tormaukin Hotel (pub/restaurant) in Glendevon. Has been very good, but we've heard the quality hasn't kept up with the rising prices.

The Tower Hotel Gastro Pub on Perth Road, the main road through Crieff. Newly redesigned the pub has bistro feel and service is very friendly, but the food is still just pub food.

Treats (tearoom) on the Square in Kinloch Rannoch. Opened in 2011 Treats is a small cafe and gift shop open all year Limited cafe menu, but more than the usual items.

Tullybannocher Farm Food Bar (cafeteria) just out of Comrie toward St Fillans. Funky cafeteria with some good food at reasonable prices.

Scottish Chocolate Centre, Iain Burnett The Highland Chocolatier in the small village of Grandtully on A827. This chocolate specialty shop and gift shop also hosts an interesting cafe in the back. Special chocolate drinks and sweets add to the soups and sandwiches to make a nice stop.

St Fillans Golf Course Tearoom at the St Fillans Golf Course. A good bet for lunch or early dinner--simple fare, good quality. Professional chef.

Willows Coffee Shop and Restaurant on St John's Place in downtown Perth. Modern cafe with full breakfast and lunch menu and a more limited dinner menu. Busy.

Yann's (restaurant) on Perth Road just up from the main shopping area in Crieff. Award winning fine dining French and Scottish restaurant in Glenearn House B&B. Best restaurant in the area, reservations recommended.

KINROSS AND FIFE

1 Golf Place (pub) on the corner just down from the first tee at the Old Course in St Andrews. A golfer's pub with typical pub menu, but the food has always been good, especially the hamburgers.

Abbot's House Cafe next to the Cathedral in Dunfermline. Excellent spot for a coffee, scone, or hearty tearoom lunch, the cafe is located in the Abbot's House Museum. Open 7 days a week.

Anstruther Fish Bar (sit-in chippy) on the east end of the harbour in Anstruther. Reputed to be the Best Chippy (fish and chip shop) in Scotland and we won't dispute that. Good Scottish fast food. Be prepared to wait, especially on weekends the lines get long.

Bella Italia (restaurant) on Bell Street in the heart of St Andrews shopping district. Chain Italian restaurant with typical decor , good service, and excellent food. Very busy.

Claret Jug Restaurant and Bar in the Dunvegan Hotel a block away from the Old Course in St Andrews. Eat in the bar if you can for the ambiance of being surrounded by photos of all golfing's greats. Food is good as well.

Crail Golf Hotel (pub) at the edge of town just before heading out to the Crail links. Always good food.

Dreel Inn (pub) on the main coastal road through Anstruther. Wonderful old (1600s) pub which serves good food. Fairly typical pub fare, but done well.

Drouthy Neebors (pub), meaning "thirsty friends," on the main shopping street in St Andrews. Decent pub food at good prices in a lively university town. Also in Stirling.

Golf Tavern or 19th Hole (pub) just off the fairways at Elie GC. Golfer's pub with decent food and good pizzas.

Kinneuchar Inn (pub) is a small village pub in Kinneuchar near Kilconquer Castle resort. A local village pub fun to visit to listen to locals and the food from a limited menu was good as well.

Red Lion Inn (pub) in the middle of the historic village of Culross. Large pub menu with some unusual items, such as fried cheese salad. Very popular with locals and tourists.

The Ship Inn (restaurant), owned by the same couple as Golf Tavern, on the shore in Earlsferry. Complete menu of good food and good prices.

Swilcan Restaurant in the Links, the clubhouse for the New and Jubilee courses in St Andrews. Golfers and non-golfers enjoy dining in the modern clubhouse lounge with views out to the Old and New courses. Extensive menu from soups to sandwiches and main courses. One of the best choices in town.

Weaver's Bar and Restaurant in City Hotel on bridge Street in Dunfermline. Large modern pub/restaurant in a building built in 1775. Typical pub menu. Lots of locals at mid-day.

LODGINGS

33 Nethergate B&B
33 Nethergate, Crail KY10 3TU
01333-451509 www.33nethergate.co.uk £70
A nice Victorian town house a little more than a block off the main road in Crail offers first class accommodations and is very golfer friendly.

Ashbank Guest House
105 Main Street, Redding, Falkirk FK2 9UQ
01324-716649 www.bandbfalkirk.com £70

Ashbank retains many of its Victorian features and has views out to the Ochill Hills, the Wallace Monument, and Airth Castle. Rooms are lovely and Betty and Bede are friendly hosts. A good location for Fife or to the west.

Errolbank Guest House
9 Dalgleish Rd., Dundee DD4 7JN
01382-462118 www.errolbank-guesthouse.com £60
A pleasant B&B in the Dundee suburbs close to Broughty Ferry.

Fisherman's Tavern Hotel
10-16 Fort Street, Broughty Ferry DD5 2AD
01382-775941 www.fishermanstavern.co.uk £ moderate
Tavern and hotel often spells a sleepless night, but at Fisherman's Tavern that wasn't a problem. Nice accommodation and good food.

Five Gables House
Dundee Road, Arbroath DD11 2PE
01241-871632 www.arbroathbandb.com £60
Converted from the old (1877-1984) clubhouse of the Arbroath GC, Five Gables is a lovely B&B with great views of the golf course and the North Sea.

The Grange B&B
45 Pittenweem Road, Anstruther KY10 3DT
01333-310842   www.thegrangeanstruther.com £80
The Grange has beautiful rooms and serves a good breakfast. Even on the high side, it's still good value.

Honeypot Guest House & Tearoom
6 High Street, South, Crail KY10 3TD
01333-450935 www.honeypotcrail.co.uk £70
Strategic location only a couple of miles from the golf courses and a short walk from the harbour. Very nice breakfasts.

Merlindale B&B
Perth Road, Crieff PH7 3EQ
01764-655205 www.merlindale.co.uk £70
Our Scottish home and one of the best B&Bs we've ever stayed in. John and Jacky Clifford are golfers and Jacky is a Cordon Bleu trained chef. The 1860s house has been significantly remodeled and is constantly being

upgraded. Rooms are large and beautifully appointed. A lovely, award winning, friendly place to stay in the heart of Scotland

No. 1 Bed & Breakfast
1 High Street, Elie KY9 1BY
01333-331157 www.bedandbreakfastelie.co.uk £75
Very welcoming B&B in a nice seaside village. Ensuite or private bath available.

The Outhouse
1 St Ayles Crescent, Anstruther
01333-312304 www.outhouseanstruther.co.uk   £ reasonable
Spacious accommodations in your own "outhouse" in the garden of the main house. Breakfast is brought out to you. Five minute walk to the harbour.

The Old Smiddy Coffee Shop and B&B
Main Street, Killin FK21 8XE
01567-820619 www.theoldsmiddykillin.co.uk £70
Three rooms, two overlooking the gorgeous Falls of Dockart. Small but comfortable.

Pitreavie Guest House
3 Aberdour Road, Dunfermline KY11 4PB
01383724244 www.pitreavieguesthouse.co.uk £60
Friendly B&B with award winning garden and views of the abbey.

Upper Hatton B&B
Dunkeld PH8 0ER
07762-2766903 www.upper-hatton.co.uk £66
Occupying several acres of forest and meadow, Upper Hatton is about a mile off the road to Blairgowrie (A923). Lovely guest lounge, pleasant rooms, good breakfast, quiet, and wildlife (peacocks, deer, pine-martens) are some of the features of Upper Hatton B&B.

Yann's at Glenearn House
Perth Road, Crieff PH& 3EQ
01764-650111 www.yannsatglenearnhouse.com £90
Glenearn House, rooms with a restaurant, is a lovely six room B&B with a supurb French/Scottish restaurant. Yann and Shari Gospellier will see that your stay is delightful.

TOURIST ATTRACTIONS

Branklyn Gardens, Perth. A lovely small (two acre) garden which always has plenty in bloom.

British Golf Museum, St Andrews. The museum, only a wedge shot from the first tee at the Old Course, houses 500 years of golf history, with photos, videos, and all manner of memorabilia.

Culross Village, west of Dunfermline along the Firth. A National Trust preserved 17th C village with several building open including The Palace.

Dewar's World of Whisky, Aberfeldy. The old Aberfeldy distillery, now home to Dewar's, has a high tech tour and the normal dram after the tour.

Dumfermline Abbey and Palace, Dunfermline. The Abbey and ruined Palace dominate the town which was at one time the capital of Scotland. The Palace ruins are interesting, but it is the Abbey which draws the most attention. Dedicated in 1147, the old church is a large room supported by eleven 30-foot tall stone pillars. In the new church you can find where King Robert the Bruce is buried, all except for his heart which is buried in Melrose Abbey in the Borders. Besides Bruce at least 22 other Royals are interred. Dating back to 1093.

Famous Grouse Distillery, Crieff. The Glenturret Distillery, now Famous Grouse, has a informative distillery tour in a lovely location.

Innerpeffray Library and Chapel, Crieff (about 4 miles east of town). The oldest lending library in Scotland is open limited hours, but is a bibliophile's treasure. Interesting history of the Drummond family.

Lochleven Castle, Kinross. Ride a small 10-passenger ferry over to the island which houses the 14th Century castle. Mary Queen of Scots, William Wallace, and Robert the Bruce all have connections to the castle. The ruins are well reserved and interesting to tour.

St Andrews Castle, St Andrews. Built around 1190, the structure you can tour today dates from the 1400s. On a point of land overlooking St Andrews Bay, several rooms are open to the public.

St Andrews Cathedral and St Rule's Tower, St Andrews. When intact, the cathedral was the largest in Scotland and would rival the largest in all the UK. Now, the ruins are an iconic image of Scotland. Wander the ruins, climb St Rule's 157 steps for a fabulous view, but be sure to find the memorial to and graves of Tommy Morris and Old Tom Morris (golfing royalty).

Scone Palace, Perth (northwest of the city). Scone Palace, the home of the Stone of Destiny used to install Scottish monarchs, is a fine grand house with lovely grounds and tons of history.

Stanley Mills, Stanley (north of Perth on the A9). Newly opened (2008) cotton mill museum. Informative self-guided tour.

The Glen GC

CHAPTER 6: SOUTHEAST SCOTLAND

GOLF

Golf in the southeast is about courses around the capital city of Edinburgh and some great links and seaside courses. Although links courses like Craigielaw and Luffness New are challenging fun, the surprises in this region are in the outlying courses such as Harburn and Baberton. Don't neglect, though, the great second course in North Berwick, The Glen.

BABERTON GOLF COURSE
50 Baberton Ave., Juniper Green, Edinburgh EH14 5DU
01314-534911   www.babertongc.com
Parkland/moorland, 6134 yards, par 69, £40

AMENITIES: Enjoy the modern new clubhouse with its comfortable lounge which serves snack all day to members and players. The clubhouse is not open to the public. The club's golf shop has been open for 20 years and is nicely supplied and staffed.

COURSE COMMENTS: The Baberton GC on the south edge of Edinburgh welcomes visitors, but can be very busy (weekdays are your best bet). This stately course was developed in 1893 out of the Baberton Estate. Extended from the original 9-hole course to 18 in 1894, the original Willie Park Jnr design was significantly remodeled by James Braid in 1926. It is pretty much the Braid course that you play today. Obviously being a Braid course, you will not be disappointed in the bunkering. About 50 bunkers will test your accuracy, but the sand is good, playable, and not very penal. The greens range in size from small to large. Most of the putting surfaces are flat (only a couple have significant borrows), and all have been brought up to US PGA standards. With no water on the course, you might think the course would be a pushover. Not true; the very undulating course is lined with ball-gobbling trees. Baberton is designed so that you play in all direction of wind in one round. You also have to be aware that several holes cross others.

Our round at Baberton on a fine spring afternoon was most enjoyable, especially because we got paired with the former club captain. It always is a pleasure to have someone who knows the course to guide us around. Right from the start we liked the holes at Baberton GC. The first, *Waugh's Knowe*, is a 403-yard par 4 which is a downhill dogleg right with bunkers left and right in the landing area. There's more room to the right than it looks from the tee, but too far right is lost. The green is large, fairly flat, and protected by one bunker. A gentle start with enough challenge. On the 507-yard par 5 second you drive between stands of trees to a fairway which bends slightly right and is dotted with a series of staggered bunkers left and right. The smallish green is tucked to the right and protected by three more bunkers. On the 4th hole, *The Knowe*, a 357-yard par 4, you drive over a low hill and down to the green. The decision is whether to play safe or go for the reachable green which rolls off on the sides and is protected by sand. A ridge behind helps those who are too bold with their approach shots. *Riccarton*, the 393-yard 7th, is a great visual hole with the entire hole in view from the tee. Shoot down a long slope to a wide fairway with bunkers on each side at the bottom. Second shot is uphill to a green guarded by more bunkers. The first hole coming in is *The Well*, the 340-yard par 4 which begins with a blind tee shot (aim at the pole). Past the pole the undulating fairway drops down to a putting surface protected at the sides and behind by large bunkers. The 388-yard par 4 thirteenth is thought by most to be the best hole at Baberton. From the left side of the tee box you can see the fairway as it descends and bends around two major slopes toward a green perched above with a hill behind, drop-off right, and bunker left. *The Gap* (an apt name for the hole) requires good decisions on all shots. The long (469-yard) two-shotter 16th starts with a drive downhill and then requires a long shot up (or two shots because most can't reach, especially into the prevailing wind) to a green with bunkers left and right. There's good reason *The Valley* is the #1 index hole. The 18th is named *Redan* (meaning defense). This 422-yard par 4 begins with a blind shot to the top of a large mound--ball will bounce left and down towards the practice area. The narrow green is surrounded by trees and bunkers. As you come down the 18th toward the green, look at the sign on a small gate into one of the neighboring yards where miss hit shots may land. The sign reads: "Trespassers Will Be Forgiven." The sign was put up by the property owners in the 1930s and has been honored by all owners since. Baberton GC is a pedigreed, friendly, challenging, busy course which should be on your to play list.

COMMENTS FROM THE FORWARD TEES: This is a delightful parkland course in Edinburgh and because of its position in the hills being surrounded by mature trees we never heard any city noise. The course has plenty of challenges with hills, bunkers, and trees and it takes good course management to be successful. Though longer than some (5489 yards) and hilly, I didn't have many sidehill lies. Par 3s are from 103 to 181 yards, and the par 5s are reasonable length ranging from 365 to 441 yards. Baberton is definitely a course on my "play again" list.

BROOMIEKNOWE GOLF COURSE
36 Golf Course Rd., Bonnyrigg, near Edinburgh EH19 2HZ
01316-639317 www.broomieknowe.com
Parkland, 6150 yards, par 70, £30

AMENITIES: The clubhouse was originally built in 1906 and has had revisions in 1954, 1960, and 1979. It hosts a beautiful lounge with views onto the 2nd green. Lunch is served from 11 until 2 pm, and full dinners after 5 pm. Mark Patchett has been the local pro for 25 years and maintains a complete golf shop.

COURSE COMMENTS: Broomieknowe is a course with excellent heritage. The original nine holes were designed by Ben Sayers in 1905 and James Braid extended the course to 18 in 1933. In 1994 five new holes were added to replace lost land. The 18 holes you play today is a beautifully forested course with a lovely variety of mature trees and some views of the Border hills. A mix of 67 greenside and fairway bunkers will challenge all players. The fairway bunkers will cost you shots, while the greenside traps are easier to play from. Only the 4th has no sand trouble. A burn is in play on 4 and 9, but only on 9 is it a bother. The moderate to large greens all have subtle slopes, and a few even have distinct levels. Even in a wet year we found them in excellent condition.

The course is easy to walk and filled with classic golf holes like the 369-yard par 4 third. The gentle dogleg right has heavy forest on both sides. Big hitters can challenge the trees on the right to be left with a short pitch to a green guarded by three traps. The next hole begins with a tough drive between mature trees. Stay as left as you can on this 321-yard dogleg right. There are no bunkers, but plenty of trees and a green which slopes away from you will be test enough. It's a lovely short challenge. The 7th at 468 yards is a long dogleg left par 4 with a bunker on the outside in the range of big hitters (260 yards). Your approach is downhill to a narrow green with no bunkers to bother you. Nine is a 350-yard par 4 where you want to stay left with your drive since 200 will reach the burn on the right, but 250 won't reach on the left. The next shot is uphill to a large green with more slope than any other on the course. One bunker short right should be avoided. Three interesting holes on the back caught our attention. The 10th, a 402-yard par 4, has a narrow fairway which doglegs slightly left. The hole plays uphill and the green slopes right to left with one small bunker on the right. For a one-shotter we like the 153-yard 15th. It's all about the bunkers here. Six traps and a smallish green make this short hole testing. The 17th at 309 yards is drivable for big hitters, but there are plenty of trees and five bunkers to get in the way. The prudent play is a medium iron straight between the trees and a short iron in avoiding the three greenside bunkers. Broomieknowe GC would be a good choice for a round anytime, but being built on a sand base with good drainage means that in wet conditions it's an excellent choice.

COMMENTS FROM THE FORWARD TEES: Broomieknowe is a good parkland course with good views of the countryside around Edinburgh. Ladies play almost the same length as men, especially on the front. Par 3s are reachable for most ladies and the par 5s are long. With some downhill help and three good shots par and bogeys are possible even on the longest holes.

CRAIGIELAW GOLF COURSE
Craigielaw, Aberlady, East Lothian EH32 0PY

01875-870800 www.craigielawgolfclub.com
Links, 6601 yards, par 71, £59

AMENITIES: Clubhouse is a modern facility with lounge and dining area. Lounge has good views out to the course, Firth of Forth, and Fife beyond. Good food is served usual hours. Open to the public for lunch every day, but dinner is for golfers only. Golf shop in the clubhouse is fully stocked and the staff is very welcoming to visitors. Club has a great teaching facility called the Foreshot Golf Academy with its own 6-hole course (The South Links) for beginners or those wanting lessons.

COURSE COMMENTS: A new course, Craigielaw is built in the tradition of links courses without the dominating dunes. Don't make the mistake, though, of thinking the course will be easy. Already Craigielaw has hosted a Scottish Amateur and been a qualifying course for the 2007 British Senior Open at Muirfield. With magnificent vista of the Firth of Forth from most holes and the links of Kilspindie GC (see *Golf in Scotland: The Hidden Gems*) next door, the course has been called "a golfer's paradise." It could also be called golfing hell if you end up in almost any of 69 greenside or fairway bunkers. All are vicious and should be avoided which is practically impossible since the fairways run off into the sand. I really loved Craigielaw, but the bunkers were my undoing. Ponds are in play on 5, 12, and 13. There's also a pond to the right of 11, but the burn which crosses near the green is the real bother. The moderate to large greens, all with significant undulations, are top quality and designed to US PGA specifications. Because the course is not far from the Aberlady Natural Wildlife Refuge, home ground of Scottish author Nigel Tranter, Craigielaw abounds with wildlife. Brown hares, swans, skylarks, grey partridges, lapwings, greenshanks (Oh, what a hideous name!), plovers, oystercatchers, and many others can be spied on the course. You don't have to listen too carefully to hear the rants of that well known species called *frustratus golfus*, as they scramble from bunker to bunker.

All the par 3s at Craigielaw (ranging from 155 to 186 yards) are strong, straight forward one-shotters characterized by strategic bunkering and undulating putting surfaces. Six is unique in that you drive over a stone fence which cuts diagonally across your line to the green with traps left. Bail out room is between the right side of the green and the fence. From there you can still make par. It isn't only the par 3s which are strong at Craigielaw. The first, *Steading*, a 327-yard par 4, is a challenging opener with bunkers at 200 and 230 yards and three more fronting the green. If the rough is light enough (like the spring we played) you can shorten the hole considerably by staying to the right of the fairway bunkers, but it means your approach will be out of the rough over bunkers. From the members' tee (291 yards) the green is drivable with the wind behind. Follow that with *St. Mary's Chapel*, the 558-yard 2nd. Trouble really begins on your second shot with a copse of trees and two traps right. The narrow green, the most swaled on the course, is protected by four more traps. Another strong par 5 is *Quarry Park*, the 540-yard 11th. A fairly open fairway begins this long hole; beware though of the two bunkers on the right at 255 yards (222 from the members' tee) because the slope of the fairway will kick a ball toward the hazards. OB runs all the way up the hole on the left and 150 yards from the green the burn begins; on the right it comes into play about 115 yards from the green. The green has the burn in front, one trap left, and some serious undulations. A stand of trees on the right is a visual challenge at *Doos Wa's*, the 346-yard 15th, but the real worry should be the two bunkers left at 230 and 250 yards. The green has plenty of bunker protection and a steep roll-off behind for those who are too strong. To finish your round Craigielaw GC's 18th is long and narrow. Aim for the marker post 282 yards out from the tee. Bunkers come into play on second shots at about 100 yards from the swaled green guarded by three more bunkers. Craigielaw GC is a demanding, yet fair test of shot-making. My score got eaten up by the bunkers, but I still put the course high on my list to play again.

COMMENTS FROM THE FORWARD TEES: Craigielaw GC is a short course for ladies at 5320 yards, but there is plenty of difficulty here. Bunkers are the main trouble and intrude on tee shots on several holes, especially the first. Strategy and accuracy are really the keys to good play. On some of the holes, the ladies' tee box is set so that visually you aim directly at trouble, especially 1, 9, and 12. Aim where you want to hit, not where the tee box directs you. For a shorter course, all the par 5s were over 450 yards long, but the links rolls can be your friend. Stay out of the bunkers and you can enjoy Craigielaw.

CRAIGMILLAR PARK GOLF COURSE
1 Observatory Road, Edinburgh, EH19 3HG
01316-670047 www.craigmillarpark.co.uk
Parkland, 5825 yards, par 70, £30

AMENITIES: The clubhouse has a lovely upstairs lounge which serves meals all day for players only, and has good views of 1, 10, and 18. Clubhouse also houses a small, but well-stocked golf shop.

COURSE COMMENTS: Hilly, but very walkable, Craigmillar Park GC came to its current location on Blackford Hill in 1906, after a having begun in 1895. The course was later extended to 18 holes upon the advice of James Braid. Sited as it is on a hill above "Old Reeky," the course can be very windy, but locals say that the worst weather often skirts around the course. A mix of 43 greenside and fairway bunkers, some quite penal, will keep players thinking. The only water on the course is a burn which is much in play on 15 and 16. The greens are moderate to large with interesting slopes and borrows. The putting surfaces are well conditioned and putts roll true. On most holes it is advisable to be below the hole. While not a tight course, holes 1 and 10 and 15 and 16 cross. The course makes pleasant visual use of old stone walls, and the views of the city below are glorious--all major sights can be seen including the Royal Observatory next door and out to the North Berwick Law.

The holes at Craigmillar Park are lovely as well, starting with the first. *Dyke* is a 352-yard par 4 that begins with a blind tee shot uphill and has a stone wall along the left marking OB. The second shot doglegs left through a narrow gap between the end of the stone wall and a copse of trees. The green isn't large and has three guarding bunkers. A testing start. The 5th, *Dip*, is 422 yards which starts with a blind drive over the crest of a hill which slopes to the right. Also on the right is a row of mature trees which complicates the approach from that side--it's best to approach from the left side of the fairway. The moderate sized green has only one bunker on the left. A tough one-shotter is *Howe Dene*, the 204 yard 7th. Beginning again with a blind drive, the last 30 yards are slightly downhill to a sloped green with a saving bunker behind. *Observatory*, the 330-yard 9th, is a downhill dogleg right with OB on the inside of the turn. The second shot goes up to a green protected by one fore-bunker on the right. As you play the green the Royal Observatory rises impressively above you. Next is *Braw View*, a dramatically downhill 354 yards with two fairway traps on the left and a stone wall on the right. Two more traps defend the smallish green. Fifteen, *The Dams*, is an exciting 167-yard long drop to a green with two bunkers left and one right. A burn crosses in front of the green. Depending upon the wind, take one club less than you think. The same burn as on 15 runs along the left side of *Westward Ho* (a popular hole name), the 399-yard par 4 sixteenth. It's a demanding hole with a tee shot over the burn and a large hill to the right. Try to find the narrow fairway to have a chance to safely reach the green guarded by six bunkers. On the downhill 18th I had a second shot of about 80 yards down a moderate slope to the pin. Since the grass was well mown I decided to try to putt and ended up about ten feet left of the hole. Definitely the longest putt I've ever tried. Craigmillar Park GC is a player's course; challenging in the wind, but still interesting in the calm.

COMMENTS FROM THE FORWARD TEES: This is a hilly parkland course on the edge of Edinburgh with great views of the city, Firth of Tay, and surrounding hills. The course is long at 5312 yards with a par of 72. Uphill and blind shots added to the challenge for me. The par 5s are all under 400 and the par 3 seventh is 193 yards, but from the elevated tee it is doable, just beware of the surrounding bunkers. Eleven and 15, both par 3s, are much shorter but require a pitch between trees and over bunkers. The 15th was easier than it looked. The hills could be an issue for some, but I liked this course and wouldn't let the hills keep me away.

THE GLEN GOLF COURSE
East Links Tantallon Terrace, North Berwick, EH39 4LE
01620-892221   www.glengolfclub.co.uk
Headland links, 6082 yard, par 70, £45

AMENITIES: Pleasant clubhouse has a lounge upstairs with views out to the sea and the course. The lounge has a well deserved reputation for good meals served usual hours. Top notch golf shop is very complete and well staffed.

COURSE COMMENTS: Golf was played here earlier than the more well known North Berwick West course, as early as the 17th Century. It wasn't until 1894 that what we know as the Glen course was built. Ben Sayers and James Braid worked on the extension to 18 holes in 1906. The current course plays over a headland and along the sea, a real combination inland and links course. The Glen offers not only exciting golf, but some of the finest views you'll find from any course. A recent (2008) commercial shows a golfer driving the Scottish countryside in search of just the perfect venue. He ends up at The Glen, and tees off in the driving rain across an expanse of ocean to a small green with a broad smile on his face. What most Americans wouldn't realize is that he is teeing up from the right edge of the 14th fairway and hitting back to the 13th green. It worked for the camera, but it's not a real golf shot. Anne, who has a photographic memory for every golf hole she's ever played, recognized it as wrong right away. Hollywood's artistic license should take nothing away from the Glen, a wonderful course which doesn't get the accolades it deserves.

The challenges are many at The Glen, including the always important coastal zephyrs. A mix of 68 fairway and greenside bunkers will test your accuracy. Many are steep-sided and all are to be avoided. The greens are moderate sized, but topography makes them seem smaller. A couple are flat, but most have significant undulations or tiers. Putts tend to roll toward the sea (or maybe that's where my eye continually wandered). Elevation changes and sidehill lies will add difficulty to The Glen. The one other hazard on the course is the distractingly beautiful views of the sea, Bass Rock (home to 70,000 gannets), 14th Century Tantallon Castle, North Berwick Law (hill), and the village of North Berwick. On a good day, the course has the most beautiful views of any course we've ever played.

The Glen GC has no weak holes and many great ones. The first is an interesting challenge. Your first shot is to a broad landing area and your second must climb 70 yards to find the almost hidden green. It's not a great hole, but it's a fun way to get up to the headland where you play the rest of the course. Getting down is even more fun, but more about that later. The 3rd, *Wantin Wa's*, is a 375-yard par 4 which doglegs left from a raised tee around a small copse of trees on the inside to a blind landing area. Two bunkers guard the narrow tiered green. *Harelaw* is the 531-yard par 5 sixth. With OB all along the right and bunkers left and right within range, the hole has a tough start. Two more bunkers complicate the approach to a very swaled green with a deep pot bunker on the right. The 9th, *Quarrel Sands*, is one of The Glen's impressive par 3s. This long, 207-yard, downhill one-shotter plays to a heart-shaped green guarded by two traps with the sea behind. The green, like many others on the course, tilts towards the sea. Dramatic! On the 348-yard 11th, *Craiglieth*, aim your drive between the first two of the three cross bunkers to have an easy shot to the green. Be careful of the valley just in front of the flat green. The Glen has an unusual signature hole, a par 3 where you can't see the green from the tee. Your blind tee shot on *Sea Hole* must go over a small hill, drop down a steep cliff, to find the green. Short of the green, the rough-covered landing area slopes right towards the green which drops off to the sea on that side. It's a hole you'll want to play repeatedly. The group who were three holes in front of us most of the time did just that until we caught up. The number one stroke index hole at the Glen is the 370-yard par 4 fourteenth called *Leithies*. It starts with a drive up as steep a cliff as you came down on 13. The blind shot has OB right and rough left. Mounds in front of the green make the approach blind as well. It deserves its rating as a testing hole. Now to get down off the headland we come to the 18th, *Jacob's Ladder*, a 365-yard par 4. Drive off the edge of a cliff to a wide fairway below (about 70 yards down) with bunkers in range and OB right. The green is protected by three forebunkers and three more greenside. Not difficult, but certainly fun! After playing The Glen GC you'll know why *Golf Monthly* said of the course: "This is a delightful links course, which enjoys panoramic views and a spectacular round of golf. It is one of the most underrated and best value courses in Scottish golf."

COMMENTS FROM THE FORWARD TEES: Unbelievable views from every hole characterize The Glen GC in North Berwick. The views are so good that it's really hard to concentrate on the golf. The golf is challenging because the course is longer than most at 5809 yards with a par of 73. There are some slopes and hill shots that make you think. Shot placement is important because of the numerous bunkers. There are only two par 3s, but both a doable. Two of the three par 5s are over 430 yards. The steeply uphill first is definitely the hardest hole for ladies. The assistant pro spent time telling me the best way to walk up number one (the right side is less steep). He also told me, with a wink and soft enough that Bob couldn't hear, that the greens all slope to the sea. After playing in the wet and wind in Wales, it didn't hurt that our day at The Glen was absolutely perfect weather.

HARBURN GOLF COURSE
Harburn, West Calder, West Lothian EH55 8RS
01506-971582   www.harburngolfclub.co.uk
Parkland, 5921 yards, par 70, £30

AMENITIES: The comfortable clubhouse was re-designed in 1961 and serves some great sandwiches. The club also has a small, but well supplied golf shop.

COURSE COMMENTS: The history of the Harburn GC is much like the history of many small village courses. The club began in 1885 as the West Calder and Addiewell GC. Play continued on the grounds of the club until 1928 when the club lost its lease on the property. Before play was discontinued at the West Calder club, a new course was put into play as the Hardale GC. A clubhouse was built in 1927, but the club's plans proved too ambitious and the club folded. Like a phoenix, though, the Harburn GC grew out of the ashes and took over the course in 1932. Eventually the West Calder and Addiewell club folded and the members migrated to Harburn, strengthening the club. In 1967, the club was able to buy the course and clubhouse land, and since has worked hard to upgrade and modernize the 1932 design.

The course you play at Harburn has the charm of an early village course, and even though relatively short, still is a demanding track ready to test all your skills. Built 870 feet above sea level, Harburn presents superb views in all directions and is susceptible to the vagaries of the Scottish winds. Thirty-one mostly greenside bunkers will challenge your approach game, but most are very playable. Water spells trouble on five holes, most particularly on the 10th with a pond 50 yards from the green. Greens at Harburn come in a full range of sizes, and all are quick and well-conditioned. Your putting stroke will be tested with significant slopes and subtle borrows. Copses of trees make staying in the fairway important at Harburn. The club is very accommodating to visitors on any day, but try to avoid Wednesday. On Wednesday there is a medal (competition) started by local shop keepers who closed down on Wednesday afternoons and played golf. Shops stay open now, but plenty of locals get away to the medal.

The members we met on the course and in the clubhouse were eager to show off their fine course to a couple of American duffers. We paired up with local member John Flockhart who gave us great suggestions for how to play the course. We didn't find any bad holes at Harburn (such a joy after playing Dullatur the day before [see Chapter 7]), and found many to highlight. The 2nd, a 385-yard par 4, doglegs right up and over a hill. Stay to the left of the marker post because the fairway slopes right towards the trees. The green isn't guarded by any bunkers, but tilts left to right. On *Faulds*, the 334-yard 6th, you drive from a low tee box to a very undulating fairway. The second shot to a two-tiered, well bunkered green is blind. A tough short hole. The tee box at *Torheaving*, the 364-yard 7th, is the highest point on the course. From it you can see the Five Sisters Bing (mine heaps or tailings) in the distance. Aim right because the fairway slopes left. The two-tiered green is protected by two deep bunkers. On the back we especially liked the 10th, *Ca' Canny*. It's a strong 364-yard par 4 dogleg left with OB on both sides. The green is fronted by a pond unusually placed higher than the green. Two traps flank the small green which sloped back to front. *Bog Burn*, the 13th, is a testing 201-yard one-shotter with rough-filled hollows between tee and green and the burn and OB on the left. It's easy to be stuck playing three off the tee. The green is severely swaled. The signature hole at Harburn GC, the 127-yard 15th, is a short tee shot through a gap in the trees to a long, narrow green protected by a deep burn in front, a stand of trees right, and a drop-off left. Demanding shot and good fun! Another interesting short hole is *The Gully*, the 315-yard 16th. A significant carry first shot down a narrow gap opens at the hole. A steep bank on the right and a steep drop on the left protect the fairway. The green has one bunker front right and is one of the flattest on the course. We completely agree with one golfer's course description that Harburn GC is "a delightful walk in meadow and woods." A true undiscovered gem.

COMMENTS FROM THE FORWARD TEES: Harburn GC sits peacefully in the heart of pleasant farmland. The lovely course has visually attractive holes which are quite different from the other holes. Besides the views from the higher points west and north across the Forth Valley to the mountains, the course is beautiful with an interesting variety of trees and wildflowers. Ladies' tees are set fairly and gave good advantage on the par 5s without taking away the challenges. Par 3s, too, are reasonable in length with plenty of challenge. I think this is a great course for ladies.

LUFFNESS NEW GOLF COURSE
The Clubhouse, Aberlady, East Lothian EH32 0QA
01620-843114   www.luffnessgolf.com
Links, 5958 yards, par 70, £80

AMENITIES: Luffness New clubhouse is a gentleman's club which requires coat and tie to enter. The lounge serves snacks on Monday and full meals other days, reputed to be high quality. The steward says the gin and tonics are to die for. No golf shop, but a few essentials are available at the bar where you check in from the side door, unless you are in coat and tie and can go in the main entrance.

COURSE COMMENTS: An Open Qualifying course when the Open is around the corner at Muirfield, Luffness New was originally laid out by Old Tom Morris in 1894. As a private club which accepts visitors, the course is relatively quiet compared to the Gullane courses next door. While the club is formal and stuffy and the members seem to believe they have priority over fee payers, the course itself is a top quality flat track played over old linksland. When we played, a group of five older members hurried to be sure they got out in front of the American and a woman. To their credit I'll admit that they were so fast that the two of us could barely keep up with the five of them. It's also not a bad place to pick if the weather is iffy. It is said that "the sky may weep over Edinburgh, but it smiles over Luffness." As a venerable championship course, Luffness New is a demanding course. The rough off the first cut can be knee or waist deep; hard to find your ball, let alone hit out of it. Almost 100 bunkers, most steep-sided and penal, keep you thinking. Often the bunkers come in sets or nests. Small burns flank a couple of holes, but they are only a concern if you are well off-line. The greens are small to moderate sized and have a well deserved reputation for being top quality. When we played they were very fast and most have interesting borrows, some subtle and some dramatic. One problem for us was that Luffness New has no ladies' tees. Anne was told to just hit off the front of the men's tee, which meant she played an extremely long course and with no ladies' par. Even without consideration for woman players, she did like the course [see Comments from the Forward Tees]. For relief, one can run to the loo between the 4th and 5th or wait and use the bushes at the 6th tee.

The testing golf at Luffness starts with the first, *Luffness Mill*, 306 yards from the members' tee (the only tee visitors are allowed to use). The first shot is fairly tight with bunkers on the right and heavy rough on both sides. Your second shot is considered by many to be the hardest shot on the course. While not warmed up, you must clear five bunkers to find a small target with several tricky slopes. It's a tough start to any round. On the 5th, *Milestone*, a 341-yard par 4, you tee over a slight rise to a fairway with traps on each side. Three more traps protect the green. The last 100 yards to the green finds numerous bumps and hollows which will affect your approach. A downhill dogleg right, the 378-yard 8th, has a small section of burn on the right. With wind behind and links rolls even a moderate hitter might be concerned with two fairway bunkers left at about 300 yards. The right to left sloping putting surface has two bunkers right and one left for protection. On the back we liked the 378-yard par 4 twelfth. The hole starts with a slightly downhill tee shot to a fairway dotted with five bunkers starting about 200 yards from the tee. Three more bunkers cross the fairway about 50 yards from the green which has a distinct ridge across the middle. The 14th, *Aberlady* (the hole looks straight toward the village), is a 495-yard par 5. The first shot is a fun downhill tee shot to a dogleg right around a bunker. Two more bunkers try to catch second shots and the green has yet two more bunkers on the sides. *Warren* is the simple 140-yard 16th where all you have to do is avoid the six bunkers around the front of the green! The wind or lack of it will severely complicate your club selection. The next hole is another bunker puzzle. *Plantation*, a par 4 of 342 yards, is a slight dogleg right with three bunkers in the landing area. A nest of three bunkers crosses the fairway about 60 yards in front of one of the course's larger greens. If you want to experience the old Scottish attitudes toward golf, Luffness is a good venue. If you want to play a challenging, easy to walk links course, and can ignore the stuffy nature of the club, Luffness New is a good choice.

COMMENTS FROM THE FORWARD TEES: This is a great links course, but it's not very lady friendly. Ladies must enter the clubhouse from an unmarked side door, if the steward has seen you and knows a lady is about. You enter into a small entry with two doors; one door leads to the women's toilet and a small area with a bench which acts as the ladies' changing room, and the other to the mixed lounge. The course has no ladies' tees. Women just tee off from the member's markers or from any area at the front of the teebox. The card offers no ladies' handicapping or par. If you want to play a fun links course, and don't care about score or amenities, you'll enjoy Luffness New.

THE MUSSELBURGH GOLF COURSE
Monktonhall, Musselburgh, East Lothian EH21 6SA
01316-652005   www.themusselburghgolfclub.com
Parkland, 6725 yards, par 71, £45

AMENITIES: The superbly located clubhouse, with views down the first and coming up the 18th, has a dining area and two well-stocked bars. Bar meals are served the usual hours and the lounge is open from 8:00 AM to 11:30 PM. A separate, very complete golf shop is beside the clubhouse.

COURSE COMMENTS: The course, except for changes to 1 and 18, is much like it was laid out in 1938 and is considered a James Braid masterpiece. The course is a championship layout and is used often as an Open Qualifying venue. As expected, Musselburgh is a challenging course from the back, but I found it enjoyably challenging from the members' tees at 6241 yards. Eighty-four typical Braid bunkers, many deep and steep-sided, are scattered throughout the course. A burn crosses four holes, but is only a concern on the 9th. The moderate sized greens are quick and tricky, with most sloped or tiered. The condition of the greens was excellent and putting at Musselburgh was fun. Most of the fairways are generous, but tough rough and trees beyond the first cut make staying in the fairway a priority.

True to its championship caliber, there aren't any weak holes at Musselburgh. We did, though, highlight several in our notes. The par 3s at Musselburgh range from 147 yards (3rd) to 187 yards (11th), but all have Braid bunkering in common. Three is the least number of bunkers (on 3 and 16), while 6 and 11 each have six bunkers. Eleven and 16 have the narrowest of openings to the putting surface, and the others have virtually no opening. All four are challenging and fun to play. Bogeys feel like pars and pars feel like birdies. The 7th, *Tunnel,* is a 479-yard par 5 which plays as a 441-yard par 4 from the members' tee. The hole is a dogleg left up a small rise with three bunkers on the right side and trees on the left. A large cross bunker in the center of the fairway a little more than 100 yards out from the green can cause concern, as well as the two bunkers on the right and one on the left of the green with a bit of slope at the front. On the 9th, *Burn,* a 408-yarder, drive to a wide fairway which drops off toward the burn at about 270 yards. The burn is in play for long hitters on the drive because of the slope. Past the water the fairway rises to the two-tiered green surrounded on three sides by heavy forest and fronted by three bunkers. A lovely hole. At *Monkton*, the 445-yard par 4 tenth, you turn around and drive over the same burn as on the 9th (it shouldn't really be in play) to a dogleg left with trees on each side. A large crossing trap about 80 yards from the green may bother second shots. Again the green is protected by several traps. The green is mostly flat past the false front. *Firs*, the 12th, is brutal from the members' tee (463-yard par 4), but easier from the medal (488-yard par 5). One bunker off the fairway right will catch wayward drives, and one on the left about 79 yards from the green is a problem for short hitters. The well protected green is quite sloped. The finishing hole, *Old Bob* (there's got to be a story there), is a 474-yard par 4. This long uphill finish usually plays into the wind. One bunker on the right will grab some drives, but length and the hill are the big problems. Once you get up to the green with the usual two bunkers right and one left, the putting surface is steeply sloped back to front. Musselburgh GC is champion's challenge, and a beautiful forest walk with nice village views. The course should be on everyone's playing agenda.

COMMENTS FROM THE FORWARD TEES: Musselburgh at 5680 yards is a long course for ladies, but since it's relatively flat, it's an easy walk. The back nine proved more difficult for me as it seemed to require more accurate ball placement and had more trouble from trees, bunkers, and water. The forward tees were well placed to keep the length reasonable while still providing challenge even though the par is 75. The 3s are fairly short, but demanding with the 11th being the toughest. The course has seven par 5s with the 4th being the longest (442 yards) and the most difficult (#1 handicap hole for ladies). My favorite though was the 11th, a 168-yard hole called *Braid's Best*. Since I can't carry the 168 yards to the green, a layup and chip shot became my best option. Overcoming the visual and physical demands of the hole is fun. At Musselburgh they've done a good job making an Open qualifying venue enjoyable for women golfers.

RATHO PARK GOLF COURSE
Ratho, Newbridge, Midlothian EH28 8NX
01313-331406 www.rathoparkgolfclub.co.uk
Parkland, 5960 yards, par 69, £33

AMENITIES: A beautiful 1880s manor house has been converted to one of the loveliest clubhouses in Scotland. The main floor lounge (available for members and visitors) is elegant and serves food most usual hours. The club also boasts a fully equipped golf shop.

COURSE COMMENTS: In 1928 famed Scottish architect James Braid designed Ratho Park GC, what today can only be described as a classy golf course. Ratho Park is a lovely parkland track, lined with Scottish pines, beeches, and poplars. The 78 fairway and greenside bunkers add to the tree trouble as most are seriously in play, but none are too penal. The small burn which runs down the left of the 7th and a pond on 15 constitute the sum of the water on the course. Greens are mostly moderate, but a few are rather large. All have subtle slopes and a few are severely tilted--never give a downhill putt on those holes. Greens are speedy, even in the wet conditions in which we played. Trees, bunkers, and quick greens are the crux of the course. There is always airport noise in the background, but the locals don't even notice it and the course isn't in any flight path.

Ratho Park GC is a lovely tree-lined track with interesting holes. The 6th, *Criss Cross*, is a testing 389-yard par 4 slight dogleg left around a series of three fairway traps. The approach to the moderate green is slightly down and the green is surrounded with three more traps. An additional forebunker on the right complicates an already tricky approach. Next comes *The Lodge*, a par 4 of about the same length. This one begins with a tight drive down a narrow fairway between two tall trees. The second shot is made more difficult by trees left and right, the road, and a large forebunker. The green, with bunkers on the side, has two distinct levels. Twelve and 13 are enjoyable back-to-back par 3s. *Seven Sisters*, the 170-yard 12th, is a straight forward shot to one of the smallest greens on the course. Traps on each side and a large forebunker mean your tee shot needs to be precise. The trees here are particularly lovely. Then comes *Roondel* at 164 yards. Facing in the opposite direction to the 12th, this marginally shorter shot is complicated by four bunkers surrounding the small green. The strength and direction of the wind make these two holes particularly interesting. *Braid's Test* is the 463-yard 14th which is played as a par 4, but should be a par 5. A large Scots pine in the middle of the narrow fairway is 270 yards out from the tee. The best approach to the green is from the right side of that tree as the second half of the fairway slopes to the right. The three bunkers around the green are not as much concern as being above the hole on the two-tiered green. *The Terrace*, a hard to drive 360-yard par 4, ends the round. Trees on the left of this dogleg left block all but the biggest hitters. A trap on the right the same distance as the trees makes for a small landing area. It's best to come into the green from the left side of the fairway since a large tree encroaches on the right. Three bunkers front the large two-tiered green. Ratho Park GC is a little hard to find, but the beautiful clubhouse, lovely trees, and Braid designed course make it worth your effort.

COMMENTS FROM THE FORWARD TEES: Ratho Park is an interesting parkland course on an old estate. Be sure to visit the castle clubhouse and enjoy all the trees as you navigate the course. The course is basically flat, but a few mounds and small hills do add challenge. Our local hosts said that the back to back par 3s, 12 and 13, are often score breakers because of the surrounding bunkers. We had a delightful time on this course. It is a pleasant place to enjoy a round.

Courses in this region listed in *Golf in Scotland: The Hidden Gems***:** Berwick-upon-Tweed (England), Dunbar, Glencorse (Penicuik), Hawick, Innerleithen, Kilspindie (Aberlady), Minto, Niddry Castle (Winchburgh), North Berwick West Links, Peebles, St Boswell, Torwoodlee (Galashiels), West Linton.

PUBS, TEAROOMS & RESTAURANTS

North Berwick seems to be one of the best places to eat in Scotland. At least we've found several good restaurants in the village. The best though is Osteria, but if you can't book in there, try Bass Rock Bistro as a quality alternative.

The 4 Mary's Pub in Linlithgow across the street from the Palace. Named for the four Marys who were attendants to Mary Queen of Scots, the pub serves good quality pub grub and especially nice soups.

Bass Rock Bistro (restaurant) just off the main shopping street in North Berwick. Upscale restaurant menu at fair prices in a lovely setting. Always a good stop.

Bella Italia (restaurant) on the main street in North Berwick. Good Italian menu and the food was well prepared.

Beancross Hotel Restaurants (family restaurant) just off the M9 near Falkirk. Highly recommended by a local B&B. Three eating areas, from fancy to more family oriented. Food was good quality off a broad menu. Look for the special writing on the walls.

The Brasserie at the Townhouse Hotel on the main square in Melrose. Known for excellent food (not pub fare), this classy restaurant is a good choice when in the area--busy, be sure to book ahead.

Corner House Hotel (pub) on the main street through Innerleithen near Peebles. A typical hotel pub, but special to us as the first pub we ate in in Scotland. Food was good for pub fare and the locals we super friendly.

Crown Hotel (pub/restaurant) on the High Street in Peebles. Several dining areas including a conservatory. Good quality pub food off a broad menu.

Deacon Brodie's Tavern on the Royal Mile in Edinburgh not far down from the Castle. Famously celebrating the notorious Deacon Brodie who was the real-life model for Stevenson's *Jekyll and Hyde*. The pub serves decent food, but is best for a relaxing drink while shopping on the Royal Mile. Stop for a brew and the history.

Golden Arms (pub) in the village of West Linton just a little ways from the golf course. Lovely old pub with over-stuffed chairs and a piano in the corner with a sign which says, "Play Me." Pub food was decent and the dogs were very friendly.

The Grange (restaurant) on the main street of North Berwick. Food was good, but the local art on the walls wasn't the best. Okay, but there are better choices in town.

Horseshoe Inn (bistro/restaurant) in Eddleston By Peebles. Award winning restaurant and bistro in a small village. Both the bistro/bar and fine dining restaurant have interesting menus and dear prices. Food is top quality. Great for a special night out.

Kailzie Garden Restaurant (tearoom) about four miles out of Peebles on the road to Traquair House. Serves snacks, lunches, and special Saturday evening dinners. Rustic decor and great food, including special "Smorrebrod" (open-face sandwich originating in Denmark). We had one of the best soups we've ever had here.

Monte Cassino Restaurante Italiano up the hill from the town square in Melrose. Top quality Italian for excellent prices means the restaurant will be busy and noisy-- still, well worth it.

Mussel Inn on Rose Street in the shopping area behind Princes Street in Edinburgh (also in Glasgow). Top fresh local seafood at affordable prices. Large portions. We always stop before heading home.

Neidpath Inn (pub) on the main road through Peebles on the west end of town. Neidpath, named after the local castle, has been a drinking pub for a long time and only recently added dining. We were there soon after they opened for dinners and the food was good and reasonably priced. Our second visit a couple of years later was even better.

Park Hotel Bar in Peebles on the east end of the High Street shopping district. The Park Hotel has a fancy restaurant with fancy prices. The bar has a good menu and better prices.

Old Aberlady Inn (pub) on the main coastal road through Aberlady. An historic golfer's pub with a good menu and tasty food. A good place to stop in the area.

The Old Clubhouse Bar and Restaurant just off the main square in the village of Gullane. Golfer's pub with interesting memorabilia and history (in 1890 it was the original Gullane Golf Club clubhouse). Upscale pub menu, good food, and all the golf conversation you want.

Osteria (restaurant) on the main street of North Berwick. Italian fine dining by a renowned chef. The food is not cheap, but worth every pence. Reservations are a must.

Ship Inn (pub) just down from the abbey in Melrose. The only public house in Melrose, the Ship Inn serves quality homemade pub food.

Traquair Arms Hotel (pub/restaurant) on the main road through the village of Innerleithen. Specializing in upscale pub and unusual Italian fare, Traquair Arms is always a good bet.

Wheelhouse Restaurant (tourist restaurant) at the famous Falkirk Wheel. One of the premier attractions in Scotland, the engineering marvel Falkirk Wheel attracts plenty of visitors. The large Wheelhouse Restaurant is a good place to eat after a visit. The extensive menu isn't overpriced considering it's at a major tourist attraction.

LODGINGS

Allerton House
Oxnam Road, Jedburgh TD8 6QQ
01835-869633 www.allertonhouse.co.uk £95
A Four Star B&B just five minutes walk from town centre, Allerton House has won several "Best Breakfast" awards. Beautiful rooms and great hosts, Christopher and Carol Longden, make a stay at Allerton pleasurable.

Braidwood B&B
Buccleuch Street, Melrose TD6 9LD
01896-822488 www.braidwoodmelrose.co.uk £65
In the heart of the village literally across the road from Melrose Abbey, Braidwood is in an excellent location for a visit to the town. Five minutes to the best restaurants and well appointed rooms make it a good place to stay.

Eildon B&B
109 Newbigging, Musselburgh EH21 7AS
01316-653981 www.stayinscotland.net £80
Georgian townhouse built in 1802 and restored in 1993. Pleasant well-appointed rooms.

Fiorlin B&B
Abbey Street, Melrose TD6 9PX
01896-822984 www.melrosebedandbreakfast.co.uk £64
Close to town center this 200 year old converted parish school is a well-located for exploring the Borders region.

The Glebe House
Law Road, North Berwick EH39 4PL
01620-892608 www.glebehouse-nb.co.uk £100
The Glebe House is a listed Georgian Manse built in 1780 and now converted to a fine guest house. Convenient to town and golf.

Glede Knowe Guest House
16 St Ronan's Terrace, Innerleithen EH44 6RB
01896-831295 www.gledeknowe.co.uk £80
Pleasant modern B&B with nice rooms and good views. Hosts Bill and Alison Mason will make your stay enjoyable. A favorite of bicyclists and convenient to the village.

Glentruim B&B
53 Dirleton Ave., North Berwick EH39 4BL
01620-890064 www.glentruim.co.uk £90
Traditional 1895 sandstone design within easy walking distance to shopping, restaurants, and golf. Serves nice breakfasts as well.

Lindores Guest House
60 Old Town, Peebles EH45 8JE
01721-7220272 www.lindorespeebles.co.uk £ reasonable
Janice and Nigel Henderson have reopened Lindores House as a B&B, and we are so glad. The B&B, when run by Carl and Kathryn Lane before they retired, was one of our favorite stays. The historic house, a former home and surgery built in 1895 by Dr. Clement Gunn, has a great location on the main road through the fine features of Lindores.

Neidpath Inn
27-29 Old Town, Peebles EH45 8JF
01721-724306 www.neidpathinn.co.uk £90
The newly refurbished rooms are separated from the bar/restaurant so there is no noise problem as in some inns. Easy walk to town. Excellent breakfast and friendly owners.

St Germains B&B
2 St. Germains House, Longniddry EH32 0PQ
01875-853034 www.st-germains.co.uk £50
Located on four acres of woodlands and gardens, St Germains has a long history including a stint in WW2 as a convalescent home for injured airmen. Dinners served by arrangement.

St Albans B&B
Clouds, Duns, Berwickshire TD11 3BB
01361-883285 www.bnbchoices.com/scotland/borders/st-albans.bnb £70
There has been a house on this site since 1694, although the present structure was built in 1789 and remodeled in 1980. As a listed historic building the Kenworthys haven't been able to add ensuite facilities, but there are two bathrooms and no more than four guests. Rooms are lovingly furnished with period decorations. Breakfast is hearty and can be very entertaining if you ask about the history of Duns. By the way, Clouds Lane doesn't refer to the sky, but to *Clud*, an early Scottish material which was made in the area.

Traquair House
Innerleithen, Peeblesshire EH44 6PW
01896-830323 www.traquair.co.uk £180
Traquair House is one of Scotland's premier lodgings. Imagine staying in the oldest continuously inhabited house in Scotland, where Mary Queen of Scots and her son, James IV, stayed. Obviously, it's not an inexpensive stay, but to stay for one night can give you lifetime of stories. Only three bedrooms are for let, each with antique furnishings, canopied beds, and private (modern) bathrooms. Take your sumptuous breakfast in the Still Room surrounded by cupboards of antique china. During your stay wander through the museum rooms open to the public. Traquair House Brewery (in the wing opposite the lodgings) which was founded in 1965 on the site of an original 18th Century brewery. Traquair House may be a once in a lifetime experience or you may find, as we have, it's a real "do again" stay.

Venlaw Farm B&B
Peebles EH45 8QG
01721-722040 www.venlawfarmpeebles.co.uk £60
The B&B is a modern bungalow working farm on the outskirts of peebles.
Friendly hosts and pleasant accommodations.

The Wing
13 Marine Parade, North Berwick EH39 4LD
01620-893162 www.thewing.co.uk £60
On the beach only about three blocks from the downtown area and only
two blocks from The Glen GC, the Wing is a great place to stay in North
Berwick. The Wing is a portion of a holiday home built in 1861 and was
used in the past as a boy's home. Owners James and Angie Sadison have
turned the Wing into a lovely B&B with an upstairs lounge with views out
to Bass Rock, the North Sea, and across to Fife. The rooms are comfortable
and breakfast in the front parlour is delicious.

TOURIST ATTRACTIONS

Abbeys. Jedburgh, Dryburgh, and Melrose Abbeys are prime
attractions in the Borders area. At Jedburgh take in the great herb
garden; at Dryburgh be sure to see Sir Walter Scott's memorial;
and at Melrose see if you can spot the bagpipe playing pig (you
can by looking up) and the burial place of King Robert the Bruce's
heart.

Abbortsford House, Melrose. The wonderful stone fantasy home of Sir
Walter Scott. Built in 1812, the "Conundrum Castle...this romance
of a house," as Scott called it, was his dream castle. The rooms
open to the public are stuffed with historic antiquities, including a
lock of Admiral Nelson's hair and a comb lost during the battle
of Culloden. One of the best things about touring
Abbotsford is that interior photography is allowed. Outside a
splendid garden completes the experience.

Robert Smail's Printing Works, Innerleithen. This print shop was started
in 1866 by Robert Smail to take care of the printing needs of the
Peebles-Innerleithen-Walkerburn area. Taken over by the National
Trust for Scotland in 1986, the shop is now open for tours of the
office, the composing room, and the printing room. A fascinating
tour and history of small village life.

Rosslyn Chapel, Roslin. Built in 1446, the chapel has been described as a "Tapestry in Stone." Thousands of some of the most impressive stone carvings in Scotland, if not Europe, adorn practically every inch of chapel walls, ceilings, and pillars. Made more famous by Dan Brown's *The Da Vinci Code*, Rosslyn has been linked to the Knights Templar and is home to numerous myths, legends, and ghosts.

Traquair House, near Innerleithen. The oldest inhabited house in Scotland, Traquair has several rooms open for touring including the library with its clever cataloging system. In the Priest's Room, where the family secretly practiced Catholicism when it was banned by Protestant reformers, be sure to see the hidden staircase in the room which allowed the priest to escape if raided. The brewery in one wing provides pleasurable tastings of the local brew.

Dunblane New GC

CHAPTER SEVEN: CENTRAL SCOTLAND

GOLF

In the Central section of Scotland are numerous fine courses we have yet to visit (look for our fourth book to cover some of those), especially those in Glasgow, but what we come away from the central area with is an appreciation for the 9-hole courses. We mean no disrespect to the fine full courses like Cardross, Helensburgh, and Dollar, but it has been the unique Bridge of Allen and Leadhills that have captured our imagination.

ABERFOYLE GOLF COURSE
Braeval, Aberfoyle FK8 3UY
01877-382493 www.aberfoylegolf.com
Heathland/parkland, 5158 yards, par 66, £20

AMENITIES: The comfortable 1973 clubhouse lounge, refurbished in 2003, has a bar and dining area, and serves snacks until 4:30. The full menu is served all days. Tasty food at great prices. It's one of the best places to eat in the village, so we've included it in the pubs section. No golf shop, but a few essentials are available at the bar.

COURSE COMMENTS: The short 5158-yard Aberfoyle GC has no par 5s and six par 3s, but is still an interesting track. The original 9-hole layout was built in 1890 and extended to 18 holes in 1980 by local efforts. Although at one point during the wars only one person used the course in a period of five weeks, today the course can be busy, particularly on weekends, though they say visitors can get on almost anytime. We played after several days of rain and found the course in very good condition because of good drainage. Playing around a large hill, Aberfoyle has some elevation changes, but is not a strenuous walk. The hillside location also means you will have good views to Ben Lomand on one side and Stirling Castle the other way, that is if it's clear. The course is surrounded by picturesque hills and farmlands. The routing at Aberfoyle can be confusing, but the course is well signed. The only sand on the course is in the 13 greenside bunkers. Though a couple are tricky, especially the one on 15, most are easy to play out of. A burn crosses several holes, but has the most effect on 2 and 6. The greens are small to tiny, and seem flat, though most have more slope than you first notice. A few of the greens are gun-turret style with tricky approaches. Especially first time players need to be aware that the course is tight and that several holes cross others--look out for stray shots from other holes. The last danger on the course is the heavy forest which lines many holes--the trees can be unforgiving.

While certainly not a championship course, we enjoyed our round at Aberfoyle and noted several holes particularly starting at the first. *Braeval*, a 318-yard par 4, is a straight forward opening hole with the road (OB) all along the right. The approach to the green is blind as the green is hidden below a ridge about 20 yards beyond the marker pole in the middle of the fairway. Nothing fancy to start, but an interesting placement of the green. The 4th, *Alma*, is the tough 256-yard par 4 signature hole at Aberfoyle. Drive to an uphill fairway with a steep heavy rough-covered slope starting about 25 yards short of the green. The green is a gun-turret green on a narrow shelf below more rough-covered slope. Should be an easy first and a short wedge, but slopes, rough, and the tiny putting surface can get in the way of a good score. A blind tee shot with trees left and bushes right begins the 305-yard 7th. Aim for the left of the marker (only 175 yards out), but don't drive much further as the fairway narrows to almost nothing. Your approach needs to thread through trees to a green with a long bunker behind and a burn on the left. Next is *Barrett*, the 158-yard par 3 eighth. The burn crosses close to the tee, but a tree and stone wall on the right complicate the shot to this elevated green. A very picturesque hole.

The inward nine starts with *Roderick*, a short 123-yard par 3, but don't think short means easy. The hole plays narrow between a stone wall on the left and a burn and trees on the right. One deep bunker covers the right half entrance to the green. A pin placed on the right side of the putting surface will be blocked by trees and fronted by the bunker--when you play, that's where the flag will be. A fascinating double dogleg (left then right) hole is the 326-yard 15th which begins with a blind tee shot. Aim at the marker pole and stay to the left because your ball will slide right. If you drive too close to the green perched on a knoll, your second shot will be blind as well. One trap on the right guards that side. *Crombie's Walk*, the 352-yard 17th, starts with a blind tee shot across the 9th fairway and up towards a narrow gap between a copse and a rough-covered hill. Two hundred and twenty yards puts you in good position for your next choice of shots. If you know where you're going, hit across the hill over the marker pole to a green with bunkers on each side. A prudent play your first time around is to lay up through the gap and have a short shot to a green where you can see the trouble. The last is downhill 368 yards to the green. Tee shot is between two stands of trees and the approach is to a small green fronted by mounds and two small bunkers. A fun drive, but a tough second shot ends your round.

Aberfoyle GC was a surprise to us. We hadn't heard much about it and it didn't look like much when we saw it. As we played the course on a pleasant fall day, we liked it more as we got into our round. Add to the fun golf an outstanding lounge/restaurant and you have an absolutely winning combination.

COMMENTS FROM THE FORWARD TEES: Aberfoyle GC isn't an easy walk, but it is good exercise. The hills are short, except for the 14th. Accuracy and strategy (aka, a willingness to layup) are important on this short (4380 yards, par 67), tricky course. The par 3s, three per side, are not easy. Two in particular caused me the most problems. The 10th is only 101 yards to the front of the green, but it's surrounded by trees and a wee burn runs along the right side. The 12th is quite elevated and required two extra clubs than the length of 108 yards implies. Hitting out of the rough on the steep side of the green wasn't a pleasure. The only par 5 at Aberfoyle, the 361-yard 14th, has at least two blind shots and can easily take 5 or 6 to finish. This course is fun and filled with one fair challenge after another.

BALFRON GOLFING SOCIETY (BALFRON GC), The Shian Golf Club

Kepulloch Road, Balfron, Sterlingshire G63 D52
07814-827620   www.balfrongolfsociety.org.uk
Moorland, 5957 yards, par 72, £20

AMENITIES: The club hosts a small clubhouse with changing rooms and a small visitor's area where soda, snacks, and coffee/tea are available. No golf shop. Honesty box for when nobody is around.

COURSE COMMENTS: Half way between the castle city of Stirling and Loch Lomand, Balfron GC is an entertaining 2001 moorland/ parkland course worthy of a visit. A course was here much earlier, but like many others was lost to agricultural needs during World War Two. Locals don't know much about that old course, but some early trophies were found recently in the attic of the local bank. The current Balfron opened as a 9-hole course in 1993, but was expanded to 18 less than ten years later. Balfron certainly didn't feel that new when we played--it has a very natural feel to it.

Not a championship track, Balfron is nonetheless a pleasant challenge with plenty of blind shots (drives and approaches), elevation changes (though not a difficult walk), and water in play on 13 holes. On some holes the water isn't the major concern it is on the 15th. Most holes have greenside bunkers, but most are avoidable as well. Thirteen is the exception with six bunkers fronting the green. You won't find many flat putts on Balfron's undulating small to medium sized quick greens. While Balfron offers plenty of challenge, especially on the short par 4s, its windy hilltop site affords fantastic vistas of the Trossachs and Ben Lawers as well as the picturesque farmland which surrounds the course. Beside the 13th green is a marker which gives a 360° notation of all the mountains visible on a clear day.

Many memorable holes make up the Balfron course and we took note of several. Three, *Fairwinds*, a par 4 of 354 yards, starts with a usually downwind drive over a burn to a wide landing area. The second shot must stay left over (around or through) a copse of trees to an elevated green with one side bunker. Take advantage of your putt here because the green is one of the flattest on the course. The 8th, *Ballikinrain*, is a 337-yard par 4 with a blind drive toward an aiming post. Your next shot should be directly over the post (ignore the illusion of a tree just past the post). A well struck ball will roll between widely spaced trees and down to a green which is quite sloped. *Stronend* is the 498-yard par 5 ninth. It's a good driving hole with sufficient room to the right on a fairway which bends left. Your second shot is over a grass dyke and between mature trees. The elevated green with bunkers on both sides is again relatively flat. *Kepulloch Muir*, the 325-yard par 4 thirteenth tees off uphill to an angled fairway with sufficient room to the right. The approach shot needs to carry or avoid the six fronting bunkers. The best views on the course are from this green. The 14th is a tough one-shotter when the wind blows against you (and it always will). The green, 163 yards away, is below the tee with a grass gully and a bothersome tree in between. Behind the green about ten feet is a stone fence, so you can't be long without risking a wild bounce. The green is wide, but not very deep. The 15th, *Drove Road*, is a 520-yard par 5 with an easy drive downhill to a generous fairway. Then the trouble starts. A winding burn runs left beside the fairway for the last 200 yards and the fairway slopes toward the burn. Even big hitters find it too risky to have a go at the green in two. After a fun round at Balfron GC we discovered a good tearoom in town for lunch.

COMMENTS FROM THE FORWARD TEES: At Balfron GC the ladies' tees were fair, but still difficult, especially the 3rd and 5th. Often second shots were blind or through narrow gaps in trees. It is a fun course with interesting holes and fantastic views.

BRIDGE OF ALLAN GOLF COURSE
Sunnylaw, Bridge of Allan FK9 4LY
01786-832332   www.bofagc.co.uk
Parkland 9-hole, 2560 yards, par 33, £15 for 18

AMENITIES: There is no golf shop, but the very comfortable clubhouse lounge serves lunches and snacks weekends. A few trolleys are available, but you are better off carrying on this hilly course.

COURSE COMMENTS: Old Tom Morris chose the Sunnylaw (*law* meaning hill) site in 1895 (a year after designing St Andrews New) and laid out the course. The site is also called "Fairy Knowe." The course is reputed to be the best preserved of Morris's layouts. The length of the holes and the greens are exactly as he designed them; some sand bunkers have been added, but the fences are original. Elevation change is by far the biggest problem to contend with at Bridge of Allan. About half the holes go up, some steeply, and the others go down, sometimes even more steeply. Besides the elevation changes 15 bunkers, mostly greenside, will demand your attention. For the most part though, the bunkers are not too penal. Bridge of Allan will challenge you with numerous blind shots, sometimes more than one on a hole. While there's no water on the course, you'll find the small, sloped greens tricky to putt. It is also easy to get distracted by the dramatic views of mountains, villages, Stirling Castle, and the Wallace Monument.

The venerable, hilly track is well maintained, and all the holes are unique. When I got home from the trip on which we played Bridge of Allan, it was *Dyke*, the 233-yard par 3 first, that I would most describe when people asked about the trip. The demanding uphill hole, now considered one of the toughest par 3s in the world for average golfers and listed as one of Old Tom's "Best 18 Holes," has a five foot tall stone wall about 20 yards in front of the even more raised green guarded by one bunker on the right. Consider a lay-up of about 180 yards and a pitch to the green, but don't chunk the pitch into the stone wall like I did. Anne got her par (4 for ladies) and I limped away with a five. The 2nd, *Fairy Knowe*, is less dramatic, but is still a tough uphill par 4. Near the green is a cone shaped mound that is the fairy knowe. Long ago the mound was excavated and ancient remains found and then replaced. The actual purpose of the mound is still a mystery. It's no mystery that the 4th, the 314-yard par 4 called *Cage*, will be a challenge. The hole starts with a blind drive over a crest and then down. The second shot must clear a stone fence, one of Morris's favored natural hazards, to find the green backed by a bunker and OB. This hole is followed by one of the most dramatic par 3s you will ever come across. *Hollow*, the 208-yard par 3 fifth, is a drop of 150 feet to a green surrounded on three sides by trees and one trap on the right. Stay straight and your ball has a chance to roll down to the green off a slope lightly covered with rough. On the fly a ball will stick on the green even though it looks as if it would bound off. I hit a good five-iron, my 160-yard club, and was just off the green to the right. Two holes later is another spectacular downhill tee shot at *Oaks*, the 289-yard par 4 seventh. The drive over the oaks has become more menacing in the last 100 years as the trees have grown, but it is still a fair shot for the average handicapper. You can try to drive the green, but there's rough, trees, and bunkers if you're off line. Bridge of Allan GC is not an easy walk in the park, but it is definitely worth the effort to play a true Old Tom Morris gem.

COMMENTS FROM THE FORWARD TEES: This is a very hilly, challenging course, but the views from the top are outstanding and well worth the climb--so too is the golf. If it is possible to rent or borrow an electric trolley, do so on this course. The holes are each unique and the par 3s are exciting and very difficult. I felt good with bogeys. The holes are not long, but have unique challenges like the stone wall in front of the 1st green or the long drop from tee to green on the 5th. My favorite is the 7th which is one of the visually hardest holes I've ever played. From the quite elevated tee you can see the green beyond the trees you have to hit over. The actual landing area for your drive is blind. I managed to find the middle of the fairway, but still had to negotiate the bunkers to reach a tricky to putt green. It's a hole I will enjoy playing again.

CALLANDER GOLF COURSE
Aveland Road, Callander, Perthshire FK17 8EN
01877-330975   www.callandergolfclub.co.uk
Parkland, 5185 yards, par 66, £30

AMENITIES: The original 1907 Callander clubhouse was remodeled in 1980. Snacks and meals are served to golfers and the public most usual hours. The lounge food is popular with locals. The well-stocked golf shop is run by the club.

COURSE COMMENTS: Old Tom Morris and Willie Fernie were responsible for design of the course in 1890. At first Callander was a six-hole course, but in 1892 was expanded to nine holes in the present location. The current holes 2, 3, and 18 are Tom Morris' holes, while number six is pure Willie Fernie. A few years later it was made a full 18. Although short, the course is known for its tough par 3s. Listed as one of the top 30 fun courses to play in Scotland by a Glasgow paper, Callander can be busy. The course is well-maintained with neat artificial turf paths around tees and over areas that tend to be wet. With good drainage, Callander is playable when others might not be. Don't let the short 5185 yards lull you into thinking the course is easy; there are plenty of challenges here. Thirty-seven heavy sand bunkers are in play, most added in the 1920s. Water is in play on several holes as burn crossings, but is only a major concern on a couple. A drainage ditch crosses several holes, but it's not a hazard and is a free drop. For the most part, the greens are on the small side. Most have interesting undulations and none are flat. A few tees, especially the 9th, are quite close to greens. Beware.

We discovered more par 4s attracted our attention than par 3s (there are no par 5s). The 3rd, *Tree*, is a 329-yard dogleg left around the tree with a blind tee shot. Aim at the conservatory room of the clubhouse. The best approach to the relatively large green with one bunker right is from the right-hand side. Enjoy the Tom Morris hole! The 6th, *Dell*, a 372-yard par 4, is probably the most typical of the Willie Fernie holes (he extended the course to 18). It's a straight hole with a tee shot over a burn to an uphill fairway. The hole plays longer than its distance because it goes up. A bunker in the middle about 50 yards out complicates the approach to a raised green protected by two more traps. Next is *Blind*, a 257-yard par 4 from the medal tees and a 228-yard par 3 from the members'. The hole plays as a tough one-shotter up and over a hill to a green protected by four bunkers. From the medal tee there has been a hole-in-one in competition. On the back the 10th is a 181-yard par 3. This uphill one-shotter demands all carry because three bunkers front the small green. Next is B*eeches*, again at 181 yards. It's the same distance as the previous hole, but a completely different shot. Trees running down the left and a burn crossing about 25 yards in front make the green with bunkers on both sides a hard target. A real beauty is the 15th, called *Avenue*. On this lovely 135-yard hole you hit down an "avenue" of mature trees to a small raised green fronted by a bunker with another on the left. The view of Ben Ledi (*Beinn le dia*, the Hill of Gods) framed by the trees adds to the beauty. The hole is so tight that locals say that 13 is as possible as a 3. I felt great with a two-putt par. The 16th, *Baigibbon*, is 365 yards from the medal tees and only 293 from the members'. The burn/pond about 60 yards from the green is reachable, so the prudent play is an iron to the left of the fairway. The green is raised and protected by two fronting bunkers. We put off playing Callander GC for several years because we knew it was short. What we didn't know until we played it was how good the golf is at this short jewel.

COMMENTS FROM THE FORWARD TEES: Callander GC was very wet when we played. It had been raining for 24 hours and we learned later that several local courses were completely closed. Callander was wet, but playable. The course may be shorter than many (4595 yards), but there is more than enough challenge for even the best players. The longest par 3 is the 14th at 201 yards which drops down at about 120 yards and helps shorter hitters. The shortest one-shot hole is the 15th at only 95 yards, but it is called "The Avenue" because it's lined with trees on both sides. There is also a large bunker directly in front of the green. Good luck to you. Callander GC will test your accuracy, but it's a fine test.

CARDROSS GOLF COURSE
Main Road, Cardross, Dumbartonshire G82 5LB
01389-841754 www.cardross.com
Parkland, 6465 yards, par 71, £40

AMENITIES: The clubhouse, last refurbished in 1994, hosts a pleasant lounge which has a main section and a conservatory with bar. Meals are served all day, but clubhouse is not open to the public--only members, guests, and playing visitors. Clubhouse overlooks the 18th green, and the conservatory looks out to the first tee. Club has a well-stocked and staffed golf shop.

COURSE COMMENTS: Willie Fernie designed the first nine at Cardross in 1895, and then James Braid did the extension to 18 in 1921. More recently the course has been updated by Donald Steele. The course affords grand views across the Clyde to Greenock and Gourock, and an old Robert the Bruce castle can be seen off the 13th fairway. In the spring Cardross GC is ablaze with rhoddies and in autumn it's a riot of fall colors. A mix of 78 bunkers, most not too penal, dot the course. The Braid fairway bunkers can cost you a shot, as will landing in either of two large, deep bunkers near the 18th green. The only water in play is a burn crossing on the par 3 fifth. The green configuration is quite interesting. There are six flat greens, six sloped, and six undulating. Most greens have subtle breaks and are well-conditioned and quick. Wind, elevation changes, and tree trouble can all add challenge to Cardross. Several fairways have undulations which are the result of row farming. With good drainage, the course is playable all year, but it will be interesting right from the first.

Hole number one, *Fernie's First*, is a 398-yard par 4. A gentle start to your round begins with a wide fairway though bunkers right and left are in range. Three more fairway bunkers can affect your approach, especially the two in the middle. A narrow green is protected by three more bunkers. There are no fairway bunkers to bother you on the 351-yard 2nd, a downhill two-shotter. Stay to the left as you come into this double green (shared with the 5th) because everything slopes left to right. Two traps on the left and two more on the right add difficulty. Be sure to aim for the correct flag--the one on the right is yours. *Clyde's View*, the 367-yard 7th, offers bunkers, bunkers, and more bunkers. The first two are on the right at about 210 yards. The next three are grouped in the middle between 50 and 80 yards from the sloped green which has two bunkers in front and one behind. As good as the front is, the back had even more attention-getting holes. The 10th, *Kilmahew*, a 458-yard par 4, begins with a blind tee shot-- aim for the left of the marker pole. The last 250 yards are downhill to a narrow green flanked by three traps. Conveniently, toilets are accessible from the 11th and the 14th tees. The front of the largest green, the 163-yard 12th, is protected by three bunkers. There are some devilish pin placements on this putting surface. A unique feature we haven't seen at many other courses were marker posts at the left edge of the 13th fairway to aid golfers in finding balls which end up in the heavy rough. It's an interesting tee shot which begins *Kirkton*, the 404-yard 14th. Draw left or fade right (for a right hander) around a small, tall copse. You could hit straight over to find a slight dogleg left fairway. The approach is then up to the almost gun-turret green with bunkers on each side. *Braid's Bend*, the 16th, is a dramatic 90° dogleg right where big hitters can try to cut the corner over tall trees. The prudent play is about 190 yards just past the marker post. Then it's downhill all the way to the green. There are two bunkers on the left of the fairway and two more around the green. The hole can be a real birdie opportunity. The last, *Douggie's Mounds*, is 470 yards downhill all the way to the green with two very large, deep bunkers at the sides and one more behind. A new tee box is planned which will make the drive even more challenging. You finish directly in front of the clubhouse. Club Captain Ian McLeod and former greenskeeper David Gall were great guides as we made our way around the wonderful, challenging Cardross GC.

COMMENTS FROM THE FORWARD TEES: I very much like this old, developed parkland course, lined with a variety of evergreen and deciduous trees as well as rhoddies on several holes. Cardross GC is long for ladies at 5794 yards with a par of 75, but it is built on a sand base (on the shores of the River Clyde), is dry and has good roll. Many of the holes are quite challenging. For example, on the 2nd the marker pole is 237 yards from the tee, so second shots will still be blind, then downhill with severe slope to the right with a tree at the edge of the fairway. The green is a double green and it has four bunkers around it and almost no greens on this course are really flat. It's a fun hole. The par 3s are all reachable, but accuracy will be important. The par 5s are fun with several having downhill runs. Pars and bogeys are possible. Cardross GC is a course worth traveling to for ladies.

CARNWATH GOLF COURSE
1 Main Street, Carnwath, Lanarkshire ML11 8JX
01555-840251   www.carnwathgc.co.uk
Parkland, 5953 yards, par 70, £25

AMENITIES: Older clubhouse has a comfortable upstairs lounge which serves good pub food (soups, sandwiches). Locals brag about the quality of their lounge staff. No golf shop, but you check in at the starters shack next to the clubhouse which has a few essentials.

COURSE COMMENTS: In the autumn of 2000 on our first visit to Scotland, Anne and I landed at Glasgow and headed to our first stay in Peebles. Because driving a right hand drive car on the left side of the road was a new (and slightly frightening) experience, I pulled over at the first decent sized village I came to. We parked and walked the few blocks of Carnwath village to a picturesque (to us) church. Across from the church was the entrance to a golf course. I stepped in and took a picture of a group teeing off on the first at the first golf course we'd visited in Scotland. Ten trips later we finally got the opportunity to play Carnwath GC; what a shame we'd waited so long. Typical of Scottish village courses, Carnwath began as a 9-hole track laid out on Gallow Hill by Willie Auchterlonie of St Andrews in 1907. The course extended to 18 in 1922, and was redesigned by then club captain, G. M. Clark, in 1963. The small, busy course welcomes visitors Monday, Wednesday, Friday, and Sunday, and is great value golf.

Even though Carnwath is short, it will test your game from the very start with 61 deep, steep-sided greenside and fairway bunkers, several hidden and all in play. A small burn is in play on four holes, but is only a problem on 17 and 18. The greens are small to moderate with the 2nd the smallest at 21 yards deep. Most are flat with only mild slopes, but they were quite quick when we played. While most of the fairways are broad, the rough is wiry and sticky, even when dry. Carnwath is an easy walk, though the course has some elevation changes, including "cardiac hill" on the 8th. It was fun to play with locals David and Margaret who could help guide us when a couple of holes crossed others.

Carnwath GC is bigger and better than your first impression from the clubhouse might lead you to believe. *Roundel*, the 193-yard first which we saw in 2000, is a testing opening hole straight uphill. Five bunkers surround the green, three in front. Following that demanding opening is *The Yett* (meaning "gate"), the longest and toughest of Carnwath's par 3s at 234 yards. It's a long shot with trees left, but that's also the easiest approach if you don't reach in one. Three bunkers gather balls that don't find the small green. The par 3 fourth has a deep gouge down the center leading to a large bunker. The topography was created when an RAF Spitfire crashed during the Second World War. The damage has been left in play. A reasonable hole is the 371-yard 5th called *Railway*, a dogleg left where the fairway also slopes left. Big hitters try to cut close to the corner trees for a short shot in, and shots too far right or long risk OB down the rail line. Second shots will be slightly down to a narrow green with one trap right. Aim for the middle of the green. Finishing the front is *Winterlaw*, a strong 375-yard dogleg right with a burn and OB on the inside, with plenty of room to the left. Stay to the left for the best angle of approach to Carnwath's largest green which has bunkers on each side and trees behind. The 11th, *Tinto* (named for the large hill in the background), at only 270 yards offers a good birdie opportunity without needing your driver. Any hit over the hill in the fairway will leave a short pitch to a small, raised green guarded by three bunkers. Another good straight forward hole is *Gallowhill*, the 321-yard par 4 twelfth. From an elevated tee hit down to a broad fairway with two bunkers on the left and trees on the right. A short approach is all that's left to a raised green with sand front left and behind. The final hole at Carnwath is the only par 5 on the back (there's only one on the front as well). *Moss Burn*, 500 yards from the medal tees (the hole plays as a 450-yard par 4 from the members' tee), has a narrow fairway with Moss burn and OB all along the left and steeply sloped rough on the right. It's a super tough finish if you aren't in the short grass. The green only needs one trap front left for protection. It took us seven years to get back to play Carnwath GC, and it certainly won't be another seven before we get back.

COMMENTS FROM THE FORWARD TEES: Carnwath is a lovely 18-hole course which is not too long for women at 5168 yards and a par of 72. Carnwath offers pleasant views of the surrounding farming area, but also the holes were visually interesting with trees and views as you play around the knock. Two of the par 3s are good successful lengths and the other two are quite long. The par 5s are reasonable length except for 18 which is 449 yards. Each hole on the course was different from all the others which I like.

CROW WOOD GOLF COURSE
Garnkirk House, Cumbernaud Rd., Muirhead, Glasgow   G69 9JF
01417-791943   www.crowwoodgolfclub.co.uk
Parkland, 6168 yards, par 71, £30

AMENITIES: An 18th Century mansion on the Garnkirk Estate was acquired in 1955 and converted into the present clubhouse which has a pleasant bar, lounge and dining room serving from 11 AM. The clubhouse is only open to golfers. A unique feature of the club's lounge is the "spike bar," named The Crows' Nest. Its available to golfers right off the course. The golf shop is small, but well-stocked and the staff is very friendly and efficient.

COURSE COMMENTS: As close to Glasgow as Crow Wood GC is, you couldn't tell it from the course, a fair parkland track. Designed by James Braid in 1925, the course retains much of its original design. We played after the wettest August in Scotland's recent history and the course showed it. It was playable but very wet; try to pick a dry time if you want to play. Sixty-eight bunkers, mostly greenside, add most of the challenge, but none are too penal. Besides the casual water, water can be in play on several holes, but will only affect play on a couple. Greens are moderate in size and because of interesting slopes can be easy to three putt. The course affords interesting views of the Campsie Hill with Ben Lomand in the background. The views are especially good from the 4th and 11th tees. Crow Wood GC is not associated with Crow Wood Hotel which you come to at the 14th tee, but the hotel was the original clubhouse for the course.

A par 3 of 144 yards starts your round at Crow Wood. *Sprot* is an interesting and challenging one-shotter. Begin from the elevated tee near the golf shop and hit down to a green surrounded by four bunkers; one in front, one on each side, and a saving bunker behind to keep you out of a burn and unplayable gunk. One of the best views is from *Campsie View,* the 341-yard par 4 fourth. The hole is downhill and a fairway bunker 250 yards out is in play for even moderate hitters (I hit 275 on this instead of my usual 220 yards). The good sized green is protected by two bunkers in front and two behind. A fun hole. The burn which crosses the fairway on *Barryknowe*, the 369-yard par 4 sixth, should not be a problem for most players. The entrance to the green is tight between two traps and the best approach is from the left. On the back I liked the 10th, *Rookery*, a 280-yard par 4. The hole, one of two short two-shotters, begins with another tee shot over a burn. Three greenside bunkers add some risk to going for the green from the tee. A birdie opportunity even for the prudent. The fairway at *Steybrae*, the 401-yard par 4 eleventh, is narrow and uphill and is hard to find even though there are no bunkers to get in the way. Bunkers 30 yards out and three more around the green will make for a tough approach. On the 16th, *Hunter*, a 328-yard par 4, a 200 yard shot is needed to crest the hill and give extra kick if it's dry (not much roll the day we played), but I still got to within 50 yards of the narrow green protected by five bunkers. While not a destination course, Crow Wood GC could be fun in the dry.

COMMENTS FROM THE FORWARD TEES: The red front nine is only 100 yards less than the men's yellow, while the back red is 133 yards shorter. With a total yardage of 5622 yards, the course has a forward par of 74. The par 3s are reasonable length, but bunkering around 1 and 15 mean you must carry the yardage or lay up. The 18th is the longest par 5 at 495 yards and plays down and then back up. It makes a good challenge at the end. Number 13 is interesting from the forward tees. A good drive in the middle of the fairway means you have a tall oak tree between you and the green. You have to be accurate as you hit right or left around the tree. The approach is to a large elevated green with many slopes. It's an interesting course if you're in the area.

DOLLAR GOLF COURSE
Brewlands House, Dollar, Clackmannanshire FK14 7EA

01259-742400   www.dollargolfclub.com
Hilly moorland, 5242 yards, par 66, £15

AMENITIES: Small clubhouse lounge open to members and players, reputed to have good food. No golf shop.

COURSE COMMENTS: The oldest golf club in Clackmannanshire (the area north of the River Forth, flanked by Stirlingshire on the west and Perthshire on the east) is also one of the least recognized of Scotland's wonderful village golf courses. We've known about a golf course at Dollar since we've been traveling to Scotland, but it took us seven trips before we finally visited the Dollar Golf Club. We are now sorry it took us so long to discover this Ben Sayer track more than a hundred years old.

The Dollar course, located in the heart of the village on the road leading up to Castle Campbell, is an 18-hole course set into the southern end of the Ochill Hills and has several interesting features. Of first note to players is that the hillside, moorland course is devoid of bunkers. When architect Ben Sayer laid out the present course in 1906 (the first nine-hole course began play in 1890), he said that the small plateau greens (often termed "gun-turret" greens because of their resemblance to a ship's gun platform) and the slopes of play would provide enough difficulty for any golfer.

The next feature noticed will be the 2nd, *Brae*, a 97-yard par 3. First time players will probably take note of this hole before they discern the absence of bunkers. The hole is straight up hill! It's only a decent wedge or 9-iron for men to clear the steep 50 foot bank (or *brae*). Not a difficult shot, but one fraught with anxiety. If a shot clears the top of the hill and holds the green or runs a little off the back, par or better should be your score. If, instead, your shot fails to reach the top, the real adventure begins. A ball that hangs up in the rough-covered hillside is a challenge to reach and an even greater challenge to hit. In the dry of summer, a ball failing to reach the green can roll all the way back down past the tee box. Terry Young, retired Club Secretary, told us about one gent, a decent player, who came in from a round saying he'd carded a 15 on number two. When everyone in the clubhouse commiserated with him, he responded, "The worse thing is I didn't hit a bad shot in the bunch!" I didn't ask how he'd scored his 15 for fear it would put evil thoughts in my head when I next play the hole. The day we played, I chipped on from behind the green and two-putted for a respectable bogey. Anne doesn't know how the local women play the hole. She didn't reach the top with her first shot, and because she was playing with a broken toe, chose to just drop at the top instead of fighting the slope on a bad foot. This might be a good time to remember that you are playing Vacation Golf. Especially for women players, this hole reminds me of the fourth at Anstruther on Fife--if you play it enough, you're bound to find the key of how to play. At one time, club discussions were held about redesigning the hole, but the committee decided that the hole is part of the character of the course. What a wise decision. As it is, it's a tough, funky, and fun challenge.

One other feature of the course that Anne and I noticed (and has been mentioned by several others) is the friendly membership. Dollar GC is a private course, but very welcoming to visitors. On the course, members who recognized that we were visitors (in other words, they didn't recognize us) would go out of their way to make sure we were finding our way (not a problem, the course is well signed), and that we were enjoying our round. Several gave us suggestions for where to get a bite after our game. All said the clubhouse food was great, but the day we played was the cook's day off. In the comfortable clubhouse lounge, all the members wanted to know how we liked their course and how we played number two. Indeed, one of the charms of Dollar GC is the friendly membership.

The golf course offers more, though, than friendly members, an intriguing second hole, and a lack of bunkers. The course is short, but has its share of quality challenging golf holes. The 9th, *Castle*, is a 200-yard par 3 that looks much easier than it plays. A long straight shot is needed to reach the small, flat green, but a canyon and trees right act as magnets to draw you into trouble. At the 10th tee you have a chance to view the gloomy Castle Campbell on the hills above the course. Number 14, *Westward Ho*, plays very differently from the medal tees and the member tees. From the member tees (which visitors will play) it's a 186-yard par 3, while the medal or championship tees play the hole as a 302-yard par 4. From either tee the path to the green is not easy. On the right hand side the length of the hole is rough-covered hillside. As a par three the shot to the green is almost all carry. From the medal tee the green may be drivable, but a ball too far right can be easily lost in the tall grass. The hole is a visual delight with a stand of trees behind the green, but a wayward shot can be a score killer. Stunning, short par fours are a staple at Dollar, and 16 and 18 are great examples. *Quarry,* the 296-yard 16th, begins with a blind shot. An aiming post points you in the correct direction even though it seems too far left--trust it. Your second shot will be to an elevated gun-turret green surrounded by a berm. If the pin is in the front, it's tough to get it close, but the hole can be a good birdie opportunity. More difficult is the finishing hole, *Brewers Knowe*, a 282-yard par 4. Your tee shot is to a split fairway with the left fairway sloped to the right and hard to hold. The right side (lower) is flat, but well below the raised green. The high road to the green is more difficult but will make the second shot easier. A fun finish however you play it.

Dollar Golf Club in the heart of Scotland has too much going for it not to be better recognized. It is hilly, but not too strenuous a walk (it does mean the club has no buggies). You face several blind tee shots and a few blind approaches to greens. The course is well conditioned and maintained (with only a grounds crew of two). It has excellent drainage and plays well all year (no winter or temporary greens). Great views abound--the Ochills, Castle Campbell, the village, and on a clear day Stirling Castle and the Wallace Monument. It took us far too long to discover this hidden beauty in Scotland's heartland.

COMMENTS FROM THE FORWARD TEES: The hilly Dollar course plays on the hill above the village. The course is only 4572 yards with a par of 68, but because of the hills plays much harder. The 2nd is the most unique par 3 I've ever tried to play. It is basically straight up 71 yards to a blind green with trees on the right. I didn't have enough power to hit a short iron high enough to reach the green and struggled off the steep slope. It's a shot I will try to have in my bag next time we play. The #1 handicap hole for women is the 450-yard 11th, the only par 5 on the course. It's followed by a 401-yard uphill par 4 which crosses the 11th and a burn. A very difficult pair of holes. Like Bob, I agree that this small village course is a great find and I would quickly agree to another round here.

DULLATUR GOLF CLUB, Antonine Course
1A Glen Douglas Dr., Craigmarloch, Cumbernauld G68 0DW
01236-723230 www.dullaturgolf.com
Parkland, 5875 yards, par 69, £24

AMENITIES: The large clubhouse serving both courses, Antonine and Carrickstone, has a lounge/bar upstairs and a snack shop downstairs. The golf shop is small, but well stocked. The day we played the golf shop was closed much of the time.

COURSE COMMENTS: The Antonine Course at Dullatur Golf Club is the newer of the two courses and is shorter and tighter than the Carrickstone Course (1896). The 2006 creation of architect Dave Thomas plays over ground containing remnants of Antonine's Wall, an ancient Roman fortification. The course is full of challenges beginning with the undulating nature of the course. It would be a good course on which to take a buggy, except that as we found, it's not very buggy friendly--poor signage, narrow gates, holes with no path for a buggy. Signage and on-course directions are quite weak. Course management is extremely important on the Antonine; it is often difficult to pick the correct line of play or the correct club. Fifty bunkers, a mix of greenside and fairway with inconsistent sand, add difficulty. Many of the bunkers are fairly severe and some are in rough condition because of no rakes (we found out that the rakes tend to be stolen by local children). A burn or ditch is in play on nine holes. The moderate sized greens can be quite swaled, but were in great condition and putted very true. The course offers some interesting views of a nearby working quarry, but pays for it by being quite noisy on the holes closest to the quarry.

The quality of golf on the Antonine Course is as mixed as our other comments. There are some interesting holes and some that are interesting for the wrong reasons. It may be a telling comment that societies and competitions play on the Carrickstone Course. The second hole is a par 4 of 308 yards which begins with a drive over rough and a small bunker (153 yards out) to a fairway which slopes to the right and downhill. Three bunkers front the raised green which slopes back to front and is fairly small. The 5th is named *Arran View* (a popular hole name in the area, see Kilsyth Lennox GC). This 354-yarder has a downhill tee shot with a series of bunkers on the left of the fairway in play with a good drive. The second shot is steeply uphill and over a burn to a small green with two bunkers front left. *Thomas's Tot*, the 7th, is a good par 3 of 185 yards. Hit off a raised tee to a raised green. A burn short of the green and a large trap dead in front of the putting surface makes the shot harder. The green is relatively large and slopes left to right.

On the back, *Braefoot*, the 337-yard 10th, is a quirky, blind hole (but less tricky than the 11th) which begins from elevated tees. Either drive over the large hill at the left of the fairway or around it to the right. If you go to the right be careful of the nest of bunkers at the outside of the fairway. The green has two bunkers around it and is heavily swaled. A good drive over the hill left me with less than 100 yards to the green. Three chips and one putt later I had my bogey. I want to play this one again. Another interesting par 3 is *Thro' the Gap*, the 171-yard 15th. Drive through the gap in the trees (sufficiently large) up to a green protected by a bunker front right and one left. The players behind us were in the trees on the right and struggling in heavy rough, trees, and rocks. Here's what the course guide says about *Lang Riggs*, the 523-yard, par 5 16th: "A 523-yard roller coaster designed to repel golfers exactly the way Romans repelled Caledonians--down the hill." The narrow, winding fairway is so sloped as to be almost unfair on most lies. You can't plan where to hit; just hit and hope. After three shots to the middle of the fairway and having my ball roll into nearly impossible rough, and finally ending up with the ball two feet above my feet, I just picked up and walked off the hole. Anne, who always is straight, had picked her ball out of the rough 100 yards before. The designer should look at the 9th hole at Killin GC to see how to create a great downhill, twisting long hole. The last two holes on the course weren't bad, but the impression left by the 16th made it hard to enjoy the end other than to be glad it was over. The friendly staff at reception and the members we met in the lounge after our round helped end our day on a brighter note. If in the area, try the Carrickstone Course at Dullatur GC; everyone else was!

COMMENTS FROM THE FORWARD TEES: The Antonine course is difficult to play. Many holes had only one good landing spot from the forward tees, and many times that was true of other shots as well. The course wound through and around the hills northeast of Glasgow and offered some interesting views. The 5205-yard course isn't too long, but it does require extremely accurate shots. Three of the par 5s were of reasonable length, but 16 was very long at 493 yards.

DUNBLANE NEW GOLF COURSE
Perth Road, Dunblane, Perthshire FK15 0LJ
01786-821521   www.dngc.co.uk
Parkland, 5930 yards, par 69, £35

AMENITIES: The 1964 clubhouse has been recently refurbished and has changing rooms downstairs and a lounge up. Lounge offers an extensive pub menu with several specials. From the lounge you order by phone down to the kitchen. Food is excellent. Club has a small but fully equipped golf shop.

COURSE COMMENTS: The club formed in 1882 and played on Laighills course (an Old Tom Morris design) until the First World War when the facility was used as a hospital. After the war the New Course was built at the present location. It then had to be again rebuilt after disuse during four years of WW II. The course is very popular with locals, so call ahead if you want to play. One story we got from the club pro was that in 1953 a group from Whitehorse Whisky rented the course for an outing and brought plenty of their own distillate. I didn't get all the happenings from that day, but "future bookings from the whisky industry have been looked on with disfavor."

Dunblane New is a joy to play, with fairways lined with a grand variety of mature trees and wonderful views out to the hills and down to the village. The turf is a pleasure to play off, and elevation changes and blind shots will add difficulty. More than 35 bunkers, mostly greenside, dot the course. The few fairway bunkers on the course are often hidden and always strategically placed. The greens, several of which are gun-turret greens carved into the side of a hill, are moderate in size, with interesting contours, and are in good condition. There are no toilet facilities on the course, but one of the lady members told Anne before we started our round that a convenient chink in the stone wall behind the 11th tee leads to a secluded area near a bike path. She also said that the cyclists are good about looking away.

To play well at Dunblane requires some precise shots even though the course is fairly open. All the par 3s are interesting and demanding. Platform or gun-turret greens, bunkers, semi-hidden pins, and long, narrow tiered greens are a few of the challenges. The longest is 190 yards and the shortest is 160. All require you to be thinking. *Gleniver*, the 418-yard par 4 second, is a dogleg left uphill with trees on both sides. The second shot is semi-blind across a road to a green with traps on both sides. There are great views from the 5th, *Panorama*. A memorial diagram on the tee of this 357-yarder shows all the hills and bens (mountains) which can be seen from the tee. The first shot is blind down the hill (use the aiming post). The approach is still downhill to a flat green with protecting bunkers. Nine and ten together make an interesting turn from out to in. *Hutcheson's Heights*, the 386-yard par 4 ninth, is a dogleg left uphill around a copse of trees--be careful, a bunker on the inside corner is hidden from the tee. Continue steeply up to a raised green with traps at the sides. Turn inward on *Wharry Glen*. The reverse of the 9th, the 402-yard 10th is a dogleg left steeply downhill with bunkers on the outside of the turn. More bunkers and trees guard the green. *Hame*, the finishing hole, is a 492-yard par 5. Slightly downhill, the 18th fairway is narrow with trees on both sides. Good shots can be rewarded with birdies, but plenty of trouble lurks in the trees and traps. Dunblane New GC is certainly on our list of play again courses in this area.

COMMENTS FROM THE FORWARD TEES: Dunblane New GC is a beautiful course with some lovely views. Sometimes you are immediately visually aware of the challenge of the hole. The front is longer than the back, but the back requires more accuracy. The par 3s have long carries for ladies and you may be stuck with steeply uphill pitches or bunker shots if you don't reach the putting surface. The 17th was the hardest for me because you either have to make it over the hill or the ball rolls off the fairway left.

HELENSBURGH GOLF COURSE
25 East Abercromby Street, Helensburgh G84 9HZ
01436-674173   www.helensburghgolfclub.org.uk
Hilltop moorland, 5942 yards, par 69, £35

AMENITIES: The 1909 clubhouse has had major renovations in 1965, 1973, and 1997, yet retains it venerable charm (look for the beautiful etched glass club logo as you go upstairs). The lounge serves snacks and light meals from 11:00 AM to 5:00 PM daily, and affords great views to the first tee and the 18th green. The small golf shop is fully stocked and well staffed.

COURSE COMMENTS: Sited above the shores of the great River Clyde, Helensburgh GC offers a village feel while being close to the metropolitan Glasgow (23 miles) and the tourist hub of Loch Lomand. The course opened as a nine in 1893 with a design approved by Tom Morris. By 1905 the course had expanded to 18 holes. Famed Scottish architect James Braid redesigned the course in 1925, mostly adding bunkers which will still find your ball today. American pro Tom Weiskoff once played the course and labeled it "fun golf." We can agree and add that it's challenging as well. Sixty-seven bunkers dot the course, and while a few are quite large, several are small and steep-sided. The 6th and the 12th are the only holes with no bunkers. Water is in play on eleven holes, but is never a major concern. Besides the bunkers and the water, an abundance of gorse adds difficulty. The small greens, most of which have significant tilts (but are not swaled), will test your flat stick skills. The greens, though, are well-conditioned and putt true. Sited on a hilltop along the river channel, Helensburgh has a couple of short, steep climbs and can be quite windy. The club has a long range plan in place for continuing course development. The views from the course across the Clyde to Greenoch and Isle Arran are outstanding. You can also see up Glen Fennan to where the Clan McGregor and Clan Calhoun had epic battles. From the tee at the 6th you can see the island in the middle of Loch Lomand on a good day. Though there is no guarantee of seeing the allusive bird, we did hear a cuckoo calling as we enjoyed the view of the loch.

An introduction to the bunkering on the course is the short (283-yard), uphill 1st called *High Hopes*. It only takes a straight 200-yard shot to avoid three bunkers on the right and one on the left on your drive. Continue up to the green which is sloped back to front and protected by four more bunkers. Welcome to Helensburgh golf! At *Ben Bouie*, the 372-yard par 4 fourth, you hit across the hill to a flat fairway, and then approach the green downhill over a burn 60 yards from the small raised green surrounded by five menacing traps. A birdie opportunity for the accurate. The next hole, *Bunker Hill*, is a short 300 yards which can be drivable by a big hitter even uphill. The prudent play is to lay back short of the top to be able to avoid the two small dangerous bunkers fronting the back-to-front sloping green. The first hole on the back, *Clyde's View*, is a long par 4 of 444 yards which starts with a downhill tee shot to a fairway which slopes left. The fairway narrows dramatically as it rises up between two fairway bunkers about 100 yards from the green. Four more bunkers protect the narrow green. A fine par 3 is next. *Clyde Arran* is 210 yards long, but is downhill. A line of three traps on the right shouldn't be in play, but one about 30 yards in front and another just left of the green are. There's enough room over the fronting bunker to bounce your ball onto the green. You don't need a driver on the tight 339-yard 12th, *Dell*. The largest green at Helensburgh is best approached from the right side. Even though there are no bunkers here, a mound on the right and trees tight around guard the front sloping green. *The Quarry*, the 150-yard one-shot 16th, presents you the flattest green on the course. The challenge is to find the green circled by nine ball-grabbing traps. An overriding principle of golf at Helensburgh is to aim to the right on tee shots because the ball will roll down to the left.

Helensburgh GC enjoys a reputation for being friendly to visitors and works hard to live up to the club's motto: "A warm welcome awaits you." The course also enjoys some interesting history. In the clubhouse from 1954 to 1980 was a Suggestion Book for member use. Several interesting entries were noted in the club's centenary book (1993). One entry from May 5, 1979, read, "Smell in the entrance hall is getting a bit overpowering." This was followed by an entry on May 14, "The body in the hall appears to be decomposing." The committee did acknowledge both comments, but did not mention a funeral.

COMMENTS FROM THE FORWARD TEES: This course is visually pleasing with grand views of the Clyde, Isle Arran, and the mountains where clans used to fight. The holes are visually interesting as well. Helensburgh is set up for makeable pars for women, especially if you can play more than once. The two par 3s are not easy. For instance, the 9th is only 89 yards, but if you don't fly the green you are in trouble because the hole is surrounded by bunkers, trees, and gorse. The green at 16 has eight traps around it. It was my sense that the front was easier, but I actually shot better on the back. On the 17th be sure to look at the hole from the men's tee because the ladies' tee is lower and the fairway isn't visible.

KILSYTH LENNOX GOLF COURSE
Tak-Ma-Doon Road, Kilsyth, Glasgow G65 0RS
01236-824115 www.kilsythlennox.com
Parkland, 6225 yards, par 71, £25

AMENITIES: The pleasant clubhouse (with plans to expand) has changing rooms downstairs and bar upstairs. The clubhouse also contains a small golf shop run by very helpful pro Billy Erskine. Shop has all your usual needs.

COURSE COMMENTS: The 1899 course was significantly modernized in 2006 by William (Rocky) Rockmore III, who built new holes in filled in quarries on the property. Still six original holes remain in play; 1 and 14-18. The current routing conveniently brings golfers back to the clubhouse after nine. Playing on the lower slopes of Campsie Hills, Kilsyth is an undulating course; hilly but not extreme. We thought the course was similar to Peebles--good exercise. The golf at Kilsyth is challenging, as well. The fifty fairway and greenside bunkers will catch your attention, but only a few are penal. Two holes, 11 and 13, have no sand trouble. A small burn is in play on several holes, but it's only a major concern on 3 and 5. Putting surfaces are small to moderately large, and some have significant contours. The sloping greens allow for difficult pin placements. Prevailing winds add some difficulty because downwind holes tend to have tight fairways and upwind holes have tight tee shots between trees. Another feature of Kilsyth is some long walks between tees and greens. The course offers some fine views of the Kelvin Valley, Lanarkshire, east to the Lothians, and even west to Isle Arran on a good day.

For all the challenges at Kilsyth Lennox GC, we enjoyed our round and scored close to our handicaps. Several holes stand out in our notes starting with *Beltmoss*, the 459-yard par 4 third. The narrow fairway slopes to the right and has a large bunker on the right about 250 yards out. Your approach shot (second for the bold or third for the intelligent) must clear a wide burn which fronts the most undulating green at Kilsyth. OB left and heavy rough right complicate the hole. An interesting par 5 is the short 6th at 477 yards. An easy tee shot sets up a true risk/reward approach over a lochan to a small green. *St Mirren's Well* plays downwind, but your ball will tend to roll to the right. This leaves the choice of whether to go over the water or not. A burn crosses about 80 yards in front of the green with two protecting bunkers. A very tight drive uphill between large trees starts the narrow 362-yard 8th, called *Arran View*. The second shot is down to a moderate sized, slightly elevated green with no bunkers. A good tee shot sets up a birdie opportunity. A great challenge on the back is the 329-yard par 4 twelfth. Stay well left on your tee shot because the right side slopes down to trees and OB. A good tee shot can lead to a birdie, but miss your first shot and double or more is likely. Next is *Colzium* (named for a nearby castle), which starts with another tight uphill tee shot between large trees. The fairway doglegs left and downhill to a long narrow green. There's plenty of slope to the fairway, but the green is more swaled than it seems. Don't give any putts here. The finishers at Kilsyth are strong. *Druntrocher*, the 512-yard 17th, has a hilly fairway, but the biggest problem will be the two large trees in the fairway a hundred yard out from the green. The tilted green is well bunkered. Kilsyth ends with *Tak-Ma-Doon*, a 210-yard par 3. Sixteen, also a par 3, is a tough uphill one-shotter, but 18 is a fun downhill shot through trees, over a burn to an elevated green surrounded by three bunkers with OB on the right. The hole is both fun and challenging, much the same as the rest of your round at Kilsyth Lennox GC.

COMMENTS FROM THE FORWARD TEES: The course is hilly, but not too difficult to walk, and at 5224 yards it's not excessively long. Because many of the holes are narrow and the greens are small, there's plenty of challenging golf here and accuracy is important. The par 3s are short, but bunkering provides enough challenge to keep your interest. All the par 5s are just over 400 yards and require some good hits, but par or bogey is possible on most.

LEADHILLS GOLF COURSE
Leadhills, Biggar ML12 6XT
01659-74456 No web
Moorland 9-hole, 2177 yards, par 33, £10 day

AMENITIES: Small clubhouse with nobody about. Honesty box. No facilities available (toilets or trolleys) the day we visited.

COURSE COMMENTS: Leadhills' 9-hole course is a perfect example of the variety of golf found in Scotland. Playing golf at Leadhills is like playing golf anywhere else 50, 75 or more years ago. Leadhills GC is rustic and empty. Rustic, as in fight the sheep for the greens. Empty, as in nobody else but the sheep is on the course. Neither rustic nor empty takes any of the fun out of playing here. As one visitor said, "Nothing can detract from the fact that it's just good fun."

On a blustery, showery fall afternoon, Anne and I drove up to Leadhills Golf Club, the highest 9-hole golf course in Britain at 1500-feet, from the south (B7040). The narrow road winds through sheep fields and past peat bogs with stacks of peat set for drying. Soon we reached the mining town of Leadhills--one street with a school, church, hotel, pub, a few shops, and a scattering of homes. We followed the sign to the golf course which sits on a hill above the village. The first things we noticed were the empty parking lot and the small, trailer-like clubhouse. An honesty box with score cards and money envelopes waits for visitors. The course itself is rough, but interesting. Hole number 3, *Gully*, at 152 yards is a one-shotter which begins with a blind shot. Aim at the post provided to try to reach the green which nestles down in a gully with rough all around. The next hole, *Guid Skelp*, is a 305-yard par 4 with a visually difficult first shot. The fairway is divided by areas of rough making it hard to find a place to aim. It's either play the correct shot or play out of heavy rough or a small canyon. As you begin play on the fifth hole, take a look at the sixth green sitting below the tee box. A well-placed tee shot on the 266-yard par 4 sixth hole, called *Valley*, will give you a peek at the green and a chance to set up a birdie putt. We only saw three bunkers on the course and one of them was marked GUR. Even with a lack of bunkers, plenty of trouble exists to run up scores at Leadhills. The greens are small; nay, they are minuscule! I've seen larger breakfast tables in B&Bs than most of the greens at Leadhills. Besides being small, the greens are only roughly mown and accessible to both local rabbits and sheep--with all that entails. The sheep are a hazard of a different sort. It's hard to hit to a green which has sheep wandering across it when your playing partner says, "Don't hit them, they're so cute."

Some may say that Leadhills GC wouldn't be a golf destination, but I say it should be. It's sheep pasture golf and a fun break from today's manicured target golf courses. You can get around nine holes in under an hour and a half or play all day for £10. Anyway, think of the stories you can tell when you get home! A stop at Leadhills GC should include a visit to the Hopetoun Arms Hotel for lunch or a pint, and a stop at the Leadhill's graveyard to find the grave of miner John Taylor, who was born in 1633, worked in the mines until he was 117 years old, and died in 1770 at the age of 137. If you continue through the village of Leadhills on B797 you reach Scotland's highest village, Wanlockhead (though Tomintoul in the Highlands also makes claim to that title). The village is quaint with sheep in most of the yards and a lead mines museum, but no golf.

COMMENTS FROM THE FORWARD TEES: This was an experience I really wasn't excited about, but one that I really enjoyed and remember with a smile. On this little course I had to carry my clubs because we travel without trolleys (carts) and there was no one around to borrow from. Be sure if you intend to play out-of-the-way courses that you bring a club bag you can carry. We didn't have the course all to ourselves, we had to share it with some cute sheep. The course is not long, only 1936 yards with a par of 34 for 9 holes. The 1st and 2nd share a wide fairway and my tee shots on both landed in the about the same spot and was good for each. When I teed off on the 4th I hit right at a group of sheep which I found hard to do. Of course, the sheep are used to golfers and they had moved before my ball came to rest. The route up to Leadhills GC from the motorway is absolutely lovely, even in misty rain. It was a fun experience and I would go back anytime.

MILNGAVIE GOLF COURSE
Laighpark, Milngavie, Glasgow G62 8EP
01419-561619   www.milngaviegc.co.uk
Parkland, 5818 yards, par 67, £30

AMENITIES: The beautiful clubhouse with views of the course was built in 1939, then extended and revised in 1969. The comfortable lounge serves lunches, but no evening meals. No golf shop, but some essentials are available at the bar. We did hear a story about the clubhouse manager who in 1928 bought a mongoose to help keep down the rat population. No one knows what happened to the mongoose, but we didn't see any rats about.

COURSE COMMENTS: Milngavie (pronounced MILN-guy) GC, down a small lane through farm fields off A809, was originally designed by the Auchterlonie brothers, Willie and Laurie, in 1895. They then redesigned the course in 1905, and that is pretty much the course you play today. A James Braid revamp in 1931 was not extensive. The course is built on several glacially formed drumlins left over from the last Ice Age (10,000 BCE). Elevation changes are used well, without making the walk difficult. There are some sidehill shots to be played, but they're never severe. Even though short, the course is plenty testing. Thirty-seven bunkers will cause trouble, mostly around the greens. Seven and 11 are the only holes with fairway traps. A small burn is in play on the 9th. The well-conditioned greens are fairly small and all have subtle slopes. Ten and 13 are the most sloped--don't ever give a 6" putt on those. Two other conditions will affect play at Milngavie. First, the wind is usually cause for concern. Second, in several places the rough beyond the second cut is lost ball territory. For all this trouble, the course is very picturesque with numerous stone wall remnants shaping the fairways, and superb views of Ben Lomand and Dumgoyne, Campsi Fells, and the Kilpatrick Hills. Most spectacular are the vistas south to Glasgow. The course is very welcoming to visitors, but is quite busy with competitions on weekends.

From the start, we were impressed with the quality golf at Milngavie GC. The first hole, called *Allander*, is a great 359-yard par 4 starting hole. Tee off over a large patch of gorse on this uphill dogleg left. A good drive on the right side will give a view of the raised green with bunkers on each side. It's a fair challenge with quite a bit of trouble about. *Drumclog*, the 162-yard 2nd, is a simple hole with plenty of trouble. Hit the green and par is easy. Miss and trees, traps, and heavy rough all bring double-bogey into play. This hole has one of the three road crossings on the course. Also catching our attention on the front was the 9th, *The Gully*. On this 374-yard par 4 you drive over the hill to a wide fairway that runs down. Your approach is over a burn to a raised green with two bunkers on each side. Here the tee shot is key--take almost any club you trust to get over the gully bluff. Starting the back, the 10th is a tough hole. Long hitters can aim at the pole or left of it and over the hill. The prudent play is just to the right of the hill and not long enough to bound out of bounds. The green is slightly raised and has one bunker on the left. Next is *Dumgoyne*, a 313-yarder. An uphill drive over a large fairway bunker, 215 yards to carry, is the best line on this straight hole. The hole continues up to the green with only one bunker front right. Be careful of being left of the green as it drops off quite a bit.

A fun one-shotter is the 12th, *Mugduck* at 175 yards. The tee shot is downhill over heavy rough. You can see one bunker on the right from the tee, but another is hidden on the left. On the 13th you have an opportunity to "walk on water." An area on the right side of the fairway is known as "the Bubble," an anomaly where the fairway floats on a bubble of water. Step on it unknowingly and it's easy to freak out. Another bubble sometimes appears in the fairway of the 10th, but it's not as consistent as the 13th. The longest par three on the course is *Cobie Ha'*, the 16th at 175 yards. The hole plays downhill across the road and then up to a green with three bunkers surrounding it. A shot to the right can run up onto the green past the front bunker (at least mine did). *Hame* is a short (307 yards), but uphill finishing hole. The green is tucked left and protected by sand. Trees left and the road (OB) right are the other hazards. It can make an entertaining end to a match. Milngavie may be a tad difficult to find, but the friendly reception and quality course make the effort worthwhile.

COMMENTS FROM THE FORWARD TEES: Milngavie GC seems longer than its yardage because of the many ups and downs. It's fun to play because each hole is unique, and at 5333 yards, it's just the right distance. The layout, away from any town or village, is extremely quiet and peaceful. Par 3s are reasonable (105 to 168 yards), but there's plenty of trouble to get into--greens are partly hidden, bunkers are in the way, and approaches are often sloped. Only one of the par 5s is downhill (the 15th at 459 yards), while both the 4th and 13th are uphill. One of my favorite holes is the 7th, a 401 yard par 4. It is open, wide, and downhill. Three fairway bunkers, trees and a boulder on the left, a fronting greenside bunker all make this hole challenging and fun. A good course for ladies.

TILLICOULTRY GOLF COURSE
Alva Road, Tillicoultry, Clackmannanshire FK13 6BL
01259-750124 www.tillygc.co.uk
Parkland undulating 9-hole, 2612 yards, par 34, £12

AMENITIES: The pleasant small clubhouse is open usual hours, except Monday and Wednesday when it's closed. No golf shop, and no trolleys available. Even though the course is hilly, it's an easy carry for nine holes.

COURSE COMMENTS: Golf has been played on the property as early as 1897, but an official club wasn't formed until 1899. The course you play today is almost the original layout. The course, especially beautiful in fall colors, has lovely views of the Ochill Hills right behind the course, including a view of the Giant's Seat, a rock formation above the course. The course can be windy, and five holes will play into the prevailing wind, while only 2 play downwind. The two fairway and sixteen greenside bunkers are not very penal. A burn crosses on 6 and 8. The moderately sized greens are not severely sloped, and several are gun-turret style.

As is true of many of Scotland's village courses, Tillicoultry has several interesting holes. The 1st, *Toosie Tap*, a 363-yard par 4, is a dogleg left up a ridge to a tree-lined fairway. The approach is blind over a hill to a double green (shared with #5) with one bunker left (actually a bunker on 2). The 151-yard par 3 third is a dramatic downhill one-shotter with a large tree blocking the left side of the green which is surrounded by bunkers. Normally, take one extra club. *The Craig*, the 353-yard par 4 fifth, is uphill toward The Craig. Your tee shot is slightly down to a small ditch running between two large beech trees. From there the approach is a long or mid-iron up a steep slope to a green shared with one. It's about 100 yards from the top of the ridge to the center of the green. If the flag is near the front, avoid being long which puts you on the lower half of the green and leaves a difficult putt. Next is *Burgle Bank*, a 131-yard one-shotter which plays longer than its yardage as you hit to a gun-turret green fronted by a burn. Trees on both sides as you cross the burn narrow the hole. The ball probably won't roll down from the right bank above the green, but will definitely roll to the bottom of a deep drop-off left. Two of the four of us playing chipped across the green from the upper bank. Four can be a good score in a match. Locals say plenty of sixes are carded here. On the 422-yard par 4 eighth, *Cantie Lie*, keep your shot high on the left as everything rolls down right. A burn fronts the green, so a lay-up is the smart play. The elevated, gun-turret green is best approached from the right to use the upper slope as a backstop. It's a hard hole to par. As a note of interest, a bomb crater sits on the right side of the 8th, probably caused by a wayward bomb dropped in practice from the nearby bombing range. The course is playable all year and is a fun, friendly track if you're in the area.

COMMENTS FROM THE FORWARD TEES: At Tillicoultry GC you have to carry your clubs or bring your own trolley; there are no trolleys for hire. I didn't play because the club had set up a men's threesome to show Bob the course. I walked and took notes and photos. The course isn't long, but it does have a bit of elevation change with several sidehill shots. It's in a beautiful location butted up against the Ochill Hills, and is well forested with a variety of trees. For a small course it has a fairly large ladies membership and would be a fun course for a lady to play, if she carried her clubs or had her own trolley.

Courses in this region listed in *Golf in Scotland: The Hidden Gems*: Glenbervie (Larbert), Muckhart, Stirling.

PUBS, TEAROOMS, & RESTAURANTS

Two pubs are the Must Stops in this area, Port Bar at Lake of Menteith for its food and service and the Clachan Inn for its history and quality food. But the surprise is the clubhouse restaurant in the Aberfoyle Golf Club. We've often eaten some fine meals in clubhouses, particularly the Macrihanish clubhouse and the tearoom at St Fillans in Perthshire, but it isn't often we say the best food in the area is at the club.

Aberfoyle Golf Course Lounge (pub) in Aberfoyle. For lunch and early dinner it has the best food in town and great prices.
Allanwater Cafe (chip shop) at the north end of the main street in Bridge of Allan. This ice cream parlour/chip shop has been in business for more than a hundred years. Famous for fish and chips and specialty homemade ice cream.

#2 Baker Street (pub) at #2 Baker Street in Stirling just down from the Castle. Good pub food, reasonable prices, traditional music on some evenings

Carbeth Inn (pub) on Stockiemuir Road, Blanefield near Drymen. Roadside pub with beer garden once known as the Halfway House (between Stirling and Glasgow). Decent pub food, popular with bikers and cyclists.

The Clachan Inn (pub) in Dryman, near Loch Lomand. Advertised as the oldest licensed pub in Scotland. Upscale pub food is excellent and reasonably priced.

The Coach House (pub) on the main street of Aberfoyle. Typical pub menu. Comfortable refuge on a cold, rainy afternoon.

Clive Ramsay (restaurant) on the main street of Bridge of Allan. Bistro named for the owner/chef has an interesting menu and is always busy.

Darnley Coffee House (tea room) on Bow Street in Stirling, just down from the castle. Housed in the bottom floor of historic Darnley's House (home to Queen Mary's second husband) the tea room is a good lunch stop. Recommended by castle staff.

Doyle's Cafe and Deli (tearoom) on the main street in Balfron. A fairly new tearoom with specialty sweets and sodas. WiFi is a bonus.

Dun Whinny Coffee Shop (tearoom) on Bridge Street just off the main road through Callander. Specializes in homemade bakery goods and soups.

The Forth Inn (pub) in the center of Aberfoyle. Typical pub food in pleasant surroundings.

The Inn at Kippin (pub) on Fore Road in the cute village of Kippin. Large pub menu with interesting selections. Serves large portions for fair prices.

Pip's Coffee House, Ancaster Square, just off the main street in Callander. Typical coffee house or tea room menu, but the sweets are good.

Port Bar, Lake of Menteith Hotel (pub and restaurant) between the parish church and the dock for the small ferry to the priory at the Lake of Menteith. The hotel restaurant is fine dining at a dear price, but the bar has a great menu and the same chef.

LODGINGS

Altskeith Country House
Loch Ard Road, Kinlochard, by Aberfoyle FK8 3TL
01835-823106 www.altskeith.com £ reasonable

First class accommodation in a lovely pastural setting. Only a 10 minute drive from Aberfoyle, the small (10 room) hotel has all the amenities necessary for a top notch stay. Not cheap, but reasonable for what you get.

Ashbank Guest House
Falkirk (see Chapter 5)

The Anchor Hotel
Harbour Street, Tarbert, Loch Fyne, Argyll PA29 6UB
01880-820577 www.lochfyne-scotland.co.uk £90
Conveniently located in the heart of the village on the harbour, the Anchor Hotel has recently been refurbished and offers lovely rooms at reasonable prices--ask for the sea view, a little higher but well worth it. Serves a great breakfast with good choices.

Firgrove B&B
13 Clifford Road, Stirling FK8 2AQ
01786-475805 www.firgrovestirling.com £75
Centrally located near both the local golf course and Stirling Castle, Firgrove is a lovely Victorian B&B known for conversation and excellent breakfasts.

Glengarry Guest House
Stirling Road, Callander FK17 8DA
01877-330216 www.glengarry-callander.com £60
Located on the main road through town from Stirling (A84), Glengarry GH is a converted 1865 Victorian villa which has been a B&B with the same owners since 1982. Hosts are particularly helpful with information about the area. Close to shopping, restaurants, and the local golf course.

Helensburgh B&B
Whistlers Dell, Rhu, Loch Lomand & the Trossachs
01436-820195 www.helensburghbandb.com £70
A comfortable luxury B&B on the banks of the Clyde. Hosts Joan and Gordon truly take care of their guests. Breakfast is delicious.

Merlindale B&B
Perth Road, Crieff PH7 3EQ
01764-655205 www.merlindale.co.uk £70
Our Scottish home and one of the best B&Bs we've ever stayed in. John and Jacky Clifford are golfers and Jacky is a Cordon Bleu trained chef. The

1860s house has been significantly remodeled and is constantly being upgraded. Rooms are large and beautifully appointed. A lovely, award winning, friendly place to stay in the heart of Scotland. Even though it is not really in the area, it is close enough to make a good hub for golf in the Central area.

TOURIST ATTRACTIONS

Balquidder Church on a minor road off A84 not far from Callander. Grave of Rob Roy MacGregor.

Doune Castle half way between Stirling and Callander. Medieval stronghold (13th C) has been used in numerous films including *Ivanhoe* (1952), *Game of Thrones* (2011), and most famously *Monty Python and the Holy Grail* (1974).

Dumbarton Castle, Dumbarton. There has been a fortification at this location since the 5th century, although what you tour today is mostly the remains of the 18th C castle. Great views over the River Clyde.

Falkirk Wheel, near Falkirk. The Wheel is a rotating boat lift which connects the Forth and Clyde Canals. Fascinating engineering to view and fun to ride.

Inchmahome Priory, on an island in the Lake of Menteith. Situated on the only lake in Scotland (all the others are lochs), the 13th C Augustinian priory is a nice visit via small ferry.

Loch Lomand in the Loch Lomand and Trossachs National Park. Soctland's second largest freshwater loch (after Loch Ness) is a fantastic spot of natural beauty and great spot for water sports.

Stirling Castle, Stirling. One of the two premier castles in Scotland (Edinburgh Castle is the other), Stirling sits majestically over the city. Plan a couple of hours or more to see it all. Great views of the surrounding town and countryside.

Royal St David's GC

CHAPTER EIGHT: NORTH WALES

Wales is a fine country to tour--more than enough to see and do, along with wonderful golf courses to play. There are, though, some special considerations when traveling in Wales. First, it seems to take longer to get places in Wales than it does in Scotland. The roads are good, but there seems to be more slow traffic. Plan to add a little to your expected travel time. Second, road signs will be just a bit more difficult to read since they will be in Welsh. They will also be in English, but the Welsh will be on top and what you first see. This can create some problems as the navigator tries to tell you to turn for Pwllheli, Llandudno, or Betws-y-Coed. Work out a system of communicating between navigator and driver ahead of time--perhaps have the navigator spell the first four letters. Even with the signage problems we didn't have much trouble (only a couple of U-turns) even on our first trip.

While on the subject of the Welsh language, which I think is beautiful when spoken by a native, I'd suggest some pre-trip study of the language so that you can pronounce the words somewhat close to the way they should be pronounced. A quick search on the internet will yield a plethora of sites to help with the basics. Most Wales guidebooks will also provide a simple introduction to Welsh pronunciation. A little preparation can pay off when native speakers recognize that you've made an effort to try to learn a little about correct pronunciation. I did my homework before our visits to Wales, but still had a few stumbles. Since most of the double-L words, like the village Llandudno, would be pronounced beginning with a guttural "CL" sound, I wondered how a native would pronounce my Welsh middle name, Lloyd. In the Tourist Office in Caernarfon I handed the native speaking attendant my middle name and asked how she would say it. She looked at me for a second and said, "Lloyd." I was shocked and asked about the double-L. She said that in place names it "CL," but in people's names it's simply "L." Even with the inevitable confusion, the effort to pronounce Welsh sort of correctly will be rewarded.

GOLF

Golf in North Wales, the area from the north Irish Sea coast along the coast south to Aberystwyth and inland. The premier courses in the north are links or seaside, but we've played a few interesting parkland courses like Abergele and the 9-hole Betws-y-Coed. Some of the courses in the area are unique. For instance, Pwllheli which is half links and half parkland and St Deiniol in Bangor which is all mountain. Surprisingly, the gem in the area is not the touted Royal St David's, but the almost unknown Nefyn and District which provides some great golf vistas.

ABERDOVEY GOLF COURSE
Station Road, Aberdovey LL35 0RT
01654-767493 www.aberdoveygolf.co.uk
Links, 6091 yards, par 71, £70

AMENITIES: Lovely clubhouse with dining room and bar/lounge. Snack menu available all day in the bar and dining room is open for dinners Friday and Saturday and lunch on Sunday. Golf shop, run by head pro Andy Humphreys, is one of the best in mid-Wales.
COURSE COMMENTS: Both Harry Colt and James Braid had hands in designing Aberdovey Golf Course which has been in existence since 1892 and is one of the premier links courses in Wales. Recently

ranked as #17 in "Britain's Top 100 Courses Under £100," the course draws consistent accolades from players of all levels. A true links design, the course throws more than 60 bunkers (mixed greenside and fairway) in the way of your shots; many are quite penal. A burn or ditch is in play on five holes as well. The greens are large and all have subtle (and sometimes not so subtle) slopes, but they are always in good condition. Besides the course's designed hazards the wind is always a factor of play on the links.

All the holes at Aberdovey are good, but some stood out in our round starting at the 420-yard par 4 first. The hole is a long start to the round especially into the prevailing wind. Drive to an undulating fairway with punishing rough at the edges. Second shots (or drives much longer than I can hit) contend with a ditch which crosses the fairway about 110 yards from the large green. On your approach the putting surface will be hidden by humps and hollows. This demanding start lets you know you're on a championship course. The impressive 3rd hole is a par 3 of 157 yards. Called the "Cedar" hole, the 3rd is blind and bunkerless. Shots short mean a blind chip as well. The punchbowl green will reward those on line and the right distance. Short and yet challenging is also the description of the 470-yard par 5 seventh. It's a fairly open tee shot which leads to a testing second and/or third as traps line the left side of the fairway (five of them) and eight more surround the large flat green--especially dangerous is the row of four pot bunkers at the right of the green. A grand short one-shotter on the back is the 12th at 131yards. The bunkerless green sits atop the dunes next to the beach and open to all the sea breezes. Any shot not finding the green can be in serious trouble down in the heavy dunes grass. Visually stunning, but very intimidating for such a short hole. Next is the 13th, a 509-yard par 5 which plays along the sea. This is the longest hole on the course. The relatively narrow fairway is studded with traps right and left to add difficulty. The interestingly sloped green is protected by fronting bunkers and a hidden one behind. The 16th, a 281-yard par 4, is a great risk/reward hole with the railway (OB) all the way down the left. Fronted by several humps and hummocks, the green is a narrow target best approached from the center of the fairway. Aberdovey, a course which illicites comments of "Magnificent," "Excellent," "The best we've ever played," should be on every golfers play list.

FROM THE FORWARD TEES: Aberdovey is an amazing links course set in the dunes and by the Atlantic. There are many strong holes so bring your "A" game. At 5850 yards the course is longer than most and some holes require a carry of 120 yards to get to the fairways. More than 60 bunkers will add difficulty. The front has two par 5s and three par 3s, while the back has four par 5s and only one par 3. Several of the short holes demand precise shots because missing the green will lead to very tough chips. The course is very challenging and beautiful as well.

ABERGELE GOLF COURSE
Abergele, Clwyd, Wales LL22 8DS
01745-824034   www.abergelegolfclub.co.uk
Parkland, 6396 yards, par 72, £30

AMENITIES: Two upstairs lounges in the 1968 clubhouse serve meals only certain hours, while the restaurant is open evenings. The club has a fully equipped golf shop.

COURSE COMMENTS: The Abergele Golf Club has been in existence since 1910, but it was in 1968 that it moved to the present course. The original Hawtree design, extended to 18 in 1970, was updated and revised in 2002, with greens brought up to USGA specifications. Views of the Irish Sea and surrounding mature forest are at times over shadowed by the looming castle (really a folly) southwest of the course. Abergele GC boasts a mix of 59 greenside and fairway bunkers, and only one hole, the 18th, with no bunkers. Many of the traps are quite large. The moderate sized greens have interesting shapes and contours, and few are severely sloped. Two ponds and one burn add to the difficulty caused by the main hazard, the heavy forest.

All the holes at Abergele are fun to play, but five caught our attention. The 4th, *Twin Copse*, is a short 298-yard par 4 which is a great risk-reward hole. Bunkers cross the fairway at 180, 215, and 225 yards. One more bunker on the right of the green awaits those bold enough to try for the green. Rows of trees on each side (the copse) pinch the fairway near the green. We found the most intriguing holes on the back. Ten, *Water Hole*, a 410-yard par 4, has a large tree in the middle of the fairway about 120 yards out. Take your drive left or directly over the tree. Don't be right because the water (a pond) awaits 205 yards out. You'll be left with a long second shot to a fair sized undulating green with one bunker left. Next is *Tan-y-Gopa*, a par 5 of 470 yards. The hole is a sweeping dogleg left with traps on the outside at 185 and 215 yards. More worrisome is the set of four traps fronting the green. Only about 10 yards exists between three of the traps and the green. Like many of the holes at Abergele, *Ty'r Wiwer* is a classic straight ahead parkland hole of 350 yards. Wide fairways lead to a green protected by two bunkers. It's the green that's the challenge-- multilevel with a tiny top shelf--and, of course, the pin was there. The finishing hole is a wonderfully challenging end to your round. *Cartref*, a 480-yard par 5, begins with a downhill drive with trees left and a large tree and burn right. The second shot must either challenge the burn or lay back of it. The large green has no bunkers to guard it. Abergele GC should be on any list of enjoyable Welsh parkland tracks.

COMMENTS FROM THE FORWARD TEES: I like the very traditional parkland Abergele course. The course is tight and plays back and forth and up and down. It seemed longer than it played. The numerous bunkers on the course are well placed for ladies to find trouble. The par 3s are reasonable length, while the par 5s are quite long at 455 yards (3rd) and 460 yards (18th). It's a very enjoyable course with enough challenge to be interesting.

ABERYSTWYTH GOLF COURSE
Brynymor Road, Aberystwyth, Ceredigion, Wales SY23 2HY
10970-615104   www.aberystwythgolfclub.com
Seaside/mountain top/parkland, 6119 yards, par 70, £25

AMENITIES: The comfortable lounge, serving pub food most hours, looks over the 15th green. Small golf shop is fully stocked.

COURSE COMMENTS: You'll get plenty of exercise at the 1911 Harry Vardon designed Aberystwyth GC. The hills add adventure to the holes and give access to wonderful views over the town and out to the sea. We thought the views from the course were better than the views from one of the town's main attractions, the funicular train which goes to the top of Constitution Hill. The elevation changes are not the only conditions golfers must contend with. Forty-five bunkers, mostly greenside, will demand accuracy. The 15th has nine of the soft sand bunkers, many of which are cut into the greens. A couple of ponds could be in play, but water is only a real concern on the 10th. A small ditch is in play on the 4th. The greens are small to moderate, but the 14th is a tiny plateau green. Some of the putting surfaces are flat, but many have interesting contours. It's also best to be short on approaches since many of the greens drop off behind. Perhaps the biggest hazard at this seaside, clifftop course is the wind. The flags are shorter than many courses because the wind tends to break them off.

For all the difficulties of Aberystwyth, it is really a friendly course. The course can bite, but good scores are readily available. We played on a moderately breezy spring day and found several holes to mention. The first (a 431-yard par 4) and second (435-yard par 4) are good starting holes. Both play uphill, fairly wide open, and straight. They allow you to get loosened up, even though the 2nd is the number one index hole. The fourth is visually tougher than its 350 yards play. The hole starts up, over and down to a burn or ditch. A good drive in the dry can reach the burn. The approach is to a raised green with three traps protecting it. The next hole, the 417-yard par 4 fifth, starts with a tough drive. The line to the green is across the slope of a hill to the left, though there's sufficient room to the right. Too high to the left will catch heavy rough. The second shot is downhill to a green with a bunker and a pond left. A challenging downhill shot is the 218-yard 7th. Bunkers are on the left and grassy mounds on the right of the green. Depending upon the wind, the hole presents different challenges for club selection. With a light breeze behind, for me the hole played two clubs shorter than the yardage. A fun short two-shotter is the 291-yard 14th. The drive needs to miss the trees left and center, but the real test is the green with bunkers on each side. It is tiny (17 by 13 yards) and an absolute plateau which drops off on all sides. Quite a test! A blind shot begins the 507-yard par 5 fifteenth. A good drive out to the marker and then down can leave even a moderate hitter a chance to reach the green in two, but be careful of the nine bunkers clustered within 80 yards of the green. The 18th is a 184-yard par 3 which plays from an elevated tee down through a chute of trees to a large green surrounded by four traps. I'm sure many matches are decided here. As we came off the 18th green heading for the clubhouse, we met a couple who asked if we were new members to the club. When we said we were just visiting, they said that was too bad since Aberystwyth GC has a very active, friendly membership.

COMMENTS FROM THE FORWARD TEES: What's not to like about Aberystwith GC? Fantastic views, wide fairways, visually interesting holes, and a workout for the muscles (the course is a good one for an electric trolley). One of the par 3s was long, but it was steeply downhill. The others were shorter, but always tricky with numerous bunkers. I was faced with several sidehill or sloping lies, but not hole after hole. One of my favorite holes was the 8th which begins with a drive over a field to a broad fairway. Then you must chip carefully to a sloping green. The Aberystwyth club is losing older lady members because of the elevation gains, but Aberystwyth is a fun course for visiting ladies.

ANGLESEY GOLF CLUB (*Club Golff Ynys Mon*)
Station Road, Rhosneigr, Angelsey, Wales LL64 5QX
01407-811127   www.angleseygolfclub.co.uk
Links, 6330 yards, par 70, £20

AMENITIES: Comfortable lounge with views out to the 18th green. Food, snacks and sandwiches available all day. The club also has a small golf shop with all the essentials.

COURSE COMMENTS: Angelsey GC is a busy course with a full membership, but it's far enough off the beaten track to still be easy to get on (in summer or weekends, be sure to call ahead). Located amongst the sand dunes and heathland in the popular resort area of Rhosneigr on Isle Angelsey in North Wales, the flat links track is enjoyable to play. The course offers pleasant views of the surrounding mountains (including Snowdonia) and farmland. During the week jets will fly out of a local RAF base right over the course and can be a dramatic distraction. Not excessively bunkered, with only 22 mostly greenside bunkers, wind becomes the major hazard.   That and rabbit holes; watch your step especially in the rough off the fairways. Besides bunnies, sheep roam the course (holes 4 to 17), and it's possible to spot some of the wild weasels which frequent the course. In the spring count yourself lucky if larks flutter above the course singing. They only sing when it's not raining. The greens are on the small side with plenty of tricky slopes, but they putt true if you can read them. Water is in play on eight holes, but is only a major concern on the 18th which has two river crossings. A final linksland hazard noticeable at Angelsey GC is the gorse (some of the sharpest we've found) and heavy marram grass which line the holes.

Angelsey GC is not tricky, but has some interesting holes. On the 377-yard 3rd avoid the two bunkers right and left on the fairway on your drive to have an easier shot in to the small green. Your second shot is blind (look for the aiming post) and hope to avoid the pot bunker front left. OB on the left (around the greenskeepers' sheds) can catch those who try to cut the sweeping dogleg left on the 378-yard par 4 fifth. Mounds all around the green make the approach more difficult, though the aiming post behind the green is helpful. The 10th, a 398-yard par 4, is a dogleg left with a demanding tee shot because there is nothing to focus on except gorse on all sides. The green is raised with mounds around, but no traps. Another good dogleg is the 371-yard 12th, which sweeps left to right with OB all along the right. Be careful with your drive; it's easy to run out of fairway and have your ball end up in rough or gorse. The green is narrow with one bunker left. On the 18th, a 369-yard par 4, you tee off across the river to the fairway. Short is in the water or in heavy rough. Then decide whether to go for the green or not again over the river (20 yards wide and 70 yards from the green). The green is small with bunkers on each side and OB behind. It's a very demanding finish to an interesting links challenge.

COMMENTS FROM THE FORWARD TEES: At Anglesey GC ladies have good advantages (as well they should) and tees are set to help drives, not hurt, but the course is not too easy. Par 3s, while not too long, do require precise shots with plenty of bunkers and mounding about. Often the trouble is more visually intimidating than physically demanding. The par 5s were relatively short and par was many times a reasonable score. The wind affected many shots, both helping and hurting. What I liked most about this course was that it allows you to get out of trouble and save the hole.

BARON HILL GOLF COURSE
Beaumaris, Anglesey, Wales LL56 8YW
01248-8102321   www.baronhill.co.uk
Heathland 9-hole, 2798 yards, par 34, £10/ 9, £18 /18

AMENITIES: Pleasant bungalow-style clubhouse has a lounge which serves snacks the usual hours. No golf shop, but check at the bar for some essentials.
COURSE COMMENTS: The course was laid out in the late 1880s on the Baron Hill estate. The mature course plays its way down through natural hazards towards the Menai Straits. Course management is a key at this small, rolling track. The course is scattered with bunkers, water hazards, and patches of gorse. Greens are small to moderate, and though fairly flat, have interesting borrows. The 293-yard par 4 first is typical of the holes at Baron Hill. The short hole has gorse on the right of the fairway and sticky rough on the left. The elevated green is a testing target. A basic start which demands your attention. The 4th has an internal OB on the right, never my favorite design feature. I did like the 186-yard 5th, an interesting one-shotter thought of as one of the best par 3s in North Wales. Two burns and a large bunker stand between the tee and the plateau green. Stay to the left if you can't reach the green to avoid the bunker. Next is the tough dogleg right 336-yard 6th. Three bunkers on the inside and one on the outside of the turn complicate your drive. Aim for the marker post (about 200 yards from the tee) and avoid straying right. The green is sheltered by trees on the right and defended by gorse on the left. A good challenge, both tough and fair. The third nice hole in a row is the 274-yard par 4 seventh. The raised green is reachable, but OB on the right and gorse left mean you pay the price for a poor shot. With the intriguing Beaumaris Castle and numerous ancient sites in the area, Baron Hill GC is good stop for a quick nine.

BETWS-Y-COED GOLF COURSE
Betws-y-Coed, Snowdonia Nat'l Park, Wales LL24 0AL
01690-710556 www.golf-betws-y-coed.co.uk
Parkland 9-hole, 2455 yards, par 32, £10/ 9, £15/18

AMENITIES: Modernized clubhouse open all year serves snacks
and bar meals from 8:00 AM until 10:30 PM and overlooks the 9th green.
No golf shop, but some essentials are available at the bar. The Cottage at
Betws-y-Coed GC has two bedrooms for up to four people, and gives
golfers the opportunity to have golf, pub, and restaurant at their doorstep.

COURSE COMMENTS: A course occupied this ground between
1912 and 1914, but was lost to agricultural uses during the war and was not
rebuilt until about 30 years ago. Reopening in 1977, the 9-hole gem at
Betws-y-Coed (BET-wis-e-koid) affords stunning views of the Conwy
Valley and the Snowdonia Mountains and plays in a lush river valley. The
tight tree-lined course is playable by all levels, and can be a tough
challenge to those who are used to wide open links courses. The course is
moderately bunkered, but the trouble is well in view. Rivers are in play on
three holes and trees add difficulty throughout the course. Greens are well-
conditioned, generally small, and have interesting slopes. They putted very
true. The short par 4 second, *Llugwy*, at 315 yards, is a dogleg left with the
River Llugwy always lurking ready to catch shots that stray left. One
bunker on the inside corner will remind you to stay right. Two more
bunkers front the fairly flat green. The very picturesque 4th hole is a 322-
yard dogleg left around a bend in the river. Big hitters can try to cut the
corner and are invited to try by the wide bailout area right. Trouble at the
green includes a ravine that runs across the front, bunkers on each side, and
a mature tree that guards the right side. A lovely challenge. *Garmon*, the
189-yard 7th is the third one-shotter in a row. With trouble in front
(bunkers and right-to-left slope) and behind (the river), the hole is not easy.
Thankfully, though, the green is one of the largest on the course and is
mostly flat. Betws-y-Coed GC has two sets of tees for those wanting a full
round.

BORTH & YNYSLAS GOLF COURSE
Aer-Y-Mor, High Street, Borth SY24 5JS
01970-871202 www.borthgolf.co.uk
Links, 5717 yards, par 70, £30

AMENITIES: Pleasant clubhouse remodeled in 2007 has a lounge
and dining room which look out to the course. Open to the public 7 day a

week. Small golf shop run by professional John Lewis. The course also has the Ryder Cup Legacy 6 Hole Course for beginners and youth.

COURSE COMMENTS: Borth lays claim to be the oldest club in Wales, started in 1885. Playing along Cardigan Bay, the present course was designed by Harry Colt in 1945 and has been continually upgraded. Besides the normal seaside wind, Borth presents other challenges. A mix of more than 40 greenside and fairway bunkers dot the course--many fairly penal. At least three holes play with the beach as a lateral hazard either left or right. Three other holes have a ditch in play. The greens are moderate sized, are quick, and have tricky subtle slopes. Many of the tees are close to previous greens which makes tricky approach shots.

We liked several of the holes at Borth, starting with the 2nd, *Traeth*, a 409-yard par 4 which happens to be stroke Index #1. With the sea on the left and OB right the drive is narrow on this long two-shotter, especially if the wind is up. The narrow green is protected by two bunkers left. Don't be bothered by a bogie here. The 7th, *Pulpud*, is a 171-yard par 3 where the wind will really make a difference in club selection--from a wedge to a long iron or hybrid. The green is surrounded by four traps. Next is *Aber* the 48-yard par 5 eighth. Playing into the wind the longest hole will seem even longer. It's a gentle dogleg right around two traps with heavy rough on both sides of the fairway. A total of four bunkers down the right side demand accuracy on all shots. Heavy rough on three sides guards the green. On the back the 11th, *Tan Y Moel,* is a beautiful 150-yard links par 3. It's all carry to a green protected by heavy rough and three pot bunkers. Next is a fine short par 4 of 281 yards. *Twyodfryn* starts with the only blind drive on the course to an undulating fairway; the fairway is a tough target. Grass-covered dunes surround the green, but most bothersome is the bunker in front. The hole reminds me of some of the grand dunes holes at Enniscrone in Ireland. The 17th, *Levi*, a 300-yard par 4, has OB all along the right and a burn down the left. Accuracy is the key on the drive and approach to the smallish difficult to read green guarded by one bunker right. Borth makes a good stop as you travel the Welsh coast.

CHESTER GOLF COURSE
Curzon Park North, Chester, England CH4 8AR
01244-677760 www.chestergolfclub.co.uk
Parkland/heathland, 6218 yards, par 71, £30

AMENITIES: Pleasant clubhouse has views over the course and the Welsh hills beyond. Lounge serves good food from a bar menu with specials. Small, but well-stocked golf shop run by pro Scott Booth.

COURSE COMMENTS: This is an English course, but it fits in so well with a trip from Scotland into Wales (or the reverse) that we thought we needed to include it here. The meadowland course inside a loop of the River Dee overlooks the Chester Race Course with the railway on one side and the river on two sides. The lovely 1901 track has more than a hundred varieties of trees for your golf ball to hide behind. Besides the trees 46 bunkers--a mix of greenside and fairway--will test your shotmaking. Three holes have water problems in the form of a ditch or pond. The greens with a reputation as the best in the area are moderate sized and have subtle slopes.

There are numerous fine holes at Chester including the 4th, *Saltney Quays*, a 526-yard par 5. The longest hole at Chester, the hole has OB left off the tee and a bunker right at about 200 yards. More bunkers right and left bother second shots and two more guard the sloping green. *Round the Bend* is the 424 yard par 4 sixth with a fairway that doglegs right about 240 yards from the tee. OB left and trees right make the tee shot more testing. The undulating green is a small target with dips and a trap on the left. An excellent one-shotter is the 8th, *Brewers Hall Farm*, at 169 yards. The recommended play is a shot over the fronting bunker which will run up to the pin. Four bunkers and OB right is plenty of protection for the flat green. The first hole on the back, *Bamford's Birdie*, is a 359-yard par 4. I don't know who Bamford is, but I didn't find his birdie. It's a good hole with a pond and several bunkers in play, but it's not my favorite. The 12th, *Vampire Point*, a 379-yard par 4 has a wonderful name. The right side of the fairway is dominated by a bank of trees and bushes on this dogleg (really angled fairway) right hole. Left in the driving area is protected by trees. Be careful of the ditch right all the way and one fairway bunker on the left about 110 yards from the green. Two more bunkers guard the entrance to the swaled green. Length is key to 499-yard par 5 fourteenth called (what else?) *The Long Hole*. The length of the hole and two strategically placed fairway bunkers, left at about 220 yards out and right about 100 yards from the green, are the main challenges. Three traps guard the large green. Chester GC makes a nice stop on your way from Scotland to Northern Wales.

FROM THE FORWARD TEES: In a beautiful setting with plenty of trees, the course is basically flat with only one pond which shouldn't impact play. Chester has six doglegs which will require good course management. From the forward tees the course is longer than some in the area at 5609 with a par of 72. All three of the par 5s are over 400 yards and the longest, the 4th, is 450 yards. On the three par 3s it is bunkers that will be the main challenge. Chester is a fun course to play.

NEFYN & DISTRICT GOLF CLUB, Old and New Courses
Morfa, Nefyn, Pwllheli, Gwynedd, Wales LL53 6DA
01758-720102 www.nefyn-golf-club.co.uk
Heathland/clifftop, 6267 yards (Old), par 71, £31

AMENITIES: Pleasant lounge in the clubhouse serves pub food most usual hours. Separate golf shop is well-stocked and has friendly staff.

COURSE COMMENTS: Nefyn (NEV-in) & District GC is an unusual set up. The first ten holes are played, then a decision is made whether to play the Old or the New. The last eight holes on the Old routing takes you out to a point surrounded by the sea, while the New routing stays inland. The Old Course is the spectacular course to play (reminiscent of Ireland's Old Head) if you only have time for one round. The original 1907 9-hole course was expanded in 1920 by James Braid and John Taylor. Ian Woosnam, the Wee Welshman, holds the profession course record of 67 (on a par of 71) on the Old. The course is popular with both locals and travelers, but is enough out-of-the-way to still be easy to get on.

Nefyn presents players with plenty of challenge, starting with 50 bunkers on the Old and 85 on the New. Forty-seven bunkers, a mix of fairway and greenside, are in play on the shared first ten holes. All the bunkers are to be avoided, if possible. Moderate to large greens populate the first ten holes, and the putting surfaces on the New are smaller while those on the Old range from small to large. All are quite swaled with interesting borrows. If you're in the water it's the sea and kiss your ball good-bye. The sea can be in play on three holes on the shared ten, and most holes on the Old. The wind will certainly be a condition of play almost everyday, as will the many holiday walkers who wander the paths especially around the Old. They don't take much notice of golfers unless they get hit. You can't blame visitors for wandering this gorgeous headland with sea views from every hole, views of the mountains, and if it's clear, Ireland. Porpoise and dolphins (as well as seabirds) can be seen off the course. Nefyn & District provides some of the most beautiful coastline vistas in all of golf.

To give you a feel for the grand golf at Nefyn and District, we've picked out some favorite holes on the first ten, a few on the New, and several on the Old. *Borthwen*, the 366-yard par 4 second, is a strong dogleg right on the edge of the sea cliffs. A drive of at least 225 yards is needed to give a safe approach to the green protected by one bunker left. A slice or a push to the right on the drive or approach will be lost to the sea. The short (472 yards) par 5 fourth has a narrow fairway which runs along the sea cliffs, and although there is generous room in the light rough to the left, the cliff is like a magnet pulling your shots to the right. For your second shot, aim to the left of the large fairway bunker about 125 yards out from the green. Any shot to the right is in danger of kicking right and over the cliff. Four small traps guard the moderate green. On the 6th, *Gwynt Teg*, three bunkers (two left and one right) complicate the drive on this 441-yard par 4. All three can be carried with a drive of 225 yards, but do try to avoid them. Four more bunkers and a sloping fairway make the approach difficult to this two-tiered green. *Dyffryn*, the 8th, is a fun downhill (past 200 yards) hole with plenty of protection (six bunkers) for the smallish green. After the 10th, turn right to the tee box of the New Course's 11th. Of note on this side is the 349-yard par 4 twelfth. Bunkers on the left at 210 and 250 yards will tend to force shots right toward the rough. The relatively small putting surface is protected by two more traps and a drop-off behind. A blind drive begins the 401-yard 14th, which is a double-dogleg (left then right). Aim for the post at 205 yards and stay left as the fairway will run to the right. The second shot must thread it's way past four traps to find the green. The last on the New is moderate length two-shotter. The hole begins with a difficult drive uphill. Three bunkers not seen from the tee await your shot. Stay to the left of the aiming post and short of 250 yards to be safe. The approach is then slightly down to a green with bunkers right and left.

If after the 10th you head back past the golf shop you'll come to the 11th on the Old Course. Eleven and 12 are good holes, but they just get you out to the point holes. On 12 though, be warned that the first green you see is really the 16th and that the 12th green is further on and across the road. *Land's End*, the 415-yard par 4 thirteenth, is a sweeping left hand dogleg along the cliff edge. The hole begins with a drive over the edge of the cliff to the fairway. The wind (and your courage) will dictate how much of the cliff you want to challenge. If you can drive 260, aim just right of the promontory, otherwise stay well right. The second shot is no picnic as the fairway narrows the closer you get to the green. Playing the 13th as a 3-shot hole makes good sense. Next is *Lifeboat*, a 157-yard dramatic, lovely downhill one-shotter. Drive from the old lookout house sharply down to a moderate green with a bunker on the left and OB behind. The wind will dictate what club to hit--and then, hope. After playing the par 4 fifteenth, you come to one of the most unique aspects of this beautiful course.

Past the green and before the 16th tee box a path leads down (about 100 yards) to the smallest village in Wales. Besides a couple of houses, the village of Porthdinllaen is home to the Ty Coch Inn, a pub since 1795. On a warm day the inn can seem like heaven. The day we played, Anne and I stopped for a quick pint while the foursome in front of us stopped for lunch. As we passed by their table on out way back up to the course, we jokingly asked if they minded if we played through. The path to the pub is accessible off the 12th green, as well, but we'd recommend you have a clear head to play 13 and 14. [More details about the Ty Coch Inn are in the pub section of this chapter.] After a refreshment stop, next play *Pot*, the 188-yard par 3 sixteenth. The green is protected by three traps and the "pot," which seems to be a giant roped-off sinkhole. The 17th, called Long, should be called Long and Narrow. Aim for the marker post about 250 yards out on this 502-yard par 5, but stay to the left as the slope will push your shots to the right and the cliff. There's a little more room on the second shot, but the fairway still slopes right. No bunkers protect the two-tiered green. Whether you play the New, the Old, or both at Nefyn & District, you're in for a treat, especially if the weather is cooperative.

COMMENTS FROM THE FORWARD TEES: The views on a sunny day from Nefyn & District GC are fantastic and totally distracting! The first ten holes are big and wide open with small elevation changes. The trouble is mostly bunkers well placed to grab your ball. The last eight (playing the Old Course configuration) require planning and precise shot-making. Par 3s are good distance for women, but seem more difficult because of bunker placement. The 11th and the 12th are especially difficult with slopes, blind shots, and some tough elevated carries. The 16th can be a particularly troublesome par 3 with a huge hole in place of a fairway. Good planning and staying short of the trouble can lead to some good scores. Ladies, you must play this course if for no other reason than the views and the chance to stop in the middle of a round at a pub in the smallest village in Wales.

NORTH WALES GOLF COURSE
72 Byniau Road, Llandudno, Wales LL30 2DZ
01492-875325 www.northwalesgolfclub.org.uk
Links, 6254 yard, par 71, £34

AMENITIES: The clubhouse has a beautiful lounge with great views of the 14th green and the 15th tee. Good food and friendly staff. The golf shop is fully equipped.

COURSE COMMENTS: Situated on Penforfa Beach (commonly known as West Shore), North Wales GC is a true links championship track with views of the sea hills and surrounding villages, Little Orme, Great Orme, the Isle of Angelsey, Puffin Island, and mountains of Snowdonia. On a good day the course, with six holes playing along the sea, is drop dead gorgeous. Founded in 1894 by Tancred Cummins, today's course will challenge players with an enjoyable variety of tests. Sixty-three bunkers, several steep-sided and some shared between holes, demand accuracy from the tee and on approaches. The greens are mostly small and flat with subtle breaks. All were nicely conditioned when we played. Water is in play on five holes, but most is easily avoidable. As on most courses it is the wind (or lack of it) which will determine how difficult the course plays. Guess how difficult it was when we played in 30-40 miles per hour gusts! Another condition which can affect play is that many locals will walk their dogs through the course and expect golfers to be aware of them. A commuter train separates this course from Llandudno GC next door. I embarrassingly found that sometimes golfers on the other course will give back wayward balls.

Aptly named *The First*, hole number one at North Wales is a brutal start when playing into a small gale. The strong 334-yard dogleg left has a bunker on the inside of the turn and OB most of the way down the left. Three bunkers guard the small green with a slight false front. Use the aiming post behind the green on your approach. The 6th is a 382-yard par 4 where you tee off over a burn and gorse to a rising fairway. Three traps in front of the green will cause problems, as will the two around the small green. The first hole to be really affected by the dunes is *Vardre*, the 384-yard 8th. A good blind tee shot over a rough-covered mound to a swaled fairway leaves a second shot which is only partially blind (aiming post behind the green helps) to the only two-tiered green on the course. The only hole with no bunkers is made tough by mounding. Nine, 10, and 11 are moderate length par 4s which play the closest to the beach. *The Warren*, North Wales' 353-yard par 4 twelfth, is fun with the prevailing wind behind you. You can hit a massive drive on this downhill two-shotter (I hit 320 when my normal drive is 220). Two bunkers guard the right of the fairway, and three steep-sided pot bunkers further protect the green. *Hades*, the 13th, is aptly named because you can barely see the top of the flag on this 177-yard par 3. Mounds block your view of the green and the right side pot bunker protecting it. The dune behind the green is covered in sticky rough. North Wales GC will give your game a test anytime you play, and it will be a stern test when the wind blows.

COMMENTS FROM THE FORWARD TEES: North Wales GC is a links course which provides plenty of roll in the fairway. Wind and water affect shots on many of the holes making the course quite a challenge. Visually, though, it's a stunning setting with views of the Irish Sea, surrounding hills and village, Great Orme, and the commuter train which runs along side the course. The finish is tough. Sixteen is especially difficult for women with a required carry of 140 yards to clear a gully or be left with a blind steep shot up and over the edge of the gully to find the green guarded by bunkers. Then on 17 you must reach the green or have another steep bank to climb. After the tough 16th and 17th, I especially liked 18. North Wales is a tough, demanding course, but with good greens it's also fun to play.

PWLLHELI GOLF CLUB (CLWB GOLFF PWLLHELI)
Golf Road, Pwllheli, Gwynedd, Wales LL53 5PS
01758-701644   www.pwllheligolfclub.co.uk
Parkland/Links, 6108 yard, par 69, £34

AMENITIES: The comfortable clubhouse has a lounge and restaurant downstairs and another lounge with outside patio upstairs. Food served the usual hours. A fully equipped golf shop is connected to the clubhouse and has friendly staff.

COURSE COMMENTS: Pwllheli GC (pronounced sort of like "pooh-cla-helee") is an unusual combination parkland/links course with nine parkland holes and nine that play in the linksland. The design was originally the work of Scotland's Old Tom Morris in 1900. The course was later extended and redesigned by James Braid. The work of both Morris and Braid shows in the 49 bunkers in play, most on the links holes and at greenside. Some of the bunkers are very deep and steep-sided. Water in the form of burns or ponds is in play on seven or eight holes, but the wind will be the most important condition of play. The parkland greens are small and flat, while the links greens are slightly larger and have more slope. The views from the course of the mountains and Bay of Cardigan are marvelous.

All the holes at Pwllheli are visually appealing and play harder than they look. The 2nd, *Yr Ala*, is a 423-yard dogleg right with a drive over a rise (use the aiming pole). The second shot is to a small green with no bunkers. Uncomplicated, straight ahead golf. A visually beautiful hole. Eight, 9, 10, and 11 are the beginning of the links holes and play along

Crugan Beach with tee boxes of 9, 10, and 11 on the seawall dunes. On 8, 9, and 11 you tee off over gorse to the linksland. On *Tanbwlch*, the 197-yard par 3 tenth, you tee off diagonally over a beach road to a green protected by vicious bunkers, gorse, and rough-covered mounds. Behind the green at 10 is an old house (now a workers' shed and toilet). An 86-year-old gentleman who is still a playing member at Pwllheli grew up in that house. Fourteen is a 342-yard par 4 (there are no par 5s for men) which is a sharp dogleg right with a copse of trees on the inside corner and two large bunkers past the trees. Only the brave (or the foolish) try to cut the corner. The approach is to a small green with a pond in front and trap front right. The number one stroke index hole is also a dogleg. The 455-yard par 4 begins with a blind drive (over the aiming pole) to a generous fairway. Only the longest of drives (275-300 yards) will have a view of the green on the second shot. Two fore bunkers and two more greenside guard the putting surface. Pwllheli GC is very accommodating to visitors, but is a popular course and can be busy. Be sure to call ahead.

COMMENTS FROM THE FORWARD TEES: Visually appealing and fun to play, Pwllheli is really two courses--half parkland and half links. Interest is maintained without numerous blind shots. Par 3s are reachable distances, but visually seem more difficult with gorse or bunkers in the way of small greens. Both the 5th and the 14th had water in play and would require lay-ups for shorter hitters. Having the two different styles in one course made the round even more fun.

ROYAL ST. DAVID'S GOLF COURSE
Harlech, Gwynedd, Wales LL46 2UB
01766-780361 www.royalstdavids.co.uk
Links, 6428 yards, par 69, £55

AMENITIES: Park in the lot and cross over the train track to the club. Pleasant clubhouse lounge serves pub meals all day, but if the weather is fair, most people take their refreshment on the patio overlooking the course. The club has a nicely equipped small golf shop.

COURSE COMMENTS: The course was built in 1894 and the Royal prefix was added in 1935 when the Prince of Wales, later to become the Duke of York, accepted the captaincy. A primary feature of the course is the domineering facade of Harlech Castle which looms over the course. The course plays across relatively flat linksland until the 13th at which point Royal St David's turns into the dunes, but you never get views of the ocean. The dunes are environmentally sensitive areas, which also inhibits course expansion. Royal St David's is the site of numerous championships, including the British Ladies (1987), the Welsh Ladies (1991), the Wales Amateur (1995), and the Wales Senior Open (2001 through 2005). To say the course is challenging is an understatement. Straight hitters can score well here, but if you're off-line scores can balloon. One hundred-fifteen bunkers, which seem to come in clusters, create major hazards on all holes except 14 and 15 which play in heavy dunes. Most of the bunkers are small and penal. Burns or ponds are in play on 12 holes, but are never as much concern as are the bunkers. The greens are moderate to large with major undulations, and as befitting a championship track, some tricky pin placements. Even as we played on average weekday, the rough was very gnarly--hard to find balls or to hit out of. One of the knocks against Royal St David's, from our experience and comments by professionals who have played the course in competitions, is that the first thirteen holes, the flat linksland holes, are rather unremarkable--tough, but not very memorable. One pro at a southern Wales course said that he had played Royal St David's twice in competitions and still couldn't describe anything but the last few holes and the view of the castle.

Looking over my notes and my scorecard, the flat holes certainly ate up my score, while I shot below my handicap on what should be the tougher dunes holes. We did pick out some holes on the front to describe. The 3rd, a 463-yard par 4, is a slight dogleg right with bunkers on the inside corner and gorse and a burn (or ditch) on the outside. Two-hundred twenty-five yards will clear the bunkers, but that's hard into the wind. The long second shot must contend with three more bunkers by the green and OB right. A dogleg left, with bunkers left and right in the driving area and gorse on both sides of the fairway if you stray, is the 371-yard 6th. A large bunker crosses most of the fairway about 100 yards before the kidney shaped green with three bunkers around it. A small pond in back of the left side of the green awaits those who get too aggressive. On the 173-yard 9th the top of the flag is all you can see from the tee; the rest is blocked by rough-covered mounding. Three traps left and one right catch off-line shots. The more exciting holes are the dunes holes, starting at the 13th. On the 15th, a 427-yard par 4, you tee off over small dunes to a narrow fairway angled right. The second shot is through an even narrower gap in the dunes to a green protected by rough-covered mounds. A good dunes hole if you find the fairway and stay straight. Next is the 16th. From the elevated tee on this 354-yard par 4 you must carry about 180 yards to find the fairway past good sized dunes. The approach is over a ridge to a green ringed by seven bunkers and several mounds. It's all about the bunkers-- all thirteen of them in play--at the 428-yard par 4 seventeenth. Stay in the middle to avoid the six traps (right and left) starting about 200 yards out. A line of three bunkers crosses the fairway just in front of the green and four more surround it. An entire course built into the dunes of Royal St. David's would rival the great dunes courses of Scotland (Cruden Bay, Royal Dornoch) and Ireland (Tralee, Carne, Ballybunion, Lahinch). As it is, Royal St David's GC is a worthy championship track, just not much fun.

COMMENTS FROM THE FORWARD TEES: We played Royal St David's GC in ideal conditions that were hot and dry, with fast links fairways and only moderate breezes. It was good to play in those conditions because the course is quite hard with a par of 74. Bunkers are the biggest problem for women (I think for men, too). They were placed where one wants to go and many greens are completely surrounded. Par 3s are reasonable distances, but shots must fly the green or be carefully rolled on. The seven par 5s aren't too long, but are still challenging. Only the 15th seemed unfair for ladies; even for long hitters, there seems to be no fairway landing area. After playing it I could at least see a better aiming point than I used. On the 14th there is a small sign directing players to the ladies tee. I missed the sign and never did find the correct teeing area. If you want to challenge your game, Royal St David's is a good choice. If you want an enjoyable round, go back to Pwllheli or Nefyn.

ST DEINIOL GOLF COURSE
Pen y Bryn, Bangor, Gwynedd, Wales LL57 1PX
01248-353098   www.st-deiniol.co.uk
Heathland mountain top, 5656 yards, par 68, £25

AMENITIES: The club has a beautiful old lounge with part going back to the World War I era. Good food is served usual hours. Golf shop is small, but well stocked. The club does have buggies (power carts) for rent, which might be a good choice because of the hilly nature of the course.

COURSE COMMENTS: St Deiniol GC is mountain top golf at its best, with stupendous views and exciting holes. Designed by Scottish architect James Braid in 1906, the course offers new vistas at every turn. Snowdonia, Penrhyn Castle, Puffin Island, the Menai Straits, and Beaumaris are visible from the course. The Braid design presents at least one par 3 to every point of the compass and some difficult par 4s. Though not long, skillful shot-making is what's needed to score at Bangor. Located in a very busy area of North Wales, the course can be crowded on weekends (women are not allowed on Saturday), but practically empty during the week. The course is very difficult to find so it would be wise to call ahead for directions. Wind will always be a condition of play as will the elevation changes throughout the course. A plethora of blind shots, sometimes more than one on a hole, characterizes St Deiniol, and eight holes cross other holes. Be especially mindful if you're not playing with a local. With all the other trouble on the course there's very little need for bunkers. Only five traps (two fairway) inhabit the course. The course has one small pond, but it's not really a problem. The greens are small to moderate sized with some slope, and the putting surfaces are great and true. The keys to scoring here are to leave your driver in the car and work for accuracy.

Don't judge St Deiniol GC by the first hole which I believe borders on being unfair. *Glan Cegin* a 327-yard par 4 would be a challenge later in the round, but is too tough as a beginning hole. The fairway is narrow with steep rough-covered slopes on each side. Without a good warmup the fairway is a hard target to find, and the green is hard to find from off the fairway. The rest of the course is demanding, but fair. A strong dogleg left with gorse on the right is the 373-yard par 4 third. The second shot must go up to a raised green with rough on both sides. The 7th, *Tros y Lon*, a 179-yard par 3 starts with an almost blind tee shot with OB right to a narrow raised green with runoff at the back. On the uphill 9th as I approached my drive, I noticed two balls in the fairway, both with my markings. I was confused. I had lost one earlier in the rough at one. As I stood over the balls a player came over the hill from the 14th fairway and asked if I had seen his ball. I pointed out my two balls and he said he'd been playing with a ball he found on the first. He offered to give my ball back, but I said finders keepers. Mystery solved, we both played on. In the lounge after the round, the player who'd found my ball said he later lost it. Maybe some balls need to stay lost. Eleven, 12, and 13 are St. Deiniol's Amen Corner--a fine set of three medium length par 4s. The 11th climbs, the 12th is downhill, and the 13th is back up to the top of the course. Eleven and 12 have blind tee shots and 13 is blind into the green. Gorse lines all three. A fun challenge. The two par 5s at Bangor are both worth a mention. At the 14th, a 530-yarder, you really need a guide the first time you play this tricky hole. We were thankful for the company of longtime member Iola Williams who directed us at *Twll y Twr*. The hole begins with a blind downhill tee shot. Stay to the left of the aiming post unless you can hit 300 yards. The second shot is uphill and again blind. At 100 yards from the green is a steep drop (steep enough to require steps down) which must be cleared. Balls short of the bottom can hang up in the rough and leave an almost impossible chip to a green protected by two Braid bunkers. As daunting as is my description, the 14th is a hole I really want to play again; I know I can do better than a two putt double bogey. The 18th, *O'r Diwedd*, is a long (512 yards) finishing hole which is complicated by a left to right sloping fairway with trees all along the high side. The two fairway bunkers on the course, which sit near the green, make the approach tougher to the green with runoff on three sides. With my personal objections to such a stern start noted, the golf at St Deiniol is both demanding and enjoyable. The golf aside, the views from the course are well worth the price of play.

COMMENTS FROM THE FORWARD TEES: Not only does St Deiniol GC have majestic views, but individual holes are also pleasing to the eye. Several holes cross other holes and several turned and twisted across the mountain top. This is not an easy walking course. Tee boxes were appropriately placed for women without reducing the challenge or taking away from the character of the hole. The course required very precise shots, and I got into a bit of trouble which isn't my norm. Three of the par 3s were long, with the 4th the longest at 226 yards. A couple of the par 5s were long as well, but they usually played downhill. The course is tricky, but not impossible to score well on.

PUBS, TEAROOMS & RESTAURANTS

North Wales offers numerous good eateries, but you have to work a little to find the best--perhaps that's as it should be. Queen's Head in a village not even on some maps, Ty Coch Pub in Wales' smallest village (and in the middle of a golf course), and Y Bryncynan are good enough to make the effort to find them worthwhile. It is San Carlo in Pwllheli though that opened our eyes. Several times we've stayed in combination pub or restaurant B&Bs with inconsistent results. San Carlo made it all work: good B&B, inviting breakfasts, wonderful dinners.

Ann's Pantry (restaurant) in Moelfre, Isle of Angelsey, Wales, across from the harbour. This nautical-themed croft restaurant has a lovely location across from the small harbour at Moelfre. Service is good, the food is excellent, and the set price dinner a real bargain.

Anna's Tearoom on Castle Street, Conwy, Wales, on the main street about 2 blocks from the castle. A beautiful Victorian tearoom above a mountain equipment shop. Pleasant classical music in the background. Soup and sandwiches were nicely done, but most interesting was the tour group who came in as we were eating. A group of quite elderly tourists came in herded by the tour guide.

The guide told the group, "This is what we're eating and the toilets are in the back, be sure to go," and put a plate of sandwiches on each table. At one table he set the sandwiches in front of a particularly senior gentleman who proceeded to eat several, one in each hand, without passing them on. We decided on a tour like that you fight for your sandwich; survival of the fastest. Made me glad we can tour on our own. Try to get a window table to overlook the busy town.

Black Boy Inn (pub/restaurant) in the heart of Caernarfon. Serving dining of distinction for more than five centuries, the Black Boy (the name may come from "black buoy") is a traditional
low-ceiling pub with its own distinct charm. Always busy.

Castle Cottage Restaurant with Rooms just off High Street close to the castle in Harlech. A tad expensive but top quality seasonal fare served in lounge/bart and dining room.

Harry's Bistro (restaurant) on 40-50 North Parade, Aberystwyth, a couple of blocks up from the Promenade. This popular modern bistro (in high season be sure to reserve ahead) is the winner of numerous AA Rosette Awards. The large portions are excellently presented and very tasty.   The only thing that was a little off-putting was a rather strange selection of music playing in the background.

Kerfoot's (cafe) on the High street through Porthmadog. Large shop selling housewares, clothes, furnishings, etc.) with a cafe on the 1st floor (which in the UK is one flight up). Mornings and lunches. Tasty Welsh Rarebit.

The King's Head Pub and Henry's Restaurant, Llandudno, Wales, just above the Orme Tram Station. The oldest pub in Llandudno (about 300 years old), the King's Head is where Lord Mostyn met with architects to design the resort town. The pub is dark and decorated with old photos, mostly related to the Orme Tram, while the restaurant is much brighter. We were greeted by one of the largest pub dogs we've ever met (a Mastiff, I think). Visit at least once for a drink and the history.

Kinmel Arms (pub) in Moelfre, Isle of Anglesey, Wales, across from the small harbour. The Kinmel Arms is a brightly lit seaside pub in nautical theme with several tables by the front windows. Everyone in the village comes here for Saturday night. One of two places to eat in the village of Moelfre (Ann's Pantry is the other), the Kinmel Arms is the best choice for meeting locals and second best for having dinner, but the food was good.

Little Italy (bar/restaurant), 51 North Parade, Aberystwyth, Wales, in the heart of the shopping district across the street from Harry's Bistro. Little Italy has a bar at street level and the restaurant is upstairs. The dining area is nicely decorated and one table has a window looking out to the busy street. The food and service are both excellent. Great to have two good choices for dining so close to one another.

Molly's (restaurant) on Hole-in-the-Wall Street, Caernarfon, Wales, just half a block up from the castle. The small bistro-style restaurant has two rooms for dining (the second room is brighter). The large portion meals are well prepared and delicious (we had seafood pasta and a sautéed seafood platter). In busy times you need to book at least a day ahead.

Olive Branch Greek Restaurant and Taverna on the promenade in Aberystwyth.   Specializing in Greek and Eastern Mediterranean fare, Olive Branch has an interesting menu and the food was excellent. Nice location just up from the historic castle.

Pilot House Cafe, Penmon on Isle of Anglesey near Black Point Lighthouse.   Nondescript cafe serving fresh, interesting fare mornings and afternoons. Does a Sunday roast as well.

The Plas Restaurant/Tearoom, High Street, Harlech, Wales, overlooking Harlech Castle and Royal St. David's GC. This Victorian tearoom/restaurant has a formal dining area, a conservatory, and grass patio for good weather dining. The food is good, but the views over the golf course, the castle, and Cardigan Bay are spectacular.

The Queen's Head (restaurant), Glanwydden (near Llandudno), Wales, in the heart of a small village not even on some maps. The motto of this fine dining restaurant with a pub feel is, "Without a doubt the warmest and most wonderful place to eat and relax in peace." The Queen's Head works hard to live up to that. Serving lunch 12:00-2:00 and dinner 6:00-9:00,   the   Queen's   Head combines large portions of great food, in elegant presentations, with exceptional service. The   food   we   enjoyed   (mushroom soup, seafood chowder, tuna steak with avocado and prawn salsa, and lamb shank) was some of the best we had in Wales.   The Queen's Head is similar to the noted Creel Inn in Scotland (near Stonehaven) and in high season or on weekends reservations are required.

San Carlo (restaurant), South Beach, Pwllheli, Wales, a short block up from the beach and near the town shopping district. Owners Susan and Carlo have created a little bit of Italy in Wales, complete with red checked table cloths, pictures from Italian movies, and Italian music in the background. All menu items are freshly prepared by Carlo and the food is outrageously good. I could have just had several portions of the fried sardine starter. Above the restaurant is their pleasant B&B (see Lodging section).

Ship Inn (pub) in Red Wharf Bay, Isle of Anglesey, Wales, on the bay. Complete pub menu with numerous specials. This seaside pub affords some great views and has plenty of outside seating for good weather (or bad weather if you're tough). Always busy.

Ty Coch (pub) in Porthdinllean, just off the 12th and 16th hole at Nefyn & District GC on the bay below the golf course. The Ty Coch is a several hundred year old beachside pub (has been a bar since at least 1795) in the smallest official village in Wales. The bar and the outside seating area look out onto Caernarfon Bay. Owners Brione and Stuart Webley serve golfers who drop off Nefryn Old at the 12th tee or the 16th tee (or both) for a bite or a brew. Tourists walk the edge of the course to get to the pub. After you're done, you walk back up the 100 yards to the course and get back into the rotation. The food and drinks are incidental, it's the location that makes Ty Coch so special. Must Stop!

Tyddyn Llwyn Hotel (pub/restaurant) located a half a mile southwest of Portmadog. Tyddyn Llwyn is off the beaten track out of town and tucked up a hill next to a caravan (trailer) park, but is only a short ways out of the village. The interior is much nicer than the surroundings, so don't be put off. The dining room has views over the patio and forest. The broccoli & stilton soup was excellent, and the manager was constantly checking on us.

Y Bryncynan (pub/restaurant) in Morfa Nefyn, Gwynedd, Wales, a couple miles inland from Nefyn & District GC. Gina and Dennis Moore have updated a more than 200 year old building to include two dining areas, a bar, and an outside seating area. Dennis was the Captain of Pwllheli GC when we met him. The restaurant was very busy on an off season Sunday and the staff hustles. We ate here two nights in a row and everything we had was excellent. I particularly enjoyed a great crab soup. I did ask Dennis about the meaning of the name, *Y Bryncynan*. He said it came with the place and nobody has ever figured out what it means. I'd suggest it means "Darned Good."

LODGINGS

Bedknobs Victorian Guest House
19 Carmen Sylva Rd., Llandudno, Wales
01492-875090   www.bedknobs-guest-house.co.uk   £26/p
Just a short walk from the promenade, formerly an elegant Victorian home, the Oldfields have refurbished Bedknobs to retain its period charm. Guests comment that the guest house is a "jewel," and that the meals are superb (a four course evening meal can be arranged for as little as £12). Very accommodating.

Bodalwyn Guest House
Queen's Avenue, Aberystwyth, Wales SY23 2EG
01970-612578 www.bodalwyn.co.uk   £55/room
Bodalwyn Guest House is an ideal location, at the north end of town about three blocks up from the seafront, for a visit to the central Wales coast town of Aberystwyth. It's within easy walking distance to all the major points of interest in town and the promenade. The Edwardian townhouse has nicely appointed rooms and your hosts, Clive and Hilary Davies, serve a hearty Welsh breakfast.

Chester Guest House
44 Hoole Road, Chester, Cheshire, England CH2 3NL
01244-348410 www.chesterhouseguesthouse.co.uk £50
Chester is a good stop if you are driving from Scotland to Northern Wales, and Chester House is a good place to stay. Centrally located just a 10 minute walk from town shopping, dining, and the cathedral, Chester House serves a great breakfast.

Deanfield House
Moelfre, Isle of Anglesey LL72 8HD
01248Deanfield House is situated in the pleasant village of Moelfre on the north coast of the Isle of Anglesey. With both sea and mountain views, Deanfield also has a residential license and small bar for guests. Chris and Neil Bannigan are fine hosts, and both cook excellent breakfasts.

Llwyn Derw B&B
Morfa Bychan Road, Porthmadog, Dwynedd, Wales LL49 9UR
01766-513869 www.gonorthwales.co.uk £54/room
.Llwyn Derw is a Grade 2 listed Arts and Crafts period house which has been extensively modernized. The house is nicely situated a half mile from

the harbour town of Portmadog toward Harlech and amongst mature oaks. Rooms are spacious and nicely furnished. The typical B&B breakfast will fortify you for most of the day. Llwyn Derw was a pleasurable find for us after having to leave Prince of Wales Hotel early [see below].

Penaber B&B
Morfa Bychan Road, Porthmadog LL49 9UR
01766-512041 www.porthmadog.co.uk/penaber £50
Comfortable B&B within easy walking distance to both Borth y Gest and Porthmadog. Large rooms in a rural setting.

Pen Y Garth B&B
Old Llanfair Road, Harlech LL46 2SW
01766-781352 www.pen-y-garth.co.uk £70
Victorian town house B&B where rooms have views over the castle and Snowdon. Friendly and welcoming, the B&B makes a great base for golf in the area.

Prince of Wales Hotel
Bangor Street, Caernarfon, Gwynedd, Wales
01286-673367 www.princeofwalesonline.co.uk £58/room
The location in the heart of town a couple of blocks from the castle is great, but the accommodations couldn't be worse. The rooms are tiny and not well-appointed. The bar downstairs was raucous until early in the morning with a private party (the birthday of one of the employees). The breakfast in the morning was straight out of "Fawlty Towers." First, no service and then bad service. No juice glasses, no spoons. The only thing edible was the packaged cereal. Immediately after breakfast we went down to check out early. Another couple was there already cutting their stay short. When we left, no one asked why we were leaving early. We went outside to find our car locked in the parking lot we'd been told to park in and had to drive over a rubbish pile to get out. Absolutely, the only good thing about our stay was the recommendation of Molly's for dinner--it was great!

San Carlo Restaurant with Rooms
Embarkment Road, Pwllheli, North Wales LL53 5AB
01758-701530 www.sancarlorestaurantwithrooms.co.uk
"Restaurant with Rooms" is an apt description of the San Carlo, a half block up from the beach just east of the harbour.. The rooms are like a pleasant European hotel, and they are set above a wonderful authentic

Italian restaurant. Carlo and Sue serve great breakfasts for guests in the restaurant, and be sure to book at least one dinner there (the best fried sardines we've ever had). The San Carlo is a friendly place with an excellent location.

Tal Menai Guest House
Bangor Road, Caenarfon LL55 1TP
01286-627160 www.talmenaiguesthouse.com £60
This lovely Victorian home is well situated for golf in the northwest corner of Wales and on the Isle of Anglesey. Accommodations are first class and the breakfast is delicious. Always a good choice.

TOURIST ATTRACTIONS

We didn't learn until our second visit to Wales that we could save money on entrance fees at many of the historic attractions in Wales. Since we belong to the National Trust for Scotland and Historic Scotland, two organizations working to preserve Scotland's historic sites, we can use our NTS cards at National Trust sites in Wales and England and we can use our HS membership for entry into CADW (Historic Wales) sites.

Rhuddlan Castle in Rhuddlan on the northern coast. The castle (open Easter to September daily) is a diamond-shape ruin constructed in the late 1200s by Edward I. Edward participated in a flurry of castle building (called "The Iron Ring") to subjugate and control the wild Welsh. The impressive hollow shell of Rhuddlan is surrounded on three sides by dry moat.

St Asaph Cathedral in St Asaph is the country's smallest. Not much larger than some village churches it is still an interesting find.

Conwy Castle (open daily), another of Edward's structures, sits dramatically over the town and the castle walls surround the entire town. The castle, built in just five years in the 1280s, provides a good self-guided tour and has some spectacular views over the town and Conwy Bay.

The Conwy Suspension Bridge is almost as impressive as the castle. The Thomas Telford designed bridge was part of the road improvement program of the 1820s.

Beaumaris Castle (open daily) on Isle of Anglesey is in Beaumaris along A545. One of the few castles to retain its moat, the castle is a joy to photograph and tour.

Llanfairwllgwyngyllgogerychwyrndrobwlllandysiliogogogoch village on Angllesey has the longest place name in Britain, which translates to "St Mary's Church in a hollow of white hazel near to a rapid whirlpool and St Tysilio's Church near the red cave," which really means "tourists leave your money here." Locally known as LlanfairPG, the village is an old rail station turned into a tourist shop. A stop to take a picture of the name of the station and buy the obligatory postcard seems to be required of a visit to Anglesey. The shop cafe did serve a decent cup of tea and a sweet and the shopping wasn't bad. I guess LlanfairPG catches us all.

Bryn Celli Ddu, on Anglesey about a mile past Plas Newyd and signposted to the north, the henge and stone circle is one of Wales most important Neolithic sites. Further north, near Moelfre, is the **Din Lligwy Hut Group**, the ruins are the foundations of several second and fourth century dwellings. The site has informative plaques to help you know what you're seeing. Not far away is a burial chamber with a 28-ton capstone. These are just a few of the many ancient sites awaiting visitors to Anglesey.

Caernarfon Castle (open daily)is the most famous of Edward's castles. Completed in 1283, the castle took 40 years to build and has walls 15-feet thick in places. In 1969 the castle was the setting for the investiture by the Queen of Prince Charles as Prince of Wales. There are good displays and videos of the investiture ceremony. You can self-guide your way through the castle or hire a private docent guide for a small fee.

Snowdonia National Park is the oldest and largest of Wales' national parks. Besides lovely villages, like Betws- y-Coed, and beautiful natural scenic areas, the main attraction in the park is the **Snowdon Mountain Railway** (operating mid-March to early October weather permitting). Leaving from the village of Llanberis, the small steam train climbs the 3000 feet to the summit in a little less than an hour. The summit cafe offers an inviting break and the views can be spectacular if the weather is right.

Harlech Castle, a World Heritage site, is open daily. Overlooking Royal St David's GC, the castle is a particularly impressive sight from the course. The song *Men of Harlech* recalls the siege of the castle during the War of Roses. The view of the golf course and Tremadog Bay is spectacular. We were led on our tour by the castle cat who eventually guided us to the exit.

Aberystwyth is an interesting town which houses the University College of Wales and the National Library of Wales. The town also has another of Edward's castles, **Aberystwyth Castle**. Much more in ruins than the other castles we've mentioned, it is still worth a quick walk about. The main attraction, other than the fine golf course for us, is the town's **Promenade**. For a panoramic view of the town and Cardigan Bay you can take the cliff railway (daily March to October) at the northern end of town up **Constitution Hill**, or get a better view from the top of the challenging Aberystwyth GC.

Devil's Bridge, by car is 12 miles east of Aberystwyth on A4120 or a one hour ride on the **Vale of Rheidol Railway**. The bridge is actually three bridges, one on top of the other, over the rapidly flowing River Mynach.

Tenby GC

CHAPTER NINE: SOUTH WALES

GOLF

South along Cardigan Bay, around St David's Head, and along the Bristol Channel some wonderful and exciting golf awaits. Most of the great golf in this area is links or seaside with Royal Porthcawl being the premier course, but Ashburnham and the Cardigan GC are great surprises.

ASHBURNHAM GOLF COURSE
Cliffe Terrace, Burry Port, Carmarthenshire, Wales SA16 0HN
01554-833846   www.ashburnhamgolfclub.co.uk
Links, 6212 yards, par 72, £39

AMENITIES: The comfortable pub lounge serves tasty meals 11 to 11 most days. Everything on the menu is reasonably priced as well. The large golf shop is well staffed.

COURSE COMMENTS: Ashburnham GC is not difficult to find if you turn to the correct page in your travel notes. I gave the directions to Anne, who is a good navigator, and she took us directly to...Milford Haven GC. When we discovered our mistake, we quickly called Ashburnham and said we were an hour away and they said they would hold our time. We arrived only about five minutes late for our scheduled time (it pays to plan to be early). Keith Williams and Mike Jones, local members who were scheduled to play with us, had patiently waited. We were certainly glad they had because they were excellent guides around a fantastic links course. Built in 1894, it's easy to see why Harry Vardon said it was the course he "liked best in Wales." Sited along the Burry Inlet (bay), if you climb to the top of the dunes at the 12th you'll have fine views of the estuary and across to the Swansea Peninsula. Bunkers are the biggest challenge at Ashburnham, with only one hole having no bunkers, most have three or more. Even the fairway bunkers are steep-faced and penal. A meandering burn or ditch on 17 is the only water in play. Most greens are medium sized, but the range at the course goes from small to large. Right now the greens have plenty of subtle slopes (none too severe), but plans are to make some greens multitiered. Off the fairways, the marram grasses make for tough play, and the wind will always be a concern as you play into it on the way out and hopefully with it on the way in. Unusual for a links course, Ashburnham has some copses of firs planted long ago for wind breaks. Much of the course is designated an area of Special Scientific Interest because of a species of wild orchid found in the area.

Ashburnham rapidly became one of my favorite Welsh courses because of the quality of interesting and demanding holes, starting at the 185-yard par 3 first. Par 3s aren't always the best opening holes (for example, at Boat of Garten in the Highlands), but this hole makes a good start. Downhill from the tee to a large green surrounded by four bunkers, the hole has ample bailout room on all sides. The 3rd, a 325-yard par 4, begins with a drive to a narrowing fairway with bunkers on each side. Past the constriction, the green is a small target circled by bunkers. Another fine par 3 is the 173-yard 6th, which plays difficult into the prevailing wind. A rough-covered hill left, drop-off right, and bunkers on both sides make this a testing shot. To add to the challenge, the green is narrow and quite sloped. Next comes the moderate length par 4 seventh. A straight drive is needed here to set up an approach from a hummocky fairway. Your approach shot to the tricky green needs to avoid a double set of bunkers on each side. Last on the front is a 410-yard par 4. The 9th is a dogleg left around very deep rough. You need to be in the fairway to have a chance at the green, which is protected by mounds and fronting traps on each side. A tough target to find in regulation. Three holes on the back really caught my attention. First is the 372-yard 12th, a swooping gentle dogleg left with rough on both sides of a wide fairway. Too far to either side can leave a blind shot behind rough-covered mounds backed by bunkers. Next is the 14th, a 509-yard par 5 which has a split fairway. Hit about 220 yards to the base of a series of mounds which separate the two parts. The second shot should be to the middle of the fairway (Don't we wish all shots were!) to give a good look at the narrow opening to the green which is protected by mounding and bunkers. I hit a 4-iron fourth shot 190 yards and stayed on the green. The 18th is a dogleg left where you want to lay up to the bottom of the hill up to the green. A second shot of about 150 yards will be left to reach a green guarded in front by bunkers with a steep hill behind and a steep drop-off right. Don't be short or the ball can roll back 30 yards. We were the last ones off the course the day we played, and as the rain came in the lounge was a welcome respite. Ashburnham GC isn't as well known (or publicized) as some of the other courses in the area, but certainly can be called a "hidden gem."

COMMENTS FROM THE FORWARD TEES: Ashburnham GC is a longer course for ladies, but the par has been adjusted to 75. Bunkers are the most obvious problem on the course; they seem to be exactly in the way. The par 3s are all reasonable distances. There are seven par 5s, and the 10th at 456 yards and 14th at 439 yards are extremely long. The 18th is a testing hole with a steeply elevated green. The whole course had a natural feel and some super holes.

BUILTH WELLS GOLF COURSE
Golf Links road, Builth Wells LD2 3NF
01982-553296 www.builthwellsgolf.co.uk
Parkland, 5197 yards, par 66, £25

AMENITIES: The clubhouse is a converted 15th Century Welsh Longhouse upgraded in 2004. Two large lounge areas and a smaller bar serve golfers and the public. Pub food available usual hours. The golf shop, staffed by pro Simon Edwards, is well-stocked.

COURSE COMMENTS: Located only a mile from town on the A483, this quiet parkland course was originally designed as a nine-hole course 1923. In 1986 the course expended to eighteen. A fairly unique feature of the course is that it has no fairway bunkers, although there are 16 greenside traps to keep you thinking. To be honest, the tree-lined course with water (ditches, ponds, and the River Chewfi) in play on six holes doesn't need bunkers to test your shotmaking skills. The course is short with no par 5s for men and six par 3s, but it's still a fun track.

Several holes highlight our notes. The 7th, a 230 yard par 3, is a tough one-shotter. The entrance to the green is narrow with trees encroaching from the left and two bunkers on the right. Next is the dogleg right 336-yard par 4 eighth. The fairway turns around a mound and small copse of trees. The approach is uphill to a raised tiered green guarded by a trap right and a fore bunker 50 yards in front. You then cross the River Chewfi over a bridge to get to the 9th tee. On the 10th, a 320-yard par 4, your tee shot should cross the river twice (it's about 195 yards to clear the second crossing). The approach is to a green with no bunkers, but severe runoff on each side and sufficient left to right slope make the hole difficult. A demanding short hole is the 273-yard par 4 twelfth. It's a dogleg right with a ditch crossing the fairway about 200 yards out and trees encroaching from the right and the fairway turn. The green is easy to putt once you get there. The next hole, a 427-yard two-shotter, has a tight drive with OB and a steep drop-off right and trees left. Second shots are downhill to a back to front sloping green with a pond protecting the left side. The double fairway on the par four 300-yard 16th is bisected by the river. OB and the river on the right make it fairly foolish not to lay up (about 150 yards). It still leaves a testing second shot over the river to a green guarded by four bunkers. Builth Wells may be a short course, but even on a nice day it will present all the test you want.

FROM THE FORWARD TEES: This woodsy course with river crossings isn't really long at 5214 yards, but it will be a lovely test. The 9th, one of three short holes on the front, is a 160-yard intimidating shot over water. A tough hole is the 18th, a 401-yard par 4. Water is big concern on Builth Wells with three holes that cross water and three more holes with ditches in play. Stay out of trouble and the course is great fun.

CAERPHILLY GOLF COURSE
Penchapel, Mountain Road, Caerphilly CF83 1HJ
02920-889104 www.caerphillygolfclub.com
Parkland, 5728 yards, par 71, £20

AMENITIES: The venerable clubhouse has been recently modernized, yet retains some features from earlier days, such as the traditional men's bar, ladies' bar, and modern mixed lounge. Snacks and meals are served in the lounge most usual hours. Small golf shop, run by pro James Lee, is fairly complete.

COURSE COMMENTS: A 9-hole Caerphilly course was laid out on the Pencapel farm lands in 1905, and remained essentially the same until 1963 when it was expanded to 18. One of the more interesting points of history about Caerphilly was that during World War I a member emergency landed his military plane on the first fairway--nice way to drop in for a round. With few bunkers on the course, the trouble really comes from the sticky rough and trees which line most fairways. A couple of holes offer chances to find ponds or ditches, and the small tricky greens add challenge as well. The gently rolling terrain is an easy walk and the slight elevation changes add some interest to the holes.

One of those holes is the 351-yard par 4 third. The challenging dramatic dogleg right hole plays down from the tee to a green guarded by bunkers on each side. The small fast green is a tough target. An interesting par 5 is the 6th at 485 yards. The fairway slopes left to right and can reward a slight draw when the ball comes down from the left to the center of the fairway. The only trouble on the hole is a fore bunker on the right of the fairway and a green tucked right behind trees. Coming in from the left side of the fairway on your second or third shot is the best approach. The 8th, redone in 2003, is the hardest hole at Caerphilly. The 342-yard hole climbs from tee to green with two ponds in play on the right of the fairway. The fairway drops as you approach the small green protected by a trap front left. The 10th, the steepest climb on the course, is a 357-yard two-shotter with OB all the way up the right side while gorse and trees line the left. A small ridge fronts the green which makes your approach to one of the smallest greens semi-blind. The 486-yard 16th may seem like a short par 5, but the slightly uphill dogleg right plays tougher than its distance. Trees in the middle of the fairway and at the inside corner add difficulty. Then more trees encroaching from the right just before the green with one bunker right make the hole a real test. A good downhill par 3 is the 162-yard finishing hole. They say that many matches are won or lost on one of the most demanding tee shots on the course. From the elevated tee, the wide, shallow green is a hard target, especially with a cross ditch fronting the green. Parkland Caerphilly, with touches of moorland-style, is a pleasant change from the tough links courses in southern Wales.

COMMENTS FROM THE FORWARD TEES: This course is not long at only 4890 yards, but the holes are unique and testing. One challenge for women is the up and downs; I thought it more hilly than did Bob. None of the five par 3s are easy, and the 7th is only 79 yards, but the green is elevated 60 feet. Short will leave a very difficult pitch. The two par 5s on the back (there's only one on the front) are very interesting. The 15th severely doglegs right with a tree-lined fairway and a ditch that came into play on my third shot. Sixteen is an opposite dogleg left with a tree in the middle of the fairway at the corner. Both are very demanding holes. With the unique holes and views this is a great course to play.

CARDIGAN GOLF CLUB (*Club Golff Aberteifi*)
Gwbert-on-Sea, Cardigan, Pembrokeshire, Wales SA43 1PR
011239-621775 www.cardigangolf.co.uk
Links, 6687 yards, par 72, £30

AMENITIES: The clubhouse is well appointed with locker rooms and a lounge with conservatory. The lounge offers great views of the course and bay, and serves snacks all day. A restaurant is open for evening meals. Locals rave about the quality food in the clubhouse. When you visit, look for the displayed Harry Vardon putter presented to the club in 1896.

COURSE COMMENTS: Another Welsh course worth playing just for the views, Cardigan is a lovely headland links course with vistas of Cardigan Bay, the River Teifi, and the Preseli Hills at every turn. The course is not difficult to find, but don't look for signs to Cardigan GC. Follow signs to *Aberteifi Golff Clwb,* the Welsh name. The championship caliber course offers plenty of challenge, and yet is playable by all levels of golfers. Thirty-five bunkers are in play and some are steep-sided and quite penal. There's a lake noted on the card, but we didn't see it. The main problems on the course, besides the wind which is always a concern on a seaside course, are the eight blind tee shots (the marker posts are well placed) and the greens. Moderate to large greens (two are over 50 yards deep) and many are multilevel. On the spring day we played the course was spectacular with the gorse in full bloom and bluebells dotting the rough.

All the holes at Cardigan are interesting. The course is definitely one you could play again and again. Among the quality holes we picked out several to highlight. Eight is a 181-yard one-shotter to an elevated two-tiered green protected by three bunkers. Very demanding! The 452-yard par 4 fourteenth is the toughest on the course. A downhill tee shot must find a narrow fairway which has gorse encroaching into the landing area. The second shot is also downhill to a relatively small green protected on the right by two bunkers. Just for an added kick, the hole normally plays into the wind. Sixteen, 17, and 18 are a fantastic finishing set. At

195 yards, the par 3 sixteenth isn't too long, but it is tricky. The hole plays downhill and into the wind. Your tee shot must avoid the three bunkers (especially one very large one) around the green. The 17th, a 321-yard par 4, is a short two-shotter with a right sloping fairway and a collection bunker. The extremely large multilevel green is tucked behind a small dune. The last hole is a par 5 of 526 yards. On your tee shot, pick a hummock and aim at it. The fairway is all bumps and humps from tee to green. A fore bunker and greenside bunker will add to the challenge. Every time you play the hole, your ball will bounce someplace different. A great and interesting finish to a spectacularly beautiful course.

COMMENTS FROM THE FORWARD TEES: Cardigan is very playable for women. It isn't easy, but the yardage of 5580 yards is much shorter than from the men's tees, and the par is 74. With bunkers, blind shots, up and downhill shots, and gorse to avoid, I really had to plan my shots. The six par 5s vary in range from 382 to 437 yards. While the 11th is the shortest par 5, it isn't the easiest, with a hill in the middle and three bunkers to avoid around the green. The par 3s were short enough to allow me a good chance to score well. With sunshine and little wind like on the day we played, this is a great course for women.

HAVERFORDWEST GOLF COURSE
Arnold Downs, Haverfordwest, Pembrokeshire SA61 2XQ
01437-768409 www.haverfordwestgolfclub.co.uk
Parkland, 5986 yards, par 70, £22

AMENITIES: Pleasant 1994 built clubhouse with modern changing rooms and inviting lounge with bar meals served most of the day. Fully equipped golf shop.

COURSE COMMENTS: The club was formed in 1904, but at a different location. During W.W.I the course at Portfield Racecourse was plowed up for cornfields. The 9-hole course was rebuilt after the war. As with many early courses it took a while to find a permanent home. The club moved to the present grounds just north of town in 1934 where a 9-hole course opened. During W.W.II the course was reduced to four holes; the rest was used for cattle grazing. Toward the end of the war a RAF Mosquito aircraft crash landed at what is now the end of the 10th hole. The course was again restored after the war and was extended to 18 holes in 1983. The course you play today is fairly convoluted with several holes crossing others and the last two reached by crossing through the parking lot. Regardless of the winding nature of the course, it's a quality track with interesting holes (just watch out for balls coming at you from strange directions). Plenty of trouble will challenge your game on Haverfordwest, including 26 bunkers, most in play around the greens. The bunkers are not deep and six holes play bunkerless. The nicely conditioned greens are moderate sized, but mostly flat. Ponds are in play on four holes, but only major concerns on two of the par 3s. The only other problems for players will be a few blind shots, plenty of mature trees, and the ever-present wind.

Several holes were marked as standouts after our round. The 5th, a 366-yard par 4, has a tee shot from the members' or medal tee directly over the 4th green and is blind over a small hill. From there the hole plays downhill with trouble (trees and OB) all along the left. Fifty yards from the green is a small burn and a series of large trees. The green is a relatively small target especially if you are coming from very far out, but there are no bunkers to complicate the approach further. The 8th is an interesting, short but fraught with danger, par 3 of 144 yards. A pond and three bunkers front the small flat green. The 12th plays as a 422-yard par 4, and has a fairway crossed by three other holes, 3, 10, and 13. Be aware of others on those holes for your safety and theirs. At 220 yards from the tee is a stand of trees that will catch any but the most accurate tee shots. More trees encroach into the fairway about 60 yards from one of the largest greens on the course. Across the parking lot the penultimate hole, number 17, has a tough tee shot. The 321-yard par 4 is a downhill dogleg right where a long fade is the prime shot. Be careful though, the prevailing wind can push too strong a fade into impossible rough. The second shot is also downhill to a small green with one bunker left. As complex as the routing is at Haverfordwest, the interesting golf and pleasant farmland views make it definitely worth a visit.

COMMENTS FROM THE FORWARD TEES: Haverfordwest was a bit of a surprise for me. It looks like any other parkland track, but the layout is interesting enough to be really fun. It's fairly short for women at 5260 yards with a par of 71, but don't be fooled into thinking it's not challenging. The course has one par 5 on each side and only three par 3s total. The test is your ability to play the moderate length two-shotters. The short holes are tricky because of hazards including water, bunkers, hills, and trees. I think this is a fine course for ladies.

MILFORD HAVEN GOLF COURSE
Clay Lane, Milford Haven, Pembrokeshire, Wales SA73 1JY
01646-692368   www.mhgc.co.uk
Seaside parkland or headland, 6035 yards, par 71, £25

AMENITIES: The lounge in the older well-appointed clubhouse serves good meals. The club also has a very fully stocked golf shop.

COURSE COMMENTS: The golf club was established in 1913 and the present course was built in 1933 as a 9-hole course. Expanded in 1978 to 18 holes, the original nine holes play as today's top nine. The course has a fantastic site with views of Milford Bay filled with tanker ships, the village, and an old fort. The best views are from the 11th tee, but every hole provides a distractingly interesting view of some sort. One unique feature of the course is a second 9th hole. If you are playing only nine (and the club offers a 9-hole price), you play the alternate 9th which brings you back to the clubhouse. While the current routing is a little contrived, a major upgrade is planned for the next few years which will change several holes and leave a much smoother flow to a round. Milford Haven makes good use of elevation changes to add interest to holes, but the course is never a difficult walk. Thirty-three bunkers, of which the greenside ones can be quite penal (steep-faced), will keep you concentrating. A pond or burn is in play on four holes and can be a serious concern. Most of the greens are moderate sized, but a couple a small and the green at the par 3 twelfth is fairly large. Wind on this headland course is the other major hazard here.

Sitting in the clubhouse after the round, Anne and I picked out several holes at Milford Haven for comment. The 2nd, *The Pond*, a 435-yard par 4, starts with a slightly downhill drive toward a burn and a pond 285 yards from the tee. The second shot is gently up to a moderate sized green with one bunker left. A good drive on the 5th, *Pimple* (we couldn't figure out where that name came from), should be just short of the burn about 100 yards from the green. Trees right and left can come into play off the tee on the dogleg right. The approach continues gently up to a green with one bunker left. The interesting configuration of the course brings you to the 6th, a 148-yard par 3, and the 16th, a 140-yarder. These two holes play from opposite hills down to greens at the bottom of the same valley. Both have protecting bunkers and drop off in front. They can play in opposite winds, or if the wind switches in the round, they can play in the same wind. Visually a unique combination. A clubhouse consensus favorite is *Westward Ho*, the 353-yard par 4 eleventh, which plays to a fairway which bends left and has a runoff along the left. The green is a tough target notched into the hillside (almost gun-turret) with two vicious traps above right and a steep drop left. A classic dogleg left around a copse of firs with another copse on the right is the 401-yard 13th called *The Fort*. It takes a drive (downhill) of about 240 yards to have a clear approach to the small green with one fronting bunker and drop off behind. *The*

Orchard has a sharp dogleg right (almost 90 degrees) with farm ruins (OB) at the inside corner. Don't try to retrieve balls in the heavy rough behind the ruins because adders live there and they're relatives of cobras. I left them a ball as my offering. A lay-up to the center of the corner (about 180 yards) is all you need. Your second shot is to a slightly elevated well bunkered green. The 17th, *Church Tower* (a good aiming point) at 505 yards, and the 18th, *The Road* at 497 yards make a good back-to-back par 5 finish. In the prevailing wind 17 will be downwind and 18 into the wind. Both are fairly straight and have ample bunker troubles with 17 having four and 18 having nine. Interesting, challenging golf and magnificent views make Milford Haven GC worthy of a spot on your Welsh itinerary.

COMMENTS FROM THE FORWARD TEES: Milford Haven GC is a visually attractive course with wide fairways. The course has a good bit of elevation change which requires good course management. The hilly nature of the course created a few blind shots for me that Bob didn't have. Most of the bunkers were avoidable. Par 3s were all reachable, and only one par five was long (the 1st at 442). The trees can create problems on this pleasant parkland course, but any trouble is more than made up for by the wonderful views of Pembroke Bay.

NEWPORT (Pembs) GOLF COURSE
Newport, Pembrokeshire, Wales SA42 0NR
01239-820244 www.newportlinks.co.uk
Seaside links, 6053 yards, par 71, £18 for 9, £30 for 18

NOTE TO THE NEW EDITION: The course has been extended to 18 holes and the name is now Newport Links & Resort. We haven't played the new design, but from the looks of it at the new website we'd like to. Use our description of the old course as an enticement to play the expanded version.

AMENITIES: The new clubhouse was dedicated in 2000 and the lounge, with excellent views of the course and the bay has a full bar and serves bar meals all day. New restaurant is lovely. The small, but well-stocked golf shop is open only when the pro is available.

COURSE COMMENTS: Newport (Pembs, to denote Pembrokeshire rather than the Newport by Cardiff) GC is one of a number of fine sited courses in Wales. Every hole on the 9-hole track has a view down to the village, the bay, and the sea. It's a course you could play for the views alone, but then you'd be missing some fine golf. It may be difficult to concentrate on your golf with all the vistas, but you'd better give some thoughts to your shots. Thirty-three bunkers, including some very large fairway bunkers in play on adjoining holes, will demand your attention. Though the bay and the sea are always in view, water is not an issue at Newport. The greens, mostly moderate in size (except for the 2nd) have some interesting undulations and a couple are bowl shaped. Though the course isn't particularly short, the prevailing wind will make the course play longer.

The golf at Newport (Pembs) is as good as the views with several holes being particularly interesting. The 2nd, a 365-yard par 4, plays downhill (and often downwind) and begins with a drive to a generous fairway with a long bunker along the right. A good tee shot leaves a short iron to the elevated, large, double-tiered green guarded by a bunker left. That hole is followed by a brutally long, 472-yard par 4, which usually plays into a crosswind. The second shot is blind with the green hidden by the crest of a hill. A large fairway bunker on the right can catch weak second shots. The green sits on a half plateau with a bunker back right. From tee to green it's a good challenge. The 6th and 7th are an unusual combination as the only par 3s on the course play back-to-back. Six is 190 yards and is a tough shot when the wind is wrong (Isn't it always!) across rough and a small canyon. A dangerous bunker is sited on the left of the green. The 7th is 171 yards and plays downhill and often downwind which makes for a fun tee shot. Three bunkers around the green add difficulty. The last hole is a good finish to either nine or eighteen. The 306-yard par 4 starts with a downhill tee shot over the road (leading to the beach) and toward the clubhouse. Be careful to time your tee shot so that you don't hit a passing car--drivers don't pay much attention to golfers. Trouble on the hole is provided by a fairway bunker left and two more by the green. We found the staff to be very friendly and helpful. When they discovered I was having trouble with a trolley, a grounds crew member went back to the clubhouse and got me another. This is a nine hole course definitely worth going around more than once.

COMMENTS FROM THE FORWARD TEES: We were lucky enough to play this course on a beautiful autumn day, so staying focused on golf and not the views was hard for me. It did help that we played the 9-hole course twice. Newport is 5261 yards with a par of 72. Different tee boxes for the second nine shorten the course by 103 yards. The fun par 3s definitely played easier the second time around. Be sure to include Newport (Pembs) in your itinerary for both the golf and the views.

PENNARD GOLF COURSE
Southgate Road, Southgate, City of Swansea, Wales SA3 2BT

01792-233131 www.pennardgolfclub.com
Hilltop links, 6225 yard, par 71, £50

AMENITIES: Pleasant clubhouse serves good food the usual hours. Small but well supplied golf shop.

COURSE COMMENTS: Called "The Links in the Sky," Pennard Golf Club is the design work of James Braid and C.K. Cotton. The course plays over a wildly undulating linksland of hummocks, hillocks, moguls, and small and large dunes. What make Pennard unique is that its links are 200 feet above the shore. The views can be spectacular or they can be nonexistent (if you play in the fog as I did), but the course will always be entertaining and difficult. As many others have said, you will either love it or hate it. Pennard is above all else a challenge, with or without wind, but even more so when the wind is up. Some say the steeply sloping, fast fairways are unfair, while others, like two-time US Open winner Lee Janzen, believe Pennard is a test of shot shaping. The forty moderate sized, strategically placed bunkers can cost strokes. The rough can be short and wispy in one place and brutally tough in another. The greens are moderate sized, play fast, and most have severe undulations. You will always find the putting demanding.

The wild contours of raised links means that there are many interesting holes at Pennard. The 3rd, *President*, is a 365-yard par 4 with a narrow fairway (typical at Pennard) bending left around two dangerous pot bunkers. As on many holes here, a driver is not necessarily the best choice. A straight 240-yard shot can run out of fairway and end up in a rough-covered hollow where the best you might be able to do is hack out to the fairway. The green has a bunker front right and another back right, but it is the subtle slopes that give the most fits. With proper care the hole can yield par or birdie. Next is *Ilston*, a 517-yard par 5. Drive uphill over the 3rd green (please, be sure no one is on it) to a blind fairway. A 250-yard drive is needed to get a good look at the rest of the hole which has OB on the right. The only sand problem is the two traps off the right of the fairway about 70 yards out from the green which is very sloped front to back and quite fast. Consider taking less club on your approach. Supposedly, there are grand views of Three Cliffs Bay as you walk up the 6th fairway, but not through the fog. Planet Golf lists *Castle*, the 351-yard 7th, as one of the best par 4s in the world. From an elevated tee you hit down to a severely moguled fairway with the ruins of Pennard Castle (hence the name) at the side. The green nestles in dunes and is tilted away from approaching shots. A real test. A fine demanding par 3 is the 180-yard 11th, named *Tower*. A small menacing pot bunker awaits front right, but a bank behind the green usually kicks balls back toward the hole. A renowned par 5 is the 16th at 493 yards. *Great Tor* plays from the high dunes along the edge of the cliff top with a right to left sloping fairway. The approach shot must find the green which is perched on the cliff edge, but thankfully is banked from back to front. Again, the views can be spectacular. Pennard may be too difficult or quirky for some, but plan a stop so that you can find out if you're on the love or hate side.

ROYAL PORTHCAWL GOLF COURSE
Rest Bay, Porthcawl, Mid Glamorgan, Wales CF36 3UW
01656-773702 www.royalporthcawl.com
Links, 6440 yards, par 72, £120

AMENITIES: The comfortable venerable lounge looks out over the sea and the restaurant looks out over the course. The golf shop is very sharp and fully equipped. The pro, Peter Evans, is very helpful.

COURSE COMMENTS: The golf club at Porthcawl was established in 1891 with a 9-hole course, but quickly moved to the present location with an 18-hole layout. Henry Colt in 1913 and Tom Simpson in 1933 are the main architects of the present course, which is constantly being upgraded without losing its Colt-Simpson character. Playing along Rest Bay, the course affords views of the sea on every hole. Some farmers' fields and a couple of hotels can be seen from the course, but mostly the focus will be on the dunes and sea. While the troubles at Porthcawl are typical of championship links courses (a wonderful combination of marram grass, gorse, and heather set upon ancient sand dunes), the wind is the biggest challenge of the course. The day we played was squally and gray (*dreich,* the Scots would call it) with wind whipping between 30 and 40 miles per hour. [see details in Chapter One.] Locals we met in the pub said it was a breezy day. Besides the wind, players must contend with more than 100 bunkers, most in play and most penal. Not only are the traps deep and steep-sided, the sand in them is thin because of the heavy wind. The medium to large greens have plenty of major slopes and small borrows. The wind can definitely be a factor in your putting, as well. One pond on the 5th is the only water on the course, but it's only in play for dramatically off-line drives. The routing of the holes is very smooth and in one round you'll play in all directions in relation to the wind.

Royal Porthcawl GC is truly a world class championship course which will demand a golfer's best for him/her to score well. Even a mediocre or poor round will still be fun on the fine links holes. The first three holes play along the edge of the bay, with the 3rd being our favorite. The last of the sea holes is a 388-yard par 4 gentle dogleg left which begins with a long carry over grass and heather. The fairway is fronted by two bunkers, mounding, and OB is down the whole left side. The narrow fairway runs slightly downhill toward an elevated green protected by four bunkers. Playing into the prevailing wind toughens the short 472-yard par 5 eighth, which has OB down the left side and gorse on the right. A line of traps on the inside can catch drives on that side. The second shot must contend with two large traps which cross the fairway 60 yards out from the long, narrow green protected by four bunkers. Next is the 366-yard par 4 ninth. Playing uphill with a long carry to the fairway, the 9th has no fairway bunkers, but gorse on the right and heavy rough left will give enough trouble. A mound in the fairway and five bunkers complicate the approach to a very back-to-front sloped green. All the par 3s (4, 7, 11, and 14) are very strong and demanding. The 14th has three bunkers, while the rest have either six or seven. Most of the greens are significantly undulating while being long and narrow. Each one is a fun challenge in any wind.

On the back we picked four holes to highlight. The 13th, a 421-yard par 4, begins with a drive up a slight hill on a dogleg left which bends into the wind. About 125 yards out from the green the fairway drops towards the large green protected by a cluster of four bunkers. On the third long two-shotter on the back, the 426-yard 16th, the left to right prevailing wind can make the hole far more difficult than it looks. Drive to a generous landing area, avoiding the bunker on the right, and stay short of the dune fronted by three bunkers which cross the fairway 265 yards out. The second shot is over the dunes to an uphill fairway, The green is the smallest on the course and has two bunkers to give problems on the right. A quirky finishing hole is a 408-yard par 4 which will definitely test your judgment. Drive out to a wide fairway which drops off into a wild area of humps, bumps, and hollows at about the 250-yard mark. The second shot is dramatically downhill (and crosses the first fairway) to the largest green at Porthcawl with mounding, bunkers, and drop-offs to protect it. The rough in this area is some of the stickiest on the course. The windy day we played we chatted with the greenskeeper who was dressing the greens. Instead of plugging and sanding, Porthcawl was hydro-aerating. Water is punched into the greens by spikes to control fungus and aerate the putting surface. The greenskeeper said it does the same as plugging and sanding, but with less damage to greens and less disruption of play. We played a couple of greens that had just been done and saw no outward affects, except water in the cups.

Royal Porthcawl GC is truly a world class venue. Even in the most challenging conditions the course is a joy to play. In good conditions the course would be magnificent. A necessary stop for any trip to Wales.

COMMENTS FROM THE FORWARD TEES: Royal Porthcawl is a visual beauty with ocean views from every hole. As a championship course, it's made even more challenging by the constant wind. At 5729 yards it's longer than most Welsh courses. Along with the wind, the bunkers cause the most concern. They always seemed to be in my landing area and were most often penal. The links bounces took the ball into unexpected areas. The par 3s aren't especially long, but all have surrounding bunkers and require accurate shots. The 12th is a tough driving hole which requires a long carry off from the tee. The pro suggested later that staying to the right plays shorter and has a better bailout area. I loved the course even though we played in extreme conditions (wind and rain). A Japanese tourist playing behind us said we he came in, "I was defeated." But he had a smile on his face.

PRISKILLY FOREST COUNTRY HOUSE & GOLF COURSE
Letterton, near Fishguard, Wales SA62 5EH
01348-840276   www.priskilly-forest.co.uk
Parkland 9-hole, 5900 yards, par 70, £14/9, £20/18

AMENITIES: The bar/lounge where you check in for golf serves good food, mostly bar snacks, all day. A more formal dining area is in the back. The club has no golf shop, but a few essentials are available at the bar. The Country House B&B could be a very nice stay, though we didn't try it.

COURSE COMMENTS: Priskilly Forest GC is off the main track enough to be uncrowded, yet the Jim Walters (from Aberystwyth) 1992 design is worth a visit. We enjoyed a late Sunday afternoon round in pleasant weather and felt we had the course to ourselves. The Priskilly Forest course may be easy to get on, but that doesn't mean the course built on the Evans' family farmland is easy. Twenty-one bunkers, most small and not too penal (though a couple are hidden), a small burn which is in play on four holes, and the forest will cause enough concern to make a round interesting. The greens are small and relatively easy to putt, but several blind shots and some sidehill play add challenge to Priskilly.

Several holes stand out in our after-round notes. It's the first shot that is most interesting on the second hole. The hole, a 199-yard par 3, begins with a semi-blind tee shot over two large trees with a small tree closer (green and flag can partially be seen through the foliage). The green slopes to the left and is protected by a bunker on that side. The first par 5 at Priskilly is the short 4th. This 461-yarder has OB all along the right side of the hole and bushes left. The hole doglegs right and then goes downhill. The green can't be seen for your second shot so use the aiming pole as a guide. Bunkers on both sides guard the small green. An uphill tee shot begins the 322-yard par 4 seventh. Your drive needs to be about 220 yards to clear the stand of trees on the inside of this dogleg left. The approach to the green will be blind downhill to a putting surface protected by one bunker front left. The finishing hole is a gem. Nine is a 523-yard par 5 with a tee shot down towards a burn and two towering oaks. A good first shot can clear the trees, but miss and you're dead. With a good tee shot even a moderately long player can hope to reach the green in two. One bunker protects the most undulating green on the course. The pleasant forest and farmland views, the friendly staff, and quality design make Priskilly Forest GC a good choice for a fun round.

COMMENTS FROM THE FORWARD TEES: The course is a pleasing farmland course and a decent challenge. The yardage for nine holes is 2670 or 5340 for 18 with a par of 72. Challenges come from hills, a burn, blind shots, and sidehill lies. The stone-walled garden by the 6th (visible from other holes) adds interest. The two par 5s are both over 400 yards, with the 9th being a downhill 464 yards. It was quite a challenge. The par 3s are both fun holes. Priskilly Forest GC made a pleasant afternoon walk in the Welsh farmland.

PYLE & KENFIG GOLF COURSE
Waun-y-Mer, Kenfig, Bridgend, Wales CF33 4PU
01656-783093   www.pandkgolfclub.co.uk
Links, 6588 yards, par 71, £55

AMENITIES: The first clubhouse burned in 1925. The current comfortable clubhouse lounge is not open to the public, only to members and players. Well-stocked golf shop is separate from clubhouse.

COURSE COMMENTS: The first 9-hole course near the tiny villages of Pyle and Kenfig was built in 1922, and proved so popular that it was expanded to 18 by 1925. The course initially plays over flat linksland, then the back 9 heads out into dunes land. Many of the 71 bunkers on the course are deep and penal, with a few tiny pot bunkers. Both 10 and 18 have a burn which flows down the side of the hole. Greens are mostly moderate in size with a mix of flat and significantly undulating putting surfaces. Wind is usually a condition of play on the seaside links, and gorse lines many of the holes.

We played P&K, as it is locally known, on a wet and windy spring day and yet enjoyed every minute of our round (except the minute I spent trying get out of a deep fairway bunker with my ball against the lip). A fun hole is the 5th, a par 5 of 494 yards. The hole, fairly straight and strewn with bunkers, goes slightly down and then up. One bunker right and one left are in play on your drive, while three others cross the fairway for your second shot. The small green is protected by two fronting bunkers. Another good hole is the dogleg left 343-yard 7th. Aim at the post on the outside of the turn, but be careful of the two bunkers within reach on the right. The smallest green on the course is surrounded by four traps, but there's room to run the ball up. Before you hit the dunes holes you play the 518-yard 9th. It usually plays downwind as you head back to the clubhouse. Two bunkers left and one right are in range on your first shot, and four more on your approach to the slightly elevated green with run-offs front and left. On the back, we liked the 190-yard par 3 twelfth. From a slightly raised tee hit straight down to a narrow green with two fronting bunkers and one more on each side. A fair, but testing one-shotter. Next is the gentle dogleg right of the 13th. On this 371-yard hole most will aim out at the pole on the left, but try to stay as much on the right side as possible to have a look at the green tucked behind a mound. The three bunkers to the right of the green make a pretty picture, but will snare any ball played too conservatively. Fourteen is a much sharper dogleg right than the 13th, especially from the members' tee. Two-twenty-five will find the middle of the fairway on this 373-yarder, and will give a decent look at the narrow green tucked between mounds and fronted by two bunkers. While P&K isn't the class track of its neighbor Royal Porthcawl, it is a strong links challenge worthy of your time.

COMMENTS FROM THE FORWARD TEES: Pyle and Kenfig is a good course with both shot and visual variety. The front and back were very different type courses, though not as extreme in contrast as Pwllheli. Par 3s are short, but not always easy. Precise shots are needed to avoid the bunkers. Par 5s are long with the longest being the 5th at 453 yards. Even with heavy winds and rain on half the holes, the course was enjoyable.

ST DAVID'S CITY GOLF COURSE
Whitesand Bay, St David's, Wales SA62 6PT
01437-721751   www.stdavidscitygolfclub.co.uk
Links 9-hole, 3040 yards, par 35, £18 for 18 holes

AMENITIES: Small clubhouse only open limited hours. Honesty box for when nobody's around. Trolleys available if the clubhouse is attended.

COURSE COMMENTS: Golf has been played on this strip of land along Whitesand Bay as early as 1898, but a club with an official course wasn't noted until 1903. The current 9-hole layout is not the original 1903 course. During World War II the local landlord was required to hand over the course so that sand could be provided for MOD building projects in the area. The entire surface of the course was destroyed by the war efforts. It wasn't long after the war, though, that locals began to rebuild their course in the same location. First, three holes were built. Over a period of several months more holes were added, until St David's had a new 9-hole course.

Today's course is wide open and very susceptible to the elements, especially the ever present sea breezes. Situated within the boundaries of Pembrokeshire Coast National Park with views of local hills, St David's head, and the bay, the course is empty much of the time--just right for a quiet round. The course offers two distinct sets of tees at all holes except 8/17 and 9/18 for a full 18-hole round, and there are two flags on the two-tiered 3rd, red for the front and yellow for the back nines. Playing through slightly undulating linksland, St David's City will present you with uphill, downhill, and sidehill lies. Early in the season when I visited the rough was wispy and easily playable, though I would guess it gets tougher as it grows. The few bunkers dotted about the course are not the challenge you'll find at other nearby courses like Tenby. The 200-yard par 3 fourth (plays at 176 yards on the 13th) is the course's best known hole. The typically small green is nestled up to the rocky cliff on the right, while on the left is thick rough and gorse. A demanding hole, but a beauty with the bay in the background. The only par 5 is the 480-yard uphill dogleg right 5th. Blind shots, trouble all around, and a tiny green create the difficulties. The course is definitely out-of-the-way unless you're staying in St David's City, the smallest cathedral city in Great Britain. Word in the village is that the members are very friendly about sharing their course, but no one was on the course when I played. If natural golf is your passion, have a go.

SOUTHERNDOWN GOLF COURSE
Ogmore-by-the-Sea, Bridgend, Wales SF32 0QP
01656-881112 www.southerndowngolfclub.com
Heath-links, 6449 yards, par 70, £70

AMENITIES: Venerable clubhouse was built in 1907 and has changing rooms, two bars, and dining room. Pub meals available usual hours and full menu in evenings. Bars and dining room have views out to the 18th green so that everyone can watch matches finish, and vistas over Ogmore River estuary and Bristol Channel offering beautiful sunsets. A separate well-stocked golf shop has a friendly, knowledgeable staff.

COURSE COMMENTS: Southerndown GC is unusual in that it is built on a Limestone Down or limestone-heath (gorse and heather) with a layer of built up sand which over the years has blown up to the course 70 meters above the sea. Southerndown GC is the only course built on such a heath and is playable all year long because of the excellent drainage. The history of the course is one filled with golf's great names. Willie Fernie first designed the course in 1905. Since then it has been modified by Herbert Fowler, Willie Park Jnr, and Harry Colt. For the past 70 years the basic course has remained unchanged except for slight modernization by Donald Steel. This litany of golf's great architects has left us with a worthy challenge. Eighty-nine bunkers, with some particularly deep and penal greenside examples, are strategically dotted around the course. Though there is no water in play at Southerndown, the large greens with interesting borrows and tiers will test a player's short game. All your game will be tested by the wind which usually blows on the coastal hilltop course. Golfers will enjoy hitting from spongy fairway turf; very links-like. This course, like several others we've played, is built on common land and sheep roam freely through the links. This leads to an interesting story told in the clubhouse bar. Several years ago there was an important match during which one player's golf ball was hit at one of the local sheep and lodged in the sheep's b... posterior. The sheep scampered away with the ball eventually dropping it much nearer the hole. The argument raged about from where the ball was to be played--the spot it first hit the sheep or where the sheep deposited the ball. Even today, the story can lead to a good discussion in the bar. [Truth or urban legend?]

All the Southerndown holes are good, but we noted several as outstanding. The 2nd, a 439-yard two-shotter, begins with a blind tee shot; aim just left of the post. Three bunkers cross the hole at 290 yards and the fairway drops down to a green sloping away from your shot and with three more bunkers right. On the 166-yard par 3 fifth, you hit over the valley to an elevated green with sand behind. The two traps in front, though, are the ones to avoid, and the right hand trap is the toughest. Nine is a birdie opportunity if you avoid the four fairway bunkers sprinkled about. Three bunkers fringe the green, but there's a good opening in front of the back-to-front sloping putting surface. The best holes were on the back, starting with the 168-yard 10th. The five traps around the green aren't as challenging as the very sloped green. Local knowledge says never give a putt on this green. Thirteen is a short 488-yard par 5 which begins with a series of three bunkers ready to catch tee shots on the left. The green is only protected by two traps and some mild mounding; another birdie chance. Big hitters (or moderate hitters if the wind is behind you) need to be aware of three cross bunkers on the drive at the 365-yard 15th. Four more bunkers protect the green, but slopes funnel the ball toward the middle of the green. I wish the pin had been there when we played. Two good holes finish your round at Southerndown. The 416-yard par 4 seventeenth has a wide fairway which is an easy target, but the second shot must clear about 70 yards of rough to find the apron of the slightly raised green. The key to the 423-yard 18th is to know where the flag is. Use the opposite side of the split level fairway to give the best approach to the large green surrounded by three bunkers.

Southerndown GC is a unique limestone-heath track with Schwyll, the Great Springs of Glamorgan (largest spring in Wales with a flow of 6 million gallons per day) only a quarter mile away, and an iron age fort just above it. Put it on your "To Play" list, especially because it's the closest championship course to the 2010 Ryder Cup venue at Celtic Manor.

COMMENTS FROM THE FORWARD TEES: Southerndown is an interesting course with grand views of the sea and the village of Porthcawl in the distance. The hilly course is long at 5548 (par 73), but the sheep add interest. None of the par 3s are long, but have other hazards to deal with. For example, if you don't land on the 5th green your ball will probably roll into difficult mounding. On the 141-yard 4th are two big bunkers between you and the raised green surrounded by trees. Sometimes there seems to be no correlation between length and par on the 4s and 5s. Take advantage of it when it's easy and gripe when it's tough. Meanwhile, just enjoy the golf, the views, and the fluffy wildlife.

TENBY GOLF COURSE
The Burrows, Tenby, Pembrokeshire, Wales SA70 7NP
01834-842978 www.tenbygolf.co.uk
Links, 5945 yards, par 70, £50

AMENITIES: Comfortable clubhouse built in 1966 has a lounge and dining room. All the locals say the meals are excellent. The golf shop is large and very complete.

COURSE COMMENTS: The oldest affiliated golf club in Wales, Tenby GC was formed in 1888. Today's course has changed quite a bit over the years (and more changes are in process), but the club still plays over the original land, or at least part of it since much was lost in the war years. The course plays out to and through some dramatic dunes, but it is not a difficult walk. It is, though, a difficult track. Blind shots, drives and approaches, and rough, hard to find your ball in and harder to hit out of, add challenge to the course that is usually windy. The 46 greenside and fairway bunkers have good sand to play from, but are penal enough that you won't want to. The greens which have a reputation for being in good condition all the time are moderate to large with tricky slopes. The only water in play is a burn crossing on 16. Besides demanding golf shots, the course also provides some beautiful views of South Beach and the village.

Play at Tenby is exciting with unique holes. The 3rd, *Dai Rees* (a famous Welsh professional's favorite hole), is a 382-yard par 4 starting with a blind drive. Aim a little right of the marker post to be in good position (about 240 yards out). The approach is difficult with trouble left (pot bunkers) and right (heavy rough). The moderate sized plateau green is severely sloped from back-to-front, so try to stay below the pin as anything off-line will fall down the slope. It's the number one stroke index hole at Tenby. The 5th, *Swm-Y-Mor* (Welsh for "the sound of the sea," which is very evident from the hole), again begins with a blind shot. On this 353-yarder there's more room left of the marker post and the fairway slopes to the right. Four bunkers fronting the green complicate the approach. The first hole on the back is a 422-yard par 4 named *James Braid* (for the Scottish architect who did redesign work on the course). The 10th is stroke index two and has both a blind tee shot and blind approach. Three fairway bunkers await miss hit shots. Your approach should be a little right because the green slopes left. The 11th is *Giltar* (the headland behind the green), a 410-yard two-shotter which yet again starts with a blind drive. The narrow fairway runs into a valley. Watch out for the trap on the right before the marker post at 210 yards out. Your second shot is to an elevated green which runs away from your shot. One bunker front right guards the sloped green. The most difficult of the par 3s is *Y-Ddau-Gwn* (Welsh for "the Two Valleys"), a 197-yard hole which is all carry to the green. Shots short will find heavy rough-covered swales. Room to miss is on the left, but right is a deep grass bunker. A demanding shot! The last hole is *Charlie's Whiskers* (named for the three mounds to the right of the green). This 375-yard par 4 is a challenging end to your round. With OB all along the left, avoid the two traps on the right of the fairway to have a good shot in. A bunker on the left 80 yards out from the putting surface is to be avoided as are the whiskers on the right. The green is the largest and flattest on the course. If you can, try to arrange to play with a local who can guide you around. Tenby GC may be a tad short, but will make up for it with challenging shots. Definitely a must play course!

COMMENTS FROM THE FORWARD TEES: Tenby GC is a lovely, challenging links course with many open fairway shots and good links roll. Distances are fair and the par 3s are reachable, but the wind can make a great difference. From the course are some stunning views of the island, bay, and village. I found the rough to be difficult to get out of. When I stayed in the fairway and planned for the roll I scored well.

PUBS, TEAROOMS & RESTAURANTS

St David's City is in the southwest corner of Wales, a little isolated from the main areas of population, but that doesn't mean the eating in the area isn't fine. Several good places are right in town, with Cwtch being very good even if you can't pronounce it. Be sure to visit the Sloop Inn in Porthgain, a classic seaside pub. Further around the coast we found another interesting pub in Kenfig, The Prince of Wales serving great food and maybe even a ghost or two. The best meal in the whole area though was at The Boathouse B&B in Laugharne--be sure to not pass up opportunities for interesting home cooked meals.

Beaufort Arms on Castle Road in Mumbles, Swansea. A real local's pub, but very friendly to visitors. Serves nice pub meals.

Black Cock Inn (pub) a mile south of Caerphilly. A family friendly pub with a small bar and dining room. Serves tasty traditional pub grub and great Sunday Roasts.

Cwtch Restaurant & Bar in St. David's City, Wales, on High Street. The small, seven table, bistro with stone wall and fireplace on one side, and on the other a nice display of wine bottles and books, is a great choice when in the area. We enjoyed a superb meal of smoked haddock stew, Greek salad, ham and cheese pizza, and panfried halibut. Prices were very reasonable considering the quality of the food.

The Drawing Room (Restaurant with Rooms) on A470 about three miles from Builth Wells. Set price meals (not cheap) with an excellent selection. Fine dining where reservations are required. If you book a room it comes with automatic prepaid dinner reservation.

Duke of Edinburgh Pub, Newgate, Wales, on the ocean about eight miles south of St David's City. This bright English pub comes with high recommendations, but failed to deliver. We stopped to eat. Even when I said we would order dinner, the barkeep had us pay for our Guinnesses, as if she knew we really wouldn't eat there. We left to find a better menu. Don't Bother, unless you want to stop just for a drink.

The Jolly Sailor Inn (pub) near the village green on Bridgend Road in Newton by Porthcawl. The 1818 inn with its quaint pub was a hit with smugglers and today serves good pub fare. Service for visitors is spotty; the management caters to locals. Stop in for a drink and look for the three local ghosts--a burley rosy cheeked sailor who holds a drink, a distressed lady with a baby, and sounds of rolling barrels in the basement.

Mallard's Wine Bar and Restaurant, The Swan Hotel in the heart of Hay-on-Wye, Wales. In the heart of the world's first "booktown," with over 30 booksellers, Mallard's has a formal dining room and two pub rooms with the same large menu in each. It also has a separate room for pool table and games (yeah). On a Friday night we had to wait for a spot, but it was worth the wait. We enjoyed a great spicy lentil and carrot soup, and the lamb chops and lasagna were good as well.

Pepe Picccante (restaurant), 33 The Explanade, Porthcawl, Wales, on the seafront. An interesting restaurant right on the seafront promenade with three different menus--an Italian, Spanish (Mexican), and Tapas--plus specials. The food is plentiful and excellent, especially the selections we had on the Italian Two Course Special (starter, main, and wine). Pepe's was busy on an off-season Wednesday, almost needed a reservation.

The Pump on the Green just north of Haverfordwest in the village of Spittal. Very reasonably priced bar and dinner menus. Always popular, so it's best to book.

Portreeve's Tafarn on Market Square, Laugharne near the castle. Known locally as "The Ranch," the restaurant is gaining a good following for the new owners who have significantly changed the menu. Give it a try.

The Prince of Wales Public House (pub) in Kenfig, Wales, on the road past P&K GC, next to the nature reserve. Built in 1504 as the Kenfig Town Hall, Prince of Wales Public House has been a bar since at least 1822. It has also been a Burgess Hall, courthouse, jail, and Sunday school. Numerous stories of ghosts and spirits in the building. As a pub it is very comfortable with historical photos and serving large portions at reasonable prices. Must Stop, for the food, the history, and possible ghost sighting.

Red Kite Restaraunt one and a half miles SE of Caerphilly off Nantgarw Road. A Marston's gastro-pub which serve good quality meals at value prices. A chain we've eaten at several times and found it acceptable each time.

Red Lion Inn (pub) in Llanafan Fawr about nine miles from Builth Wells on the main road. Wales' oldest pub which started serving in 1188 with the current building dating from 1472. Quintessential traditional Welsh pub owned by the same family for the past 350 years. Good menu and reasonably priced.

The Sampler Tearoom, 17 Nun Street, St David's City, Wales, down the street from the Cathedral close. This themed tearoom has its walls filled with framed samplers, some as old as the 1850s. The food is outstanding and the decor entertaining. Makes a pleasant lunch stop or a break from visiting the beautiful cathedral.

Sloop Inn (pub) at the harbour of Porthgain, near St David's City, Wales. The old pub, nautical in theme and decorated with items relating to ships (nets, bells, pulleys, etc.) including a dingy overhead, has four eating/drinking areas and a patio outside for good weather. We visited twice (lunch and dinner two different days) and it was busy both days with locals and tourists. We had an interesting conversation with a local council member who was collecting for a charity. Everything we had was good, but the mildly spicy fish soup (muscles, shrimp, whitefish, prawns) in a tomato base served with crusty bread was outstanding, as were two sweets we tried (Sticky Toffee Pudding, and Granny's Hot Apple and Carmel Pie). You may have to park a ways up the road from the harbour, but a visit to the Sloop Inn is worth the walk.

LODGINGS

Blue Seas B&B
72 Beach Road, Newton, Porthcawl, South Wales
01656-786540 www.blueseasbnb.co.uk £50/room
A pleasant small hotel-like B&B on the beach front through the village of Newton with an outstanding location right on the seafront. Rooms are decent and breakfasts are large.

The Boat House B&B
1 Gosport St., Laugharne, South Wales
01994-427263 www.bed-breakfast-holiday.co.uk £70/room

Ann is a spectacular host at one of the loveliest bed and breakfasts we've ever visited. The location is outstanding, tucked as it is in the small township with the castle, the estuary, and poet Dylan Thomas' Boat House within easy ambling distance. The rooms are large and elegant, and the breakfasts offer up some of the area's best products. A great feature of the breakfasts is that it doesn't have to be the same every day--Ann works hard at varying the menu items. Home cooked dinners can also be arranged. "Magical," "gorgeous," and "spacious" are all comments from the guests of The Boat House.

Bryn Awel B&B
45 High Street, St David's, Pembrokeshire SA62 6SB
01437-720082 www.brynawel-bb.co.uk £70
Located conveniently near the coastal walking path and a few minutes from the shopping area of town right across from the Oriel y Parc Visitor Centre and Gallery. Jane and Pete make the B&B a warm and cosy place and serve an excellent breakfast.

Firs Guest House
Church Street, Hay-on-Wye, Wales
01497-821800 www.hay-on-wye.co.uk/firs £30/p
Firs Guest House is a beautiful B&B, centrally located in the heart of a great shopping town if you love books. Rooms are large and comfortable, and hosts David and Esther Davies serve a great breakfast. Hay-on-Wye is a fun place to visit, with good eateries, and Firs B&B should be the place you stay.

Marllew Guest House
39 Esplanade Ave., Porthcawl CF83 1EJ
01656-789319 www.marllewguesthouse.co.uk £60
Near the seafront this 1912 home retains its Eduardian charms. Lisa is a fantastic host. Good value.

Ramsey House Guest House
Lower Moor, St David's, Pembrokeshire SA62 6RP
01437-720321 www.ramseyhouse.co.uk £115
Luxury boutique hotel-style B&B close to the center of town and the cathedral. B&B has designer furnishings of leather and oak and an enclosed garden. Host Shaun is a gourmet chef who serves a broad breakfast selection. Pack lunches and dinners can be arranged. Visit Wales Gold Star winner.

Tides Reach Guest House
388 Mumbles Road, Swansea SA3 5TN
01792-404877 www.tidesreachguesthouse.com £75
Overlooking the promenade, Mumbles Head, and Swansea Bay, Tides Reach is a comfortable and spacious B&B well located for the golfing tourist. Nice rooms and a good breakfast are features of Tides Reach.

Ty Castell Guest House
Station Road, Nantgaredig, Carmarthen SA32 7LQ
01267-290034 www.ty-castell.co.uk £80
Lovely modern (1990), purpose built house with stunning views over the gardens and River Towy. The guest house is only five minutes from the National Garden of Wales and four minutes from town. Paul and Steve serve great breakfasts and evening meals can be arranged.

The Woodlands Guest House
Hay Road, Builth Wells LD2 3YL
01982-552354 www.thewoodlandsbuilthwells.co.uk £60
The 1904 home is welcoming, relaxing, and cozy, and it's an easy walk to town. We had a nice view of the gardens from our room and a very good breakfast.

TOURIST ATTRACTIONS

From Aberystwyth south along the coast to St David's City and east toward Cardiff and north in the interior toward the Brecon Beacons and Hay-on-Wye is the realm for this section Welsh attractions. Castles dominate the sites, but there are several surprises as well.

Cilgerren Castle, late 13th century, overlooking the River Teifi is a large and impressive ruin which is well worth a visit.
Pentre Ifan, just south of Cardigan off A487, is the largest burial stone in Wales and has a 16-foot top stone balanced on large stone legs and dates to about 2000 BCE. Very stirring to the imagination.
Carreg Coetan Arthur (one of many Arthur's seats in Wales), a well-preserved capped dolmen set in a tract of homes just into the village of Newport past the 9-hole golf course. The dolman is interesting, but it is the juxtaposition of the ancient and the modern that is most fascinating.

Porthgain, with its cute harbour and good pub, and **Aberieddi**, with the remains of an old mine and quarry are good stops along the Pembrokeshire coast. We watched a group of wet-suited adventurers paddling around the rocks at the entrance to what is known locally as **The Blue Lagoon**, quarries flooded with seawater which because of the chemical makeup of the rock have a deep blue color.

St David's City is the smallest city in Britain. What is really a small village gains its city status by hosting the rather magnificent **St David's Cathedral** (open daily). The 125-foot stone tower of the cathedral has clocks on three sides--the story is that the parishioners in the north couldn't raise the money for a clock on their side of the tower. The cathedral is lovely both inside and out. Look for the interesting interior sundial which gives you the time from window light. One evening we visited the cathedral for Evensong where we heard a girl's choral group and the great pipe organ. Beside the 12th C cathedral is the ruined mid-14th century **Bishop's Palace** built by Bishop Henry de Gower. The cathedral and palace are worth your time to explore.

Pembrokeshire Coastal Path follows the edge of the shore and cliffs. If you only want a short hike, explore **St David's Head** starting at **Whitesand Beach** north of the city and near the interesting 9-hole golf course. Numerous interesting views and ancient sites (including another Arthur's seat dolmen) can be accessed in a couple of miles of path.

Pembroke Castle (open daily) predates Edward's castles. The castle is good for touring and it has one of the best castle gift shops we've been in.

Laugharne Castle in Laugharne (open March to September daily) was built in the 13th C and poet Dylan Thomas called it "castle brown as owls." The Thomas quotation is appropriate, not only because of the appearance of the castle, but because Laugharne was home to Thomas. Along the bay from the castle be sure to visit.

Dylan Thomas Boathouse, where he did much of his writing. The Boathouse is filled with Thomas memorabilia and is open for touring May to October, but sometimes at inconsistent times.

National Botanic Garden of Wales is off A48 at Porthythyd east of Carmarthen. The 500-acre garden is open daily and will take half a day to do it justice. Besides the typical outdoor gardens (heather, oriental, walled) is the Glasshouse, which is reason enough to visit the gardens.   Inside are plantings from several regions of the world, all within one climate controlled facility.

Carreg Cennen Castle neath the National Botanic Garden is southwest of Llandeilo.   One of the most impressively sited castles in Wales, Carreg Cennen affords   some fantastic views of the countryside.

Caerphilly Castle (open daily) is the center of the town and surrounded by homes and shops.   It is also surrounded by an impressive moat which was reflooded in 1958.   Begun in 1268, the 30-acre castle looms out of the moat with massive towers and partial walls standing at strained angles. Take time not only to tour the interior ruins, but to walk all the way around the outside of the castle to see it from all angles.

Booktown, the village of Hay-on-Wye just off A438, is a unique place to visit.   In 1961 Richard Booth opened Hay Castle Bookshop in an old castle. Today, Booktown boasts over 35 new and used bookstores, including stores that specialize in golf books, murder and mystery, poetry, children's books, antiques, music, as well as plenty of general book dealers.   The last week of May is time for the Hay Festival of Literature, when accommodations get booked up years in advance. Hay-on-Wye, like its copy Wigtown in southern Scotland, is a bibliophile's mecca.

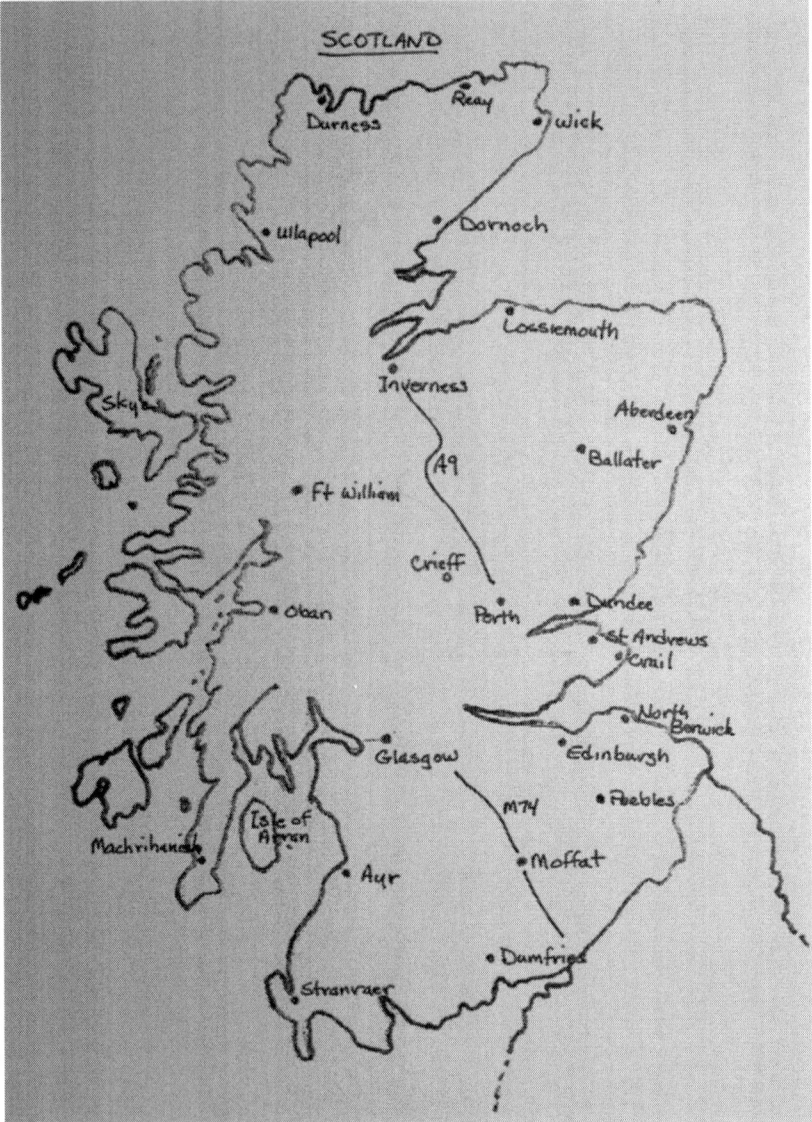

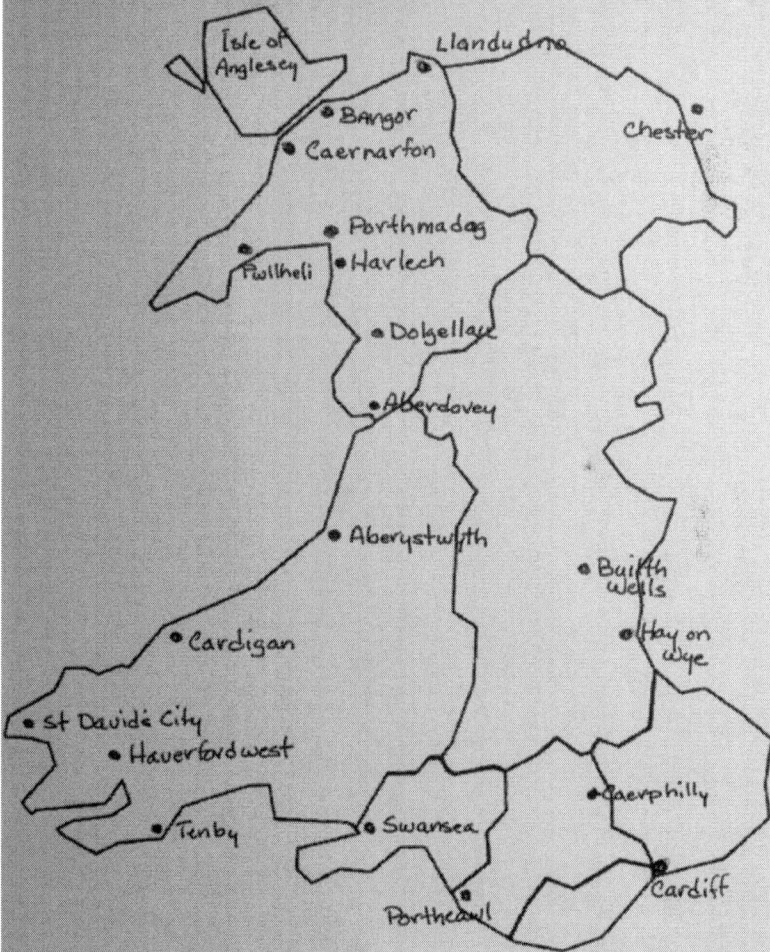

WALES

Isle of Anglesey

Llandudno

Chester

• Bangor
• Caernarfon

• Porthmadog
• Harlech

Pwllheli

• Dolgellau

• Aberdovey

• Aberystwyth

• Builth Wells

• Cardigan

• Hay on Wye

• St David's City
• Haverfordwest

• Caerphilly

• Tenby

• Swansea

• Cardiff

Porthcawl

INDEX OF GOLF COURSES

Scotland Courses

Aberdour 131-32
Aberfoyle 192-95
Abernethy 36-38
Alford 74-76
Alyth 106-07

Baberton 169-71
Balfron 195-96
Ballater 76-77
Ballindollach 38-39
Blairgowrie Landsdowne 107-09
Blairgowrie Rosemount 109-11
Braemar 77-79
Bridge of Allan 196-98
Broomieknowe 171-72

Callander 198-99
Canmore 132-34
Cardross 199-201
Carnwath 201-03
Carrbridge 39-40
Craigielaw 172-74
Crail Craighead 134-36
Craigmillar Park 174-76
Crow Wood 203-04

Dollar 205-07
Downfield 111-13
Drumoig 136-37
Dullatur Antonine 207-09
Dumfries County 12-13
Dunblane New 192, 209-11
Dunkeld & Birnham 113-15
Dunniker Park 137-38
Durness 36, 40-43

Edzell 115-16
Elie 138-40
Forfar 116-18
Forrester Park 140-42
Fort William 43-45
Fraserburgh 82-83

Gairloch 45-46
The Glen 169, 176-78
Glencuitten 13-15
Gleneagles Kings 120-22
Gleneagles Queens 118-20
Glenrothes 142-43

Harburn 178-80
Helensburgh 211-13
Huntly 83-85
Inverallochy 85-87
Inverness 46-47
Isle of Skye 47-48

Keith 87-88
Kingsbarns 105, 143-46
Kilsyth Lennox 213-14
Kinross Bruce 148-49
Kinross Montgomery 146-48
Kirkcudbright 15-16

Largs 16-19
Leadhills 214-16
Leven Links 149-51
Lochgilphead 19-20
Loch Ness 48-50
Luffness New 180-82

Milngavie 216-18
Moffat 20-22
Monifeith 122-24
Montrose 124-26

Moray Old 74, 88-90
Murcar 91-92
Musselburgh 182-83

Nairn 50-51
Newburgh-on-Ythan 92-94
Newtonmore 51-53

Panmure 126-28
Peterhead 94-96
Piperdam 128-29
Portpatrick 22-24

Ratho Park 183-85
Rosehearty 96-97

St Andrews Dukes 151-53
St Andrews Links Trust
    Castle 153-55
    Jubilee 155-57
    New 157-59
Spey Valley 53-55
Stranraer 11, 24-26
Strathmore 129-30
Strathpeffer Spa 55-57
Struie (Dornoch) 57-58

Tarland 98-99
Tillicoultry 218-19
Torvean 58-60
Traigh 60-62

Ullapool 62-64

Wick 64-65

Welsh Courses

Aberdovey 224-26
Abergele 226-27
Aberystwyth 227-28
Anglesey 228-30
Ashburnham 252-54
Baron Hill 230
Betws-y-Coed 231
Borth & Ynyslas 231-32
Builth Wells 254-55
Caerphilly 255-57
Cardigan 257-58
Chester 232-33
Haverfordwest 258-59
Milford Haven 259-61

Nefyn & District 234-36, cover
Newport (Pembs) 261-62
North Wales 236-38
Pennard 262-64
Priskilly Forest 266-67
Pwllheli 238-39
Pyle & Kenfig 4, 267-68
Royal Porthcawl 264-66
Royal St Davids 223, 239-41
St Davids City 268-69
St Deiniol 241-43
Southerndown 269-71
Tenby 252, 271-73

11745958R00158

Printed in Great Britain
by Amazon.co.uk, Ltd.,
Marston Gate.